Contents at a Glance

Contents

Chapter 9: Keys to the Kingdom: The App Store Submission Process... 303

Foreword

The mobile landscape is very different than it was just a few years ago. The iPhone's powerful software, revolutionary user interface, and powerful developer platform has driven an almost overnight explosion of apps. Consumers have shown through their actions that apps are how they want to consume content on mobile devices.

The rapid change in the mobile landscape provides an excellent opportunity for entrepreneurship. In June 2008, I left a nearly four-year tenure at Apple because on the eve of the App Store launch, I felt the old guard of the mobile industry, who had been the gatekeepers, were about to lose their stranglehold, giving way to a new generation of entrepreneurs. My adventure in the iPhone space has been highly rewarding emotionally, intellectually, and, yes, financially. I have also never worked harder in my life.

My firm, Double Encore, has been offering iPhone consulting and development services since July 2008. Since that time, I have met with a countless number of perspective clients from individuals to large brands. There is no shortage of enthusiasm and optimism. Yet the App Store is not the fountain of youth. Nor can it turn coal into gold. There are many more failures than successes in this young market.

To be successful in the new mobile industry, you must not merely develop an app. You need to own the enter life cycle of your app from conception, design, development, and ultimately distribution. The journey doesn't end when your app appears on the App Store.

Your job is to figure out where the rubber meets the road, to paraphrase an entrepreneurial expression. Have you done market research to determine whether you're addressing a need in the market place? How big is the addressable market? How are you going to generate revenue? How are you going to market the app? Why is your app better?

These are some of the key questions you should be asking while you are considering building an iPhone application business. I have seen too many people, some of whom were my own clients, who put too much faith in the App Store to sell their product for them.

There is good news! *The Business of iPhone App Development* is the most comprehensive, easy-to-use resource for planning a sustainable iPhone application business. The book is extremely thorough and will guide you through the critical considerations you will face. From generating buzz to defining your business model, *The Business of iPhone App Development* offers a depth and breadth of knowledge that I believe will equip you with the tools necessary to achieve success. Are you ready?

Dan Burcaw
Founder and CEO
Double Encore, Inc.

Cofounder
Push IO LLC

About the Authors

 As the founder of Electric Butterfly, **Dave Wooldridge** has been developing award-winning web sites and software for 15 years. When he's not creating Mac and iPhone apps, he can be found writing. Dave is the author of *The Developer Sketchbook for iPhone Apps* and has written numerous articles for leading tech publications, including a monthly software marketing column for *MacTech Magazine*. Follow Dave at `Twitter.com/ebutterfly`.

 At the beginning of 2009, **Michael Schneider** left Silicon Vally technology firm Wilson Sonsini Goodrich & Rosati to found HiveBrain Software. HiveBrain publishes a variety of applications on the iTunes App Store, the most notable of which, TouchType, peaked at #13 in the U.S. App Store. Michael continues to practice law under the name Bitwise Legal, focusing on software and interactive media clients. Notable clients include Bungie and Innerfence. Follow Michael at `Twitter.com/hivebrain`.

About the Technical Reviewer

Mark Johnson has been building and selling iPhone apps full-time since the App Store opened; he splits his time between running an iPhone consulting practice in San Francisco and publishing his own apps. He has nine diverse apps in the App Store including free, paid, ad supported, and an affiliate sales app. Mark has 15 years of experience developing software but is now a rabid student of marketing and believes that it doesn't matter how cool or useful your idea for an app is; if you don't know how to market it, then it's a bad idea.

Acknowledgments

Dave and Michael would like to thank the entire Apress family for believing in this book. None of this would have been possible without the many amazing people who were involved in this project. The wonderful Kelly Moritz not only kept us on track, but her positive spirit was a great motivator. The talented Douglas Pundick and Mark Johnson provided invaluable feedback and technical expertise. The copyediting wizardry of Kim Wimpsett truly made us better writers. The production team's usual magic ensured our humble words looked good in print, and the marketing and sales staff worked hard to deliver those words to readers everywhere. We greatly appreciate all your efforts and dedication!

A very special thank-you goes out to Clay Andres for his insightful guidance and having the faith in us as authors to realize his vision.

Dave would like to personally thank Michael Schneider and Dan Burcaw for their important contributions to this project, and especially Mark Johnson for patiently testing all of the book's example code. A big shout-out to my good friend, Dave Mark, for introducing me to Clay and the Apress gang. And special thanks to my supportive family. I certainly wouldn't be an author today without the writing skills I learned from my mother long ago. Thanks, Mom! Finally, I am eternally grateful for the immense love and support from my wife, Madeline, throughout this long journey. You are my rock and soul mate!

Michael would like to personally thank Dave Wooldridge and Clay Andres for involving him in this project, and Mark Johnson for making the introductions that got everything started. Many thanks to my parents, Mark and Nancy, for nurturing my interest in learning, and to my wife, Stacy, for supporting me in my contribution to this book and in my decision to leave corporate life and pursue my dreams.

Chapter 1

Seeing the Big Picture in a Crowded App Store Marketplace

Living in Los Angeles, there's no shortage of Hollywood clichés. There was a time when it seemed like everyone I met—no matter their profession—was working on a screenplay.

Now they're all working on their own iPhone apps!

And who can blame them? It's a testament to the soaring popularity of the iPhone. There's money to be made in the App Store, and everyone wants in on the action.

We've all read about the success story of indie developer Steve Demeter. His Trism game, along with many of the 500 other apps that were included in the initial July 2008 launch of the App Store, experienced an overwhelming explosion in sales. With some price tags as low as 99 cents, iPhone and iPod touch owners were impulsively downloading these inexpensive apps at a feverish pace. In the months that followed, several of the most popular apps were already netting their creators hundreds of thousands of dollars, allowing programmers like Steve Demeter to quit his day job to focus full-time on this lucrative opportunity.

The media quickly proclaimed the seemingly overnight sensation of the App Store as a "gold rush" for developers. With the lure of potential riches, inspired entrepreneurs from all over the world have downloaded the iPhone SDK, racing to learn Objective-C and Cocoa Touch in the hopes of cashing in on this software phenomenon.

Fast-forward one year to June 2009. More than 40 million iPhone and iPod touch users have downloaded more than 1 billion apps through the App Store. You'd think that with stats like that, it'd be easier than ever to make money in the App Store, right? Think again....

Why a Business Book for iPhone Developers?

With more than 100,000 applications in the App Store and developer interest continuing to grow at a stunning rate, industry analysts predict that number will likely double before the end of 2010.

Think about that for a moment. When browsing through the App Store, how many new apps do you stumble upon weekly or even monthly? 25? 50? According to Apple, approximately 8,500 new apps and updates are submitted each week to its app review team!

In such a crowded marketplace, it's becoming increasingly difficult for new apps to get noticed. Without the necessary exposure, your app may simply get lost in the endless stream of new software that floods the App Store on a daily basis. Gone are the days when you could quickly cobble together a simple app, throw it into the App Store, and then sit back waiting for the large royalty checks to roll in.

The media hype machine is so good at celebrating the underdog stories of a few indie developers who found instant wealth in the App Store that newcomers often assume that if they build an app, the sales will come. When the anticipated avalanche of profit turns out to be nothing more than a trickle, surprised developers quickly discover that a *Field of Dreams* philosophy is no longer enough in this highly competitive market.

"Ah, but what if I've just created the next killer app?" you ask. "Surely Apple will want to showcase it as a 'Featured App' in the App Store."

Having a great product is certainly the underlying key in this equation, but it won't be enough. It's true that being a "Featured App" can instantly propel your sales into the stratosphere, but unfortunately, those "Featured App" spotlights are not purchasable advertising spaces. Apple chooses only a select few apps every month for those coveted spots. With thousands of new apps vying for attention, your chances of getting that life-altering call from Apple are pretty slim. In fact, you may have better odds winning the lottery.

But don't despair. Your killer app can certainly make a lot of money without being a "Featured App." Like anything else in life, finding success in the current App Store environment will require some hard work and planning, but who says the journey can't be fun along the way?

Tackling the New World of Mobile Marketing

If you have the benefit of working for a large software company with deep pockets, then there's probably a dedicated department to handle all of the marketing for the products you create. But if you're an independent developer who's responsible for managing every aspect of your own business, then you're all too familiar with the haunting questions that arise when wondering how to implement effective marketing strategies to increase app sales.

And you aren't alone…just take a look online at the various iPhone developer forums and mailing lists, and you'll quickly see countless posts (some with generous amounts of cursing) from frustrated programmers, all asking similar questions:

- "How do I promote my app?"
- "My app just got approved in the App Store. Now what?"
- "How do I get reviews for my app?"
- "Yikes! My 99-cent app is selling only a few units a week. What do I do?"
- "How do I make a video trailer for my app?"
- "Is there anything I can do to avoid one-star customer reviews?"

Although this all may look quite daunting, trust me—it's really not as overwhelming as it might appear. My goal here is to provide answers to those questions and much more. A lot of innovative marketing tactics, tools, and resources are available to iPhone developers that you simply may not be aware of. Just like you wouldn't want to bring a knife to a gunfight, the key to success is in choosing the right weapon for the task at hand. This book's primary objective is to arm you with the ammunition you need, humbly serving as your definitive reference guide to the business of iPhone app development.

Rest Easy—This Is Not Your Typical Business Book

If just the thought of reading yet another stale book on over-generalized marketing concepts causes your eyes to roll back in your head, then don't worry! This is not your run-of-the-mill business book. You do not need a Harvard MBA to grok this material.

Like all Apress books, this one was written by developers for developers, taking you step-by-step through marketing solutions that have proven successful for professional iPhone app creators. We won't just tell you what you need to do; we'll also show you how to do it.

This is not about expensive advertising campaigns. This is about cost-effective marketing alternatives that can help you sell more apps! In fact, most of the business strategies described in this book cost little to no money—perfect for all of us indie developers on shoestring budgets. All you need is some dedicated time, patience, a little creativity…and of course, this book.

Planning Your Own Success Story

I know what you're thinking. This all sounds very time-consuming, and free time is something you simply don't have to give. As a full-time developer myself, I understand this all too well. Whether I'm feeling the pressure from self-imposed work deadlines or racing to finish a project for a client, time often feels like the enemy. With what little free time I do manage to salvage, I just want to spend it programming the next killer iPhone app. I don't want to be bothered with marketing concerns, at least not until my app is finished. But that would be too late.

Without a solid game plan in place, you'll find that one solitary publicity push when your app is released may not be enough to generate substantial sales. Once upon a time, sending out a press release, landing a few magazine reviews, and listing your product updates on the popular online software directories may have worked fine to promote traditional desktop applications, but many of those old shareware techniques don't apply here. In the unique world of the App Store, you'd most likely see a momentary sales bump on launch day that quickly plummets in the week that follows (see Figure 1–1). Then you'd end up spending a lot of extra time that you had not originally allocated in desperate scrambling to figure out how to improve sales.

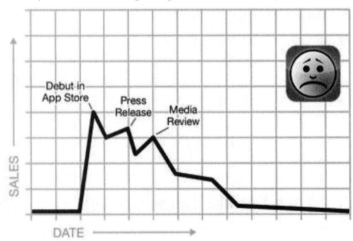

Figure 1–1. *Without a long-term marketing plan in place, you risk drastically shortening the life span and profitability of your iPhone app.*

If no one knows about your app, it won't matter how many cool new features you add in the future. Did you build an app that consumers will want, satisfying an existing need in the marketplace? Did you do anything to create prerelease interest in your app? And what about your app's longevity in the App Store? Have you thought about how to sustain and grow your sales beyond the initial release? Wouldn't you prefer your sales to look more like the graph in Figure 1–2?

The reality is that if done right, your marketing efforts should actually help save you time in the long run. It's not just about time management. Sure, carving out a few hours every week to focus on promoting your app is important, but that's only part of the solution.

Think like a marketer. Think big picture.

It's not just about what to do after your app is available in the App Store. Did you know that as a developer, you can integrate several elements directly into your app that can encourage sales, produce additional revenue streams, help users "spread the word" via built-in social marketing, and improve customer support and reviews? Your iPhone app itself is one of your most powerful promotional tools, but to take advantage of these valuable tactics (and many others), you should start planning your marketing strategy before you've even written a single line of code.

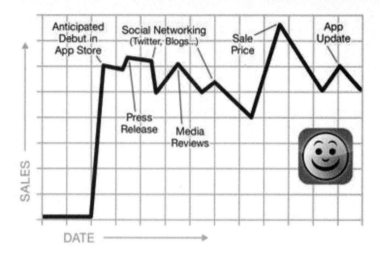

Figure 1–2. *Wouldn't you prefer your sales graph to look more like this?*

In fact, this is such an important point that I feel obligated to say it again…

Start planning your marketing strategy before writing a single line of code. By incorporating marketing and business savvy into every aspect of the development process, you're giving your app the best possible chance of succeeding in the App Store.

Now just to be clear, I'm not suggesting that you turn your app's interface into a walking billboard—that's a task better suited for your App Store description, your web site, and publicity materials (which we'll also cover extensively in this book). What I'm talking about here are essential components that can be integrated into your app's functionality and UI design that will help promote your app in very subtle ways that your users will perceive only as convenient, quality-enhancing features.

The iPhone SDK 3.0 introduced more than 1,000 new APIs, many of which can actually make your job easier as a marketer, such as In-App Purchase and In-App Email—both of which will be explored in this book.

Yes, you read that correctly. Several chapters of this book will be focused on what you love doing most: designing and programming your app! Got your attention now? And you thought marketing wasn't going to be fun!

How to Use This Book

The sequence of chapters takes a very systematic linear approach, working step-by-step through the planning, development, and release of an iPhone app. Along the way, important business solutions will be presented in each phase of the process to help you produce an app that sells! Although you may be tempted to jump around, reading only the chapters that appeal to you, I recommend reading the chapters in order to benefit from this strategic, organized workflow (see Figure 1–3).

Figure 1–3. *For best results, follow the linear workflow of this book.*

Chapter 2—Doing Your Homework: Analyzing iPhone App Ideas and Performing Competitive Research

So you think you've got a great idea for an iPhone app? Learn how to discover untapped markets and refine your app concept to be unique and highly marketable, setting it apart from your competition. We'll also explore the invaluable advantages of doing some good old-fashioned detective work by analyzing what your competitors are doing right *and* wrong.

Chapter 3—Protecting Your Intellectual Property

This just might be one of the most important chapters in the book! Although we probably all hate dealing with legal matters, it's crucial to the long-term health and success of your business not only to protect yourself but also to protect the intellectual property of your original concepts and code. **Michael Schneider**, an expert lawyer turned iPhone developer, will walk you through everything you need to know to safeguard your iPhone business.

Chapter 4—Your iPhone App Is Your Most Powerful Marketing Tool

Your app icon and screenshots are often the first visual elements users see in the App Store when evaluating your app. Bad first impressions can cost you sales and invite negative reviews, so fine-tuning your app's design is a critical component to success. Your iPhone app is your most powerful marketing tool, so Chapter 4 includes useful tips on prototyping, creating eye-catching app icons, designing intuitive user interfaces, and turning your app into a social marketing powerhouse.

Chapter 5—Money for Nothing: When It Pays to Be Free

Unlike the traditional desktop software world, the App Store does not currently allow time-limited or feature-crippled trial versions. To work around this restriction, many developers offer an In-App Purchase–supported "freemium" model or a free "lite" version of their apps, hoping users will buy in-app content or the separate paid version to gain access to premium features. Learn the benefit of *free* to promote paid versions, monetizing your free apps with in-app advertising, and the value of in-app cross-promotion and social gaming platforms, as well as when and how to use these strategies for effective results.

Chapter 6—Exploring New Business Models with In-App Purchase and Affiliate Programs

With In-App Purchase (accessible via iPhone SDK 3.0's Store Kit framework), developers can now construct new business models within their applications such as offering subscriptions, selling add-on content and services, and unlocking premium features. In Chapter 6, you'll explore the additional revenue opportunities of In-App Purchase and affiliate programs.

Chapter 7—Testing and Usability: Putting Your Best Foot Forward

Did you know that many of the one-star customer reviews in the App Store are caused by user frustration with hard-to-use app interfaces or buggy features? Low customer ratings can really hurt your app's perception and sales, so avoiding those situations when possible should be your top priority. Chapter 7 is all about the value of conducting thorough beta testing, providing built-in help, and tracking usage and performance through in-app analytics.

Chapter 8—Get the Party Started! Creating Prerelease Buzz

Your app is finished, but before you submit it to the App Store, it's time to start generating some prerelease buzz for it. Chapter 8 will show you the best way to stir up some excitement and anticipation for your app by promoting it on your web site, blogs, Twitter, and other social networks, as well as by getting basically anyone you can to review or talk about your app.

Chapter 9—Keys to the Kingdom: The App Store Submission Process

Your product page in the App Store is the world's gateway to your app, so its presentation is essential in properly communicating the value of your app. Chapter 9 will walk you through the app submission process in iTunes Connect, helping you optimize your app's text description, keywords, rating, screenshots, and other required elements, as well as discuss how to set the price to maximize your sales potential.

Chapter 10—Increasing Awareness for Your iPhone App

Once you're in the App Store, it's time to rev up the publicity engine to increase consumer awareness of your app's availability. Even if your prerelease marketing efforts resulted in an initial sales surge, there's still vital work to be done. It's your job to ensure that your iPhone application does not get buried amidst the thousands of new apps flooding into the App Store. Chapter 10 reveals how to craft effective press releases, utilize promo codes, gain exposure through interviews, and sustain momentum in the App Store with promotions, giveaways, and carefully timed sales events.

Getting Started with Your First iPhone App

We have a lot of ground to cover here, so before we get too far along, this book assumes that you've already downloaded and installed the latest Xcode tools and iPhone SDK (3.0 or higher). If not, then make your way over to the Apple Developer Connection web site:

`http://developer.apple.com/`

If you do not yet have an ADC membership, then sign up (it's free) so that you'll have access to the latest SDKs, tools, documentation, tutorials, and even sample code. And while you're there, take the time to apply for the required iPhone Developer Program:

`http://developer.apple.com/iphone/program/`

Do not wait to do this when your iPhone app is ready to be submitted to the App Store, since it can often take weeks to receive acceptance into the iPhone Developer Program, which would delay your progress unnecessarily. After being accepted, pay the applicable fee to complete your registration. After your payment has been processed, now when logged into the iPhone Dev Center, you'll see an iPhone Developer Program column on the right side of the browser screen. Click the iTunes Connect button listed there.

On the main page of iTunes Connect, be sure to visit the Contracts, Tax, & Banking Information section to view the contracts you currently have in effect. By default, you should have the "Free Applications" contract already activated, which allows you to submit free iPhone apps to the App Store. But if you want to submit paid apps to the App Store, then you'll need to request a "Paid Applications" contract. Apple needs your bank and tax information so that it can pay you when you've accrued revenue from app sales. Since Apple transfers money via secure electronic deposits, you'll need to provide your bank's ABA routing number, name, and address, as well as your account number, so make sure your bank supports electronic transactions with third-party vendors. If you plan on selling your app in several regional App Stores, then in order to receive international payments, Apple will also require your bank's SWIFT code. Although most large national banks support the SWIFT system, some smaller independent banks and credit unions do not, so it's important to use a bank that can supply a SWIFT code. Until you complete their required steps (see Figure 1–4), Apple will hold any money it owes you in trust. And since this can also be a fairly lengthy process, I highly recommend completing the "Paid Applications" contract long before submitting your app to the App Store.

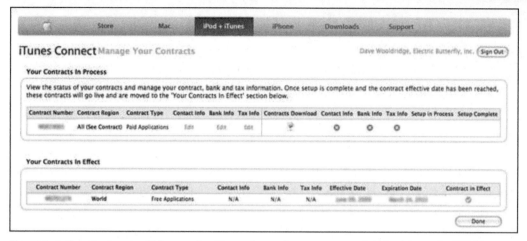

Figure 1–4. *To order to get paid for your App Store sales, make sure you complete Apple's required "Paid Applications" contract in the iTunes Connect online portal.*

In this book, we'll also assume that you're already familiar with Objective-C and iPhone application programming. If you're looking for in-depth guidance beyond the documentation and tutorials available in the Apple Developer Connection, I highly recommend the following books:

- *Learn Objective-C on the Mac* by Mark Dalrymple and Scott Knaster (Apress, 2009): http://www.apress.com/book/view/9781430218159

- *Beginning iPhone 3 Development: Exploring the iPhone SDK* by Dave Mark and Jeff LaMarche (Apress, 2009): http://www.apress.com/book/view/1430224592

Already in the App Store? It's Never Too Late to Boost Sales

Even if you're an iPhone developer veteran with one or more apps currently available in the App Store, you can still do a lot to increase exposure and sales for those apps. You've already invested valuable development time and money to get to this point, so it'd be a shame to give up now!

But don't make the mistake of skipping ahead to the post-release chapters. Many of the solutions presented in earlier chapters can be utilized with great effect, especially when planning new versions and updates for your existing apps.

Take the time to work through all the chapters in the order they're presented. You may be surprised by the tips you pick up along the way that can help even older apps that have been stagnating for months in the App Store.

Developing iPhone Apps for Clients

This book can benefit not only the people who want to sell their own apps in the App Store but also consultants who develop iPhone apps for third-party companies. You're being hired for your expertise, so anything you can do to help your clients succeed in the App Store will serve to strengthen your worth to them.

What better way to secure a consulting contract than by offering a full turnkey service, guiding your clients from app concept to launch, providing both code and marketing support? By offering an optional marketing/publicity package to your list of iPhone development services, you're also establishing new income opportunities for yourself!

The success of your clients directly affects the success of your relationship with them. Add this book's business solutions to your existing toolbox so that you can prove to be an indispensable superhero for all your clients' iPhone app needs.

Ready to Dive In?

Now that you've taken a broad look at the current state of the App Store, it's apparent that several challenges await all iPhone developers as they navigate their way along the road to success. As programmers, problem solving is what we all do on a daily basis, so I'm confident you'll enjoy each step in this process. And just think, put together the right puzzle pieces, and you may just find that elusive pot of gold at the end of the road. Mmmm, app sales!

First shake off all that Objective-C code bouncing around in your brain. You'll want a clear head for the next two chapters. Don't worry, you'll be diving into design and development issues soon enough, but before you do that, you need to do a little competitive research and business planning. So, roll up your sleeves, put on your detective hat, and let's get started.

Doing Your Homework: Analyzing iPhone App Ideas and Performing Competitive Research

So, you think you've got a good idea for an iPhone app? Make sure it's a great idea. No amount of marketing will help sell a bad app. Sure, you may have excellent coding skills with the ability to produce a performance-optimized, quality application, but if it's based on a poorly conceived concept, it won't stand a chance in today's crowded App Store.

In this chapter, you'll learn how some good old-fashioned detective work can help test the validity and marketability of your app concept. Analyzing what your competition is doing right *and* wrong will give you the insight needed to truly refine and improve your ideas into a unique app that stands apart from the rest.

Even if the thought of doing a little competitive research seems elementary to you, keep reading. You may be pleasantly surprised to learn some new tricks here.

Fulfilling a Need

People buy software to solve a problem or satisfy a need. To-do lists keep us organized. Weather and news apps keep us informed. Games feed into our desire to be entertained. Even silly novelty apps serve our basic need for acceptance by enabling people to bond over a few shared laughs. Although these general examples may be easy to recognize and understand, what about more specific needs?

If you're looking to build a nongame, such as a productivity or utility app, here are a few factors to consider:

- Pinpoint a need or issue that is currently not being addressed by existing apps.

- Does your app fulfill that need in a way that makes the mobile experience significantly easier than performing the same tasks on a desktop computer?

- If your app is similar to other existing apps, what feature(s) can you add that would solve the needs not currently addressed by your competitors?

Discovering Untapped Markets

Thousands of iPhone apps have very few users. AdMob, a popular mobile advertising network, reported that of the 2,309 iPhone apps that actively displayed embedded AdMob ads in May 2009, a whopping 54 percent of them (1,246) had fewer than 1,000 users each. Granted, that's a small cross section of apps compared to the sheer size of the App Store, but it's still a shocking wake-up call nonetheless, especially when you consider that most of the apps in AdMob's network are free.

Even if an app is free, it does not guarantee that people will use it. And if you expect people to pay for it, it's that much more important that your app provides a desperately desired service, feature, or experience—something users will feel compelled to download. Just because iPhone apps are inexpensive compared to traditional desktop software prices, they are no longer considered impulse buys like in the early days of the App Store. In the past year, users have packed their iPhones and iPod touches with so many apps that they've gradually become much more selective about which apps they choose to download. Just think about your own decision-making process when purchasing a new app. You may not think twice about spending $12 for a movie ticket, but for some curious reason, you more than likely contemplate at great length whether to spend a mere $2.99 on an iPhone game. I'm guilty of doing the same thing, even though as a programmer myself, I'm fully aware of how much hard work goes into creating an iPhone application.

Part of the problem is that with so many iPhone apps priced at only 99 cents in an attempt to boost volume sales and rank higher on the App Store charts, users now have a distorted perception of app worth. Unfortunately, this has conditioned users to expect a lot of value for very little money. To cut through this purchase barrier, your app *must* be special, providing a unique experience and/or satisfying an existing need.

With more than 100,000 apps in the App Store, at first glance it might appear that all the original ideas have already been taken. When Apple says, "There's an app for that," the company is really not kidding...or so it would seem. But then every so often, a pioneer comes along with a new app that causes iPhone developers worldwide to slap their own foreheads while shouting, "Why didn't I think of that?"

Sometimes the coolest ideas are the simplest concepts, hiding right under our noses. As developers, we're so captivated (and envious) over the success stories of our peers that one of the first instincts to strike is often the most fatal: how to take advantage of current trends by riding the coattails of what's popular. When iFart Mobile became a runaway hit in 2008, a flood of copycat fart apps bombarded the App Store, hoping to cash in on the popular novelty. Jumping on the bandwagon, the first handful of copycat apps probably generated enough sales to justify their development, but at a certain point, the App Store became over-saturated. With more than 500 fart-related apps currently available, the odds of consumers finding and purchasing your new fart app are highly unlikely. When having to choose from such a large assortment, it's simply too overwhelming to look at them all, so consumers will more than likely settle for the most popular ones currently residing near the top of the charts.

Wouldn't you much rather be the visionary who develops *that* app—the one that hundreds of developers rush to emulate? Of course, we all would. So, how does one go about finding new untapped ideas?

First take a look at your own needs and interests. Sure, you're a developer, but first and foremost you're also a user. Is there some missing functionality that you'd love to see added to the iPhone? If so, do any existing apps already provide that functionality? No? Well, if it's a feature you want, then odds are, there are others out there wishing for the same thing…and maybe even willing to pay for it. Bingo.

It's worth noting that some wish-list items might make great features but not great apps. For example, the heavily requested feature Copy & Paste was finally added to the iPhone OS 3.0, but it doesn't really make sense as its own stand-alone app.

What interests do you have outside of technology? There are successful apps for bird-watchers, comic book collectors, sports fans…and the list goes on. If you're passionate about a specific hobby and have not found any related apps, then that might be a great space to fill. Just remember that the more niche it is (underwater basket weaving, anyone?), the smaller your potential customer base will be. If you develop a journal log for the small yet dedicated group of arctic nude swimmers, you may make a few shivering, blue-lipped individuals happy, but you may not make much money doing it. By broadening that idea to encompass all water sports (including custom log templates for surfers, boaters, swimmers, and scuba divers), your journal app dramatically expands its potential customer base, making it a much more viable app concept.

If you're feeling particularly void of any original ideas, try turning to your friends and family. See what specific needs and interests they have that might be well suited for a mobile app. But whatever you do, please do not solicit for app ideas on your blog, on your Facebook page, or via Twitter. Although your followers may provide some great suggestions, accepting their feedback leaves you legally vulnerable. If your app becomes successful, you run the risk of a stranger suing you for stealing their idea without providing adequate credit or compensation for it, producing evidence in the form of an archived tweet or blog comment they posted to you. You're better off limiting your inquiries to only your trusted friends and family.

Another great source for original ideas is your local newsstand. Although that may seem a little "old school," don't discount the ease of flipping through the pages of the latest magazines. The Internet is a vast treasure chest of data, but you have to know what you're searching for in order to find anything of relevance. At a newsstand, you can quickly browse through dozens of popular magazine genres. Print is expensive, so if there's a monthly magazine dedicated to a topic, the odds are good that enough people are interested in it to justify further exploration. The real question then lies in figuring out whether a decent percentage of those readers are tech-savvy and either plan to own or already own an iPhone. If the magazine has a web site, that's a good place to start, checking to see whether they have an active online forum, RSS feed, podcasts, or Twitter account. By just taking a few minutes to read some of the posts there, you can get a good feel for that magazine's reader base.

Also look to see whether any of the magazine advertisers are promoting computer- or mobile-related solutions. For example, writing magazines include several ads for software tools that assist authors with various elements of the writing business and the story-building process. The App Store already has several mobile writing tools to help authors organize their notes and story ideas, but what about giving freelance writers the ability to track the status of submitted queries to potential publishers?

Now that you have a general idea of what to search for, it's time to take your investigation to the Internet. Although there are several desktop software programs and subscription-based web sites that offer that query-tracking service, there do not seem to be any iPhone apps that handle that particular task (yet). Of course, by the time you read this, there very well may be several apps in the App Store that do just that, so if you do stumble upon an untapped market such as this, it's best to start developing your app quickly. If you discovered a new niche, I can guarantee there are *at least* a dozen other developers thinking about similar app concepts. Time is of the essence.

It's important to note that if you introduce an entirely new product concept that is unlike anything else in the App Store, be aware that your marketing efforts will require educating consumers on why they should buy an app they do not yet know they need or want. When fulfilling an existing demand, you're selling to a known target audience. In either case, just remember this famous (and very relevant) saying: "There's no such thing as an original idea. It's who does it first that counts."

Enhancing the Mobile Experience

Expanding on the writing-related app idea that I previously mentioned, don't just emulate the feature sets of similar desktop software programs and/or web sites. Not only is that disrespectful to those developers (not to mention the potential legal infringement issues involved), but you're not bringing anything new to the table. Why would writers opt to buy your query tracking iPhone app instead of a competing desktop program?

Are you simplifying the task? Are you adding any significant mobile advantages that would make it easier for traveling writers who are constantly away from their office? Do you plan on integrating Mail and iCal support to save them several steps when communicating with their editors and publishers?

A perfect example of a product that enhances the mobile experience is Bump, a free iPhone app that makes swapping contact information as easy as bumping hands with another Bump user (see Figure 2–1). Exchanging contact information is not a new concept in smartphones. For years, numerous mobile apps have tried to streamline this process in handheld devices, but they typically involve too many button clicks with complicated methods of "beaming" vCard-formatted data. Some of them are even limited to sending vCards via email, which adds even more steps. The developers of Bump utilized the iPhone's built-in technologies to simplify this need into a single action, which swaps contact information instantly and securely.

Figure 2–1. *Bump enhances the mobile experience by greatly simplifying the exchange of contact information between two people.*

"Our primary goal when designing Bump was to create a simple, fun, and intuitive way to connect two phones," says David Lieb, cofounder and president of Bump Technologies, Inc. "The accelerometer and location services allow us to do that: Bump monitors the output of the accelerometers and sends the output of the accelerometers up to the global Bump servers whenever a physical bump is felt. The servers then match up any pair of phones that felt the same bump at the same time in the same location. This allows connections to be made between any two phones with just a simple bump of the hands."

Lieb adds, "The idea for Bump came out of a moment of frustration (well, actually two moments). Back in 2005, I was working as an engineer, and it really bothered me that in order to get some simple data like names and phone numbers from one phone to another one not 12 inches away from it, I had to ask someone to read out their information, and I had to type it in. I wanted to be able to just touch the phones together and transfer the information—but the phones of 2005 didn't have what it takes to make that work. Fast-forward to 2008, when I went to business school and found myself typing in the phone numbers of dozens of new classmates. Same frustration, but this time, I noticed everyone was carrying smartphones, many of which had accelerometers and location awareness. So we decided to build Bump."

Even though the app's idea stemmed from the needs of its own developers, it appears to be fulfilling a common need that many people have. In July 2009, Bump surpassed a million downloads in the App Store.

The same logic of simplifying mobile tasks also applies for those developers who want to port their own Mac or Windows software apps into companion iPhone versions. Don't just repackage the same features in an iPhone interface. By designing your iPhone app to be easier to use for the often one-handed, fast-paced world of mobile users, not only will you strengthen the loyalty of your existing customers, but your iPhone app may also attract new users to your desktop versions.

Some people have even been known to switch from another mobile device (such as BlackBerry or Window Mobile) to an iPhone just so they could utilize a specific app that's not available on any other mobile platform.

Competing with Similar Apps

Does the world really need any more to-do lists, shopping lists, tip calculators, music jukebox quizzes, or fart apps? If you think it does, then it must be because you've identified some new feature that none of the other apps has tapped into—a feature that people want and need. If not, then trying to compete with the hundreds of existing tip calculators, to-do lists, and so on, may be futile, especially if there are really good ones that have captured that particular niche market well.

Perform an App Store search for *tip*, and you'll discover that there are currently more than 100 tip calculator apps in the App Store. True, it's a great idea for a mobile app, but how do you find an audience for your new app when competing with so many existing tip calculators, especially when some of them are very well done and have been heavily featured in the media? One of the most popular ones, Tipulator, was even showcased in an Apple iPhone ad.

Sure, it might be a lot easier to quickly churn out a tip calculator app than it would be to develop a complicated 3D game, but looking at such heavy competition in this space, would even such a simple app be worth developing if you couldn't sell any? It's difficult to justify putting any amount of time into a venture—no matter how small—if it turns out to be a bad investment. If you can't offer a new approach or new features that would motivate users to choose your app over the hundreds of other similar apps, then you may want to try another app idea.

Ah, but if you do know how to build a better mousetrap, then that along with some creative marketing may be enough to gain a toehold in the market. Just look at how many Twitter apps there are, yet new ones pop up all the time with bigger and better features or a more intuitive mobile interface, causing users to switch.

If you think you have a winning concept and do decide to tackle a specific niche that's already saturated with similar apps, just know that you'll have your work cut out for you.

It'll be an upward battle to grow your customer base when users have so many choices vying for their attention. You'll take a more in-depth look at how to analyze and outmaneuver your competition at a later point in this chapter.

If after releasing your app you find that competing in such a crowded space is too difficult and choose to abandon the app to develop a different product in a less crowded category, then you run the risk of tarnishing your reputation and the future of any new apps you release. Why would any users buy any other apps from you if they can't trust that you'll continue to support them with updates and new features? The App Store is littered with dozens of apps that have been abandoned by their developers from lack of sales. Their product pages are full of angry customer reviews, and although it may sound petty to complain about losing 99 cents, their complaints are not really about the money but about the principle at stake. You have to be passionate about your app with a commitment to continue maintaining it for the long haul in order to preserve the relationship with your customers.

When to Avoid Over-Saturated Categories

When it comes time to submit your app to the App Store, you'll be asked to select an appropriate category to place it in. Sometimes the most obvious choice is not always the best choice.

When researching similar apps in the App Store, take a good look at what categories they're located in and how well they are faring in those categories. Just this little bit of detective work alone can help you choose the best category that will give your app the greatest chance for exposure in the App Store.

A good example of this is DistinctDev's best-selling novelty app, The Moron Test. Even though the app includes several levels of game play, the developers made a conscious decision to avoid the massive Games category, opting instead to place it in the smaller Entertainment category. This turned out to be a smart move. The Moron Test quickly rose to the number-one paid app in Entertainment. That exposure as a top Entertainment app fueled even more sales, which in turn elevated its position to the top of the U.S. App Store's Top 25. Would The Moron Test have sold as well if placed in the Games category? Maybe not. Even though the main Games category is divided into 19 subcategories, such as Action, Arcade, and Board Games, it still would have proven difficult to compete against the immersive, high-action 3D games that dominate the overall Top Games chart.

Depending on the kind of app you have, sometimes this strategy can work against you. Obviously having the right keywords in your app name is vital so that you're included in related App Store searches (which I discuss later in this chapter), but people also like to browse their favorite categories to find new apps. With this in mind, don't pick a category just because it's smaller. It's important that you choose the category where most people will think to look for your type of app. So, even though DistinctDev bypassed the large Games category, placing The Moron Test in the smaller Entertainment category instead, it's still a very appropriate and intuitive location for this app.

For apps that would fit well in several different categories, the decision may not seem so obvious. When this happens, it's best to investigate the categories that similar apps have chosen, especially the apps that are selling well. For example, there are dozens of note-taking apps in the App Store, but would that kind of app be best placed in Utilities, Productivity, or Business? Do a quick App Store search for *notes* to see where most of those apps reside.

It's highly recommended that you use the desktop iTunes for all your competitive research since it displays much more information than the iPhone version of the App Store. For example, if you click an app from the search results, the app's category is not displayed in the iPhone's App Store listing, but it is displayed in the desktop version of iTunes (see Figure 2–2).

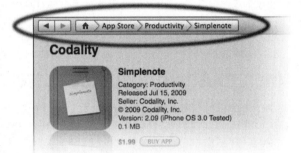

Figure 2–2. *If accessed from search results, an app's category is not listed in the iPhone's App Store (left), but it is listed in the desktop version of the App Store in iTunes (right).*

When I shop for writing software, my goal is to find writing tools that will help me be more productive as an author, so instinctively, the Productivity category would be my first choice to look, and it would appear that I'm not alone in that thinking. Although some note-taking apps are located in Utilities and Business, the majority of them reside in Productivity.

Sometimes, a particular category can limit your potential audience. In the case of Bump, the contact-swapping app I mentioned earlier in this chapter, the developers wanted the app to appeal to more than just business users. Although similar apps are rooted firmly in the Business category, the simplicity of Bump made it an easy data-sharing solution for anyone, so the decision was made to place it in the Social Networking category.

"At its core, Bump is much more than contact information exchange; it is a technology that lets two devices intuitively interact. We didn't want to pigeonhole Bump as a business app, nor did we want to position it as an iPhone-only utility," says Lieb. "By choosing the Social Networking category, we positioned Bump as a tool for connecting with the people around you. Also, we knew that if we were successful, being in the Social Networking category would put us right next to world-class brands like Facebook, MySpace, LinkedIn, AIM, Yahoo, and Loopt."

So when in doubt, check out your competition's category choices and the possible advantages they may gain from those locations.

Assessing the Competition

If you know your app idea faces some existing competition, don't rely on investigating only the ones you know. It's now time to do the legwork of finding all your major competitors in the App Store. After doing some initial searches, you may already have a rough idea of how many similar apps exist, but now you'll want to start compiling a list of them for later reference. And every time a new one pops up in the App Store, you should add it to your list.

Staying on top of what your competitors are doing is one of your primary jobs as a developer. The only way to grow your customer base and prevent users from switching to the other side is to make sure you're staying one step ahead of your competitors, and that requires keeping an eye on their updates. Believe me, if your app is a contender, then they're watching your every move too.

You'll want to perform several searches using different keywords and phrase variations in order to find any similar apps that exist. It's worth taking the time to create a list of keywords that you, as a user, might try in order to find these kinds of apps. Also, use a dictionary and thesaurus to discover additional related words. There's no telling what keywords other people may search for, so it's best to be thorough.

For example purposes, let's say you're looking to build an app that helps people locate where they've parked their car. Since forgetting where one has parked their car after a sporting event or a long day of shopping seems to happen to the best of us, it's actually a fitting concept for a mobile app—one that is the basis for at least 20 different apps currently available in the App Store.

To find all of these parked-car finder apps, let's run through a few searches in the App Store. The search results for keywords like *car* and *park* included too many nonrelated apps, so let's narrow our search to a phrase. Interestingly enough, *car finder* delivered very few results, but searches for *parked car*, *car locator* (see Figure 2–3), and *car park* (see Figure 2–4) returned plenty of relevant apps.

Figure 2–3. *Searching the App Store for* car locator *found six related apps on the first screen.*

Figure 2–4. *Searching the App Store for* car park *found seven related apps on the first screen.*

Now this part is important. Did you notice that a select few apps, such as G-Park, Where's My Car?, and iCarPark are coming up in almost all the related searches? It's no coincidence that at the time of this search, these three apps are ranked higher in Top Paid Navigation Apps than any of the others.

Sure, G-Park has a slick interface and has benefited from publicity outside of the App Store, such as being featured in Apple's International iPhone commercial, *USA Today*, *Los Angeles Times*, and *New York Times*, so in regards to G-Park sales, there's more at work here than just keywords.

But for all three of those apps to outperform their competition and consistently show up in most of the relevant searches—and in the first screen of results, no less—proves they're utilizing important keywords and strategic app names to help achieve this. When most consumers search for a type of app, they usually won't read past the first few screens of results, so it's important that you study the description and name of your major competitors' apps to figure out which keywords are crucial for you to include. Although descriptions are no longer searchable in the App Store, they do often include eye-catching text phrases that could prove valuable in your keyword quest. Getting placement in the first or second screen of related search results will provide much needed exposure for your app, which, ultimately, can also help boost sales.

Another tip for hunting down your competition is to read the customer reviews for the apps you already found. Often, customers will compare apps in their reviews, recommending one over the other. Make sure to add any new mentions to your growing list of competitive apps and also take a close look at them. Were the reviewers correct in their comparison of the apps and their features?

Alternative App Directories for Competitive Research

You'll perform most of your searches within your regional App Store in iTunes, but don't forget about competitive apps that may be available only in other countries. This is especially important if you plan on eventually making your app available in several country-specific App Stores outside your own. Here are several web-based, third-party app directories that are worth exploring. This is by no means an exhaustive list but merely a select group of sites to get you started. New iPhone app directories are springing up all the time, so beyond this list, you may want to search the Web for other sites.

- Appolicious: http://appolicious.com/
- AppShopper: http://appshopper.com/
- Apptism: http://www.apptism.com/
- Fresh Apps: http://www.freshapps.com/
- Macworld AppGuide: http://www.macworld.com/appguide/
- Yappler: http://www.yappler.com/
- AppSafari: http://www.appsafari.com/
- iGoApps: http://www.igoapps.com/

- VersionTracker: http://www.versiontracker.com/iphone/
- MacUpdate: http://m.macupdate.com/iphone.php

Analyzing App Ranking Statistics

After getting a handle on how much competition is out there for your particular niche, it's also important to find out how your competitors are faring in the App Store. Are they ranked high in the App Store charts? Have any of them broken out of their primary categories to rank well in overall downloads? Do those apps perform better in some countries but not in others? This information can also help you determine whether a particular niche is popular or profitable enough to warrant your own development investment in it. Your iTunes Connect account limits you to only your own app statistics, but thankfully, some amazing alternatives can assist in your competitive research quest.

Mobclix

http://www.mobclix.com/appstore/

Beyond offering a compelling platform of iPhone services, ranging from embedded mobile advertising to sophisticated app analytics, Mobclix also provides comprehensive app rankings for the U.S. App Store (see Figure 2–5). Want to investigate the charting trends of your competition or even your own apps? You can find a wealth of valuable information here. The Mobclix web site should be a required destination for all iPhone developers.

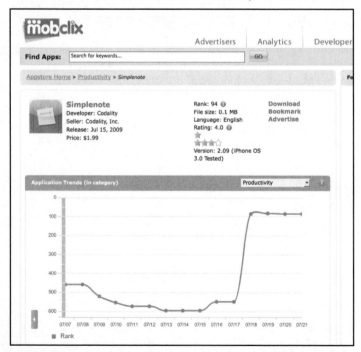

Figure 2–5. *Charting the app ranking history of Simplenote at Mobclix.com*

MajicRank

http://majicjungle.com/majicrank.html

Majic Jungle Software's David Frampton has created a very handy free Mac OS X application that allows you to easily track iPhone app ranking statistics across "The Big Eight" countries, as well as many other countries (see Figure 2–6). David has put a lot of work into this free software tool, so if you find it useful, consider buying one of his iPhone apps as your way of saying thanks.

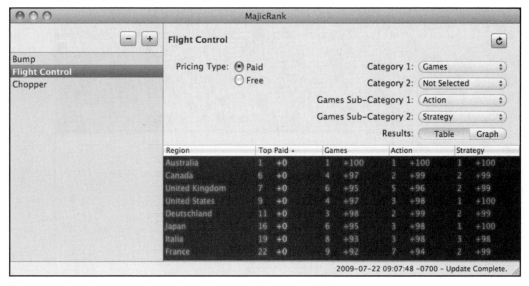

Figure 2–6. *Tracking app rankings with the free Mac OS X app, MajicRank*

APPlyzer

http://www.applyzer.com/

APPlyzer is a popular web-based source for free and paid app ranking statistics (see Figure 2–7). It's a subscriber-based service for tracking paid apps, but it offers the service free for tracking free apps. This site really provides an extensive amount of information for both regional App Stores and overall worldwide stats, so it's well worth the small fee to upgrade to the premium service.

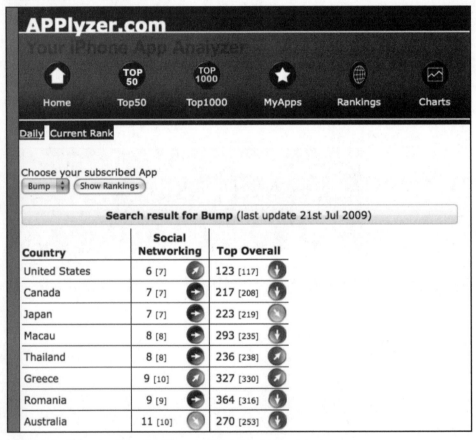

Figure 2–7. Comparing the rank of Bump in different countries at Applyzer.com

App Store Metrics by 148Apps.biz

http://148apps.biz/app-store-metrics/

This is a great web site, chock-full of iPhone development news and business insights. But beyond all of its wonderful content, 148Apps.biz may be best known for its comprehensive App Store metrics, which include statistics on active app count, submissions, approvals, app prices, and distribution of apps across the various categories (see Figure 2–8).

Figure 2–8. *148Apps.biz reveals the number of iPhone apps in each category.*

Top App Charts

http://www.topappcharts.com/

Top App Charts offers a unique spin on app ranking statistics by charting the big movers and shakers on the lists. Similar to APPlyzer, this free site uses visual markers for big debuts, jumps, and drops to reveal the actual movement of apps through the ranks.

Yappler's App Store Stats

http://www.yappler.com/Apple-iPhone-App-Store-Stats/

Even though Yappler was already listed earlier in this chapter as an app directory site, it also provides some interesting App Store statistics worth checking out.

Other Resources for App Ranking Statistics

Although several other app analytics services, web sites, software tools, and even a few cool iPhone apps track App Store ranking—such as AppFigures, AppViz, and Heartbeat—they're more focused on analyzing your own app's statistics and collecting data from your iTunes Connect account's sales logs. So, even though these resources may fall beyond the scope of competitive research, don't worry—they'll be profiled here in later chapters.

Finding Inspiration in Your Competitors' Customer Reviews

Continuing with the competitive research example on parked-car finder apps, now that you've compiled a list of all similar apps, it's time to take a closer look at their individual feature sets and their customer reviews. All of these apps use the iPhone's built-in GPS location awareness to first store the user's parked-car location and then again to determine the user's current location to help them map a route back to their parked car, displaying an embedded map framework, such as MapKit. Some of the apps don't offer much more than that basic functionality. Others offer some additional features such as saving a text note, voice memo, and/or photo of your parked location for logging the actual row, level, spot number, and so on (perfect for parking structures). And even a select few include the ability to log your arrival time, and if you parked at a meter, they can track the amount of time remaining on your meter so you can return to your car before it expires.

The interesting thing about comparing these apps is that they all deliver similar features in vastly different interfaces. And based on the posted customer reviews, you can quickly determine which interfaces have proven to be easy to use and which are less intuitive, causing user frustration.

Now, I'm not going to direct any criticism toward any specific apps here. Nor am I going to reveal which apps received negative customer reviews. The goal of this book is to help developers make more money with their iPhone apps, so I don't want to unintentionally make it any harder for them by pointing out their weaknesses. You can easily see for yourself which apps are receiving poor ratings in the App Store. So, for the purpose for this example, I'll give you a general look at customer reviews as a gauge of what some of these apps are doing right and wrong without naming any names. Let's dive in.

Learning from the Mistakes of Others

For those apps that log the remaining time left on your parking meter, some customers posted negative reviews, wondering why the app does not notify them with an alert, reminding them when their meter is about to expire. For example, one reviewer gave a low two-star rating, citing "needs a timer for meters that can alert you when the app is closed." As developers, we see these types of comment as a feature request, but disappointed consumers tend to view them as missing features. Unfortunately, their "feature requests" are posted as negative ratings, which hurt the overall perception of the app and can impact sales. The goal is learn from the mistakes of your competitors in the hopes of avoiding (as much as humanly possible) those kinds of reviews.

Most, if not all, of these apps also fall prey to a ton of negative reviews that complain about slow GPS performance and inaccurate GPS results. More often than not, these two factors aren't caused by faulty programming but rely more on the user's current signal strength and the GPS shortcomings of older iPhone models. Most people (especially nontech users) don't understand the limitations of their mobile devices, so they simply blame the app for these issues.

To work around those GPS-related complaints, most of the developers have stated in very clear language in their App Store descriptions that for best results they highly recommend using an iPhone 3G or 3GS, which offers much improved GPS location accuracy. But it would appear that many users are not taking the time to read the disclaimers in the App Store descriptions so then are upset when the app does not perform well on their iPod touch devices (which lack true GPS).

These developers also warn that if you're located deep within an underground multifloor parking structure, the thick concrete obstructions above you may prevent the app from pinpointing your exact location. The GPS built into a user's car loses its signal underground, but somehow the iPhone app's GPS is expected to still work flawlessly? It's not always about logic but about anticipating user expectations.

The apps that have fewer GPS-related complaints have successfully attacked the problem from within. Instead of relying solely on their App Store descriptions, these select few developers have taken a proactive approach by also integrating status indicators into their apps' interfaces. These UI indicators range from showing users the progress of retrieving the GPS location data (for impatiently dealing with slow signals) to location accuracy ratings (for notifying users if the retrieved GPS data is weak or not). A couple of these apps have even taken it one step further by enabling the user to manually adjust the location position on the map screen when the retrieved GPS results prove inaccurate—this also helps prevent frustration from iPod touch and first-gen iPhone users (the ones who missed the 3G disclaimer).

From just our little example of parked-car finder apps, you can see that customer reviews can teach you a lot about what users expect in this kind of app. By monitoring their likes and dislikes with similar apps, you can better plan what features you need to build into your own app to be competitive in this space. Anything less, and you'll be receiving the same feedback from your customers.

Going Beyond the App Store's Customer Reviews

Although the App Store's customer reviews are very helpful in the course of doing competitive research, it's important to keep in mind that Apple's current implementation of it is somewhat flawed. When deleting an app from your iPhone, Apple asks whether you'd like to rate the app first. Obviously, if you're deleting an app, either you didn't like it or you no longer have any use for it, so this automatically invites negative ratings. Whereas to leave a positive rating for an app you love (and plan on using indefinitely), you have to go out of your way to find the app in the App Store to post your review. So, with this in mind, don't assume that the App Store's customer reviews are always a fair representation of an app's quality and value.

You should also take a look at the many web sites and blogs that offer extensive app reviews. Many of them also post video walk-throughs of the apps with audio commentary.

Like the iPhone app directories I mentioned earlier, this is not an exhaustive list, but there should be enough third-party app review sites here to get you started. A lot of podcasts and YouTube video app reviews are available online that are worth searching for as well.

- AppVee: http://www.appvee.com/
- AppCraver: http://www.appcraver.com/
- 148Apps: http://www.148apps.com/
- Touch Arcade: http://toucharcade.com/
- App Store HQ: http://www.appstorehq.com/
- Appmodo: http://appmodo.com/
- iPhoneAppReviews: http://www.iphoneappreviews.net/
- iPhone Application List: http://iphoneapplicationlist.com/
- The iPhone App Review: http://www.theiphoneappreview.com/
- What's on iPhone?: http://www.whatsoniphone.com/
- The App Podcast: http://iphoneapppodcast.com/

- User Recommended iPhone Apps: http://iphone.iusethis.com/

- iPhone App Ratings: http://www.iphoneappratings.org/

- AppChatter: http://www.appchatter.com/

- TouchMyApps: http://www.touchmyapps.com/

Plus, here are a few general iPhone-related sites that publish app reviews:

- Macworld AppGuide: http://www.macworld.com/appguide/

- iPhone Alley: http://www.iphonealley.com/reviews/apps/

- Ars Technica: http://arstechnica.com/apple/iphone/apps.ars

- AppleTell:
  http://www.appletell.com/apple/archives/category/iphone-sdk/

- The Unofficial Apple Weblog: http://www.tuaw.com/category/app-review/

- Apptism: http://www.apptism.com/reviews

- AppAdvice: http://appadvice.com/appnn/category/reviews/

Taking Your Competition for a Test-Drive

So, you've spent hours reading the reviews, but have you tried the apps yourself? Don't just take their word for it. Nothing beats firsthand knowledge. Download your competitors' apps, and kick the tires a little.

I know you're probably hesitant to put money in the pockets of your competitors, but with app prices hovering between 99 cents to a few dollars, you don't have to worry about them getting rich off of your small purchase. Besides, it's in your best interest to play with the interfaces and functionality to see how well the apps accomplish their task. It's a good way to learn which UI pieces work and which elements feel awkward or nonintuitive—something you may not be able to properly evaluate by just viewing screenshots.

Even if lite/free versions of the apps are available, it's important to also download the paid versions as well in order to try the premium features that aren't available in the free editions.

The good news is that with app prices being as low as they are, even developers on a tight, shoestring budget can typically afford this, since purchasing a dozen iPhone apps probably won't cost you more than a single DVD movie.

Defining Your Differentiator

Now that you've done your homework, researching your competition, I'll talk about your app's feature set. Mimicking the same features as similar apps won't propel your sales ahead of the pack. You have to offer something more, something better than the existing solutions.

What can your app do that makes it better than the rest of your competition? If you're building a parked-car finder app, what makes your app different from the others? You need to define one or more unique differentiators that make your app stand a cut above similar apps.

Upon reading customer reviews, you've discovered that some of the apps that track the remaining time left on a parking meter do not (yet) support the ability to notify the user with a reminder alert before their meter expires. If none of the other apps offers this functionality, then parking meter time notifications would be a nice differentiator to add to your own app, especially since many customers have already requested this feature.

Say you're meeting your friends at the mall and you want to let them know your exact location without having to call or text them all individually. If your competitors aren't addressing this potential convenience, then enabling your app to broadcast your current map location to your friends via Twitter, email, or Facebook with a single button click could prove to be a great differentiator.

Basically, your differentiators should be exciting enough that when promoting your app, these unique features make the purchase decision very easy for people who are evaluating your app along with several other similar apps. If users want that differentiating feature and no one else has it, then buying your app becomes a no-brainer.

But you can't stop there. Sooner or later (usually sooner than you'd like), your competition will add those same features to their apps to remain competitive. And they'll probably "one-up" you with a few new features of their own, forcing you to come up with some new differentiators in subsequent updates to ensure that people remain interested in your app.

Having multiple differentiators defined, along with a loose road map of new features you plan on adding to future versions, will help keep your app relevant and competitive. For example, earlier versions of the iPhone OS did not support a landscape keyboard in Mail, Notes, and Messages. To satisfy the demand for easier two-thumb typing, a slew of wide keyboard apps flooded the App Store, offering the ability to type emails and notes in landscape mode. Many of those apps were one-trick ponies with the landscape keyboard being their only key selling point. When iPhone OS 3.0 added landscape keyboard support to Mail, Notes, and other built-in Apple apps, it instantly invalidated the usefulness of many of those one-function apps. The ones that survived were the apps that still had something unique to offer, such as syncing notes with Google Docs, organizing notes into groups, posting notes to Twitter, and so on.

Just keep in mind that the more features you add, the more streamlined and intuitive your interface design needs to be, especially on a small mobile screen. After several updates, if your app begins to feel bloated and cluttered, then it is failing its primary objective, which is to provide an easy-to-use mobile experience. Take a look at atebits' popular Twitter client, Tweetie. The developer, Loren Brichter, continues to add dozens of new features with every release while spending a great deal of time simplifying the UI design so that additional features never interfere with enjoying the app's core Twitter functionality. Each new feature he implements serves to further empower the user without diminishing the app's usability.

What's in an App Name?

While researching the competition, you undoubtedly performed a countless number of searches within the App Store. Along the way, you discovered that the words used in an app's name and related keywords can affect its placement in App Store searches. I'll discuss how to refine your App Store display name, keywords, and description in Chapter 9, so for now let's focus on your app name. Obviously, in the App Store, you're able to add short captions to your app's display name to help ensure inclusion in relevant search results, but we won't worry about those long App Store names just yet.

Your app name is the one you will use to promote your app everywhere, both inside and outside the App Store. Coupled with its icon, your app name is a brand—one that you hope to build into a recognizable name that is both symbolic of its core function and appealing enough to be memorable. If people can't easily remember your app's name, they can't recommend it to others.

This is also the name that is listed in the very small space under your app icon when displayed on an iPhone's home screen. You've got approximately 12 characters to play with. Anything longer than that, and you risk your name being truncated (with "…"). For example, Rebisoft's Jack Nutting developed a stellar retro shooter game called Diabolotros, which makes great use of the iPhone's Accelerometer. Having grown up in the 80s, I spent a fair amount of time in the arcades playing Space Invaders, so I quickly downloaded the free Diabolotros Lite to check it out. It's an addictive, fun game, and I soon purchased the full version. I noticed that Diabolotros, at 11 characters long, displays quite nicely under the app icon on my iPhone home screen. DiabolotrosLite, however, is too long, so in order for it to fit, the name is automatically truncated to "Diabol…sLite" (see Figure 2–9).

Figure 2–9. *Try to keep your app name to 12 characters or less to avoid a truncated display on the iPhone's home screen.*

Since adding the word *lite* or *free* would put most app names over the 12–character max, many developers have inserted a *lite* or *free* badge into their app icon as a visual marker for users to easily distinguish it from the full version. This alleviates the need to clutter your app name with those words.

In comparison, Digital Chocolate's 3D Rollercoaster Rush has quite a long name in the App Store, but its actual application name is shortened to 3D Coaster to ensure that it fits under the app icon on an iPhone. Luckily, users would still recognize the nickname *coaster* as meaning "rollercoaster." And for the free version, Digital Chocolate simply modified its app icon with a "free" badge (shown in Figure 2–9).

If you do use an abbreviated name for your application binary that's displayed on the iPhone home screen, take great care that it is not radically different from its App Store name. If the two names don't appear related in the eyes of Apple's app review team, it can be grounds for rejection from the App Store.

While Chapter 9 will be exploring app name conventions in more detail as it relates to App Store submissions, the point I'm trying to make here is that you need to think about these issues in advance when you're deciding upon your app name. Take extra care not to use long words that can't be broken down into nicknames or abbreviations. *Supercalifragilistic* is a memorable word but impossible to trim into a 12–character app name.

So now that you've figured out your length limitation, what would make for a good name? Finding the perfect name can be very challenging, but it's worth spending the time to get it right. In previous App Store searches, app names that included relevant keywords ranked well in the search results, but don't get too caught up with trying to integrate keywords into your app name. Remember, your app's name in the App Store can be much longer with a keyword-laden caption, so you should concentrate primarily on creating a name that's unique and memorable.

Although a name like Parked Car Locator is very descriptive, is rich with keywords, and can be easily shortened to the 11-character "Car Locator" when needed, it's probably too generic to be registered as a trademark. Since U.S. trademark law prevents the trademark ownership of common words that describe a service or function—common words that other companies need to be able to use to describe similar things—it would be very difficult to legally protect a name like Parked Car Locator.

Instead, try coming up with something a little more creative. To prevent getting lost in the forest, travelers would often place markers on branches or leave a trail of breadcrumbs so that they could find their way back home. Since finding your way back to your parked car involves a similar strategy, you might want to play around with a cute app name like Breadcrumbs, which is only 11 characters long. To ensure placement in relevant search results within the App Store, you could pack your app submission with important keywords and even expand your App Store name to Breadcrumbs—Parked Car Locator.

If another iPhone app is using a similar name, then you'll definitely want to come up with a different name. Even if you've locked in on a name that no one else is using in the App Store, you can't stop there. You should also search the Internet and all major software directories—Google.com, MacUpdate.com, and VersionTracker.com to name a few—to check for any possible conflicts on other software platforms.

You'll also want to search the United States Patent and Trademark Office's TESS database for any filed trademarks on that name (TESS stands for Trademark Electronic Search System):

`http://www.uspto.gov/main/trademarks.htm`

Searching TESS in no way obligates you to file a trademark. That's something you can do later when you're ready. For now, you merely want to make sure the name is not already trademarked by another party.

And if you're planning on making your iPhone app available in multiple regional App Stores beyond your own, then you'll also want to check for registered trademarks and any usage of that name in those respective countries. For guidance on securing and protecting your application name rights internationally, you may want to consult with a trademark attorney.

Why would it matter if a Mac or Windows software product is already using that name if you only plan on using it for your iPhone app? Well, it causes brand confusion for consumers who might incorrectly assume your app is the iPhone version of the Mac or Windows software of the same name. If another software company was using that name first and can prove prior art (prior public use of the name and logo), especially if they've already registered the trademark, you'll find yourself legally vulnerable. You don't want to spend months developing your app only to receive a cease-and-desist letter from their attorneys. Even worse, if your iPhone app has become a successful best-seller in the App Store, you don't want them to sue you for trademark infringement and a percentage of your app royalties.

My intent is not to scare you but simply to make you aware of the potential land mines to watch out for when picking a unique name for your iPhone app.

This is the kind of legal safeguarding that you'll want to do for your original app name, icon, and logo, so check out the section in Chapter 3 where Michael Schneider explains the benefits and process of registering a trademark.

Registering Web Site Domain Names

Now that you've decided upon an app name, you'll want to snatch up a domain name for it before someone else does. Having a dedicated web site for your iPhone app is critical to its success. It's a central place for promoting your app and providing customer support. Don't worry about the design and structure of it yet. I'll discuss methods for shaping it into a thriving promotional tool and support center in Chapter 8.

The important task at hand is to secure a good domain name for your app. To find out whether the domains you want are taken (and if so, who's using them), you'll want to search the WHOIS database. Here are a few sites where you can do this:

- Domain Tools Whois Lookup: `http://whois.domaintools.com/`
- Whois Domain Search: `http://www.whois.net/`
- Network Solutions WHOIS: `http://www.networksolutions.com/whois/`

The advantage to doing your searches via WHOIS instead of just searching for domain names at a domain name registrar is that those simple availability searches will only tell you whether a domain is already taken, whereas a WHOIS search will often provide detailed information on the owners of taken domains.

If you're having trouble finding an available domain name that matches your app name, then try adding the word *app* to the end of it, or *game* if it's a game. For the popular iPhone app Simplenote, the domain Simplenote.com was already taken, so the developers registered SimplenoteApp.com.

To register your domain, GoDaddy.com and NetworkSolutions.com are popular registrars, although I prefer Register.com. Plenty of alternatives exist, with many of them offering cheaper registration prices, so do a little shopping online first to find a domain name registrar that offers the features you need at a price that fits your budget.

If you currently maintain your own blog or web site, you don't have to create a stand-alone site for your iPhone app. You can add a directory to your existing site for your iPhone app-related web pages and then redirect your iPhone app URL to that new directory in your site. Why have an iPhone app URL if your existing web site or blog already has a custom URL? It just looks a lot more professional to point consumers to the following:

```
http://www.breadcrumbsapp.com/
```

than to the following:

```
http://www.mywebsite.com/software/iphone/breadcrumbs/
```

In addition, the short, dedicated iPhone app URL is a lot easier for people to remember. And most domain registrars offer web-forwarding services so that you can easily set your iPhone app URL to redirect to wherever you want. Driving traffic to your existing web site is also a great strategy for cross-promoting other iPhone apps, software, or services you offer.

Building a Unique Identity for Your iPhone App

Before I dive into effective app icon design in Chapter 4, I wanted you to start thinking about app icon ideas now. With all that competitive research done, you've had the opportunity to see the app icons that you'll be competing against.

It's important to have an app icon that's unique yet still reflective of your app's core function and UI design. This may sound obvious, but it's always surprising to me how many developers design an app icon in their own isolated vacuum without regard to the icons their competition are already using. Because of this, many similar apps unintentionally have similar icons. When doing a search in the App Store for a particular kind of app, the results are a page full of app icons that often all look very much the same, which in turn makes the entire group look rather generic on the surface.

If you're building a writing app and all the similar apps utilize notebook-themed icons, try coming up with a clever visual that's different yet still communicates writing. If most of your competitors are using blue icons, think about using a contrasting color for your app icon (such as red or orange). You're attempting to package your iPhone app as a brand, but in order for this to succeed, the brand identity you're pitching has to be unique and eye-catching.

Like I said, since you have your list of competing apps sitting in front of you, your app icon design is merely something to think about between now and Chapter 4, especially since the next chapter will include helpful facts about filing a trademark for your app name and icon. So percolate on it. We'll revisit this design topic again soon.

Making Progress

You covered a lot of ground in this chapter, so take a moment to breathe. The next chapter is an important one. Yes, it tackles all of that daunting legal stuff that programmers would rather not deal with, but this is vital knowledge for safeguarding your iPhone business. Michael Schneider, an expert lawyer turned iPhone developer, will walk you through the essentials of protecting both yourself and your intellectual property.

Chapter 3

Protecting Your Intellectual Property

This chapter was contributed by Michael Schneider, a technology transactions attorney and iPhone developer. As an attorney, Michael works with clients on intellectual property and technology-related contracts, helping them build, monetize, and protect their products. As an iPhone developer, Michael has published a number of successful applications, including TouchType, Private-I, and Andrew Johnson series of self-help applications.

When you build an iPhone application, you are creating intellectual property by building software. Unlike traditional businesses, software companies typically don't build their value through physical assets. As you build your business, you probably won't build factories or buy fleets of trucks. The value of your business is not going to be in real estate or equipment; it is going to be built on the intangible assets that you create. Your products and your ownership of them will be your company's core assets, so it is important to understand how to identify and protect the intellectual property that will become the basis of your company's value.

In addition to being something that you can sell or license to other people, intellectual property rights are a way that you can stop competitors from stealing your work. Even if you have no intention of monetizing your intellectual property beyond selling your application to end users, understanding your rights can help you fend off copycats.

Similarly, as an app developer, you will want to avoid infringing the intellectual property rights of other people. Understanding the strengths and limitations of intellectual property will help you understand what is and isn't permissible under the law, so you can fend off those who try to bully you with trumped up claims and so you can better understand where the lines are to avoid violating someone else's rights.

In this chapter, you will explore how to obtain the different types of intellectual property protection available to you and which ones make the most sense in the context of app development. You will also explore some of the common pitfalls that can hurt your intellectual property rights and the value of your business.

To give you a sense of where this chapter is coming from, before venturing into iPhone development, I worked as a lawyer for technology companies helping to build, protect, and monetize products. As a disclaimer, even among iPhone developers, every person's legal needs are different. Although I will try to explain in general terms some of the legal issues surrounding iPhone development and app sales, this chapter should not be taken as legal advice. My hope is that you will use the information in this chapter to become aware of some of the legal issues to watch out for and use that information to engage in a more meaningful way with a legal professional.

What Is Intellectual Property?

I talk to a lot of developers who have heard about intellectual property and understand that it is something that they should care about but are unclear on exactly what intellectual property is.

Intellectual property (IP) is a term that refers to the intangible rights that you or your company can possess in your creative work. In our case, this creative work will likely be an iPhone application, but it could also be components of that application, such as music or graphics.

The primary benefit that intellectual property gives you is the right to exclude others from using your protected work. In other words, this is the right to stop other people from using your creative work, assuming it is protected properly. If a competitor or another company takes something that you have properly protected (for example, your icon, your graphics, and in some cases your idea), intellectual property rights give you the ability to sue to stop them and possibly recover damages (that is, money).

Each type of intellectual property protects a different type of content in a different way. In the case of a copyright, the authors are granted the right to dictate who can copy, distribute, publicly perform, modify, or create derivative works from their original work of authorship. In the case of a patent, the inventor is granted the right to stop other people from using, making, or exporting the subject of the invention. Trademarks are intended to keep others from confusing your customers into thinking that the other company is you (or somehow affiliated with you).

Determining Your Intellectual Property Strategy

As you read this chapter, consider which types of intellectual property make sense in the context of your business and the apps that you are creating. These decisions about which types of protection to pursue, and why, are your company's intellectual property strategy. Like making a business plan, defining and understanding your company's intellectual property strategy will help you make better decisions and avoid pitfalls that could jeopardize the intellectual property assets you are trying to build.

Although every company has its own factors to consider when determining what type of IP protection to seek, some characteristics are specific to iPhone applications. So in this chapter, I will focus on the issues that are common to most iPhone developers.

iPhone Apps Are Different

Although iPhone applications share common origins with desktop software, certain differences influence the types of intellectual property that is worth pursuing. Our applications typically have a rapid time to market, and the barriers to entry are extremely low. iPhone applications are typically less expensive than their desktop counterparts, with most apps in the iTunes App Store priced at less than $5.

The iPhone platform is an unprecedented opportunity for one- or two-person teams to make apps that can compete against apps from giant, well-funded companies. A developer account with Apple costs only $99, and the tools you need to build apps are bundled with every new Mac. From a technology standpoint, Apple has built an incredibly robust framework for creating compelling user interfaces, which takes much of the work out of otherwise complex features such as animation.

On mobile devices, simple programs are often more valuable to users than more feature-rich applications. Where the best desktop application is typically determined based on the extent of its features and capabilities, the best iPhone apps do one thing very well, intentionally keeping features limited.

The simplicity and ease of development fostered by Apple's tools mean that apps can move from concept to publication extremely quickly. Development of iPhone apps is typically measured in weeks and months, as opposed to years, and many successful apps have been created in as short as a weekend.

For these reasons, independent developers dominate the iPhone application marketplace. Some of the biggest hits on the iPhone have been fairly simple independently developed apps. My original TouchType application took less than a week to make and was among the most popular apps in the App Store for about a month. Other simple apps, such as The Moron Test, currently top the charts. As I look through the list of top apps on the App Store, 15 out of the current top 25 apps on the App Store are developed by independent developers, with no preexisting brand. This new landscape requires a slightly different approach to intellectual property.

Developing an iPhone Specific Game Plan

As a developer of iPhone applications, a traditional intellectual property strategy may not fit your business. The speed with which apps can be developed and published makes some forms of IP less useful in the iPhone app context. You may have limited financial resources to pursue protection. The strategies described in this chapter are based on some assumptions that are tied to the nature of the App Store. These won't apply to everyone, but they should serve as a backdrop for your analysis.

- **Speed.** If your app is simple in nature, the competitors will appear almost instantly, so you may want to focus your efforts on IP protection that can be established fairly quickly. Rights that take years to establish are probably not well suited to the platform. Although you probably hope that your app will still be selling years from now in some form or another, there is a good chance mobile devices and applications will look very different in five years. With exceptions for app developers working on long-term business plans, developers should focus their energy on obtaining rights that can be protected immediately, such as copyright.

- **Cost.** The vast majority of apps fail commercially. As of the publication of this book, there are more than 100,000 applications in the App Store. When you combine the list of top 100 paid applications overall, together with the top 100 paid applications in each of the 40 categories (including the subcategories in Games), there are fewer than 4,000 apps represented in those top app lists at any one time. I estimate that 96 percent of iPhone applications published today haven't made more than $5,000. This means, depending on how ambitious your application is, you may want to focus on low-cost IP protection. Depending on your goals, it may make sense to wait and see whether you achieve a degree of success before spending money pursuing protectable rights in your work.

- **Geography.** You should also consider the worldwide nature of the App Store and whether you are going to focus your IP strategy solely in the United States or in other countries as well. This chapter is focused primarily on U.S. intellectual property law, but most other countries have some form of copyright, trademark, or patent protection available. Each additional country adds a layer of expense, and it would likely be impractical to pursue protection in all 77 countries that the App Store targets. Identify the jurisdictions that you care most about from a business standpoint, and then prioritize where you will spend your money. Most developers see the vast majority of their sales generated from the U.S. App Store, so protecting your interests in the United States is a good place to start. If you are developing your application outside the United States, you should be sure to do a trademark search in the United States to determine whether anyone else is using the mark already. A simple trademark search can be run yourself using Google, but if you want to conduct a more thorough search, including records, at the U.S. Patent and Trademark Office, there are trademark search services that you can pay to do a more comprehensive search. Whether to pay for a comprehensive search will depend primarily on how much you are investing in your new mark. If changing the name of your company or application would be workable, you might just rely on your Google search to determine whether anyone is using a similar mark. On the other hand, if you were about to embark on an expensive advertising or PR campaign to establish your brand, it would make sense to have a more thorough search performed before investing in the brand.

Copyrighting Your App

The concept of "copyrighting" an app is a little misleading because it implies that obtaining copyright protection for your work requires you to take proactive measures to have protection. In fact, in the United States and most other countries that follow the Berne Convention, some degree of copyright protection is established automatically the moment you put pen to paper (or start working in Photoshop or Xcode), assuming the thing you are creating is original to you. Copyright protects original works of authorship. This includes literary, dramatic, musical, and artistic works, such as poetry, novels, movies, songs, computer software, and architecture. In the case of iPhone applications copyright can provide protection for your source code, graphics, and sound effects in your app; the text of your instructions; app description; or creative video or audio content that you bundle with your app. Copyright does not protect facts, ideas, systems, or methods of operation, but if those facts, ideas, systems, or methods of operation are implemented in creative/artistic way, copyright might provide some protection for the way the these things are expressed.

How to Obtain a Copyright

A copyright automatically comes into existence when you create a work of authorship and fix it in a tangible medium. In app development terms, this means it starts when you type a line of code, draw some graphics, record sounds, or write your app's description. Assuming the work is creative and recorded somewhere (for example, on your hard drive or printed to a page), there is a copyright coming into existence.

Copyright protection is very affordable. A base level of protection exists at the time of creation without the need to pay lawyers or file a copyright application. That said, filing with the U.S. Copyright Office provides some important additional benefits. Registered works, for instance, may be eligible for statutory damages and attorney fees if you decide to sue an infringer. This means that although you can protect an unregistered copyright, you might not be able to win as much in the lawsuit as you would if it were registered. Fortunately, copyright applications are relatively inexpensive compared to patent or trademark filings. The current filing fee for a copyright application in the United States is $65 and can be as low as $35 if you file online. It is fairly common for authors and software developers to pay an attorney to handle their copyright registrations for them, but if you are comfortable with legal concepts and willing to ask questions when needed, filing a copyright application on your own behalf is an option that the U.S. Copyright Office supports. The place to start is http://www.copyright.gov/eco/. ECO stands for "electronic copyright office," and the Copyright Office has done a nice job of making the application process fast and easy through its site. Keep in mind that the government is not always on the cutting edge of technology. According to its most current documentation, their system supports Microsoft Internet Explorer 6.0 and Netscape Navigator 7.02 and apparently is not compatible with Safari. Since you probably don't have a copy of Netscape, you may need to run some Microsoft code to get things working properly.

If you are interested in filing a copyright on your own behalf, the Copyright Office has a detailed tutorial posted at http://www.copyright.gov/eco/eco-tutorial.pdf.

Limitations of Copyright Protection

A copyright is a strong and affordable means of protecting your apps content and code, but copyrights protect creative expression of ideas; they don't protect the ideas themselves. For instance, if you have an idea for an app that recommends new music to users based on the contents of their music library on their iPhone, a copyright could provide protection for your creative graphics or the text of your instructions. Copyright, however, would not provide protection for the concept of the application. In the context of iPhone applications, this is a huge limitation.

Filing Trademarks for App Icons and Logos

I'll spend more time discussing trademark protection than any of the other forms of intellectual property because I believe trademark represents an iPhone developers' most affordable and effective means of fending off competitors. In the "Copywriting Your App" section of this chapter, I discussed the limitations of copyright protection. An important limitation being that copyright does not protect ideas, so your app idea or concept will not have protection under copyright law. Patents can provide protection for concepts and ideas, but obtaining a patent is relatively expensive and time-consuming when compared with copyright and trademark. Trademark doesn't protect concepts or ideas but can protect the logos or name that you give your app if that name or logo is distinctive enough. Trademarks are a way to keep other developers from exploiting the goodwill you establish with your application or concept.

Let's say that you have created the first credit card processing application for the iPhone. You want to protect yourself, but filing a patent on the idea would take years before it resulted in an issued patent, assuming that your idea meets the criteria for patent protection. Without a patent, you don't have much protection for the concept, but you do have the advantage of being first to market. Your application, as the first of its kind, is likely to get media attention and could even be featured by Apple . Once your app has achieved a degree of success, the competitors are likely to start making similar apps. Without a patent, you may not be able to stop this from happening, but you can stop your competitors from tricking customers into thinking that they are you. Similarly, Apple's approval process does not provide any filter for copycat apps, so you can't assume that the approval process or Apple will be doing anything to stop knock-offs from hitting the store. By creating an icon, name, and interface that people associate specifically with your company, you can establish trademark rights. These trademark rights give you a tool that you can use to prevent other people from using confusingly similar branding on their app.

If a competitor copies your app in a way that is likely to cause customers to be confused as to whether the app came from them or from you, your trademark rights should give you a means to stop them. But all names and logos are not equally protectable. This section describes the basics of trademark protection and how to choose a protectable trademark to identify your company and apps.

How to Get a Trademark

Like copyright, with trademark you can obtain some rights automatically by simply using a name or symbol as an identifier of the source of your app. These "common law" trademarks are fairly limited, though, and there are significant benefits to filing a trademark registration with the U.S. Patent and Trademark Office.

A federal trademark registration provides notice to the public that you are claiming ownership of the mark. The registration also creates a legal presumption of your ownership of the mark and your exclusive right to use the mark nationwide in connection with the types of goods and services listed in your registration. Most important, a federal trademark registration is required to bring an action concerning the trademark in federal court.

The best way to find out more about the trademark application process is to visit `http://uspto.gov`. The Patent and Trademark Office has a wealth of information on its website about the process, and it offers step-by-step instructions on how to file a trademark application online. The federal government even operates a help line that you can call to get more information about the filing process. The help line cannot give you legal advice, but it is an extremely helpful, amazing resource. The Trademark Assistance Center's number is 1-800-786-9199.

There are advantages, however, to hiring a lawyer to help prepare your application. Often there is a back and forth required with the Patent and Trademark Office in the process, and having a professional working on your behalf can help you obtain the broadest possible rights for your mark.

Picking a Protectable Trademark

Some trademarks are stronger than others. Made-up names (for example, Exxon or Google) or those that have no literal connection to the company (for example, Apple for a computer company) are best to establish strong intellectual property rights. Names that require a slight leap of logic or merely suggest a company's products or services (for example, Titanium for a travel bag company, suggesting strength and durability) are protectable and often strike the right balance between developing strong brands and educating the public about the company.

On the other hand, names that describe what a company does (for example, Online Advertising, Inc., for company that sells Internet ads) tend not to be initially protectable. Companies often gravitate toward descriptive names—wanting the public to immediately understand the company's business. However, choosing a descriptive name can adversely impact a company's long-term bottom line. For example, it may be impossible to stop a competitor from using the same name, a descriptive name (which, by its nature, may be similar to others' names) may require additional marketing spend to differentiate it from a crowded field, and there may be additional expenses caused by the increased burden of "policing" others who want to use similar names.

As an app maker, you have two important opportunities to brand your app, your app name, and your icon. You also have the ability to specify your company name. First let's discuss your app name as a brand. The App Store places some unusual business constraints on the app name that you choose. In a non-iPhone app store context, I typically recommend picking a name that is does not describe or suggest the function of your product. Descriptive or suggestive trademarks are much more difficult to protect than arbitrary or fanciful ones. With iPhone applications, however, arbitrary marks pose a discovery problem. The problem is that on the iPhone the App Store will only display the first 17 or so letters of your application's name when listing apps. If you give your application an arbitrary a name, casual browsers of the App Store catalog may not find your app or realize that it is something that they need. For this reason, there are business advantages to choosing a less protectable mark; however, you should still seek to make your app name distinctive in some way. you sell a tip calculator and name it Tip Calculator, it is going to be nearly impossible for you to successfully obtain trademark protection for that name. On the other hand, if you name your tip calculator app TipStar and add a distinctive icon featuring a star, you have something that you can argue identifies the app as coming from you, as opposed to simply describing the app's purpose. In the TipStar example, if another developer published a tip calculator that featured a star-shaped logo or used the word *star*, Ryan Rowe, the developer of TipStar would have a legitimate claim of infringement. The distinction, Ryan's TipStar trademark goes beyond simply describing the app but adds something distinctive that exists for the purpose of distinguishing his apps from others. The star name and symbol are unrelated to the purpose of the app, so if Ryan put out an app called WeightStar or ConvertStar, he could build on the goodwill that he created with his initial app. Your goal should be to create a distinctive name that can identify your app as coming from you but without completely obscuring the purpose of your app. It is a fine line.

If you choose an app name that suggests the function of your app, you may want to take extra effort to make your icon distinctive. Figure 3–1 shows some examples of distinctive icons, compared with some icons that are less distinctive.

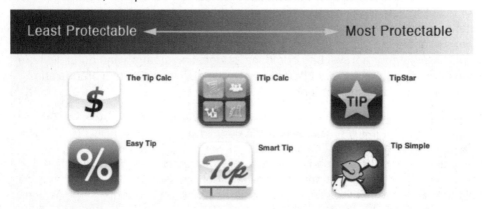

Figure 3–1. *Tip calculator names and icons from least to most protectable*

Trade Secrets

As a developer, you probably have some secrets worth protecting. Maybe it is the concept for your next game or app, an algorithm that makes your apps more efficient, or the source code behind one of your app's features. Trade secret law is one way you can protect those secrets, and qualifying for the protection is fairly simple. Trade secret law varies from state to state but typically provides protection for information that provides the owner of the information with an advantage over competitors in the marketplace and that is treated by the owner in a way that can be reasonably expected to prevent the information from being learned by other people, absent some improper action, such as breach of contract or theft. In simpler terms, if you have a secret that gives you a competitive advantage and you take sufficient steps to keep it a secret, you can sue someone if it is stolen from you.

How Do You Establish a Trade Secret?

Trade secret protection doesn't require any application or filing with the government. In fact, you don't need to do anything but take reasonable steps to keep the secret confidential. For protecting source code, this might mean keeping the code on a secure server. For protecting your unpublished product ideas, this might mean not talking about your app idea with people that haven't signed an NDA. The following are some minimum steps to take toward maintaining the confidentiality of information that you want to protect as a trade secret:

- **Education.** Be sure to educate all of your employees and contractors on the importance of maintaining confidentiality of company information. Being able to show that you took efforts to make sure everyone was aware of their responsibilities will help demonstrate that your company acted reasonably.

- **Contractual Protection.** Every full-time or part-time employee and all consultants (including founders and officers) should sign an employment agreement that contains provisions protecting confidential information of your company before commencing work and before any company trade secrets are revealed to them. Use nondisclosure agreements to protect confidential information disclosed to any other third parties.

- **Control of Tangible Materials.** Confidential documents and tangible materials should be marked as "Confidential," and access to these documents and materials should be limited to those employees and contractors who have a need to know such information for the performance of their duties to the company.

- **Control of Electronic Data and Code.** Be sure that source code and other confidential data is stored on secured computers that require a login and password to access.

Nondisclosure Agreements

Nondisclosure agreements, also referred to as *confidentiality agreements*, are used to create a confidential relationship that legally binds a party to protect the trade secret information of another party. Although a confidential relationship can be created through an oral agreement or can be implied by the conduct of the parties, I recommend that you always use an NDA when disclosing confidential information because oral or implied agreements are much more difficult to prove than written agreements.

At the core of most nondisclosure agreements is the obligation not to user or disclose the other party's confidential information.

If you are in a situation where both you and the other party will be disclosing confidential information to each other, the appropriate agreement would be a mutual nondisclosure agreement. Mutual NDAs tend to be drafted in an even handed manner, since the rights and obligations apply equally to both parties.

If you are in a situation, however, where you expect to disclose but not receive confidential information, you should consider using a one-way nondisclosure agreement that protects your confidential information but does not create any obligations for your company with respect to information received from the other party. An example of a situation where a one-way NDA would be appropriate would be if you are pitching a product idea to another company or hiring a contractor to perform work for you. In those cases, you might not want to be restricted in how you use information received from the other party, since it will likely apply to the product you are pitching or the work you are hiring the contractor to perform.

Nondisclosure agreements are a critical part of maintaining protection for your trade secrets. Trade secrets are protectable only if they are kept secret, so failure to put a confidentiality agreement in place with a third party before disclosing a trade secret even once can cause a loss of your trade secret rights.

Limitations of Trade Secret Protection

An important limitation to consider, however, is that trade secret protection applies only to nonpublic information, which means there is no protection for information that others can gather by simply inspecting your product. The secret recipe for Coca Cola is a famous trade secret, but its trade secret protection does not stop Coca Cola's competitors from buying a can and trying to reverse-engineer the finished product. This limitation applies equally to the observable elements of your iPhone application. Information that your users can access by analyzing your application are not protected under trade secret law because they stopped being secret once you published the app.

To help illustrate this distinction, let's imagine that you created a new search engine that runs on the iPhone. Imagine that this search engine is powered by a top-secret and highly effective algorithm that you invented to determine which search results are most relevant to the user. If it works, this algorithm would probably be your company's most valuable intellectual property asset. The key then would be putting out your application in a way that gives your users the benefit of the algorithm, without exposing exactly how it works.

Now let's assume the Google has learned of your amazing app and wants to incorporate the technology into its search engine. As the developer of this technology, you will clearly want Google to need to license or buy it from you or, better yet, acquire your company to get access to the secret. Before Google can do that, you can assume that they will probably buy a copy of your app and try to figure out how it works. Assuming you haven't patented your algorithm, if their engineers can figure out what how your algorithm works by testing and observing your program, they likely won't need to buy your company to implement something similar.

If you take sufficient efforts to protect the algorithm and it isn't ascertainable by simply observing your product, you can keep your competitors from using it. If they hack into your computers or bribe one of your employees to disclose the algorithm, you could sue them for trade secret misappropriation.

The fact that trade secret law covers only things that you can keep secret is an important limitation to consider and means that you will want to look to other forms of intellectual property protection (for example, copyright and/or patent) to protect aspects of your products that are visible to the user.

Patents

If you think of the various forms of IP as weapons, patent protection is the doomsday device. Patents are expensive to obtain and expensive to litigate, but they can offer extremely strong protection for inventive ideas and should scare the pants off of your competition. Entire business models or core technology can be sunk by a patent on preexisting technology that covers what the company is doing. For this reason, many areas midsize to large companies amass an arsenal of patents purely for defensive purposes so they will have something to fire back at their competition if they get sued.

Despite their strength, patents tend to be a bad fit for most iPhone developers. Costs vary, but typically hiring an attorney to file a patent application and take it through to publication costs more than $10,000. The process often takes two to three years, so your iPhone application would need to be long-term venture for the patent to become relevant. Games, for instance, have a fairly distinctive sales curve on the App Store. If a game is successful, it will see a spike in sales at or near launch, and then typically sales deteriorate over time. For a patent to be worthwhile, your inventive idea must still be valuable in three years. Meanwhile, having a patent in process doesn't give you any enforceable rights until the patent issues. Telling your competitors that you are coming for them once your patent issues might keep them investing too greatly in a competitive app, but if the competitive app is inexpensive to create (or the competitor already created it), they are likely to continue selling the app until your patent issues. Combine that with the fact that there are iPhone developers all over the world. Your patent may not scare a 14-year-old kid in India that is creating a competitive app and doesn't have much to lose by being sued.

All that said, there are cases where patents make a lot of sense for iPhone developers. The biggest downside of pursuing patent protection is the cost. If you are working on a particularly big budget or ambitious application and the $10,000+ it will cost you to pursue a patent is not a huge expense in the scheme of the overall project, obtaining a patent might be a smart move to try to protect your overall investment in the project. Another time when patent protection makes sense is if your application is a long-term venture. If three years is short in the grand scheme of your product's expected life cycle, the lengthy application process may not be an issue. Seriously think about your ambitions for your application, and decide whether you think people are going to still care in three years.

Is Your Invention Patentable?

Patents protect new and useful processes, machines, articles of manufacture or compositions of matter, or any new and useful improvement to those things. In general terms, among other requirements, to qualify for a patent, your invention must be new and useful, and you have to be able to describe it in a way that would instruct a person reasonably skilled in the area that your invention applies to make the invention work.

The requirement that the invention be "new" means that you have to be the first one to invent it. In the United States, if two people file a patent on the same invention, the patent would go to the first to conceive the invention, not the first to file the patent application. In fact, whether the other inventor files a patent at all, if they conceived of the invention first, your later filed patent can be invalidated. Even if no one conceived of the invention before you, the invention itself must be "nonobvious" to a person having ordinary skill in the area of technology related to your invention. This can be a tricky burden, since often the best inventions seem obvious once they have been invented. To this point, the test is whether the invention was nonobvious at the time it was invented. Because this is a difficult thing to determine once the invention is known, often the fact that no one had previously conceived of the invention despite having access to the same information as the inventor is used as evidence that the invention was not particularly obvious.

Another requirement for protection is that your invention must be described in your application in a manner that demonstrates that you have "reduced the invention to practice." This means that you have done more than conceive of the invention, but you have actually determined how to make it work with enough detail that a skilled person in your area of technology could produce it. For example, if I claim to have invented a time machine or a teleportation device, to qualify for a patent, I need to be able to describe how to build the machine or device in a way that actually enables someone to build it.

Assuming your invention qualifies for protection, a U.S. patent gives its owner the right to exclude others from making, using, offering for sale, or "selling" the invention in the United States or "importing" the invention into the United States for a period of 20 years from the date on which the application for the patent was filed in the United States. These rights are particularly powerful compared to copyright or trade secret protection because your right to prevent other people from making or selling your invention applies whether or not they copied or stole the invention from you. Even if they independently invent the same thing, if you conceived of it first, you may be able to stop them.

Avoiding the On Sale Bar

An invention will not qualify for patent protection unless its patent application is filed more than one year after it is first published, used in public, or on sale in the United States. This means if you demonstrate your invention or app to a potential investor or customer, you write a blog post about it, or your app is submitted to Apple, the clock is running. If you don't file your patent application within one year, you will lose the right to do so. For this reason, if you are considering pursuing patent protection, you should contact a patent attorney fairly early in the process so that they can help you determine how much time you have to file your application.

How to File a Patent

Although it is possible to file a patent application on your own, you will almost certainly get a broader and more defensible patent if you work with a patent attorney. Unlike contracts, where a plainly written agreement is actually preferable to a complex one, patent applications have a certain vocabulary that applies specifically to patent applications. Using the wrong phrasing to describe an invention can cause weaknesses in your patent claims. Patent attorneys and the Patent Office have their own language, and it is worth hiring someone that speaks it to translate your invention into the right terms to maximize the value of your patent. If you do try to draft an application on your own, you might at least hire a patent attorney to look it over before you file it to see if there are any obvious fixes that they can recommend.

Filing a Provisional Patent Application Yourself

Although the patent process is expensive and generally requires an attorney, there is a preliminary step that you can do yourself for a modest filing fee. This preliminary step is called a *provisional patent application*. A provisional patent application is basically a description of your invention that you file with the Patent Office to establish an early effective filing date if you decide to file a full patent application on the invention. The provisional patent application just holds your place in line so that if you file a full application, you can get the benefit of the earlier filing date. Generally speaking, provisional patent applications are pretty weak. They don't give you any enforceable rights and won't result in a patent unless you later file a full patent application before your time runs out (see the earlier "Avoiding On Sale Bar" section).

So why bother? A provisional patent application gives you the ability to use the term *patent pending* in connection with your product. The term *patent pending* doesn't mean that you have any legally enforceable rights, but it puts your competitors and potential competitors on notice that you have a patent application in the works. Depending on how expensive it will be for potential competitor to enter your market, making them aware that you are pursuing patent protection may be enough to dissuade them from making the investment. Many people simply don't know what patent pending means and won't want to find out.

If you don't file a nonprovisional patent application within the time allotted by the on sale bar, you will lose the ability to claim patent pending status, but by then, you should know whether your app has a future and decide whether it is worth spending the money to continue pursuing a patent.

You can file provisional patent applications online through the United States Patent and Trademark Office website at `https://sportal.uspto.gov/secure/portal/efs-unregistered`.

The USPTO has some instructions and information on its website, and there are some additional resources available from legal publishers like Nolo Press. Nolo has a book called *Patent Pending in 24 Hours* that can walk you through the process. If you think you are going to follow up with a nonprovisional patent application, you might also want to consult with the attorney who will be filing your full application. They would be able to file your provisional application for much less than a full application would cost, and they might be less restricted when filing the nonprovisional application than if they have to work from a provisional application that you drafted yourself.

Addressing Intellectual Property in Contractor and Employee Agreements

If you are hiring contractors or employees to help you create your application, it is imperative that you get an agreement in place with them to govern ownership of the intellectual property that they contribute to your application. It is a common misconception that the person hiring a contractor or employee automatically owns the rights to the work he or she creates. In reality, if you hire a contractor to create the code for your application or design your user interface, unless you have a written agreement indicating that you own the work product, it is unlikely that you will have all the rights you would like in the work delivered.

Hiring Contractors

Drafting an independent contractor agreement that protects your company involves more than just having the requisite intellectual property assignment provisions. You may want to work with an attorney to get a form in place that will cover your company from a variety of problems that can arise. You may want to include acceptance provisions for deliverables so that you know you will get what you expect. Or add liquidated damages for late delivery to motivate your contractor to deliver work product in a timely fashion. If your contractors are overseas in countries where intellectual property protection is not particularly strong, you may want to include additional protective provisions around confidentiality.

This section, however, is focused on making sure you get the intellectual property rights that you expect from your independent contractor agreement. In the independent contractor context, the customer does not own the intellectual property rights in the work product created by the contractor, unless there is a written agreement that assigns the rights to that intellectual property to the customer. This is contrary to what many people hiring contractors expect. You may have heard of the "work-for-hire" doctrine. The work-for-hire doctrine does not mean that if you hire someone to do work for you, you own the work product. In fact, if you hire a contractor without a written agreement assigning the intellectual property rights, you will most likely only have a limited license to use the work product. This is problematic for a number of reasons. First, since your license to the work product is not in writing, it can be difficult to determine what is permitted and not permitted. For instance, under this unwritten license, it may be unclear whether you have the right to hire other contractors to modify the work or whether you have the right to sublicense it to other companies.

If you are fortunate enough to have someone try to buy your company or the rights to your application, the lack of written license agreement or assignment of IP could jeopardize the deal. I have seen an IPO and more than one acquisition almost go south for this reason. In each case, the company that didn't get the agreement in place with their contractor had to find them and negotiate a deal to buy the missing rights. This negotiation is not an easy one, because the company on the eve of a liquidation event has very little leverage, particularly if the contractor knows of the pending acquisition. Hoping to get an agreement in place retroactively also assumes that you will be able to find the contractor. Years from now, they contractor's company may not exist, or the contractor may have moved to a remote part of the Andes. If you can't find them, no matter how much money you have to try to buy the rights, they won't be available.

If there is one thing that you take from this chapter, it should be to get an independent contractor agreement in place with anyone that you hire to create anything that will be incorporated into your app. This includes, coders, artists, and user interface designers. Everyone.

I recommend that you work with an attorney to create an independent contractor agreement that is customized for the needs of your company, but for your reference, I have posted an example independent contractor agreement at www.bitwiselegal.com/iPhone. It should give you an idea of the type of provisions that you, as the hiring company, would want to see in an agreement to hire a contractor.

Hiring Employees

Hiring employees has its own set of complications for your business. From an IP perspective, however, it is simpler than with independent contractors. Unlike with contractors, when you hire an employee, you do get some ownership rights in the work product that they create. Like contractors, however, you don't get all the rights that you might expect. Patent rights in particular are not assigned automatically as part of an employer/employee relationship. Without a written assignment, the employer gets what are referred to as *shop rights*, which mean that the employer can use the invention in its business but does not own the underlying intellectual property in the invention.

Like when working with independent contractors, you will want to have a written employment agreement assigning intellectual property rights to you as the employer. You should have all employees sign this agreement.

> **NOTE:** Intellectual property assignments apply to founders too. Often when friends come together to form a company, they jointly develop the company's products without signing employment (or contractor) agreements with the company. If there is a falling out and the founders part ways, the company could be left without full rights in its technology. Founders who didn't sign an assignment agreement could later try to sue the company for infringement or use the work that they created to create a competitor to the original company.

Inbound Licensing of Third-Party Intellectual Property

So, every developer hates to have to re-create something that another coder has already nailed. Sometimes it is more time and cost efficient to get code from other people. The third-party code might be better tested and more stable than something you write from scratch. It might have useful features that you might not have had time to build into your own code. The problem is that it isn't yours. Since you didn't build it yourself or hire an employee or contractor to build it for you, you need to obtain the right to use the code from the person or people who made it. This section addresses how to acquire the rights you need to use content or technology in your application that are owned by other people.

Document Your Inbound Licenses

Whenever you use code or other materials that you obtain from a third party, you will want to be sure that you have documented and understand the scope of your license. Sometimes these inbound license agreements will be negotiated and executed between you and the licensor. Other times, you may have clicked through an agreement with the provider as part of your purchase. In the case of code that you find on the Web, you may be bound by the terms of a license that accompanies the code, or if there is no license posted, you might not have the right to use the code at all.

Know What You Are Getting

The main purpose of license agreement is to grant the licensee the right to use the licensor's code or other content, but licenses also can provide the licensor with certain assurances regarding the quality of the code or content. If you are negotiating an inbound license, you will want to secure some warranties from the licensor that they in fact have the right to grant you the license to the code or content. You may also want the licensor to defend you if for some reason your company is sued for infringement caused by the in-licensed materials.

Many click-through or shrink-wrap licenses will not include these types of warranties or indemnification. The result is that you alone may be responsible if something harmful is included in the code provided by a licensor. Freely available code, like Joe Hewitt's Three20 framework, are incredible resources, but it is important to understand that code like Three20, licensed under the BSD license does not come with any warranties. It is effectively "as-is," which means that although it is a great way to save time in your development of apps, you alone will be responsible if that code fails, includes a virus, or infringes. Surprisingly, the same applies to most artwork that you license through stock photography sites, like iStockphoto.com. This is not to say that you shouldn't use Three20 or stock photography, but only that you should be aware that there is a risk that your company bears by doing so.

Avoid Viral Licenses

Some freely available software is licensed under open source licenses that are viral in nature. These open source licenses, like the GPL and the LGPL, have contributed immensely to the advancement of software, but they carry a fairly strong obligation on anyone that uses the code in their own programs to license the resulting application under a similar open source license. This means that if you accidentally include some open source code that you found on the Internet into your application, you may be contractually obligating yourself to provide access to your source code and allow other people to redistribute your apps. For commercial software, this is a real problem.

The take-away here is that you should be sure to review the license agreement for any piece of third-party code or content that you incorporate into your application. Everything in your app should be traceable back to its original licensor and linked in your records to a license agreement that you are comfortable provides you with sufficient warranties and does not contain viral provisions that could taint your commercial products.

Don't Use Apple's Trademarks

It is important to know that Apple's developer agreement prohibits the use of Apple's trademarks in your applications. This means that you want to avoid using toolbar icons that look like an iPod, and avoid including pictures or images of an iPhone in your app. You similarly shouldn't use the word iPod or iPhone in your app or company name. Using these marks is a violation of your agreement with Apple, and could get your app rejected or possibly stuck in a lengthy and unpredictable approval cycle.

Creating a Custom End User License Agreement

Your end user license agreement (EULA) is the agreement with your user that gives them the right to use your application. In terms of intellectual property, this agreement is where you grant your user a license under your intellectual property rights to use your work.

The Purpose of a EULA

Your end user license agreement is the document that governs your relationship with your users. Among other things, it grants your users the right to use your application and sets out any limitations you want to impose on how it can be used. Like any license agreement, your EULA can grant narrow or broad rights depending on your goals. Most app developers will want to grant users only a very narrow license that limits the users to just using your application, but not modifying or redistributing it. This model is to some extent baked in to the App Store, since Apple embeds technological restrictions on users' ability to share apps with others.

One of the most important reasons to have a EULA is that the EULA can be used to limit the warranties that users get with your application and therefore limit your liability to the end user.

Warranty Disclaimers

What should your customer expect when they purchase a copy of your application? The ways these expectations are set from a legal standpoint are with warranties. When you say in your app description that your game has 20 levels or that your Twitter client enables users to post tweets from the application, these are "express warranties" about the app. If a customer buys your app and it doesn't do the things you said it would do, the user could claim that you breached your warranty.

Most app developers are not looking to disclaim their express warranties, but without the proper warranty disclaimer language in your EULA, you could end up making warranties to the end user that you do not intend. These are implied warranties that can come into existence based on the circumstances of the sale. Examples of these implied warranties are the "warranty of merchantability" and "warranty of fitness for a particular purpose." The problem with these warranties is that they are often based on what the customer expects your product to do, rather than the things that you told them it would do.

A detailed description of the various implied warranties and how they come into existence isn't necessary to understand how they fit into your EULA. The point is that with proper disclaimers in your end user license agreement, you can disclaim these implied warranties and limit the user's ability to sue you if your application does not live up to their expectations. As you launch your application on the App Store, you will see how important this is. There are all types of customers in the App Store. Some are mature, and some are immature. Some are reasonable, and others are crazy. Once you start seeing some of the reviews that people post for apps, it will be clear that often users' expectations for what an application can do are not based in reality (for example, customers complaining that your app doesn't run in the background on the iPhone).

Limitations of Liability

Another important benefit for developers in an end user license agreement is a provision limiting the developer's liability in connection with the sale of the application. A limitation of liability provision is an agreement between you and your user that sets the maximum liability under your agreement at some amount. Most often, these caps on liability are set at the amount the customer paid for the product. Sometimes they are set even lower than that. Not all jurisdictions enforce limitations of liability. Often the judges evaluate whether the limitation of liability provision is fair to the user. Generally, however, courts in the United States will respect people's right to decide for themselves what contracts they want to agree to, and most often limitations of liability are considered enforceable.

A limitation of liability is particularly important if your application, like many iPhone applications, sells for only a few dollars. If your customer pays only a dollar for your application, you would not want to be exposed to customers suing you for thousands of dollars if they are feel they are harmed by the application. The limitation of liability provision in your EULA can help reduce this risk and can allow you to keep selling your application for $1, instead of having to raise the price to factor in the risk that the customer sues you. The customer gets a better price on the application but agrees that if it doesn't work, they won't sue you for more than some fixed about (most likely, the amount they paid for the app).

Apple's Default EULA?

You absolutely should have an end user license agreement that governs your relationship with your users, but you might not need to create a custom agreement for yourself. Apple has a standard end user license agreement that they apply as a default if you don't upload your own.

Apple's End User License Agreement

Apple's default end user license agreement includes some of the basic protections discussed, such as the limited license grant, disclaimer of warranties, and limitation of liability. Apple posts a copy of its App Store Terms and Licensed Application End User License Agreement at http://www.apple.com/legal/itunes/us/terms.html#APPS.

Apple's current App Store Terms and Licensed Application End User License Agreement (dated September 9, 2009) provides most of the basic protection that you would want in an end user license agreement, and it requires no additional effort to implement. There are some reasons, however, that you might want to create your own agreement.

Reasons to Use Your Own Agreement

In my opinion, the biggest weakness in Apple's default end user license agreement is that the user is not presented with it for acceptance when they download or install your application. They have agreed to the terms as part of Apple's other click-through agreements, but one could argue that the agreement would be more likely to be enforceable if users were required to agree to the terms at the time that they decide to purchase your application. This is not to say that the Apple default agreement is not enforceable, only that is gives the user an argument that they otherwise wouldn't have if the agreement was presented to them for agreement at the time of the download.

Another good reason to create your own EULA is if your application or business has specific risks that are not accounted for in Apple's default agreement. For instance, if you are developing a medical app that helps doctors evaluate the needs of their patients, you may want to include some specific disclaimers reminding the doctors that they shouldn't rely solely on your application in providing care. If you are creating an application that involves user-generated content, you may want to include a Digital Millennium Act Safe Harbor provision that can help protect your company if your users upload infringing content.

Lastly, the privacy provisions in Apple's default end user license agreement may not match how your company uses and/or discloses user information. In fact, the language in Apple's default agreement if fairly vague with respect to how this information can be used by developers. If you plan on collecting any personal information from your users, such as their name or email address, or will be accessing data on their device, such as their music library or their address book, you should seriously consider implementing your own end user license agreement with privacy provisions specific to your business. This is particularly important if you plan to use the information that you receive for any purpose beyond providing the user with the service that they are downloading your app for or if you want to preserve the right to share that information with other companies.

How and When to Pursue Legal Action

So, you have taken the necessary steps to secure yourself some intellectual property rights in your application. Now the competitors have emerged, and you think they may be treading your rights. What do you do? In the remainder of this chapter, I will cover the prelitigation and litigation options in the context of an application that I believe infringed the trademark of one of my applications.

This fact pattern involves one of my early applications called Private-I. Private-I is an application is intended to help iPhone users recover their lost or stolen iPhone. The application features an intentionally intriguing icon with the word *Private* displayed in red letters. The icon is intended to lure someone that finds or steals the user's iPhone into opening the app to find out what the user considers private. When the app is opened, it displays a loading screen that appears to be loading some private information, when in reality it is secretly sending the iPhone's owner an email message with a map to the phone's location. I had modest hopes for the application, since it was inherently limited by the fact that the thief would have to open the application for the location tracking to be activated. To my surprise, the app struck a chord with people. It was featured on a number of prominent blogs, like TechCrunch and Engadget.

Like all apps that achieve notable success on the store, similar apps started appearing shortly after my app launched. The total market for the app didn't warrant seeking patent protection for the concept, and I am not sure that the concept would even warrant patent protection, so I accepted that others would be using the idea to make apps. One competitor in particular, however, decided to use my exact icon to sell his app, which caused me to consider taking legal action. The following is an explanation of some of your prelitigation and litigation options and how I evaluated these options in connection with my own copycat situation.

First Steps Toward Dispute Resolution

In my experience. Apple tries to avoid getting involved in disputes between app developers. Nonetheless, before you start considering real litigation, it is worth pursuing a remedy through Apple since working with Apple costs nothing, and if the company is responsive, it could result in immediate results. Litigation, on the other hand, can be time-consuming and expensive. Trademark-related issues can be submitted to Apple for consideration through the following email address: appdisputes@apple.com.

In my case, the appdisputes@apple.com email address didn't exist yet, but I sent a request to Apple's copyright officer, as registered with the U.S. Copyright Office. My request was not answered, which led me to the conclusion that Apple would prefer not to get involved in interdeveloper disputes. Truthfully, I can't blame them. Copyright and trademark disputes can be complicated, and Apple shouldn't want to have to make a determination in each case as to the respective rights of the developers. It would be understandable if they simply waited for the developers to resolve their dispute through litigation or negotiation and then act in response to a court order or the agreed instructions of the developers.

Nonetheless, emailing Apple should be your first step in pursuing an infringer. You just should not assume that Apple is going to resolve the dispute for you.

Prelitigation

If you think a competitor is infringing your intellectual property rights, the first step in the litigation process is to identify rights they are infringing. If they have used some of your graphics in their application, you would be focused on your copyright in the graphics. If they have given their application a name that is confusingly similar to your application, you would want to focus on your trademark rights. If they have an app that has taken the same concept or idea that you created for your app, if you have filed a patent application, or you still have time to file before the "on sale bar" restricts your right to do so, you may want to focus on your potential patent rights.

Talking with a lawyer at this stage can help you identify the ways in which your rights are being violated. A lawyer can also help you understand if there are any additional steps you need to take to shore up your rights before you start trying to assert them against others. A lawyer can also help you understand the relative strength your weaknesses of your rights and your likelihood of prevailing in a lawsuit against the competitor.

Going to court is extremely expensive. Fortunately, most disputes are resolved well before going that far. If you and your lawyer conclude that you have a valid infringement claim against your competitor, your next step will likely be to send the competitor a cease and desist letter. The purpose of this letter is to notify the other party that you believe they are infringing your rights and demand that they stop. Depending on the circumstances, your competitor may not realize they are infringing. A cease-and-desist letter serves the dual purpose of notify them of the alleged infringement to get them to stop and creating documentation to show that they were aware of your rights, should they choose to continue infringing.

So, how did I approach this in the case of Private-I? I evaluated the rights that I believed the copycat infringed. In my case, I believed that the copycat infringed my copyright in the icon because the artwork had been copied, and the trademark was infringed because the use of the same icon on another product was bound to cause confusion with customers. More important, I evaluated the harm that the infringement was causing me and the potential benefit that would come from pursuing a claim. My conclusion was that pursuing the copycat wasn't worth the effort. His duplicate of my app never sold very well and didn't have a large effect on my sales. I was offended that someone would be so underhanded as to copy an entire application and post it on the App Store but had to make a decision as to whether I wanted to spend my time writing letters and interacting with someone who I found distasteful or whether I wanted to focus my energy on making apps. I don't regret the decision. Private-I continues to be a strong contender in the Travel category, and the copycat application has almost no exposure on the store.

Litigation

In my case, the copycat application wasn't causing much harm, but if your rights are being infringed and it is causing real harm to your business, litigation is the way to stop the infringement and potentially recover monetary damages from the infringer. Litigation is expensive and time-consuming, but it is an extremely strong weapon. If the potentially infringing competitor does not stop infringing your rights as a result of your cease-and-desist letter, and your discussions with them have broken down, your next step is to file a claim against them. I use the work "you" fairly loosely here. This is not something that you would want to attempt alone. If you think you have a claim, you should work with an intellectual property litigator to draft and file the complaint.

Summary

Intellectual property law and the general legal issues in running a software business can be difficult to wrap your head around. Fortunately, you don't need to understand everything about intellectual property to be an IP-savvy developer. Even lawyers who work in this space tend to focus on specific portions of the law. My practice, for instance, is focused primarily on helping people draft contracts related to intellectual property, while other lawyers are specifically focused on litigation, and others spend their time helping people file patent or trademark applications. Since even lawyers in this field don't know everything about IP, your goal should simply be to get enough exposure to the issues so that you will recognize when it is time to explore more on a particular topic. Think of these legal issues like the frameworks included in Cocoa. For example, you don't need to know how to use a `UIImagePickerView` until you write an app that requires use of the camera or photos, but when that time comes, it will be important to know that the class exists and roughly what it is capable of. Just like learning a programming language, the key to success in business legal issues is knowing what resources are available and how to access them.

Chapter 4

Your iPhone App Is Your Most Powerful Marketing Tool

Your app icon and screenshots are often the first visual elements users see in the App Store when evaluating your app. A bad first impression can cost you sales and invite negative reviews, so fine-tuning your app's design is a critical component to success. In this chapter, I'll reveal some useful tips for prototyping, creating eye-catching app icons, designing intuitive user interfaces, and turning your app into a social marketing powerhouse.

This book is focused on how to improve the marketability of your app, so although this chapter should not be seen as a comprehensive guide to interface design, I will be providing important concepts to consider when designing your UI, along with pointing out common pitfalls to avoid.

Getting Your Foot in the Door: First Impressions Are Everything

After performing several App Store searches during your pursuit to collect competitive research information in Chapter 2, you undoubtedly noticed that there are a *lot* of low-quality apps clogging the pipeline—shoddy apps quickly churned out by developers concerned only with exploiting short-term trends. One of the biggest problems that plagues new iPhone developers is app discovery. In a sea of more than 100,000 apps, it's hard for users to successfully wade through the crud to find the true gems. But no matter how much publicity you do to drive traffic and awareness to your app, discovery is only part of the equation.

When people finally do seek out or stumble upon your app's product page in the App Store, you've managed to capture their interest, but only for a moment. You have precious few seconds to convince them to continue exploring your app. This means your app's icon and screenshots need to "hook" them into wanting to learn more.

In general, most people are both lazy and extremely busy, placing an immense value on their time (and a short fuse on their patience). If your app does not captivate them within the first few seconds of viewing your App Store page, they will move on, especially if there are many similar apps to choose from.

Your app icon is the first visual cue your app has to offer. Consumers see your app icon first in the App Store listings. Your icon combined with your app's name will be the first key factor that determines whether a user is interested enough to click through to your app's product page. It also represents your app's brand identity and must be uniquely memorable. If your icon doesn't look professional, it leaves the distinct impression that your application may not be professionally made. So, with this in mind, an eye-catching, quality app icon should be your top design priority. It is your proverbial "foot in the door," granting you a little more of a consumer's time and short attention span.

When people land on your app's product page in the App Store, your screenshots are the second important visual cue. You cannot rely on people reading your app's entire text description in the App Store. They may read the first couple lines of your app description but will be immediately drawn to the displayed screenshot. That first screenshot must be one that best represents the core functionality of your app. Don't waste the opportunity by posting your app's splash screen or settings screen as that first visual. Although those screens may technically come first in the flow of using your app, they communicate nothing to potential customers. In those vital few seconds, that first screenshot has to convey your app's functionality or defining feature. After one look, you want consumers to have that "ah-ha" moment where they immediately understand how your app generally works and/or why they should buy it. At the very least, it should spur them to continue clicking to see more of your screenshots, read more of your app description, and explore your customer reviews and official web site. And if you've done your job right, that winning first impression convinced them to download and evaluate your free lite version (if you offer one).

And while I'm on the subject of free lite versions, I'll mention that giving your users the ability to evaluate your app before purchase will help promote the paid version, but it becomes that much more important that your app's UI is designed to impress. If a user downloads your app, tries it briefly, and then decides to delete it, they are automatically prompted to rate the app upon deletion. Although this flawed approach invites negative reviews, it sure provides extra incentive to make as good of a first impression as possible. Unfortunately, your app's UI design and functionality are now responsible not only for attempting to win a sale for the paid version but also for avoiding negative reviews (that may be unfairly "judging a book by its cover"). This task may seem overwhelming at first, but after reading this chapter, you'll be armed with some practical design methodology for tackling this problem head on.

I'll discuss the merits of free lite versions to promote paid apps in Chapter 5, but first things first. It's time now to lay the groundwork for your app's design.

Playing by the Rules in Apple's Sandbox

Violating Apple's iPhone Human Interface Guidelines (commonly known as the HIG) is probably the most frequent cause for submitted iPhone apps to be rejected. Although the App Store does contain some exceptions to the rule—approved apps that have broken a few of those UI design rules—it's best to adhere to the guidelines the best you can. There's no sense playing with fire unless you have a very good reason to do so, and even then, you need to ask yourself whether it's truly worth the risk. Design innovation can give an app that "sexy" visual appeal that helps drive interest and sales, but before you attempt to break too many conventions, keep in mind two very important factors:

- If your design violates too many critical guidelines, Apple won't think twice about rejecting your app, no matter how cool it is. And if you're not in the App Store, your app can't make money.

- Apple's interface guidelines serve the vital purpose of supplying common interface controls and architecture. Familiarity greatly eases the learning curve, which makes the user experience much more intuitive.

Some developers familiar with Apple's infamous rejection letters have lost faith in playing by the rules, especially when the rules often appear to be a somewhat moving target. Apple's app review process has been under quite a bit of scrutiny during the past year as developers and the tech media have questioned the inconsistent reasoning behind the rejection of several high-profile apps. One such example is the beautifully designed Eucalyptus ebook reader. The app was initially rejected because it allowed users to download and read any book from the Project Gutenberg site, which happens to include the erotic Kama Sutra among its vast catalog of 30,000 books. Even though that same ebook is also accessible through other approved iPhone app ebook readers such as Stanza and Amazon's Kindle for iPhone, as well as Apple's built-in Mobile Safari browser, Eucalyptus was rejected. After a public outcry from the developer community, Apple eventually approved the app, but it now sports a 17+ age rating, even though the ebook reader itself does not include any adult content. Ironically, both Stanza and Amazon's Kindle for iPhone are rated for ages 4+.

But nothing caused an uproar like the rejection and removal of Google Voice–related apps from the App Store in late July 2009. With Google Voice offering enhanced voicemail options, free text messaging, inexpensive international calls, and universal phone number routing, not only did it have the potential to command quite a bit of network bandwidth, but it also stood to compete with many of AT&T's existing services (the iPhone's exclusive U.S. carrier). Critics fear that app rejections like this not only stifle innovation but could also cripple the integrity of the App Store. Plenty of blogs and news reports covered the event in excessive detail, so I won't rehash the story here, but suffice it to say, the App Store's blocking of Google Voice caused the FCC to take notice, sending inquiries to both Apple and AT&T. Obviously, everyone wants Apple's app review process to be much more transparent with a clearly defined set of rules to help developers better prepare for app submissions. Ideally, by the time you read this, Apple will have already made the modifications needed to greatly improve its app review system.

But even if nothing changes by the time you're ready to submit your app to the App Store, it doesn't matter. Sure, the inconsistency of why some apps are rejected may seem unfair. And yes, having an app that's been selling in the App Store for months suddenly be removed for some new reason is definitely discouraging and can be a major blow to any business. This seemingly blurred, moving line has made many question whether developing for the iPhone has become a substantially riskier investment than it used to be. Whether you agree or disagree with Apple's App Store policies and decisions, it ultimately does not matter.

The bottom line is that if you want the opportunity to make money in the hottest, most lucrative mobile platform, you have to remember that it's Apple's sandbox you're playing in. To stay in the game, you need to adhere to the company's rules. You may not like its rules, but that's the real price of admission (beyond your iPhone Developer Program fee).

My intention is not to make light of the serious nature of app rejections. I know that some independent developers have invested their entire businesses in iPhone app development only to see their primary source of income destroyed by app rejections or app removals. Being the exclusive sales channel for iPhone apps is the App Store's greatest strength, as well as the biggest concern for developers. My goal here is merely to keep you focused on the design, development, and marketing elements that *are* within your control.

In the larger scope of things, it's important to remember that the App Store only celebrated its first birthday in July 2009. It's still very young, and yet it grew in size much faster than Apple (or anyone else) ever anticipated, so it's showing the obvious growing pains. Apple has admitted that it's working hard to streamline the app review process and make the App Store easier to use to improve app discovery. It has already made a few steps in the right direction with new changes to the iPhone Dev Center, iTunes Connect, and the App Store, so I for one remain hopeful that playing in Apple's sandbox will eventually get easier for app developers.

For the immediate future, although it may be impossible to foresee all the possible reasons for rejection (especially if new ones arise), you can at least do yourself the favor of avoiding the known issues that will earn you a rejection letter. Throughout this book, I'll be spotlighting known rejection causes as they apply to the related design and development topics being discussed, but those select tidbits alone are not enough. Here are two additional resources that should be required reading for all iPhone developers.

Apple's iPhone Human Interface Guidelines

http://developer.apple.com/iphone/library/documentation/UserExperience/Conceptual/Mobile HIG/

This is the bible for iPhone interface design. Obviously, you're encouraged to be creative and inventive, but let the HIG serve as your foundation. This online guide also provides a link to download a handy PDF version. You can also access the HIG within Xcode's built-in documentation browser. With so many viewing options, you really have no excuse, so read it, embrace it, live it!

Application Submission Feedback

http://appreview.tumblr.com/

This blog posts reported reasons for app rejections, as submitted by anonymous developers. This unauthorized site is a great source of information, although Apple's app review team can't be thrilled with its existence.

Creating an Effective App Icon and Logo

As I mentioned earlier, when consumers browse the App Store listings, your app icon is the first visual cue your app has to offer. Your app's icon and name will be the first key factors that determine whether a user is interested enough to click through to your app's product page. Since the icon represents your app's brand identity, its design must be memorable and eye-catching enough to stand apart from your competition.

At the end of Chapter 2, I recommended reviewing your competition's app icons and starting to think about ideas for your own app icon. If you're building a note-taking app and most of the similar apps currently use a notebook-related app icon, then you won't want to emulate that same look, or else your app may be perceived as an unoriginal "also-ran" app that's simply hopping on the same bandwagon. But your app is going to be different, better. So, let your app icon reflect that with contrasting colors and an original visual theme that set your app apart from similar apps when all displayed together in the App Store listings.

Although some app icons utilize photographic imagery, you'll find that most apps use illustration-based icons. Often photos include too much detail that when shrunken down into a tiny 57 × 57 pixel iPhone app icon, the image looks too cluttered and busy. The most successful icons boast a simple, crisp, and clean design that looks vibrant and appealing at any size—big or small. Because of this, illustrations tend to work best to meet those design goals.

Designing a Custom App Icon

Taking the fictional app example from Chapter 2, the parked-car locator called Breadcrumbs, let's design an original app icon for it. Many of the competitive apps in this space use icon imagery that look suspiciously like royalty-free clip art. Using royalty-free stock art can serve as a great foundation for mocking up the initial prototype design of your icon, but you'll want to create your own original artwork for the final icon, especially if you have plans to register a trademark for your app logo and icon. You can't trademark someone else's artwork or imagery unless you own all the rights to it.

App Rejection Warning: Do not use copyrighted or trademarked art or names in your app icon or UI. This also includes any Apple trademarks—iPhone imagery is strictly hands-off, so don't include it in your icon or interface design. Although a few select apps do display an iPhone in their app icon or UI icons, they are the rare exception. Breaking this rule without receiving prior permission from Apple will quickly earn most new apps a rejection letter. It's also important to note that Apple will also reject your app if it uses unauthorized images of public figures or celebrities. And believe me, Apple is doing you a favor by enforcing this before granting entry into the App Store. The last thing you want is some large Fortune 500 corporation suing you for trademark infringement.

Let me just state for the record that although I know my way around Adobe Photoshop, I'm definitely not an artist. But that's the beauty of designing a simple icon. As long as you know a few layering and filtering tricks, you can still create an attractive icon. You don't have to be Michelangelo, but having a good eye for composition—how to structure the layout of an icon—is definitely a valuable trait to have. But not to worry, even if your graphics skills ended with kindergarten drawings displayed on the refrigerator, the "Tips for the Artistically Challenged" section later in this chapter provides helpful advice and links to online resources.

However, I will say that if you're not a talented artist, then it's definitely worth finding room in your budget to hire a professional designer. Your app icon will greatly benefit from the skilled eye of an experienced graphics guru. And since your app icon is such an important visual component of your overall app marketing strategy, if you're truly serious about succeeding in the App Store, then hiring a professional designer to develop your icon, your logo, and even some of your UI elements is a very smart investment.

But for those of you who are struggling independent developers working with small, shoestring budgets, let's see what you can do on your own to produce a worthy, quality icon.

Most professional design work is done in either Adobe Illustrator or Photoshop (http://www.adobe.com/). You can create the Breadcrumbs app icon example in either program since we'll be taking an illustration-based approach. For those of you unfamiliar with Illustrator, it is a vector-based drawing program, which means it creates illustrations that can be set to any size without losing any pixel quality—perfect for designing software icons and logos that may need to be available in many different sizes for anything ranging from a small desktop icon to a large trade-show poster. Photoshop, on the other hand, is a bitmap-based graphics program that also includes many vector-based tools. I tend to be partial to Photoshop, but most designers would probably recommend Illustrator for this specific task.

If Illustrator or Photoshop is too expensive for your needs, other cheaper graphics tools are available as well. Just search your favorite online software directories (such as VersionTracker.com, MacUpdate.com, or Download.com) for comparable alternatives. But if you plan on creating your own graphics for all your software products, web site, and marketing materials, then I highly recommend investing in Adobe's applications. If you buy the Creative Suite, you'll get all of Adobe's best design apps bundled together for a discounted package price.

Enough talk about rules and tools. Let's dive into some design work! Since the fictitious Breadcrumbs app will help locate your parked car, you obviously know that including a car in the icon would be beneficial. But you don't want to look like any other competing app icons, so you'll draw your car from scratch using very simple shapes. You'll also incorporate a trail of dots (to emulate breadcrumbs) leading up to the car to help visually communicate the logic behind the app name.

It's very important to remember that when submitting your app to the App Store, you'll need to provide Apple with a large 512 × 512 pixel icon. So if you're creating your icon in Photoshop, make sure your master design is at least that big. Since you'll probably want to use your icon in marketing materials as well, you should strongly consider creating your master icon at an even bigger size. Keep in mind that print advertising (magazine ads, trade-show posters, and so on) should be at least 300 dots per inch (dpi), so if your biggest icon is only 512 × 512 pixels, then your icon is only 1.7 inches big when used in 300 dpi print materials. If you create your master icon at a large size that's several inches big, then you'll always be sure to have the right size for any occasion. You can always resize the icon smaller with great results, but you can't increase the size of an existing bitmap-based icon without it looking terribly pixelized. If you're creating a vector-based icon in Illustrator, then resizing up or down is not an issue.

Since Apple requires a 512 × 512 pixel icon and your app is compiled with a 57 × 57 pixel icon (both need to be saved as PNG images), then you'll want to make sure your design looks good in both sizes. The trick is for your icon to look professional and sophisticated, while remaining simplistic enough to still display well in almost any size. This is no easy feat, especially for a nondesigner, but we'll take a stab at it by using a few clever little graphics tricks.

App Rejection Warning: Your 57 × 57 app icon and 512 × 512 App Store icon must match! Don't try to work around icon legibility issues by crafting a complex, detailed 512 × 512 icon and then a vastly simplified version for the 57 × 57 app icon. The icons don't need to be precisely identical, so you can do minor touch-ups to the small icon if the resize muddied a few elements. But when placed next to each other, both icons should look like the same design. If there's a major difference between the two, your app risks being rejected by Apple's app review team.

First, let's start with a rough sketch of the icon by drawing the objects in outline form (see the left icon in Figure 4–1). I recommend using a graphics program that supports layers (as Photoshop and Illustrator do) so that you can place each separate object in its own layer. For example, the car windshield is the top layer, with the car bumper layer beneath. And under that, we have the car frame layer and the car tire layer. Another separate layer holds the breadcrumb dots. The bottom layer is the background. Why go to all the trouble of maintaining so many layers? By keeping the objects separated, it allows you to easily move around individual layers or groups of layers until you have a composition that looks balanced and complete. Separate layers also allow you to modify the outline stroke and filter effects of a selected object without affecting the other objects.

Keep the basic icon outline very simple. Its raw, unfinished appearance will tempt you to add detailed lines and textures, but resist the urge. Too many fine lines will not translate well when the icon is resized into the small 57 × 57 iPhone icon, so it's best not to enhance the design in that way.

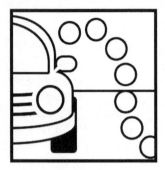

Figure 4–1. *After designing an initial outline (left icon), you can experiment with contrasting colors (middle icon) and then add a professional polish with easy-to-use effects and filters (right icon).*

Once you have a layout you like, you can then start experimenting with color (see the middle icon in Figure 4–1). Leaving the outline stroke black, I filled the car frame object with red, the bumper with light gray, and the windshield with light blue. I also added a blue gradient for the sky and a light tan gradient for the ground. Notice that the gradient fades lighter toward the middle horizon—this helps give the background a little more dimension with the illusion of sunlight shining from the horizon line. Since this book is printed in grayscale, you won't be able to see the nice contrast of the red car against the blue sky, but try to visualize it in your mind. Although this color version is an improvement from the previous black-and-white outline, it still looks very childish, like it was drawn by an amateur illustrator. Remember, I'm a programmer, not an artist.

Now for the fun part! With just a few tricks using the built-in tools and effects included in both Photoshop and Illustrator, you can transform that amateurish icon into a polished work of art (see the right icon in Figure 4–1).

The current black outlines give the icon a cartoonish, comic-book look, so the first thing you need to do is change the color of the stroke outlines for all the objects. Select the layer that contains the car frame object, and change its stroke outline to a dark red to nicely complement the car's bright red color. Make the headlight and bumper's stroke outline dark gray. Then decrease the opacity of the white dots' stroke outline to 60 percent, allowing the stroke to take on the subtle shades of blue and tan from the background behind the dots. By just changing the stroke outline colors, you've already made a huge improvement.

Next up, you can use the built-in Bevel and Emboss layer style on the car bumper object and the white dots to give them a three-dimensional feel. Adjust the Highlight and Shadow modes until you get the look you want. Since you want to create the illusion that there's one central light source, make sure all your Bevel and Emboss modified objects use the same Shading Angle value for consistency. You can then add the Drop Shadow layer style to the car's grill and drop its opacity to 60 percent.

Using the Gradient tool, continue shading and highlighting strategic areas of the car to enhance the three-dimensional effect. In Photoshop, when the Gradient tool is chosen, you can modify its settings to customize how the gradient will draw itself. For example, with the car's headlight object selected, I changed the Gradient tool's mode to Radial so that the white to yellow gradient would make the headlight's surface appear rounded. Changing the Gradient tool's mode to Linear and selecting the car frame object, I added a light red to dark red vertical gradient, which provided shading near the bottom of the car frame. A small, lighter gradient was added to the car's hood as a highlight.

With the car windshield object selected, I added a horizontal Linear gradient of white to light blue. But the windshield still did not yet look like glass. So, I added an artificial "glint" of light near the top of the windshield. Create a new layer above the existing car windshield layer. Draw an arced, white sliver on this new layer, and then change its opacity to 60 percent. Ahh, much better. Now it looks more like glass.

Now here's the hard part: creating the angled sunbeams in the sky. These sunbeams really give the icon that extra "pop," so it's worth the additional effort. First, darken the existing blue background, making it a darker blue vertical gradient (with the lighter color ending at the middle horizon line). Then create a new layer above the background (but below the car object layers). Draw a white rectangle that fills the entire sky area, and then change its opacity to 30 percent. This will make the sky look washed out, until you start cutting out angled slices that allow the darker sky underneath to shine through. The cut-out angled slices are actually the spaces between the sunbeams, so space them evenly with all of them angled toward the same central point on the horizon. In this case, the central reference point I used is directly behind the car's headlight.

The very last task is to create a shadow below the car. This is as easy as creating a new layer below the existing car object layers and then drawing a fairly flat, horizontal oval that is slightly wider than the car. Fill the oval black, change its opacity to 50 percent, and then apply the built-in Blur filter until it looks like an authentic shadow.

And that's it! By using Photoshop and/or Illustrator's built-in shapes, stroke outlines, the Gradient tool, layer styles, and the Blur filter, you were able to transform a basic design idea into a professional-looking app icon. I hope you'll be able to put these simple little tricks to good use when designing your own app icons. If you're having trouble locating the various tools, effects, and filters described in the previous steps, consult the documentation of Photoshop and Illustrator for details.

The true test now is in resizing the finished icon to the required sizes. If the design still looks good in both 512 × 512 pixel and 57 × 57 pixel icon sizes, then you accomplished your mission. Don't worry about the rounded edges and glossy beveled look that iPhone app icons typically have. The iPhone and the App Store automatically add those elements to the icon for you. Although you can't do anything about the dynamically added rounded edges, you do have the ability to disable the beveled gloss effect from your app icon if desired. The Breadcrumbs app icon would probably look better without it, but let's test it by previewing the app icon in Xcode's iPhone Simulator (see Figure 4–2).

Figure 4–2. *You have the option to disable the default beveled gloss effect if your app icon looks better without it. Previewing the example Breadcrumbs app icon with the glossy effect (left) and without (right).*

As you can see in Figure 4–2, the default beveled gloss effect interferes too much with the underlying icon design, so let's disable it. After you've added your 57 × 57 pixel icon PNG file—named `Icon.png`—to the Resources folder of your iPhone app project in Xcode, you'll need to open your project's plist file. Xcode displays the contents of your plist file as a nicely formatted list (see Figure 4–3).

Key	Value
▼ Information Property List	(13 items)
Localization native development region	English
Bundle display name	${PRODUCT_NAME}
Executable file	${EXECUTABLE_NAME}
Icon file	Icon.png
Bundle identifier	com.yourcompany.${PRODUCT_NAME:rfc1034identifier}
InfoDictionary version	6.0
Bundle name	${PRODUCT_NAME}
Bundle OS Type code	APPL
Bundle creator OS Type code	????
Bundle version	1.0
Application requires iPhone environment	☑
Main nib file base name	MainWindow
Icon already includes gloss and bevel effects	☑

Figure 4–3. *Adding a new plist property, "Icon already includes gloss and bevel effects," and setting it to True will disable the default beveled gloss effect from your iPhone app icon in Xcode.*

First you'll want to add your `Icon.png` filename to the Icon property. Then click the gray plus (+) symbol button on the bottom-right side of the list to add a new entry to the plist file. In the new blank row, click the tiny arrows in the left Key column to display a contextual menu of additional properties. If you have iPhone SDK 3 installed, then you should be able to select "Icon already includes gloss and bevel effects" from that menu. It may not seem like the intuitive choice, but setting its value to True will disable the default beveled gloss effect from your app icon. Save the plist file, and run your Xcode project in the iPhone Simulator to preview your app icon. When displaying your 57 × 57 pixel icon on the iPhone or the 512 × 512 pixel icon in the App Store, Apple checks your app's plist file first, so your preferred setting is honored with both icon sizes.

Don't Forget About a Logo

After sweating over your icon design, let's keep the creative juices flowing and tackle a logo for your app. This is another visual element that would benefit from the wizardry of a professional designer, so if you hired a designer to create your app icon, you should also have that same expert create a logo to match. But don't worry if a constrained budget forces you to continue carrying the graphics burden on your own. A logo does not need to be complicated. In fact, like your icon, the more simplistic your logo is, the more flexibility you have to use it in various small sizes while still maintaining readability.

Like your master icon, you'll want to create a master logo that's at least several inches long with a 300 dpi resolution so that it'll look good in any and all print-related marketing materials you may create in the future. For best results, you may want to choose the vector-based Illustrator for creating your logo, especially if your icon was constructed in Illustrator.

Since I'm not a trained artist, I opted to follow my own advice and keep things simple with the Breadcrumbs logo example. Take advantage of the design work you've already done, and incorporate the existing icon into the logo design. Not only does this save you a lot of design time, but it also helps reinforce the branding you already established with the app icon. Sometimes crafting an appealing, simple logo is just a matter of finding an interesting font. I opted to use a rounded, condensed serif font for the name Breadcrumbs. After trying several different fonts, a font with rounded edges seemed to perfectly complement the rounded lines within the app icon. To add a little flavor to the font, let's give it a thick black stroke outline with a white fill color and then employ a Drop Shadow layer style. Nice!

If you do use a third-party font, it's important that you purchase the proper font licensing to use it in commercial projects. Some fonts can be quite expensive, so if money is an issue, I recommend using royalty-free fonts when possible. See the "Tips for the Artistically Challenged" section later in this chapter for some helpful font library resources.

With only the icon and adjoining app name, the logo still feels too basic. To really drive home the breadcrumbs metaphor, let's extend the trail of white dots to flow from the icon to a "Parked Car Locator" caption beneath the app name (see Figure 4–4). Wow, such a simple element, and yet it really pulls the entire logo together to form an original and cohesive design.

Figure 4–4. *This fictional Breadcrumbs logo is a simple extension of its app icon design.*

Creating an app icon for inclusion in your Xcode project seems like a no-brainer at this early stage in the game, but why design a logo now when the app hasn't even been developed yet? Obviously, you'll want to have your logo ready to use on your app's official web site, as well as available for any prerelease publicity efforts you do, but the biggest reason to do it now is for trademark registration (as explained by Michael Schneider in Chapter 3). The trademark application and approval process can take several months, so if you plan on registering a trademark for your app logo, then it's best to start this ball rolling as soon as possible. If all goes well, you'll ideally have the trademark officially registered before your app is available in the App Store.

Maintaining a Consistent Brand Identity

To reinforce your brand identity, you'll want to use the same app icon and logo across all your marketing efforts. If you use too many visual variations for promoting the same iPhone app, you're likely to cause confusion among consumers. By consistently using the same icon and logo, your app's brand will start to become recognizable by people. This familiarity will help consumers easily recall your app name by memory when searching the App Store and recommending your app to friends and family. Having a recognized brand also helps you promote new iPhone apps to those users who are familiar with the visual branding of your previous app.

To reinforce the logo branding of Touchgrind, a popular skateboarding game app, Illusion Labs included the same logo and color palette within various screens of the app, as well as in the app's YouTube video trailer and official web site (see Figure 4–5). For all you nonartists out there, notice that even though the Touchgrind logo is a very simple design, its consistent use is nonetheless quite effective.

Figure 4–5. *Illusion Labs uses the same Touchgrind logo within the app itself (top left), its Touchgrind YouTube video trailer (bottom left), and its Touchgrind.com web site (right) for consistent branding.*

If you're porting an existing app to the iPhone from another platform, such as Mac OS X or Windows, then take advantage of the brand equity you've already established by using a similar icon and logo for the iPhone version. This is a great way to attract new customers who are already familiar with your app from another platform.

When Cultured Code created an iPhone version of its award-winning Mac application, Things, it utilized the same branding but modified the icon slightly. The icon is still instantly recognizable as Things and cements the fact that the iPhone app is directly related to its Mac cousin. But the minor design tweak to the iPhone version's icon plays an important role in that not only does it help the image display better as a small 57 × 57 pixel iPhone icon with rounded edges, but it also helps position the iPhone app as its own stand-alone version (see Figure 4–6).

Figure 4–6. *The Things Mac icon (left) and the Things iPhone icon (right)*

The Things iPhone icon is another great example of an image that is both simple and sophisticated at the same time. Although there are dozens of competing to-do lists and task management apps in the App Store with similar check mark–themed icons, the Things iPhone app stands out from the pack because of its photorealistic icon. It's really quite a simple image, but upon closer examination, what gives the icon that high-quality feel are the little design nuances such as the high-contrast colors, the inner drop shadow on the white square, and the subtle gloss effect on the surrounding blue box. In my opinion, the Things icons for Mac and the iPhone are perfect models of effective app icon design, where less is more—delivering sheer simplicity with visual impact.

As you discovered while experimenting with Photoshop effects and filters during the design of the Breadcrumbs icon example, sometimes the only things separating an amateur drawing from a professional-looking design are a few minor graphical touches.

Interface Design: Think Like a User, Not a Developer

After discussing it earlier in this chapter, you've taken the time to read Apple's iPhone Human Interface Guidelines, right? No? This is important, so go ahead. I'll wait....

You're back already? Great! Now that you understand Apple's suggested boundaries and recommended design practices for iPhone user interfaces, your first step in the development process is to put that knowledge to good use. No, I'm not talking about writing code just yet. Think about your app's core functionality and the key features it will include. How do you package that feature set into a compact user-friendly interface for a small mobile device? Answering that question should be your first development task. You may already be an experienced iPhone programmer, well versed in Objective-C and Cocoa Touch (and if you're not, plenty of great iPhone development books are available from Apress), but many developers have trouble translating their app concept into an efficient user interface that's intuitive and easy to use.

When showcasing your app in the App Store, users want to see its interface. It's the front end that they will be interacting with on a daily basis when using your app, so they'll be checking to see whether it satisfies their specific needs and is easy to learn. Since they may have many alternatives to choose from, your app needs to be more visually appealing than your competitors. It's not just about being the app with the most features. Offering the features that consumers want may initially grab their attention, but the app with the best overall user experience will win their hard-earned money.

Take off your "developer hat" for a moment to think about your own purchasing habits. When you compare several similar apps of interest, trying to evaluate which one to buy, it's your visual senses that first kick into gear. You're looking at an app's screenshots in the App Store and maybe even watching a video demo trailer on the developer's web site or playing with a free lite version. Obviously, customer ratings and reviews play a huge part in your decision, but let's say two similar apps offer the same features and have received roughly the same glowing reviews. When compared side by side, if one app offers a very plain, boring UI and the other offers a slick, attractive UI, a consumer is going to gravitate toward the app that's more visually enticing.

This type of thinking does not apply only to games, which require unique interfaces and original game play. Even if you're developing a utility or productivity app that performs mundane tasks, there's no reason why it can't be exciting and fun to use. Your customers will thank you for it.

The Immense Value of Prototyping

Prototyping can reveal awkward workflows and unintuitive architecture in your app. An interface concept can play like a good idea in your head, but once you map it out on paper and scrutinize a semi-working prototype, you may change your mind. In fact, sometimes a prototype can lead you to new ideas that end up enhancing the marketability of your app. At the very least, prototyping will expose actions that are overly complicated, leading you to find new solutions to streamline the user interaction—something that's crucial to the success of a mobile app.

Prototyping can also save you countless hours of development time and prevent you from writing unusable code. How is that possible? you ask. Wouldn't it be faster to just jump into Xcode right now and start hammering out a quick and dirty demo?

If you're developing an app for a client or your boss, they may want to see your ideas before they'll sign off on the project. The key word here is *see*. More often than not, many business executives—especially those with no creative background—have trouble visualizing an interface. No matter how well you communicate your idea in a meeting, they just can't picture it in their head. Putting together wireframes or screenshot mock-ups of your interface concept is an easy, timesaving method to quickly show your client or boss what you're proposing. This way, if they come back to you with lots of changes or (gasp!) a major shift in direction, you won't have wasted a lot of precious time in Xcode and Interface Builder.

If you're outsourcing your app development, then prototyping can also be extremely valuable in properly communicating your UI concept to third-party programmers, especially if there's a substantial language barrier. When they're charging you by the hour, the less time you have to spend explaining your ideas and goals, the less money the outsourced development will cost you. A picture is worth a thousand words.

Even if you're an independent developer working solo on an app, the most important benefit of prototyping is the amount of valuable time and potential headaches it can save you later during the beta testing stage. You don't want to spend months slaving over an app only to then receive overwhelming feedback from your testers that the UI is impossible to grasp, making it difficult for them to figure out how to use the app or access certain features. Those are issues best solved before you get too deep into the development process.

Drawing Your Ideas on Paper

Don't overlook the value of sketches on grid paper! Getting your ideas down on paper is a quick way to map out the basic look and feel of your app. Designing a game that requires a completely custom interface? Drawing your concept on paper may be your only rapid option, since this would be impossible to do with only the standard controls available in Interface Builder. Sketch it first by hand to work out the design kinks, and then construct the final custom artwork in Illustrator or Photoshop.

Tired of drawing the same buttons and other standard interface elements over and over again? Thanks to the generous contributions of several prominent designers and developers, predrawn iPhone sketch templates are available online (see Figure 4–7):

- Erik Loehfelm's iPhone UX Sketch Templates (offered in multiple formats such as PDF, Photoshop, EPS, PNG, and OmiGraffle): http://erikloehfelm.blogspot.com/2009/05/iphone-ux-sketch-templates.html

- Boulevart's iPhone Sketchpaper (PDF and Photoshop PSD): http://labs.boulevart.be/index.php/2008/06/05/sketch-paper-for-the-mobile-designer/

- UI Stencils iPhone Stencil Kit (stainless steel stencil): http://www.uistencils.com/iphone-stencil-kit.html

- Kapsoft's iPhone Stencil (durable IMA acrylic stencil): http://www.mobilesketchbook.com/

Figure 4–7. *iPhone-related sketching templates and stencil kits are available from third-party designers.*

Although all the downloadable templates are truly well done, I couldn't find a comprehensive solution that matched my personal design needs, so I opted to publish my own unique, grid-based templates in *The Developer Sketchbook for iPhone Apps*, which includes more than 500 pages of portrait and landscape UI templates, app navigation flowcharts, and app icon design templates. Also available is Dean Kaplan's *iPhone Application Sketch Book* from Apress, with 150 pages of handy templates. If you're looking for an iPhone design notebook to take with you when you're away from the office or simply a central place to keep all your app ideas organized, these two printed solutions are worthy additions to your development arsenal.

- *The Developer Sketchbook for iPhone Apps* (Electric Butterfly): http://www.developersketchbook.com/

- *iPhone Application Sketch Book* (Apress): http://www.apress.com/

Beautiful Mock-ups in Illustrator and Photoshop

If drawing on paper is not your thing and you're more comfortable working in Photoshop or Illustrator, other resourceful designers have graciously donated comprehensive sets of interface elements to the iPhone developer community, conveniently stored in layered files, making the creation of pixel-perfect mock-ups extremely easy (see Figure 4–8).

- Mercury Intermedia's iPhone UI Vector Elements (for Illustrator): http://www.mercuryintermedia.com/blog/index.php/2009/03/iphone-ui-vector-elements

- Teehan+Lax's iPhone GUI (for Photoshop): http://www.teehanlax.com/blog/

- ThreeTwentyFourEighty's iPhone Interface PSD (for Photoshop): http://www.320480.com/

- Smashing Magazine's iPhone PSD Vector Kit (for Photoshop): http://www.smashingmagazine.com/2008/11/26/iphone-psd-vector-kit/

Figure 4–8. *Just a small sample of the many iPhone elements available in layered Photoshop files and vector-based Illustrator files from third-party designers*

Other Software Tools for Designing Mock-Ups

If you don't own a license for Photoshop or Illustrator or you're looking for a more budget-conscious prototyping option, then OmniGraffle is an inexpensive solution for Mac users. Although originally developed as a diagramming tool, OmniGraffle has become a popular choice for constructing wireframes and interface design mock-ups.

- OmniGraffle: http://www.omnigroup.com/applications/omnigraffle/

The third-party web site Graffletopia offers an extensive free library of user-contributed OmniGraffle stencils. Several iPhone-related stencils are available for download, which I've listed here for your convenience:

- Graffletopia: http://www.graf[f]letopia.com/

    - Ultimate iPhone Stencil by Patrick Crowley

    - Mobile iPhone by Yahoo! (part of the Yahoo! Design Stencil Kit)

    - iPhone Wire Frames by Theresa Neil

    - iPhone Sketch by Soup Industries

If you prefer using presentation software for client meetings, then you may want to check out Dotan Saguy's MockApp for Apple Keynote (Mac) and Microsoft PowerPoint (Mac/PC):

- MockApp: http://mockapp.com/

One of my personal favorites is Balsamiq Mockups, a robust, cross-platform Adobe AIR application that features a vast toolkit of "hand-drawn" UI elements for both desktop apps and iPhone apps. This unique approach produces mock-ups that are very clean and professional while still looking as though they were drawn on paper.

- Balsamiq Mockups: http://www.balsamiq.com/products/mockups/

Paper Prototyping

Whether you've designed your initial mock-ups via desktop graphics software or hand-drawn sketches, many developers have found it beneficial to create printed paper prototypes of their user interfaces. With scissors, glue, and even a little tape, you can emulate a very rough look and feel of the app's navigational flow. You may decide to get fancy with moving pieces of paper that slide within an iPhone frame or stick to a more conventional storyboard approach that spans several pages (like directors do before shooting movie scenes). Either way, this is a convenient method for performing very basic usability testing, working out any major flaws before crafting a more refined prototype in Interface Builder.

Of course, if you're simply designing an app for yourself as a solo developer, then this step may seem a little excessive, especially if you're skilled enough to cobble together fast prototypes in Interface Builder. But if you're working with a client whose infamous for requesting countless UI changes, then creating functional paper prototypes may allow you to quickly refine the design and get your client's approval without wasting any actual programming time.

Moving to Interface Builder

After you've created and tweaked your design and you're finally happy with the way your interface looks, it's now time to fire up Xcode and Interface Builder. Creating a new Xcode project, you could immediately go to work re-creating your UI design with real UIKit components or your own custom controls in Interface Builder, but before you put too much effort into writing a lot of code, you may want to first test the usability of your new UI design.

You can quickly create a semi-functional prototype of your app by coding only the bare minimum of UI elements needed to emulate the intended flow of actions. Although you may assume this would include writing at least basic code for most of the controls in your app, there's actually a lot you can "fake" to avoid that and save time. This is especially handy if you just want to quickly test a UI concept in the iPhone Simulator or compile and distribute a quick prototype to others to receive feedback. This step can be immensely valuable in finding questionable areas of your app's navigational flow that could benefit from streamlining or simplifying actions. And when allowing a select group to test such an early prototype, you gain important insights about what interface elements are not intuitive to other people, allowing you to make important changes to your design before investing months of time pursuing a wrong direction.

For example, if your app is managed by a navigation controller or tab bar controller, then add that controller to your window in Interface Builder. In Xcode, write only the controller code necessary to enable moving from one screen to the next. Don't worry about re-creating the individual UI controls in every screen. If you've already created mock-ups of your app's various screens in Photoshop, Illustrator, or some other graphics editor, then simply crop and save those screens as PNG files. Import those PNG files into your Xcode project. By adding new subviews with UIImages to display each PNG file, those temporary UIImages can serve as "dummy" placeholders for those screens in Interface Builder (see Figure 4–9).

As shown in Figure 4–9, a navigation controller is wired up with enough code to move between your app's various screens. On the selected subview in the example, a UIImage is added and set to display the PNG mock-up of the default background with a fake text field. To enhance the prototype with additional functionality, a few lines of code can be added so that a mouse click on that UIImage would trigger the display of a new UIImage subview layer that displays a PNG mock-up of a fake iPhone keyboard. Based on your own needs, you can decide how much extra interactivity you want to add to your prototypes.

Figure 4–9. *Create quick prototypes by adding a minimum amount of navigation code needed to move from one screen to the next. Each screen subview can be "faked" by displaying Photoshop PNG files of your interface mock-ups in UIImages.*

After testing the prototype, receiving valuable feedback, and making any improvements to your app design, you can then strip out the small amount of temporary code and related UIImages. Now you're ready to build the real subviews and controls on top of your existing controller code to start fleshing out the finalized interface and feature set of your newly optimized app architecture.

As an alternative, many iPhone developers have found the innovative Briefs Cocoa Touch framework to be a nice solution for quickly generating live wireframe-based prototypes. Using PNG or JPEG images of your mock-up interface screens, Briefs enables you to assign, run, and test basic control schemes live on an iPhone OS device or within the iPhone Simulator.

- Briefs: http://giveabrief.com/

Pushing the Envelope with a Custom Interface

Creating a custom UI for a nongame app can be very rewarding. Why should games have all the fun? There's no reason why utility and productivity apps can't be just as visually appealing. Unique and exciting user interfaces can get people talking, which results in free publicity for your app. Mac OS X users saw this strategy work wonders for Delicious Monster with the cutting-edge UI of its successful Delicious Library software application.

If you have your heart set on creating a custom interface, here's one important rule to remember: don't over-think the design. Being innovative is good as long as it does not make your UI less intuitive to use. In such a small screen for mobile usage, less is more. Take special care that your custom design does not add extra complexity to your interface.

Convertbot by Tapbots breaks convention with a totally unique interface design (see Figure 4–10). The app provides unit conversion for hundreds of formats such as currency, speed, temperature, length, mass, time, and so on—a very utilitarian service that could have easily been presented in a basic screen layout using standard UIKit controls. Instead, the developers opted to produce a very clever and innovative design, turning the typically mundane task of unit conversion into a fun user experience. The beautiful interface of Convertbot has earned Tapbots a lot of free buzz in the iPhone community with countless reviewers and users praising the thoughtful and creative design behind its UI.

What makes the design so effective and easy to use is that behind the meticulously crafted UI is an extremely simple concept: a single large dial. So, even though the interface is unlike any of the usual UIKit elements, everyone knows how to use a dial (especially iPod users).

Figure 4–10. *The Convertbot UI effectively balances beauty and simplicity to provide a satisfying and intuitive user experience.*

Another good example of an app that delivers a beautiful custom interface while remaining very easy to use is BRID's Awesome Note. Although there are already dozens of note-taking apps in the App Store, most of them use standard table views to organize and list groups of notes. Instead of a simple table view row for each notes category,

Awesome Note sets itself apart from its competitors by wrapping the same functionality into a graphical, cascading tab folder theme (see Figure 4–11). Because we're all familiar with using folders in the physical world (and also on our desktop computers), the elements in this design remain instantly recognizable. The custom UI of Awesome Note succeeds in offering a unique user experience with no additional learning curve.

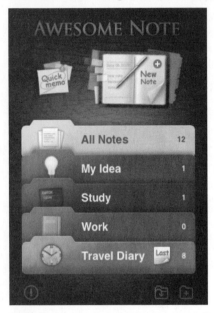

Figure 4–11. *The stunning UI of Awesome Note remains easy to use by integrating familiar tab folders and sticky note elements.*

You'll notice that Awesome Note also breaks convention by using a custom-designed navigation controller at the top of the right screenshot (in Figure 4–11). The design is careful to mimic the functionality and button placement of UIKit's navigation controller. So, why not just use the standard navigation controller to benefit from its "out-of-the-box" functionality? The subtle difference here is that this custom toolbar design reinforces the tab folder theme, as well as the selected category note's icon and color scheme from the previous screen. By placing the Back Arrow button and New Note buttons in the same location with similar functionality as the standard buttons from UIKit's navigation controller (see Figure 4–12), no one is left guessing how to use Awesome Note. This approach also helps conserve screen real estate in that the Back Arrow button takes up far less space than UIKit's breadcrumbs-style navigation button, which allows a longer title name to be displayed with its related icon. The custom UI is unique yet familiar at the same time.

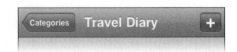

Figure 4–12. *The custom navigation controller in Awesome Note (left) emulates the familiar functionality and button placement as its standard UIKit counterpart (right), making the UI easy to learn.*

As long as you avoid known issues that can get your app rejected by Apple and remember to think like a user to maintain a UI that's intuitive and easy to use, pushing the envelope on interface design can offer an attractive user experience with the potential to garner increased publicity and sales.

The Comfortable Familiarity of UIKit

Before choosing to design a custom interface instead of using the standard UIKit controls provided by Apple, make sure you have very valid reasons to do so. As previously mentioned, the custom controls in BRID's Awesome Note app help reinforce its unique tab folder theme while staying true to the familiar functionality of similar UIKit components. In that particular situation, BRID's design intentions appear well served and justified, but don't reinvent the wheel just for the sake of being clever.

If you're building a complex, feature-rich app that's intended to store a lot of data, you may want to think twice about introducing a custom UI with new visual metaphors. If your app's interface appears to be too cluttered and complicated, you run the risk of overwhelming users. Your custom design elements may seem intuitive to you because you created them, but to newcomers, your unique visuals may feel foreign and confusing. Anything that causes frustration can lead to negative customer ratings and reviews, which obviously won't help your app sales.

With thousands of apps already using Apple's standard UIKit framework, users already know how to operate those standard components. By relying on UIKit, your app minimizes the learning curve for new customers. This allows people to focus on your app's core functionality and not get bogged down figuring out how to use your interface.

Cultured Code takes advantage of this with its iPhone version of Things, which specializes in making task management as easy as possible. The main Things iPhone screen consists of standard UIKit components such as a navigation controller and grouped table views (see Figure 4–13). To brand this basic UI with its own unique visual identity, Cultured Code integrated beautiful custom icons that match the ones used in its Mac OS X version of Things.

By keeping the interface extremely simple, Things provides a very clean and uncluttered working environment, enabling users to focus only on creating and organizing their tasks. No matter how many tasks are added, the simplicity of the design gives the content room to breathe on the screen. For a productivity app like Things, sheer simplicity can prove to be the most alluring trait. With an interface that never appears cramped in such a small mobile screen size, even long lists of tasks fail to overwhelm users—an impressive feat that underscores the power of UIKit. Apple has put a lot of thought into its native interface elements to ensure they visually communicate their function in a highly compact, streamlined approach. If you can't create something better than what's already included in UIKit, then don't.

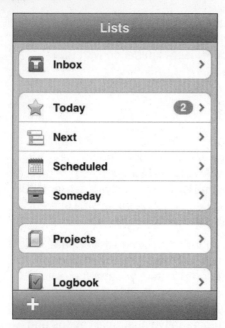

Figure 4–13. *The Things iPhone app utilizes a combination of standard UIKit components with custom icons to create a very clean and straightforward working environment.*

In the case of Things, one look at the first screenshot in the App Store, and you automatically understand how it works. There's no learning curve. You just "get it" upon first glance. That screenshot alone is a powerful marketing tool, making Things extremely attractive to people looking for an easy-to-use task management app.

Extensibility is an important factor to keep in mind when designing your interface. If there are four distinct sections in your app, a tab bar controller may seem like the best UI choice for easily accessing each of the sections. But before you decide to go that route, you should think about what features you have planned for future updates. If you plan on integrating additional sections at some point soon, then a tab bar controller is probably not the best choice since it can only comfortably hold a maximum of four or five tabs in portrait mode. To give your app room to grow in the future, you may want to consider using a table view to list those sections. A grouped table view, like the one used in Things for iPhone (Figure 4–13), can be scrolled, so it can accommodate an endless number of new additions while still remaining easy to use. Extensibility is an important consideration for every aspect of your UI design since you don't want to be forced to radically change the interface in version 2.0 or 3.0 because you ran out of room. Requiring your customers to learn how to use a new UI after they've grown accustomed to using your original UI will only agitate them. It may even cost you a few customers who decide to switch to a competitor's app out of frustration.

If you're interested in using UIKit elements in your app but worry about your interface looking too much like other similar apps, you can do several things to make your UIKit-driven interface unique. Here are a few options.

Icons and Images Within Your App

As you saw with Things, the icons and imagery you use within your app's interface can make a huge difference in giving your app a unique visual identity. Try not to use stock clip art for your icons, which will only cheapen the look of your UI. You want your icons to all be consistent in design and not a motley collection of stock clip art from different styles. You also do not want any of your users to recognize any of your icons as clip art they've seen in other places—that automatically lowers the perceived quality of your app. If you don't have the design chops to create your own artwork, then like I've said before, I highly recommend hiring a professional graphic designer. And if you already had someone create your app icon and logo, then see whether that person is also able to design your UI icons and imagery for a consistent overall theme.

Toolbar Colors

You can modify the color of navigation controllers and toolbars. Don't feel obligated to use the default blue or black choices. Upon browsing the App Store, you'll see a lot of apps using distinct toolbar colors such as dark blue, red, brown, green, or pink. Just make sure to choose a high-contrast color so that embedded text labels and buttons are still easy to read. Set the color of those components to your own signature shade within Interface Builder:

1. Open your XIB file in Interface Builder, select the Navigation Bar or Toolbar component, and then open its Attributes Inspector palette.

2. Under Attributes, keep Style set to Default, and then change Tint to your desired color, using the included Color Picker button.

3. The navigation bar or toolbar may not reflect your new color change within Interface Builder, but your new color will be visible when running your project in the iPhone Simulator.

Background Colors and Images

If you use a custom color for your navigation bar and/or toolbar, then you'll also want to modify the background of your views from the default blue striping to a new color or image of your choice. For example, if your navigation bar is dark brown, then you might want to change the selected grouped table view's background to a complementary color such as orange. You can set this by adding the following line of code to the `viewDidLoad` function in the related view controller's `.m` file:

```
self.tableView.backgroundColor = [UIColor orangeColor];
```

Of course, you may want to choose a more subtle color scheme that doesn't look so stark behind white grouped table view cells, such as a background image of a gradient or texture pattern. To fill the background with an image instead of a color, you can modify the previous code line to read as follows:

```
self.tableView.backgroundColor = [UIColor colorWithPatternImage:[UIImage
imageNamed:@"BG-Gradient.png"]];
```

The only problem with this simple approach is that the background image may display darker along the sides of the grouped table view cells than it appears on the rest of the screen. You can avoid this issue by adding a new `UIView` with your background image that sits beneath your grouped table view. Then simply clear your grouped table view's `backgroundColor` property to see the seamless background image of your new `UIView` underneath:

```
self.tableView.backgroundColor = [UIColor clearColor];
```

Toolbar Button Icons

Designing single-color white icons for use in buttons and tabs is a lot harder than most people assume. With no additional colors, you must design white icons that distinctly communicate an action or topic by its unique symbolism. Not to sound like a broken record, but this is yet another occasion when simplicity works best to ensure that the user can easily understand the meaning behind each and every icon. Showing a rough prototype to a select group can help pinpoint icons that people are having trouble identifying so that you can modify their design accordingly long before you start beta testing a finished app.

> **App Rejection Warning: Use system-provided icons only in the way that users expect them to work.** Apple has generously included several icons in the iPhone SDK that developers can use in their own apps, such as Add, Compose, Reply, Action, Search, and many more. This can save you from having to create custom icons for common tasks that are already covered by Apple's system icons. Just keep in mind that Apple provides these icons to represent consistent behavior across all apps that use them. When employing these system icons in your own app, be sure you're using them in their intended manner, or else your App Store submission may get quickly rejected. For example, don't use the Reply icon for a back button, and don't use the Bookmarks icon to open an ebook.

Designing for Accessibility

Although the iPhone 3GS's new VoiceOver audio feature has gained the lion's share of media attention, another important new accessibility feature is White on Black, which enables any user to change the display to white text on black backgrounds in any application. When turned on, this high-contrast feature inverts the screen's colors, making the text easier to read for some vision-impaired folks. As a developer, you should test your app's interface design in White on Black mode to ensure that it remains readable and its usability does not suffer from the inverted colors. It does not appear that the iPhone Simulator in the 3.0 SDK supports the White on Black mode, so for now you'll need to test your app on an actual iPhone 3GS device. In the Settings panel of an iPhone 3GS, choose General, then select Accessibility, and finally tap the White on Black switch to ON.

Here's an important subject that's often overlooked by software developers: color blindness. Although complete color blindness is a rare condition, quite a large percentage of the world population suffers from some form of color-deficient vision. This means their eyes still see full color but are unable to differentiate between some key colors like red and green. Although very few females exhibit color problems, would you believe that a whopping 8 percent of males demonstrate some sort of color deficiency? To put that into perspective, roughly 1 in 12 males of European descent have color-deficient vision. Considering that many iPhone developers create games and other apps specifically geared toward guys, being aware of color-deficiency issues when you're designing your interface is crucial in making your app accessible to the broadest audience possible.

Vischeck

http://www.vischeck.com/

This web site should be a required stop for all software developers. It provides helpful online tools for revealing color problems in your applications. Upload screenshots of your interface into the online Vischeck simulator to see how your UI design will look through color-deficient eyes. Upload screenshots to the online Daltonize tool to color-correct your interface for the three most common color deficiencies. The site also offers downloads of the Vischeck simulator as a free Photoshop plug-in for testing your interface screenshots directly within Photoshop.

Sim Daltonism for Mac OS X

http://michelf.com/projects/sim-daltonism/

This timesaving desktop application by Michel Fortin is a simple floating palette that allows you to test your iPhone app's interface in real time. Run your Xcode project in the iPhone Simulator while running the Sim Daltonism floating palette along one side. Select a color-deficiency type from the palette's menu, and then move your mouse pointer over the iPhone Simulator to see how your app's UI looks through color-deficient eyes in the palette window. If you find Sim Daltonism useful, then you're encouraged to support its continued development by making an online donation at Michel's web site.

Tips for the Artistically Challenged

The do-it-yourself route is not for everyone, especially when designing something as important as custom artwork for your iPhone app icon, logo, and user interface. It's important to remember that Photoshop, Illustrator, and other graphics programs are merely tools. Those tools are only as useful as your ability to wield them. To put the tools to good use, you must have the creativity and patience to translate the ideas from your head into actual pixels on the screen. Need some help? Here are a few tips and resources that might give you just the boost you're looking for.

Graphics and Icons

If you're interested in improving your Photoshop or Illustrator skills but have grown beyond the included documentation, you should check out the many tutorial-based web sites and design books that reveal cool techniques for achieving beautiful effects in those feature-packed graphics applications. Beyond searching Google, Amazon.com, and other common sites for solutions, here are a few more:

- Adobe Design Center: http://www.adobe.com/designcenter/

- Adobe Photoshop Killer Tips: http://www.photoshopkillertips.com/

- Layers Magazine Online: http://www.layersmagazine.com/

- Photoshop User TV: http://www.photoshopusertv.com/

- IllustratorWorld: http://www.illustratorworld.com/

eddit and PixelPressIcons offer stunning collections of premade white icons for use in tab bars and toolbars. Available in both bitmap and vector-based editions, their respective icon sets are inexpensive and royalty-free. Perfect for commercial app development, these icons are a great, timesaving solution for both nonartists and budget-conscious projects.

- eddit's iPhone UI Icon Set: http://eddit.com/shop/

- PixelPressIcon's Whitespace Icon Collection:
  http://www.pixelpressicons.com/?page_id=118

As far as full-color icons are concerned (for use in your table views and other related UI elements), dozens of web sites offer either icon design tutorials, free stock icons, commercial icon sets, custom icon design services, or all of the above. If you do find some free stock icons that you'd like to use in your iPhone app, be sure to check the licensing terms to ensure that the icons are royalty-free and can be used in commercial software. Some free icons require giving credit to the designer in your app or documentation. Also, as previously mentioned, if you do decide to use stock icons in your iPhone app, consider modifying them so that you app retains a unique feel (provided you still adhere to the related license terms). You don't want to cheapen the quality perception of your app by using the same stock icons that people have already seen countless times in other software and web sites. Here are a select handful of online resources:

- The Iconfactory: http://iconfactory.com/

- Stockicons: http://stockicons.com/

- IconDock: http://icondock.com/

- Icon Archive: http://www.iconarchive.com/

- Free Icons Web: http://www.freeiconsweb.com/

- IconsPedia: http://www.iconspedia.com/

- Iconfinder: http://www.iconfinder.net/

- iPhone Toolbox Icons: http://iphonetoolbox.com/category/icons/

Another great source for graphics is iStockphoto. Although most people know it as a destination for purchasing inexpensive stock photography, iStockphoto also has an extensive library of beautiful vector-based background imagery and icons.

- iStockphoto: http://www.istockphoto.com/

Fonts

For most iPhone apps, using the native iPhone system fonts will be sufficient, so font licensing will not be a concern. If you're developing a game, kids app, or entertainment app that uses a special font in its interface, then you'll want to make sure the unique font you've chosen has affordable licensing terms. Royalty-free fonts are obviously the most cost effective, as long as they allow use in commercial projects. Pay close attention to the licensing agreement of each custom font you're interested in using. At first glance, many font libraries appear to be free or royalty-free, but often the fine print specifies personal use only, with separate licenses (and higher price tags) available for commercial purposes, such as web sites, software, and so on. Do your homework before you purchase specialty fonts for use in your iPhone apps. Here are a few font directories to explore:

- DaFont: http://www.dafont.com/

- MyFonts: http://www.myfonts.com/

- Search Free Fonts: http://www.searchfreefonts.com/

- Discover Fonts: http://www.discoverfonts.com/

- Fonts.com: http://www.fonts.com/

- FontSpace: http://www.fontspace.com/

- UrbanFonts: http://www.urbanfonts.com/

- 1,001 Free Fonts: http://www.1001freefonts.com/

Audio and Music

If you're building a game or entertainment app, audio and music are often big factors in the enjoyment of it, so if you're not a sound designer or have very little experience composing and editing audio, then you may want to hire someone to do the music and sound effects cues. If you can't afford to hire a digital musician or sound designer, then you may want to consider licensing stock sound libraries. As with fonts, make sure any stock audio or music you purchase is royalty-free and licensed for commercial use.

- Sound Effects Library: http://www.sound-effects-library.com/

- SoundMATTER: http://soundmatter.thegamecreators.com/

- IndieSFX: http://www.indiesfx.co.uk/

- NEO Sounds: http://www.neosounds.com/

- The Music Bakery: http://www.musicbakery.com/

- Sounddogs.com: http://www.sounddogs.com/

- Soundrangers: http://www.soundrangers.com/

- iStockaudio: http://www.istockaudio.com/

Professional Design Services

If creating artwork or custom audio proves difficult for you—like pulling teeth—then instead of allowing the experience to become overly frustrating and unrewarding, you may want to consider hiring a professional designer. Don't succumb to any egotistical notions that you must create and control every aspect of the design and development process if your app stands to suffer from your own creative limitations. The success of your app is far too important. Knowing your own limitations as a developer will give you the freedom to bring on outside help so that you can build the best-quality app possible. Even when delegating the work to professional designers, you're still in charge of the project.

If money is an issue, then be creative. Do you have any talents that a professional designer may need? Does he or she need some web site or software programming assistance? If so, then there's an opportunity to barter services. Another option is to offer a small percentage of your app sales in exchange for their ongoing graphics support. In essence they're becoming a partner, sharing in the risk. If the app fails to reach an audience, then no one involved makes any money. Some designers, depending on their availability, may not be open to such a gamble. Even if you have a great concept, they may prefer to get paid up front. But if a profit-sharing option is your best option, then it can't hurt to offer it.

Although there are far too many professional design services and freelance artists to list within these pages, here are a just few notable resources worth considering:

- 99designs: http://99designs.com/

- oDesk: http://www.odesk.com/

- Elance: http://www.elance.com/

- Guru.com: http://www.guru.com/

When exploring outsourcing marketplaces, online search engines, or even your local yellow pages, never settle for the first listing you find. Ask for recommendations from your peers either directly or via developer mailing lists and online forums. It's good to find out from other developers which companies and consultants are trusted and respected for their design work on icons, logos, music, sound effects, and other outsourced creative elements. Even when you find a designer you like, ask to see their portfolio to make sure their design style and skills are capable of bringing your specific vision to life.

Communication is key when working with a designer. Although they may be extremely good at their craft, they can't read minds. The more information you give them about your creative needs, the better equipped they will be to deliver exactly what you want.

How You Like Me Now? Encouraging User Reviews Within Your App

You've put a lot of work into perfecting your app's user experience in the hopes that your efforts result in sales and positive customer ratings. If a user decides to delete your app from their iPhone, Apple's system automatically prompts the user to first rate the app before completing the uninstall. Although this is a convenient way to solicit customer feedback, it's not necessarily the most opportune time to ask their opinion. If the user has chosen to delete your app, then they probably don't like it or haven't found it useful. In either situation, if they do opt to post a rating, then odds are it will likely be a negative one. For happy customers—ones who have chosen to keep your app—to post a rating, they have to go out of their way to visit the App Store on their own accord, which is not as convenient. This shows the inherent flaw in Apple's rating system.

We all know that customer ratings and reviews in the App Store can greatly affect the sales of an app, so how does a developer combat the uneven emphasis on negative feedback? Why not prompt the user for positive feedback at the time of your choice? It's as easy as having your app display its own `UIAlertView`, asking users who like the app to please rate it. Here's how to do it with only a handful of code lines.

First, fire up Xcode and create a new iPhone project, using the View-based Application template as the foundation. Let's name the project AskForRating. You may want to give the user the option to rate your app at any time by including a button on your Settings screen, but for example purposes, you'll simply be adding a button to the AskForRating project's main screen.

Next, you'll need to add a reference to the `UIAlertViewDelegate` in the `@interface` call of your `AskForRatingViewController.h` header file. You'll also want to add an `IBAction` for the button you'll be creating in Interface Builder later. Your `AskForRatingViewController.h` file should now consist of the following code:

```
#import <UIKit/UIKit.h>

@interface AskForRatingViewController : UIViewController <UIAlertViewDelegate> {

}

- (IBAction)buttonPressed:(id)sender;

@end
```

After saving that file, now open the AskForRatingViewController.m implementation file, and add the following code:

```
- (IBAction)buttonPressed:(id)sender {
    UIAlertView *buttonAlert = [[UIAlertView alloc] initWithTitle:@"Help Spread the
Word" message:@"If you like this app, please rate it in the App Store. Thanks!"
delegate:self cancelButtonTitle:@"Maybe Later" otherButtonTitles:@"Rate It Now", nil];
    [buttonAlert show];
    [buttonAlert release];
}

- (void)alertView:(UIAlertView *)alertView clickedButtonAtIndex:(NSInteger)buttonIndex {
    if (buttonIndex == 1) {
        NSURL *url = [NSURL URLWithString:@"YOUR APP STORE URL"];
        [[UIApplication sharedApplication] openURL:url];
    }
}
```

The (IBAction)buttonPressed code receives the tapped button action and proceeds to display the UIAlertView, asking the user to rate the app. The alertView code is called when the user chooses either the Maybe Later or Rate It Now button in the UIAlertView dialog box. If the Rate It Now button is selected, your App Store URL is launched, sending the user directly to your app's page in the App Store.

Don't forget to replace the placeholder string "YOUR APP STORE URL" with your unique App Store URL. To grab the correct URL, simply locate your app in the desktop Mac version of iTunes, and then Ctrl+click your app icon. In the contextual menu that appears, select Copy iTunes Store URL, and then paste it into the URL string in your code.

Save the file in Xcode, and move on to the last task: creating your button. Double-click the AskForRatingViewController.xib file to open it in Interface Builder. Add a Rounded Rectangle Button to your view. Rename the button's title to Rate This App. If desired, you could create your own custom button instead. Then wire the button's Touch Up Inside connector to the File Owner's buttonPressed connector. Save and close the XIB file.

If you run your Xcode project in the iPhone Simulator, you'll see that pressing the Rate This App button successfully prompts you to rate the app with a UIAlertView dialog box (see Figure 4–14). It's important to note that if you click the Rate It Now button, the App Store URL won't load within the iPhone Simulator, so you'll have to test your app on an actual iPhone device in order to ensure it properly displays your app's page in the App Store.

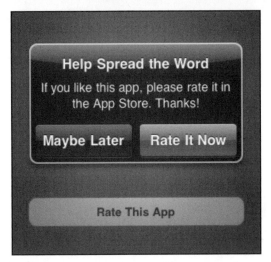

Figure 4–14. *Encourage users to rate your app with a built-in custom prompt.*

Take note of the wording used in Figure 4–14's UIAlertView. By using the title "Help Spread the Word" as the call to action, you're inviting fans to help evangelize your app. And with the message "If you like this app, please rate it in the App Store," you're specifically addressing your satisfied users. Of course, that won't stop haters from using this feature, but the wording does set a very positive tone. Even the Cancel button is labeled Maybe Later, letting users know that their feedback is always welcome at any time.

Although this is a nice solution, it's still a passive one, relying on the user to press the button to initiate the action. If you place that button on your Settings screen, they may only stumble upon it while looking for help with your app. And if they're searching for help, they may be frustrated—not a good time to hit them up for a review. You want to ask users to rate your app when they're in the best possible mood, such as moments when they are enjoying your app. You may want to consider taking a more proactive stance, initiating the display of your UIAlertView at strategic times such as the following:

- After several days of usage, if users haven't deleted your app yet, they must have found some positive value in it. Include code in your main view controller's viewDidLoad event to check the NSUserDefaults' firstRun key, determining how many days the app has been installed upon app launch. Depending on how often your app is likely to get used (daily or weekly), pick an appropriate time to pop up the rating request dialog box—maybe after 5 to 15 days of being installed.

- If your app is a game, then display the rating request dialog box when they're feeling good after finishing a difficult level or achieving a high score.

■ If it's a productivity app, then you may want to display the rating request dialog box when users have a positive sense of accomplishment after writing a document, editing a photo, checking off a list of tasks, and so on.

With any of these approaches, take care not to be overly aggressive. If you annoy users by constantly asking them for a rating, this ploy will backfire on you. The users you annoy will be driven to post negative ratings, complaining about how much they hate being pestered for their feedback. For best results, ask only once or in a very few select places. If customers choose Maybe Later, they can always do it when it's convenient for them by accessing the Rate This App button on your Settings screen.

Check Out This Cool App! Tell a Friend with In-App Email and Social Networking

Similar to the concept of a Rate This App button, you can also include a Tell A Friend button in your app, enabling your customers to recommend your app to their friends and family. This is good old-fashioned grassroots marketing. By supplying your users with convenient options to talk about your app, it's a proactive step in the hopes of increasing your app's exposure and sales through the proven power of word of mouth. Nothing helps sell a product more effectively than recommendations from trusted peers.

What options would you want to offer? With the introduction of iPhone OS 3.0, you can now send email directly from within your app, so that's an easy yet powerful feature to include! And with Twitter and Facebook being such popular social networking sites, you may want to consider adding support for those platforms as well.

If you do decide to connect with a third-party web service, you'll want to first read the API license agreement to confirm that it allows you to access the API in a commercial software application for mobile devices. And even if they do allow commercial use, take into consideration that their terms may change in the future, possibly forcing you to remove that feature. If your app lists supported web services as buttons on a UIActionSheet, then that gives you the flexibility to easily remove one of the buttons if needed in a future app update. Delicious Monster had to remove its Delicious Library for iPhone from the App Store when Amazon.com changed its Product Advertising API licensing agreement, forbidding developers to use the API in mobile applications. Let's hope Delicious Monster will find a replacement API from an alternative web service so that its Delicious Library iPhone app can once again see the light of day.

Even beyond licensing terms, a third-party web service might make an API change that could break your app, causing you to scramble to submit a new fixed update to the App Store. Remember Twitpocalypse—the Twitter API change that briefly disabled many of the iPhone Twitter client apps back in June 2009? Unlike the instant availability of posting new software downloads on your web site, you may have to wait days for your updated version to make its way through the App Store review process before customers can get their hands on it.

Web services offer amazing content that are perfect for mobile app consumption, but definitely keep these potential issues in mind when deciding how much of your app's functionality will be dependent on a third-party web service.

Without any further ado, let's try our hand at a little code, shall we? Just like the RateThisApp example, create a new iPhone project in Xcode, choosing the View-based Application template and naming it TellAFriend. You'll want the app to include a Tell A Friend button that when pressed, a UIActionSheet is displayed with various buttons for email, Twitter, and Facebook. Why use a UIActionSheet? It allows you to add the Tell A Friend feature with a single button, so as not to be intrusive in your existing interface design. It also consolidates all of the supported social networking services into a single list, making it easy to add or remove options as needed. Want to add support for another social networking platform? Just add another button to your UIActionSheet without disturbing your app's main UI design.

Open the TellAFriendViewController.m header file, and modify the code to read as follows:

```
#import <UIKit/UIKit.h>

@interface TellAFriendViewController : UIViewController <UIActionSheetDelegate> {

}

- (IBAction)buttonPressed:(id)sender;

@end
```

Notice the added reference to the UIActionSheetDelegate and the IBAction for the button you'll be creating in Interface Builder. Save that file, and now open the TellAFriendViewController.m implementation file. Change the code to read as follows:

```
#import "TellAFriendViewController.h"

@implementation TellAFriendViewController

- (void)viewDidLoad {
    // Implement viewDidLoad to do additional setup after loading the view, typically
from a nib.
    [super viewDidLoad];
}

- (IBAction)buttonPressed:(id)sender {
    // Button was tapped, so display Action Sheet.
    UIActionSheet *actionSheet = [[UIActionSheet alloc] initWithTitle:@"Like This App?
Tell A Friend!" delegate:self cancelButtonTitle:@"Maybe Later"
destructiveButtonTitle:@"Send Email" otherButtonTitles:@"Post on Twitter", @"Share on
Facebook", nil];
    [actionSheet showInView:self.view];
    [actionSheet release];

}

- (void)actionSheet:(UIActionSheet *)actionSheet
didDismissWithButtonIndex:(NSInteger)buttonIndex {
```

```
    if (buttonIndex != [actionSheet cancelButtonIndex]) {
        if (buttonIndex == [actionSheet destructiveButtonIndex]) {
            // Add Email code here.
        }
        if (buttonIndex == 1) {
            // Add Twitter code here.
        }
        if (buttonIndex == 2) {
            // Add Facebook Connect code here.
        }
    }
}

- (void)didReceiveMemoryWarning {
    // Releases the view if it doesn't have a superview.
    [super didReceiveMemoryWarning];

    // Release any cached data, images, etc that aren't in use.
}

- (void)viewDidUnload {
    // Release any retained subviews of the main view.
    // e.g. self.myOutlet = nil;
}

- (void)dealloc {
    [super dealloc];
}

@end
```

As in the RateThisApp example, the (IBAction)buttonPressed code receives the tapped button action. This is where you display the UIActionSheet with the title "Like This App? Tell A Friend!" Buttons for email, Twitter, and Facebook have been added (see Figure 4–15), but their functionality has not yet been implemented.

To minimize the amount of screen real estate that the Tell A Friend button requires, let's use an icon instead of actual text. A small icon button will be much easier to integrate into an existing UI design. Although plenty of web sites use the plus (+) symbol as the standardized icon for sharing, do not use that symbol as your icon in an iPhone app. That symbol is already reserved for Apple's system-supplied Add button. If you use a plus symbol for any other purpose than the intended Add functionality, your App Store submission will be quickly rejected. Try using different imagery to serve your needs here. A megaphone icon might be a nice symbol for communicating this feature (see Figure 4–15).

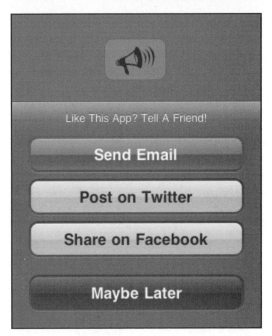

Figure 4–15. *The Tell A Friend example app in action*

I created a megaphone icon, saved it as a PNG file, and then imported it into the Xcode project's Resources folder. Now I can double-click `TellAFriendViewController.xib` to open the view in Interface Builder. Add a Rounded Rectangle Button to the view, and wire up its Touch Up Inside connector to the File Owner's `buttonPressed` connector. Then instead of using title text for the button, assign the button's Image to the megaphone PNG file. Resize the button accordingly, and then save the project.

In-App Email

With the basic foundation of the TellAFriend app finished, now you need to add functionality to the Send Email button. In previous versions of the iPhone SDK, sending emails required launching the built-in Mail app, which forced your app to quit, since only one app can run at a time. The iPhone SDK 3.0 solves that problem by including support for an In-App Email feature. This new feature allows users to compose and send an email directly within your own app!

It should go without saying that the example code you'll be writing will require you to have the iPhone SDK 3.0 installed. If you want your app to be compatible with both iPhone OS 2 and 3, then you'll want to take a look at Apple's MailComposer example project, which shows how to support both OS versions via code. To download the MailComposer example, log into the iPhone Developer Program site, and then head over to the following location:

`http://developer.apple.com/iphone/library/samplecode/MailComposer/`

For the purpose of the TellAFriend example app, I'll keep things simple and only focus on sending emails using the new In-App Email feature in iPhone SDK 3.0. Before you write any code, the required `MessageUI.framework` has to be added to the Xcode project. To do this, Ctrl+click the project's Frameworks folder, and from the contextual menu that appears, select Add ➤ Existing Frameworks... (see Figure 4–16). Select the `MessageUI.framework`, which can be located in the Xcode tools' parent Developer folder at the following path:

Developer ➤ Platforms ➤ iPhoneOS.platform ➤ developer ➤ SDKs ➤ iPhoneOS3.0.sdk ➤ System ➤ Library ➤ Frameworks ➤ MessageUI.framework

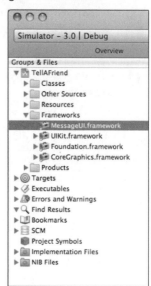

Figure 4–16. Add the `MessageUI.framework` (left) for inclusion in your Xcode project (right).

Once the `MessageUI.framework` is included in your project, you can now dig into some programming. Open the `TellAFriendViewController.h` header file, and modify the code as follows:

```
#import <UIKit/UIKit.h>
#import <MessageUI/MessageUI.h>
#import <MessageUI/MFMailComposeViewController.h>

@interface TellAFriendViewController : UIViewController <UIActionSheetDelegate,
MFMailComposeViewControllerDelegate> {

}

- (IBAction)buttonPressed:(id)sender;
- (void)showMailComposer;

@end
```

As you can see from the new code elements highlighted in bold, the `MessageUI` classes have been imported, a new Mail delegate was added to the `@interface`, and a

showMailComposer function is referenced. Save this file; then open the
TellAFriendViewController.m implementation file, and change the code accordingly:

```
#import "TellAFriendViewController.h"

@implementation TellAFriendViewController


// Implement viewDidLoad to do additional setup after loading the view, typically from a
nib.
- (void)viewDidLoad {
    [super viewDidLoad];
}

- (IBAction)buttonPressed:(id)sender {
    // Button was tapped, so display Action Sheet.
    UIActionSheet *actionSheet = [[UIActionSheet alloc] initWithTitle:@"Like This App?
Tell A Friend!" delegate:self cancelButtonTitle:@"Maybe Later"
destructiveButtonTitle:@"Send Email" otherButtonTitles:@"Post on Twitter", @"Share on
Facebook", nil];
    [actionSheet showInView:self.view];
    [actionSheet release];

}

- (void)actionSheet:(UIActionSheet *)actionSheet
didDismissWithButtonIndex:(NSInteger)buttonIndex {
    if (buttonIndex != [actionSheet cancelButtonIndex]) {
        if (buttonIndex == [actionSheet destructiveButtonIndex]) {
            // In-App Email, requires iPhone OS 3.0
            [self showMailComposer];
        }
        if (buttonIndex == 1) {
            // Add Twitter code here.
        }
        if (buttonIndex == 2) {
            // Add Facebook Connect code here.
        }
    }
}

// Displays an email composition interface inside the application. Populates all the
Mail fields.
- (void)showMailComposer {

    Class mailClass = (NSClassFromString(@"MFMailComposeViewController"));
    if (mailClass != nil) {
        // Test to ensure that device is configured for sending emails.
        if ([mailClass canSendMail]) {

            MFMailComposeViewController *picker = [[MFMailComposeViewController alloc]
init];
            picker.mailComposeDelegate = self;

            [picker setSubject:@"Check out this cool iPhone app!"];
```

```
                // Fill out the email body text
                NSString *emailBody = @"Check out this cool iPhone app, now available in the
App Store!\n\nBreadcrumbs - Parked Car Locator\n\nWatch a video and learn more
at:\nhttp://www.breadcrumbsapp.com/";
                [picker setMessageBody:emailBody isHTML:NO];

                [self presentModalViewController:picker animated:YES];
                [picker release];

        }
        else {
                // Device is not configured for sending emails, so notify user.
                UIAlertView *alertView = [[UIAlertView alloc] initWithTitle:@"Unable to
Email" message:@"This device is not yet configured for sending emails." delegate:self
cancelButtonTitle:@"Okay, I'll Try Later" otherButtonTitles:nil];
                [alertView show];
                [alertView release];
        }
    }

}

// Dismisses the Mail composer when the user taps Cancel or Send.
- (void)mailComposeController:(MFMailComposeViewController*)controller
didFinishWithResult:(MFMailComposeResult)result error:(NSError*)error
{
    NSString *resultTitle = nil;
    NSString *resultMsg = nil;

    switch (result)
    {
        case MFMailComposeResultCancelled:
            resultTitle = @"Email Cancelled";
            resultMsg = @"You elected to cancel the email";
            break;
        case MFMailComposeResultSaved:
            resultTitle = @"Email Saved";
            resultMsg = @"You saved the email as a draft";
            break;
        case MFMailComposeResultSent:
            resultTitle = @"Email Sent";
            resultMsg = @"Your email was successfully delivered";
            break;
        case MFMailComposeResultFailed:
            resultTitle = @"Email Failed";
            resultMsg = @"Sorry, the Mail Composer failed. Please try again.";
            break;
        default:
            resultTitle = @"Email Not Sent";
            resultMsg = @"Sorry, an error occurred. Your email could not be sent.";
            break;
    }

    // Notifies user of any Mail Composer errors received with an Alert View dialog.
```

```
    UIAlertView *mailAlertView = [[UIAlertView alloc] initWithTitle:resultTitle
message:resultMsg delegate:self cancelButtonTitle:@"Okay" otherButtonTitles:nil];
    [mailAlertView show];
    [mailAlertView release];
    [resultTitle release];
    [resultMsg release];

    [self dismissModalViewControllerAnimated:YES];
}

- (void)didReceiveMemoryWarning {
    // Releases the view if it doesn't have a superview.
    [super didReceiveMemoryWarning];

    // Release any cached data, images, etc that aren't in use.
}

- (void)viewDidUnload {
    // Release any retained subviews of the main view.
    // e.g. self.myOutlet = nil;
}

- (void)dealloc {
    [super dealloc];
}

@end
```

Let's step through the new code (highlighted in bold) so you can see exactly what's happening. First, in the buttonPressed action, the following comment:

```
// Add Email code here.
```

was replaced with this:

```
[self showMailComposer];
```

This line calls the showMailComposer function, which does all the heavy lifting of crafting an email message and then displaying it in a new embedded MFMailComposeViewController. For this example, the message tells a friend to check out the fictional Breadcrumbs app in the App Store. It even includes a link to the official web site. By supplying all of this for the user, it makes sharing extremely convenient and simple. All the user has to do is type a friend's email address in the To field and tap the Send button (see Figure 4–17).

Working our way down, below the showMailComposer function is the mailComposeController event, which gets called when the user presses the MFMailComposeViewController's Cancel or Send button. This is the place to add code that notifies the user of the status of their email action. As you can see from the listed code, you can test the received results for the status of the email and then report a confirmation to the user either if the email was successfully delivered or if the process failed for some reason.

It's always a good idea to provide users with frequent status updates, especially when sending data via an online connection. If a user clicks the Send button and the

MFMailComposeViewController is dismissed without any further communication, the user is left waiting, wondering whether the email was delivered. In the example mailComposerController event, if the received result signals a successful delivery, then the user is notified via a UIAlertView. Likewise, the user is also notified if the email could not be sent. In your never-ending quest to avoid negative customer ratings in the App Store, communicating the current status of email actions will help prevent users from getting frustrated.

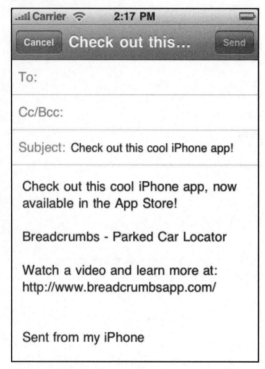

Figure 4–17. *When users tap the Send Email button in the example, the iPhone OS 3.0's Mail Composer is displayed within the iPhone app.*

Before running the TellAFriend project in the iPhone Simulator, make sure you have Xcode set to Simulator - 3.0 | Debug so that your In-App Email code compiles and runs correctly. Even though the iPhone Simulator will report that your email was successfully delivered, it does not actually send your email message. For best results, test your In-App Email code on an iPhone device.

And that's all there is to it! Adding In-App Email support to your app actually requires very few lines of code compared to how much functionality you get in return.

Twitter and Facebook Connect

Beyond sending emails, you may want to also give users the ability to post messages to their Twitter and Facebook accounts. And although it's nice when users blatantly promote your app, another more subtle way to increase awareness for your app is to deeply integrate social networking with other core features in your app. For example, if you're building a game, enabling users to share their high scores via Twitter and Facebook will not only breed synergy among players but may also attract new customers who want to get in on the action. NimbleBit's Moon Drop includes a seamless user option for Tweeting high scores (see Figure 4–18). A more comprehensive extension of community building is to integrate one of the many social gaming platforms currently available for iPhone games, which I'll be talking about in Chapter 5. For now, let's look at Twitter and Facebook.

Figure 4–18. *After finishing a game in NimbleBit's Moon Drop, users are prompted to tweet about their high scores.*

Many open source iPhone Twitter clients are available for download. A quick online search reveals at least a dozen of them. Many of them appear to rely on the popular open source framework, MGTwitterEngine, developed by prominent Cocoa developer Matt Legend Gemmell. Originally developed for Mac OS X software applications, Matt's Twitter framework has since been updated for use in iPhone app projects.

MGTwitterEngine is an Objective-C class library that encompasses the entire Twitter API and returns data as native Cocoa objects, making it extremely easy to use. And you'll be happy to know that Matt's license terms are very generous, allowing developers to use MGTwitterEngine royalty-free in commercial products. All he requires is that you credit him as the author of the MGTwitterEngine code included in your app. Of course, if you find his code helpful, I suggest emailing him a personal "thank you" or posting a comment on his blog. Open source developers put a lot of hard work into their contributed code, so they always appreciate knowing when people find their efforts useful.

For details on how to use MGTwitterEngine, visit Matt's blog. You can download the source code from his Subversion repository. For those who don't know, Subversion is a popular open source version control system. If you don't have Subversion installed or need help using it, check out `http://subversion.tigris.org/`.

- Mike Legend Gemmell's MGTwitterEngine: `http://mattgemmell.com/2008/02/22/mgtwitterengine-twitter-from-cocoa`

- Download MGTwitterEngine: `http://svn.cocoasourcecode.com/MGTwitterEngine/`

- Matt's Source License: `http://mattgemmell.com/license`

Facebook allows developers to access their platform using their Facebook Connect API. Recently, it released Facebook Connect for the iPhone, and already some iPhone apps in the App Store are taking advantage of Facebook Connect's extensive features. Having access to your list of friends and their profile information, as well as connecting with them in real time, brings the full power of the Facebook platform into your iPhone app. It may seem like overkill to integrate such an extensive framework into your Xcode project just so your users can post status updates to their Facebook page. But if you're developing an iPhone game or any kind of peer-to-peer community app, you may soon find yourself utilizing additional Facebook Connect features in other parts of your project.

The beauty of Facebook Connect is that you, the developer, need not worry about programming a secure environment for users to share their personal data. Facebook Connect handles the security for you by providing users with Facebook's simple and trusted authentication process for logging into their accounts.

On the official Facebook Connect for iPhone web site, Facebook provides links for downloading the SDK, reading the documentation, and even watching the online video *How to Implement Facebook Connect on the iPhone in 5 Minutes*.

- Facebook Connect for iPhone: `http://developers.facebook.com/connect_iphone.php`

Before you can use the Facebook Connect SDK in your iPhone app, you'll first need an API key and secret in order to authenticate your Facebook Connect requests. This requires you to have an active Facebook account of your own. Once logged into your account, visit the following Facebook Developer site:

- Facebook Developer: My Applications: `http://www.facebook.com/developers/apps.php`

On that Developer web page, click the Set Up New Application button to create a new Facebook application. Be sure to give it the same name as the iPhone app you're building since that application name will be listed as the source when users post status updates from your iPhone app. This is a subtle yet effective way to get your app's name displayed on users' Facebook pages—great exposure for your app.

Once your new Facebook application is created on their Developer site, the application's "Essential Information" will list your unique API key and secret. Save those two text strings in a safe place because you'll need them when customizing the Facebook Connect code in your own iPhone app.

App Rejection Warning: Your app must notify users when an online connection attempt fails. If your app relies on connecting with a third-party web service, you must include appropriate error-handling code so that in the case of a failed connection or data request, your app handles the failure gracefully and notifies the users of the current status. If a bad data request freezes your app or leaves the user waiting without any indication of what's happening, then the App Store review team will most likely reject your submission. If you provide a demo account for use during the review process, make sure that demo account works! Or provide two demo accounts, just in case one fails during the review. It's also a good practice to always notify users if and when your app requires an online connection, especially since iPod touch devices may not always be logged into a WiFi network.

Now you're ready to integrate social networking into your own iPhone apps! Following the documentation and example code included with the MGTwitterEngine framework and the Facebook Connect for iPhone SDK, see whether you can add support for posting to Twitter and Facebook in the existing Tell A Friend example project. I bet you'll have it up and running in no time!

Earning Your Stripes

Wow, that was a lot of information packed into a single chapter! I hope you were able to absorb all of that *and* have some fun along the way. You even played around with some code in this chapter...yeah, I thought you'd appreciate that. I told you we'd be talking about more than just research and marketing concepts.

You've definitely earned yourself a pat on the back and a well-deserved break after all of the things you've tackled so far. So, go kick your feet up and enjoy a few levels of your favorite iPhone game.

When you're ready for more, just turn the page to dive into the next chapter.

Chapter 5

Money for Nothing: When It Pays to Be Free

In the previous chapter, you explored the value of designing an eye-catching app icon and elegant user interface so as to help make your app more visually attractive in the App Store. But once you have people's attention, will your screenshots be enough to convince them to purchase your app? Don't think that just because your app is priced at only 99 cents that everyone will automatically buy it. If you haven't noticed lately, most of the apps in the Top 25 are 99 cents, so why should consumers pick your app over the thousands of other 99-cent apps? Unfortunately, the current App Store ecosystem has a very skewed outlook on pricing, with everyone racing to the bottom with lowered prices to gain traction in the Top 100.

So, what's a developer to do? Don't forget the big lesson from the previous chapter: your iPhone app is your most powerful marketing tool. Let's take that concept to the next level by giving consumers something for free.

Free? Yes, you read that correctly. Don't worry. The objective here is still to make money. Free is a very powerful motivator to get people to download your product. Who doesn't love to get free stuff? I know I do, and according to the App Store statistics, I'm not alone. Although free apps account for only 25 percent of the App Store's catalog, they represent a whopping 95 percent of the total downloads!

You can take advantage of this demand for free by employing one or more of the following strategies:

- Offer a free "lite" version of your app to help drive sales for the paid version, or utilize a "freemium" model with premium features available through In-App Purchase.

- Give away your app for free to get as many people using it as possible. After you've cultivated a large loyal customer base that depends on your app, use that basic free version to up-sell a separate premium version that includes additional "must-have" features.

- Make your app free, supported by in-app advertising.

Which of those scenarios will work for your particular situation will greatly hinge on what kind of app you're developing. For example, in-app advertising may not be an appropriate solution for an educational kids app because parents may not condone apps that advertise to their young children and because the majority of users may be playing the app safely offline on an iPod touch, unreachable by ad network servers.

In this chapter, I'll be covering when and how to utilize the power of *free* for effective results. Plus, I'll explore how in-app cross-promotion and social gaming platforms can help advertise your paid apps across not only your own free apps but also within apps from other developers.

The Benefits of Free to Promote Paid Versions

As an iPhone developer, you're undoubtedly no stranger to the concept of free "lite" apps. Like me, your iPhone home screen is probably littered with several "pages" of lite apps downloaded from the App Store. And after evaluating them, you've probably even bought the paid versions of at least a few of them. Without the ability to try the lite version first, would you have purchased the full paid version? Maybe not. So, it's easy to see the enormous value that free lite versions can have in boosting paid app sales.

Developers of desktop software have known this important fact for decades. Making trial demo versions available for free download is one of the primary marketing tools for selling commercial software. The trial versions of most modern Mac and Windows applications offer built-in purchase mechanisms for enabling users to easily buy a license online and receive a serial number that unlocks the demo app, instantaneously transforming the trial version into the full-featured application.

Try before you buy. It sounds like a no-brainer for the App Store, right? Unfortunately, Apple does not currently allow iPhone app developers to offer free trial demos with crippled features that can be unlocked by purchasing the app. This limitation forced developers to work around the issue by producing two separate versions of their app: one is a free lite version, and the other is a paid version that offers additional features not found in the lite version. For the first year of the App Store, this was the closest anyone got to the "try-before-you-buy" concept.

When Apple announced the inclusion of the new In-App Purchase feature in the iPhone SDK 3.0, developers were hopeful that maybe it would finally solve this problem, but that was not quite the case. Even though In-App Purchase does enable users to purchase App Store items within an iPhone application, Apple is very particular about how In-App Purchase is utilized. Free apps are now allowed to offer In-App Purchases, but this built-in ecommerce API cannot be used to unlock previously crippled features, because apps are still prohibited from presenting features as disabled. If a feature is included in the free app—such as a button in the toolbar—then it must be a functional feature. The current implementation of In-App Purchase enables developers to provide *additional* features that are not currently included in the app, such as subscription services, new content, and add-on game levels. Even though In-App Purchase does not directly solve the "try-before-you-buy" issue, it does provide a powerful path for additional revenue streams beyond initial app sales.

With the advent of In-App Purchase, many developers were quick to predict that it would render lite versions obsolete, but with the various complexities and guidelines for implementing In-App Purchase, a free lite version is still a very valid and effective business model. Which approach is best for you depends on the kind of app you're developing.

Choosing a Path: Lite Version vs. In-App Purchase

The most obvious reason many developers still opt to produce both a free lite version and a separate paid version is that it is much easier to implement than In-App Purchase. If you've ever taken the time to glance through Apple's Store Kit documentation, you'll notice that In-App Purchase requires quite a bit of additional programming and back-end infrastructure. For newcomers to the iPhone developer platform, the Store Kit API may seem a little overwhelming, whereas it's easy enough to compile two versions of your app within Xcode, one being a lite version and the other a more robust paid version.

If your app's functionality can be divided neatly into a free feature set and additional premium features made available for a small upgrade fee, then In-App Purchase may just be the better model to suit your needs. For example, if your free app is a first-person shooter that includes five levels of game play, then additional levels and weapons could be offered as In-App Purchase items. It's important to note that you can't replace the existing app binary with a new binary via In-App Purchase, so for most games, this requires including the extra game levels and content within the free app in a hidden or locked capacity. When the customer purchases that item, your app would then unlock that new weapon or game level. ngmoco has found success with this model in its popular Eliminate Pro app, which is offered for free, and additional game play, weapons, and armor can be bought via In-App Purchase. If you're interested in learning more about Apple's Store Kit API, check out the extensive coverage of In-App Purchase in Chapter 6.

But In-App Purchase may not apply well to every type of application. Some single-function utility apps are structured in such a way that attempting to target specific features to be offered via In-App Purchase can be problematic. In the case of most games, it seems to be a good fit, but keep in mind that unlocking additional content via In-App Purchase requires your application to be that much bigger (to store that hidden content). And when dealing with the download bandwidth limitations on mobile devices, the file size of your free app can make a huge difference in its effectiveness as a promotional sales tool. Many phone carriers, such as AT&T, limit file downloads through their mobile networks to only 10MB, so if users want to download your 35MB free game onto their iPhone, they'll have to wait until they are logged into a local WiFi network. That defeats potential impulse buys and spur-of-the-moment downloads. By the time they are within range of a WiFi network, they may have already forgotten about your app. With a lite version, only the content that it is offered for free is included, which in turn compiles to a much smaller file size than the larger, full-featured paid version. If the free lite app binary weighs in at under 10MB, then it will be accessible to a much broader audience of potential customers, since they'll have the ability to download it onto their iPhones through their carrier's mobile network if WiFi isn't available.

With all that said, the one major drawback to the free lite model is that purchasing the paid version is a separate app download, so transferring any existing user data from the lite version to the paid version is quite a logistical headache for developers (which I explain later in this chapter). In-App Purchase unlocks the new features or content directly within the app, so there's no need to transfer existing user data.

I do believe In-App Purchase is a very powerful avenue for mobile sales and will soon become one of the most popular methods for monetizing app development on the iPhone OS platform. If this model fits nicely with your application's feature set and architecture, then stay tuned! I'll be providing detailed coverage on when and how to implement In-App Purchase in Chapter 6.

But for now, let's focus on the current topic at hand: using a free lite version to promote your paid application. As you already know from browsing the App Store, free lite versions are acceptable by Apple's app review team, but there are very strict rules that you should follow when developing your Lite app.

Playing It Safe: Lite Version Restrictions

To avoid rejection from the App Store, make sure your lite version adheres to the following guidelines. It's important to note that although these rules may not be written in stone anywhere, this checklist appears to have worked for countless lite versions currently available in the App Store.

Lite Version Must Be a Fully Functional App

Your free lite version can contain fewer features than the paid version as long as this limited feature set allows the user to enjoy the lite version as a complete, stand-alone experience. The core functionality of the app should be accessible in both versions. For example, if your app's primary functionality is writing documents, then both the lite and paid versions should include the ability to create, edit, and save documents. To entice users to purchase the paid version, you can make additional enhancements exclusive to the paid version, such as file syncing services, extra style formatting options, and so on. You may even limit the number of documents a user can store in the lite version (lite: 10 files, paid: unlimited files), as long as the core functionality remains intact.

Lite Version Cannot Contain Crippled Features

A free lite version may not contain disabled features that, when accessed, inform users that the selected functionality is available only in the paid version. For example, if your app is a game and the ability to save high scores is limited to the paid version, do not include a reference to high scores in your lite version's interface. Don't include a High

Scores button in the lite version that, when selected, notifies the user that high scores is a full-version, paid-only feature with a blatant Buy Now button. In the eyes of Apple, that's considered a crippled feature. If your lite version includes a High Scores button, it must include that functionality.

Lite Version Cannot Remind User to Buy Paid Version

Although you can definitely include a Buy Full Version button in your lite version's main Info screen, you cannot prompt the user to upgrade via dialog boxes while they are using your app. This constant "nag" window may be acceptable for desktop shareware, but it'll quickly earn you a rejection letter from Apple's app review team.

Lite Version Cannot Time Out or Disable Features

In the world of desktop software, a common approach to expedite the full version purchase is to create time-limited demo versions that disable either certain features or the entire app after being installed for a set number of days. This is a big no-no in the App Store. iPhone apps are not allowed to ever expire or time out in any way.

Lite Version Cannot Be Referenced As a Demo

Since all iPhone apps are required to be fully functional, you'll have trouble getting approved in the App Store if you use words like *demo* or *trial* in your app name or any where in your user interface. Your app can include the words *lite* or *free* to denote a lite version.

Can a Free Lite Version Really Boost Paid App Sales?

If done right, your lite version can be a finely tuned sales machine, turning thousands (or hopefully millions) of users into paying customers. So, how many free lite downloads does it actually take to see a spike in paid app sales?

On average, most iPhone developers report conversion rates between 0.5 percent and 3 percent. This means that for every 100 downloads of their free lite version, they're selling approximately one to three paid versions. If you're selling your paid version for 99 cents and your lite version is getting only 100 downloads per day, then your app sales may bring in only a few dollars each day. That's not going to generate enough revenue to financially support yourself or your development costs.

This is where success really becomes a numbers game. Volume is king. You'll need to heavily promote your lite version to increase the number of downloads it receives. The more lite downloads you have, the more your paid app sales will rise. Ethan Nicholas, the developer behind the best-selling iShoot app, reported conversion rates as high as 8 percent. The popularity of Ethan's iShoot Lite helped propel iShoot to the number-one spot in the App Store's Top Paid Apps. Although 8 percent may not seem like a lot, the numbers quickly add up if your lite version becomes popular. The free iShoot Lite received millions of downloads, and with iShoot priced at $2.99 at the time (January 2009), that small conversion rate reportedly earned Ethan more than $700,000 in just the first few weeks of release.

Specialized niche apps often see higher conversion rates since interested users are looking for specific features that only a handful of apps may offer. A popular niche app may not rank high enough to be listed in the Top 100, but it could potentially benefit from conversion rates of 10 percent to 20 percent. Why such a big difference? Popular apps that hover in the Top 100 have much more visibility, drawing the attention of a broader, general audience who may download many free lite versions out of sheer curiosity. Special niche apps are usually found by consumers with a genuine interest or need for that specific functionality, so the odds they'll purchase the full version are much better. This is why many niche apps are often priced higher than games and novelty apps. What they lack in sales volume, they try to make up with a higher profit margin.

With all of that said, very few developers will experience overnight success like Ethan Nicholas, especially now that there are more than 100,000 applications competing for attention in the App Store. A lot of factors go into building an effective lite version. But if you develop a solid lite version strategy across several apps, there is still potential to make quite a bit of money. Here's where attention to detail can really pay off.

They Won't Buy the Cow If the Milk Is Free

Most developers immediately understand the marketing value of offering a free lite version, but since Apple requires lite apps to be fully functional, a major concern is giving too much away. If your lite version includes enough functionality to satisfy people's needs, then why would users buy the paid version?

The answer lies in all of the market analysis and competitive research that was discussed in Chapter 2. If you know the audience your app is targeting, if you know who your competition is and what features they offer, and if you know what key features are important to users, then planning your lite version strategy will be that much easier.

The trick is to understand what features to include in the lite version without cannibalizing your paid app sales. If your competitors offer specific features in their lite versions, then you'll want to take a similar approach, especially if users are expecting those features. But if your app has some cool new feature that no one else is yet offering—that innovative X factor that sets your app apart from the competition—then you'll want to figure out a way to allow users to test-drive that feature in your lite version, while providing a more comprehensive version of it in your paid app.

You want to whet their appetite without giving away the whole meal.

For games, this is usually very simple. Game developers typically include the first level or two in the free lite version. If users want more, then they have to upgrade to the paid version, where they are rewarded with dozens of additional levels, enhancements, and special features.

For productivity, utility, and other nongame apps, this can be challenging, which is why many of them do not offer free lite versions, relying instead on reviews, external publicity, video trailers, and screenshots to help sell the app. How do you limit the lite version functionality enough to encourage paid app sales and yet still get approved into the App Store?

Major League Baseball solved this problem by omitting some key features from its free MLB.com At Bat Lite. The lite version contains plenty of functionality with tons of baseball statistics and short video clips from past games, making it a very attractive stand-alone app, but if you're interested in enhanced, premium features such as live game-day audio, video highlights during the games, and 10-minute video recaps following each game, you need to purchase the $9.99 full version, MLB.com At Bat 2009.

Figure 5–1 shows how the lite version has seamlessly integrated a banner ad within its main interface that promotes the paid version. Although this blatant advertisement may seem questionable when considering Apple's strict rules for acceptable lite versions, it should be noted that this approach is really no different from displaying in-app advertising (such as AdMob banners) that promotes other iPhone apps. Plus—and this is probably the most important distinction—Major League Baseball is a beloved, high-profile brand that Apple surely wants in the App Store, so exceptions may apply here. For best results during the App Store submission process, you may want to play it safe, confining your Buy Full Version button to your app's central splash screen and Info screen.

Figure 5–1. *Although MLB.com At Bat Lite is a fully functional app that includes plenty of content, strategic banner ads entice users to upgrade to the paid version for additional premium features.*

By keeping bandwidth-heavy features such as streaming media exclusive to the paid version, MLB also prevents its free lite version from becoming a costly venture. This allows the expensive premium features to be used and paid for solely by customers of the MLB.com At Bat 2009 full version.

As mentioned in a previous example, if you're building an app for writers, then you'll need your lite version to be fully functional, allowing users to create, edit, and save their notes. Since all writers will want the ability to import/export their documents via email or sync files with a remote server (such as Google Docs), then obviously those are features your app will need to remain competitive in the App Store, but they could be offered as enhanced features available only in the paid version.

For fear of cannibalizing paid app sales, many nongame developers shy away from lite versions. Some developers wait until app sales drop off, thinking that introducing a free lite version at the tail end of an app's life span will help resuscitate sales. Although that may drum up a little extra business, you're really not maximizing the true potential of the lite version as a promotional tool. The timing is all wrong. Developers who have taken this delayed approach do see an increase in paid app sales when introducing a free lite version at such a late stage, but by then, all of the free publicity generated from the initial launch has long since faded, so the new sales bump is often not enough to push the paid version back into the App Store's Top 100. If only those developers had made a free lite version available when their app's release was benefitting from the initial wave of publicity....

If you plan on releasing a free lite version, you should make it available from the very beginning when you first launch your paid version. This way, your free lite version can take advantage of all the publicity and word-of-mouth generated during the app's initial release. The more traffic you drive to downloading the free lite version, the more conversions you'll have for the paid app. Many developers who advertise their apps online link the ads to their free lite versions to encourage click-throughs. This makes their advertising campaigns much more effective since people love free. Then let your lite version work its magic, giving users a small taste of what they'll get if they buy the paid version.

If you worry that the exclusive features in your paid version are not enticing enough to get users to switch from the free lite version, then either you need to rethink the division of features between the two versions to make the upgrade more appealing or you may want to consider adding in-app advertising to your free lite version. Offering a paid version without any advertisements can be a powerful lure, and it also provides a way to monetize your free lite version with ad revenue. I'll talk more about in-app advertising later in this chapter.

Of course, not all applications lend themselves well to the concept of a free lite version. But if you can figure out a way to make it work in your favor to generate app sales, then it's a gamble that will pay off in the long run.

Perfecting Your In-App Sales Pitch

To design a more effective lite version, you need to think of it as a virtual sales assistant. You can't personally be there to walk each user through the benefits of your app, so you need your lite version to do the talking for you. This means you need to carefully craft the sales pitch within your lite version to properly communicate your message. You already know what the guidelines are for lite versions, so for the moment, take off your "developer hat." It's time to think like a user, putting yourself in their shoes.

Many lite versions promote the paid version on their splash screen that is displayed for the first few seconds when the app is launched. Although this is a great way to take advantage of your users' undivided attention as they briefly wait for the app to load, it should not be the only place that the buy button is located. After users finish a session with your app, if they are interested in learning more about the paid version, they will look on your app's main screen, Info screen, Help screen, and/or Settings screen (depending on which of those screens you've included in your app). This may sound like common sense to you, but I'm always surprised at just how many lite versions I encounter that don't make that buy button easily accessible within the app or, worse yet, don't even include it at all!

If people can't find the buy button, they can't purchase your app. Don't rely on them remembering to manually visit the App Store on their own. Odds are, they might forget, and then you've just lost those potential customers. When it comes to selling anything, especially software, make the act of buying your product as easy and painless as humanly possible. And unlike most online ecommerce systems that overly complicate the process with too many steps, Apple has designed the iTunes App Store to be the simplest, most convenient way to buy software, so you really have no excuse. If someone loves your free lite version and is interested in upgrading to the paid version, that next step should only be a finger tap away.

So, now that you've integrated a buy button into your lite version's main screen or Info screen, what should it say? That may sound like a stupid question, but the answer is really much more subtle and complicated than you might think.

Words like *buy* and *purchase* communicate one thing to iPhone users: tapping that button will take them to the App Store. Yes, your refined sales pitch is already there in the App Store—complete with a detailed description and screenshots—making this very convenient from a development standpoint. As you already learned in Chapter 4, launching your iTunes store URL within your app can be done in only a few lines of code. Although many apps do this and have found success with this simple approach, it is not necessarily the most effective.

Jumping to the App Store from that buy button takes the user out of your app, something they may not want to do at that very moment, especially if they mistakenly think it will automatically initiate a purchase. As developers, we understand that's not possible without the user first entering their iTunes password in the App Store, but some iPhone users may not be tech-savvy enough to recognize that. Why would they want to buy the app without first knowing what additional features they would gain? They wouldn't, so they might ignore the button. And if that happens, your free lite version just failed its one and only mission.

Any known reason that might make a user hesitate from tapping that buy button should be eliminated whenever possible. If there's anything you can do to remove that hesitation or fear, then it's worth the extra development time to implement it.

So, how do you solve the problem at hand? Instead of instantly redirecting users away from your app to the App Store, why not include your sales pitch directly inside your app? Once you've sold them on upgrading to the full version, then you can safely close the deal with a buy button linked to the App Store.

On the main screen of Gameloft's Assassin's Creed: Altair's Chronicles Free (see Figure 5–2), your eye is immediately drawn to the big red Full Version button. Tapping it takes you to a new screen that's chock-full of screenshots and key selling points on why you should upgrade to the full version. All this is communicated without forcing the user to leave the app. That promo screen gives users the choice to either buy the paid app or tap the Back button to return to the game. Although this screen definitely does its job well, users may not know that the Full Version button will take them there. The button does not include the word *buy*, but it doesn't exactly indicate that more information will be provided either (instead of redirecting to the App Store). The red button's title is still a little too vague. And curiously enough, the Full Version button on that second promo screen does not say *buy* either, which is where I would expect that word, especially since that nested button does take users to the game's page in the App Store.

Like Gameloft, ATOD AB also does a nice job of promoting its full version within Fastlane Street Racing Lite (see Figure 5–3). In this example, the up-sell is done on the Info screen, which is a very smart move. From the main screen, tapping the Info button is a nonthreatening decision that's easy for any user to make. Based on the behavior of most apps, users know that an Info button will not force them to leave the app or automatically prompt them to spend money. *Info* is harmless. Tapping that button takes you to a screen similar to the one shown in Assassin's Creed, with the exception that it feels a bit more straightforward and simplified. The text is concise and to the point, and the nested "Purchase full version" button is obviously very descriptive.

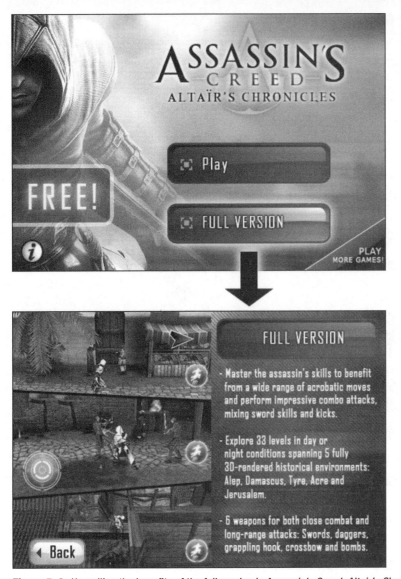

Figure 5–2. *Up-selling the benefits of the full version in Assassin's Creed: Altair's Chronicles Free.*

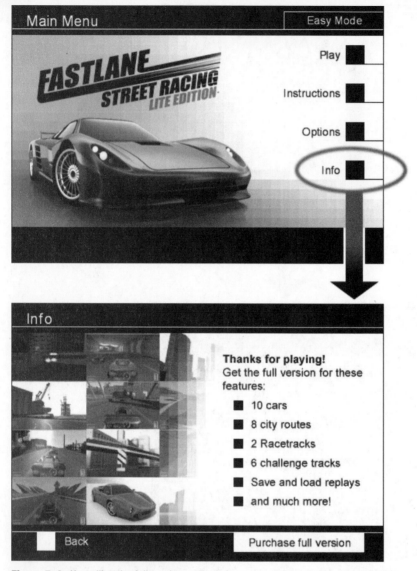

Figure 5–3. *Up-selling the full version on the Info screen of Fastlane Street Racing Lite.*

Marketers are always debating whether *buy* or *purchase* is more effective. In a global marketplace, most ecommerce sites tend to gravitate toward the word *buy*. The iTunes App Store uses a Buy App button, so when in Rome.... Besides, the shorter word *buy* is a lot easier to fit into your interface design, especially if you're designing a portrait-view app.

One of my favorite examples is Digital Chocolate's 3D Rollercoaster Rush Free. On the app's main screen, the What's Full Version? button tells me exactly what I'll get if I select it. I'm expecting detailed information on what features are included in the paid version, and that's precisely what I receive (see Figure 5–4). Within the app, a UIView (consisting of a `UIImage` with a transparent border) is displayed on top of the main screen. It is very visually appealing and well designed. The bullet points with bold highlights are crafted for maximum impact. It convinced me to tap the Get the Full Version button, and I'm a very jaded iPhone user who rarely plays games, so the sales pitch is definitely effective.

Figure 5–4. *3D Rollercoaster Rush Free is a great example of the up-sell done right.*

APP REJECTION WARNING: You should not display the app's price within your application. When promoting the full version within your free lite version, don't list the price. Apple has localized App Stores in many countries around the world, supporting many different currencies, so it frowns upon hard-coded prices displayed in your app. Apple's app review team does not always flag this as a cause for rejection, but it happens enough that you'll want to avoid doing it yourself. Beyond the risk of rejection, it's important not to list the price in your app so that you have the flexibility to change the App Store price at any time for special sale offers without having to submit an update.

It's important to include analytics in your lite version so that you can track how many people are tapping that buy button. Those analytics reports combined with your iTunes Connect statistics will help you determine the effectiveness of your lite version as a promotional tool. You'll know how many people are downloading your lite app, how often they use it, how many users click the buy button, and how many sales your paid version is pulling in. With all that data at your fingertips, if the conversion rate of lite-to-paid sales is much lower than expected, you can experiment with the wording and button placements in subsequent updates in an effort to improve results. Of course, knowing how customers also use your paid app can be just as valuable as well, so if you do add analytics to your development strategy, make sure to wire it into all your apps—both lite and paid—for the most comprehensive picture of how they are performing. I'll be examining the various analytics services available for iPhone app development in Chapter 7.

Another important tip worth mentioning: if you're an iPhone developer, you should join the iTunes Affiliate Program. Any links you have pointing to the App Store should be affiliate links. There's no reason not to earn some affiliate commissions for all the traffic you're sending Apple's way. This means all the buy buttons in your lite version, cross-promotions, web site, and so on, should be coded with iTunes affiliate links. I'll be exploring the lucrative world of affiliate programs in Chapter 6.

Bulletproofing Your Lite Version

As developers, we all work hard to create quality products, so no one purposefully releases buggy software. Showstopper bugs happen to the best of us, but if there was ever a time to ramp up your testing and quality control efforts, it's with your free lite version.

Since users will be evaluating your lite app to determine whether the paid version is worth their hard-earned money, they'll be test-driving it with a very critical eye. As previously discussed in Chapter 4, if a user deletes your app, Apple prompts the user to rate the app. As evident by the lower ratings of most lite versions compared to their paid-app counterparts, people have no problem giving an app a dismal one-star rating for the most minor of reasons. Even though the lite version was free, their reviews can often be harsh if the experience left them frustrated.

Ensure that your lite version includes ample built-in instructions to help alleviate any potential confusion that might arise if someone can't figure out how to use the app. Many lite versions ask users upon launch if they would like to watch or read a brief tutorial before exploring the app. Although this does require a little extra development effort, it is a very proactive approach that may help avoid many of those unwarranted one-star reviews.

Migrating Data from the Lite Version to the Paid Version

If a user purchases your app, they should not be penalized by losing the data they had in the free lite version. If that happens, then prepare to receive a slew of negative customer reviews in the App Store. For most games, there's nothing to lose since high-score leaderboards are usually stored on a remote server. But what if it's a productivity app that saves files or database records?

Unlike the more flexible environment of desktop operating systems, the iPhone OS restricts each app to its own data "sandbox" for storing files. App A is not allowed to access the saved files from app B, and vice versa. This protects each installed app from malicious behavior but makes it incredibly difficult to share data between apps.

Syncing with the "Cloud"

Some developers have solved this problem by implementing a syncing service that enables customers to sync their app data to a remote server. Popular apps like Flixoft's Grocery Gadget encourage users to sign up for a free group account so that data from the lite version can be easily transferred to the separate paid version. If your app stores large amounts of complex data or if you simply want to give customers a way to access their data from alternative locations (such as their computer's web browser), then maintaining a syncing service might be your best bet. If this sounds like an appealing solution for your app needs, then here are a few affordable "cloud" services worth checking out:

- Amazon S3: http://aws.amazon.com/s3/
- Google App Engine: http://code.google.com/appengine/
- Rackspace Cloud: http://www.rackspacecloud.com/

If you don't want the hassle of developing and maintaining a web application to handle the syncing of data between your iPhone app and the "cloud" or if you need to transfer only a very small amount of data from one app to another, then there is another option.

Transferring Data via URL

Some developers have found success transferring data across a unique URL command. For example, if an iPhone app makes an open URL request for an HTTP web site address, Mobile Safari automatically launches and processes the request since it is the default app registered to handle HTTP. In a nutshell, your iPhone app just sent data to

Mobile Safari. You can put this same concept to work for your own apps by setting up your own unique URL protocol handler. For this to work, it needs to be a prefix that is not already being used by any other application. Since you have no idea what unique protocols other iPhone apps might be using for this same purpose, you should come up with your own prefix that is obscure enough to prevent conflicts with those other apps.

For the purposes of this exercise, let's create a unique protocol for our fictional parked-car locator app, Breadcrumbs. I want users of the lite version to be able to transfer their saved parking locations to the paid version. Since the amount of data is very small (just a few GPS coordinates) and does not contain any confidential information, then transferring the data via an open URL command would work quite well.

For our URL prefix, we'll use bcrumbs. If your app has an original name (which it should), then that name (or a variation of it) might lend itself nicely as a unique prefix. First, the bcrumbs URL protocol needs to be registered with the iPhone OS as being assigned to the full version of Breadcrumbs. This is done by adding a new URL type to the paid app's Info.plist file in Xcode (see Figure 5–5).

Key	Value
▼ Information Property List	(13 items)
Localization native development region	English
Bundle display name	${PRODUCT_NAME}
Executable file	${EXECUTABLE_NAME}
Icon file	icon.png
Bundle identifier	com.electricbutterfly.${PRODUCT_NAME:rfc1034identifier}
InfoDictionary version	6.0
Bundle name	${PRODUCT_NAME}
Bundle OS Type code	APPL
Bundle creator OS Type code	????
Bundle version	1.0
Application requires iPhone environment	☑
Main nib file base name	MainWindow
▼ URL types	(1 item)
▼ Item 1	(2 items)
URL identifier	com.electricbutterfly.${PRODUCT_NAME:rfc1034identifier}
▼ URL Schemes	(1 item)
Item 1	bcrumbs

Figure 5–5. *Open your full version's* Info.plist *file within Xcode's plist editor to add a new URL type.*

Click the gray plus (+) symbol button on the right side of the plist editor to add a new entry to the Info.plist file. In the new blank row, click the tiny arrows in the left Key column to display a contextual menu of additional properties, and from those choices, select "URL types." With the new URL type added to your Info.plist, now open its disclosure triangle to configure its nested properties. Under its Item 1 key, you'll need to add the unique com.company.Application property of this paid app to the "URL identifier" field. For the fictional Breadcrumbs app, that would most likely be com.electricbutterfly.Breadcrumbs. Now, you'll need to click the plus button again to add another nested key directly below "URL identifier," and then you'll choose URL

Schemes from the new key's contextual menu. The URL scheme is where you define your unique URL protocol handler, so in the case of the Breadcrumbs example, that would be bcrumbs.

> **IMPORTANT NOTE:** If you have a single Xcode project set up with two compile targets—one target build for your lite version and one target build for your paid version—then you'll need to create a separate plist file for each target. Only the plist file of your app's full version can contain the unique URL protocol handler definition. If your lite version's plist file references this same URL type, then your lite version will end up receiving its own URL requests, which will cause a conflict. When your lite version sends the unique URL request, you want only your paid version to respond to it.

Now that the unique bcrumbs URL protocol is assigned to the full version of Breadcrumbs, the next step is to add code to the lite version for transferring the data via URL. Let's say you've added a new button to the lite app's Settings screen called Transfer My Data to Full Version, and it's already been wired up in Interface Builder. Let's also assume that the event handler already includes code for obtaining the data from the lite app's sandbox (such as content from an XML file or plain-text file).

You can't send raw data via a URL query, so it first must be Base64-encoded. The iPhone SDK does not include Base 64 encoding and decoding, but several third-party Objective-C libraries are available that provide Base64 support for iPhone, such as Google Toolbox for Mac (http://code.google.com/p/google-toolbox-for-mac/).

Once the data is Base64-encoded and stored in an NSString—let's call it encodedData—it can be sent as part of the unique URL query:

```
NSString *urlQuery = [NSString stringWithFormat:@"bcrumbs://localhost/importData?%@",
encodedData];
NSURL *url = [NSURL URLWithString:urlQuery];
[[UIApplication sharedApplication] openURL:url];
```

When a user taps the Transfer My Data to Full Version button, the lite version makes that URL request. The iPhone OS recognizes the bcrumbs URL protocol handler as being registered to the full version of Breadcrumbs, so the lite version quits, and that unique URL is passed to the paid app. The full version of Breadcrumbs launches to receive and parse that URL command.

For that last part to succeed, the paid app must include the application:handleOpenURL handler in the application delegate's implementation. For example, my BreadcrumbsAppDelegate.m file includes the following code:

```
- (BOOL)application:(UIApplication *)application handleOpenURL:(NSURL *)url {
    if([@"/importData" isEqual:[url path]]) {
        NSString *urlData = [url query];

        // First, you should ask users if they want existing
        // data replaced by the new imported Lite data.

        // Then you'll need to decode the Base64 string.
```

```
        // Lastly, you'll want to parse and save the data
        // to this full version's own app sandbox.

        return YES;
    }
    return NO;
}
```

And that's all there is to it! As previously mentioned, just keep in mind that transferring data via URL is practical only for small amounts of data such as XML files or text files that are less than a few hundred kilobytes. You'll also want to defend your paid app against hackers who figure out your unique URL protocol by coding your `application:handleOpenURL` handler to only accept the specific data you want and to ignore invalid URL strings.

Securing Market Share: Give It Away Now, Up-Sell Later

Is the success of your iPhone app dependent on being adopted by as many people as possible, such as a social networking app that requires multiple participants in order for it to be useful? If so, then you may want to consider giving away the app for free. The only way to get millions of people to adopt your service on such a grand, global scale is to make it freely available to everyone. Think Facebook and Twitter.

The goal is to get everyone and anyone to use your app frequently enough that it eventually becomes an indispensable part of their daily lives. The fewer barriers to entry, the easier this task is to accomplish. Beyond being free, for best results, your app should also be void of any potential deterrents such as advertising.

After your app has cultivated a large loyal following, you can introduce a premium version of the app that offers additional features for a price. An alternative option is to offer premium features as In-App Purchase items (which is discussed at length in Chapter 6). The basic version will always be available for free, which is what the majority of users will choose.

So, how do you make any money if most people only use the free basic version? This is yet another example of how volume will ultimately dictate your success. If you've created an innovative user experience and you've done your job right as a marketer, then your free app has penetrated the mainstream as a "must-have" app and is currently used by millions. For example purposes, let's say the free basic version is frequently used by 10 million people. Even if only 8 percent of that user base decides to upgrade to the $1.99 premium version, after subtracting Apple's 30 percent App Store fee, you would still net more than $1.1 million in revenue.

Again, volume is the name of the game for this strategy to work. Most apps will not be appropriate for this kind of business model. But if your app relies on peer-to-peer interaction between users, then this approach might just be your ticket to capturing the lion's share of the market for that particular niche. If your app is the market leader, you'll fare much better at successfully up-selling more users to the premium version.

In Chapter 2, I mentioned the cool iPhone app Bump by Bump Technologies, Inc., which enables users to instantly send contact information to each other by bumping their hands together. But for it to work, the two people must both have Bump installed on their iPhones. The more people who have Bump, the more useful it becomes (see Figure 5–6). The hope is that it will eventually be ubiquitous enough among mobile phones that it becomes the standard method for users to swap virtual business cards and other data. And the plan seems to be working. As it stands now, the app has become quite popular among iPhone users and has even been featured in one of Apple's iPhone commercials.

Will Bump always be free? To continue the adoption momentum, the developers plan to offer the basic version of Bump free of charge for the foreseeable future. But at some point, I imagine Bump Technologies will need to monetize its development efforts in order to grow, so I wouldn't be surprised if it one day releases a premium edition with additional features for those power users who want more.

That's exactly what Infinite Labs did with its Mover app. At first, only the free Mover app was introduced, allowing people to easily share photos, contacts, text clippings, and bookmarks by flicking them from their iPhone screen toward a nearby iPhone. If someone slides a photo your way, it will show up on the main screen of your iPhone's Mover app. Like Bump, in order for this sharing process to work, everyone involved must have Mover installed on their iPhones (see Figure 5–6). By offering the basic app for free, it makes it easy for everyone to utilize it and integrate it into their daily lifestyle. Benefiting from great word-of-mouth and the exposure from an Apple iPhone commercial, Mover enjoyed several months of widespread adoption before the separate Mover+ was introduced as a paid app. Although Mover will always be free, users who want Bluetooth support and additional new features need to upgrade to the Mover+ premium version.

If you need to earn revenue sooner rather than later to finance your development efforts, then this may not be the right path for you. But if your development is currently supported by existing cash flow from investors or other products/services and you can afford to wait several months for your free app to gain traction in the mobile marketplace, then this can be an effective business model with the right app.

Figure 5–6. *Since mass adoption is the key to the success of Bump (left) and Mover (right), both free apps include a Tell A Friend option, encouraging users to spread the word. Chapter 4 includes detailed instructions and an example project for implementing Tell A Friend via In-App Email within your own apps.*

Monetizing Free with In-App Advertising

Everyone knows that in-app mobile advertising is the next great frontier with marketers racing to target that growing audience. At one time or another, we've all downloaded a few of the many free iPhone apps that display in-app advertising, and some of us have even tapped the ads. Based on current trends, research experts Gartner anticipate mobile ad spending to surpass $13 billion by 2013. But the big question is, can iPhone app developers make any money from it? The answer depends on what kind of app you're building.

If you're developing a free app that would appeal to a broad mainstream market and experience frequent usage, then you might be able to earn quite a bit of revenue from in-app advertising. Like the other free strategies mentioned in this chapter, the key is volume. The more people who use your app, the more ad impressions and click-throughs that will accrue.

If your free app has limited appeal to a niche market, then it may not generate enough advertising revenue to support your business. On the other hand, catering to a niche market may earn you higher rates from premium ad networks whose brand advertisers are eager to target that audience. Even though this kind of niche app will ultimately attract fewer users than a mass-market app, it may be able to make up the difference in revenue by earning more money per ad.

Taking a Hard Look at the Numbers

Ad sharing revenue is based on cost per thousand (CPM), so if you're averaging a CPM that hovers around $1 to $2, then to make more than $1,000, your in-app advertising will need to receive at least 1,000,000 ad impressions. With more than 40 million iPhone and iPod touch users out there, it shouldn't be too hard for your free app to drum up 1 million ad impressions, right?

Just because your app is free does not guarantee an avalanche of downloads. There are simply too many apps in the App Store vying for people's attention. According to AdMob, the largest iPhone ad network, only 5 percent of the free apps in their network have more than 100,000 users, while a staggering 54 percent have fewer than 1,000 users. If your app falls into that later category, you'd net only a few dollars a day—definitely not enough to sustain a full-time salary for yourself.

For that 5 percent of free apps that do enjoy a large user base, Pinch Media CEO Greg Yardley believes that small top percentile may be the only apps capable of making more money with in-app advertising than from being sold as paid apps. "Unless there is something inherent about the app that screams free, sell it," says Yardley.

When trying to decide whether you should release your product as either a paid app or a free ad-supported app, it's important to do the math. A paid app sale would earn you at least 70 cents (based on a 99-cent price). If it was an ad-supported free app, would it generate enough ad impressions and click-throughs to net you more than 70 cents per user? With a heavily used app, you could confidently answer "yes" to that question, but with very few users, the answer may be a surprising "no."

Mobile app analytics leader Pinch Media has reported that the average free app usage declines rapidly in the first few weeks after download, with less than 5 percent of users returning to the app after 30 days. For in-app advertising to be a lucrative revenue source, your app needs to serve up as many advertisements as possible, which requires continued usage by a large number of users. If your app is supported entirely by in-app advertising, it's crucial that you have marketing and development strategies in place that not only drive new users to your app but also extend your app's life span beyond that initial 30-day average. So, even when offering free apps, developers cannot rest on their laurels, waiting for the ad revenue to roll in. You should expect to work just as hard promoting and continuously updating a free, ad-supported app as you would for a paid app to ensure that your in-app advertising solution pays off.

But if your free app becomes a runaway hit, rising into the App Store's Top 100, it's possible to make a lot of money from in-app advertising. The popular iPhone ad exchange network AdWhirl says that top apps can make $400 to $5,000 per day from in-app advertising. And if you have several top-ranking free apps generating ad revenue at the same time, you could have a very profitable business on your hands.

When to Use In-App Advertising

In-app advertising may not be an effective business model for all apps. You need to take an in-depth look at not only what kind of app you're building but also how people will be consuming your app.

If your app requires an Internet connection, such as accessing information from GPS, web services, or an online social network, then adding in-app advertising will not be an imposition for your users since they will already be online when running your app. And if your app is "sticky" enough to retain the user's attention for a long span of time, your app will be able to display many more banner ads, which will net you more ad-sharing revenue.

If your app is a game or educational app aimed at a younger demographic, then in-app advertising may not be appropriate. For one, parents may not appreciate apps that directly advertise to their kids. And advertising to young children may be illegal in some regions, so it's important to do your legal homework. Also, if the majority of your users tend to play your app safely offline on an iPod touch, then your in-app advertising will not be making you any money. If your app cannot communicate with the ad network servers, then it can't serve up ads. No ad impressions equals zero earned revenue.

Many entertainment apps, especially casual games and board games, can fare quite well with in-app advertising. If the user interface design is done right, banner ads inserted at the very top or bottom of the screen should be unobtrusive to the game play, which is essential.

On the other hand, in-app advertising can be very difficult to successfully integrate into full-screen, immersive 3D games. Often the only option in those cases is to display advertisements in between game levels. This is usually not ideal since that would drastically reduce the number of ad impressions your app could generate, especially if game levels take a long time for users to complete.

If you do decide to monetize your free iPhone application with in-app advertising, be sure to do it from the very beginning with your initial 1.0 release. If your app has always included advertising, then users will simply accept it as the "price" for a free download. If your app has already gained a loyal following of users who have enjoyed several versions of your app ad-free, then the sudden introduction of in-app advertising in a later update is bound to upset many of your fans. As always, you want to avoid receiving negative customer reviews in the App Store, so carefully plan your free app strategy up front.

If you're not sold on relying entirely on advertising revenue and decide to release a free lite version to promote your paid app, then you might want to consider using in-app advertising in only your lite version. Depending on the kind of app you're developing, it can be an effective way to not only monetize that free app but also help motivate users to upgrade to the paid app if they want an ad-free version.

Which Ad Network Is Right for You?

Although there are dozens of mobile advertising platforms, I'll limit the focus here to only the major iPhone players that offer an in-app advertising SDK for iPhone developers. Many of the ad network exchanges like Mobclix and AdWhirl support and display ads from several other mobile ad companies not listed here.

Beyond the lure of easy-to-use in-app advertising SDKs that can be integrated into your app within five to ten minutes, all of these ad networks are also free and promote 100 percent fill rates. Most of them offer very similar features and competitive CPM rates, so which one should you choose? It really comes down to the actual needs of your app. For example, some ad networks specialize in full-screen, interactive, rich-media ads, which may be a good fit for games and landscape-only apps. Some ad networks only offer 320 × 48 pixel banner ads designed for portrait-view apps. Others allow you to assign some of your ad inventory to promoting your apps within your own products, as well as across their entire ad network of apps.

If you know what your specific needs are, then it is well worth your time to investigate all the iPhone-compatible ad networks to find the one that offers the solutions you want. It's important to differentiate which ad networks pay out only for actual click-throughs on ads vs. the ones that also pay out for ad impressions (views). Some ad networks claim high CPM rates without mentioning that those attractive rates are often only a small fraction of their ad inventory and available only to select apps, so be sure to do your homework before choosing one.

AdMob

http://www.admob.com/

As the largest iPhone ad network, AdMob's distinct text-based banner ads can be seen in many of the most popular ad-supported free apps. AdMob uses recognizable black icons in every ad to visually communicate what the ad's link function is if tapped (shown later in Figure 5–7). The download arrow icon represents a link to the App Store. The compass icon indicates a web site link, which will launch Mobile Safari. The phone icon lets users know that tapping the ad will initiate a phone call (on an iPhone). The video icon represents a direct link to playing a video clip in the built-in video player (such as a film trailer). There are several other icons, but you get the idea.

Unlike a static graphic image ad, the primary advantage to AdMob's text-based ads is that the colors can be customized for better integration with your app's user interface design. In Figure 5–7, the AdMob banner ad displays a brown background color to best match the existing wood background theme of Optime Software's Checkers app. Of course, if you choose banner ad colors that blend in *too well* with the app UI, then you run the risk of it going unnoticed, which could result in fewer taps and less ad revenue earned.

AdMob also offers house ads, which allow you to use some of your app's ad inventory to cross-promote some of your other apps. Having a few house ads in place also provides a safety net for filling the banner space if an online ad request fails.

Another popular feature is AdMob's Download Exchange, which enables you to promote your apps across other apps in their network by giving up some of your app's ad inventory to reciprocate. This is a great way to increase app discovery and boost your App Store chart ranking.

Like a couple other ad networks, AdMob recently introduced interactive video ads as an option, so if you're looking beyond traditional mobile banner ads for a more immersive advertising format that enables users to interact with video and web content, then this might be a viable solution.

In November 2009, online advertising giant Google announced plans to acquire AdMob, so it'll be interesting to see how that affects the mobile advertising playing field if and when that acquisition takes place. Although such a combined juggernaut may prove worrisome for competing ad networks, it can only be a boon for AdMob vendors.

AdWhirl

http://www.adwhirl.com/

AdWhirl is a very popular mobile ad network exchange, which uses mediation layers to display ads from multiple ad partners to ensure maximum CPM and fill rates. Using its web-based dashboard, AdWhirl enables you to switch between different ad networks dynamically on the fly without any changes to your actual iPhone app. Their exchange currently includes AdMob, Mobclix, JumpTap, VideoEgg, Millennial Media, Quattro Wireless, and others. AdWhirl's iPhone SDK also provides support for generic notifications so that developers can set up ad networks that AdWhirl has not explicitly partnered with, such as Greystripe and Google AdSense for Mobile Applications (see Figure 5–7).

Like AdMob, AdWhirl allows you to cross-promote your other apps by using some of your own ad inventory to display your own custom ads. Even AdMob's Download Exchange program works seamless within AdWhirl.

Interestingly enough, AdMob acquired AdWhirl in August 2009, most likely in an attempt to stave off the newcomer exchange network from Mobclix. Although AdMob promises to leave AdWhirl untouched with its functionality and open exchange of multiple ad partners intact, the acquisition has definitely left many developers and advertisers curious about the future direction of AdWhirl. And with Google's plans to acquire AdMob, I would not be surprised to see other ad networks consolidating into merged entities in the near future as they all jockey to be the market leader.

Figure 5–7. With AdWhirl, developers like Optime Software can optimize their in-app ad inventory by switching between ad networks on the fly (AdMob banner ad on the left) and even support additional ad networks through a generic notifications channel (Google AdSense on the right).

Google AdSense for Mobile Applications

http://www.google.com/ads/mobileapps/

Predicted to be a major player in the mobile space, Google's widely successful AdSense program definitely has a massive inventory of existing advertisers to offer. Its mobile AdSense platform was currently in beta at the time of this writing, but for those of you interested, you can sign up for it online. With Google AdSense ads already showing up in AdWhirl and Mobclix's network exchanges, as well as directly integrated within a few select, high-profile iPhone apps, Google AdSense for Mobile Applications may be out of beta and officially launched by the time you read this book. And with Google's November 2009 announcement to acquire AdMob, you can expect Google's presence in the mobile advertising world to continue growing at an exponential rate.

Greystripe

https://www.greystripe.com/

Greystripe has set itself apart from competing ad networks by offering a proprietary method for displaying Flash ads within iPhone apps. Although the Flash format is not natively supported on the iPhone or iPod touch, Greystripe has an innovative system for converting Flash ads for seamless performance within their iPhone advertisements.

Since Flash ads represent the majority of online ads seen on web sites and various mobile platforms, this allows Greystripe to support online ad servers like Google's Doubleclick and Microsoft's Atlas, bringing big brand advertisers to the iPhone. Utilizing rich-media interaction and mini-games embedded in ads, it offers an immersive advertising experience that promises more creative marketing options for advertisers and higher CPM revenue for developers. Greystripe's unique CPM Protection Program offers to beat any other mobile ad network's eCPM by at least 25 percent for 60 days.

Medialets

https://www.medialets.com/

Medialets specializes in rich-media advertising on mobile devices. What sets it apart from its rich-media ad competitors is the fact that it also offers an analytics platform, similar to Mobclix's integrated advertising/analytics approach. Medialet's iPhone SDK includes its mobile advertising framework for inserting in-app ads and its Medialytics framework for tracking user activity.

Mobclix Mobile Ad Exchange

http://www.mobclix.com/

Already well known as a leading analytics provider for iPhone developers, Mobclix is the latest player to jump into the in-app advertising arena. Out of the gate, it announced support for 20 mobile ad networks including Google, Yahoo, JumpTap, VideoEgg, Quattro Wireless, Millennial Media, Point Roll, InMobi, and many others. Mobclix now represents the largest mobile ad network available for both advertisers and iPhone developers. Notably, its biggest competitor, AdMob (and its own AdWhirl exchange network), has opted not to participate in Mobclix's ad exchange.

Since app developers will go wherever they can get the highest price for their ad space, while advertisers will choose the ad networks with the most inventory and widest reach across the most mobile apps, Moblix definitely offers a very attractive package. Especially of interest to iPhone developers, Mobclix app analytics are integrated into its mobile ad exchange SDK, providing a very powerful all-in-one solution.

Quattro Wireless

http://www.quattrowireless.com/

Although Quattro Wireless participates in the major mobile ad exchanges from AdWhirl, Mobclix, and Tapjoy, it also offers a Quattro iPhone SDK for only serving ads from its network. Catering to leading direct marketers and Fortune 500 brands, it's known as a premium ad network with the largest presence across multiple mobile platforms. Quattro Wireless is the exclusive ad network for the popular location-aware iPhone app WHERE.

As you might expect from a premium ad network, to receive the highest possible CPM rates, your app may be required to pass demographic analytics data back to Quattro so that their advertisers can be paired with the most appropriate audience. It also helps if your app appeals to a particular niche market that their advertisers want to reach. For example, a popular money-tracking app might be very attractive to premium advertisers such as banks, financial services, and credit card companies.

In January 2010, Quattro Wireless announced that it was being acquired by Apple. Although it is unclear how Apple will utilize Quattro, I can only imagine that under Apple's stewardship Quattro Wireless will undoubtedly play a much larger role in the iPhone arena in the near future.

Tapjoy

http://www.tapjoy.com/

Tapjoy has an interesting ad exchange platform in that it has partnered with several companies to offer an appealing and comprehensive package for developers. Besides supporting AdMob, Quattro Wireless, Mobclix, and other ad networks, it's the official ad platform for Pinch Media analytics and the recommended iPhone SDK for selling virtual goods via Offerpal Media.

It also offers an innovative Pay Per Install program that utilizes a finder's free incentive for cross-promoting your app within other apps in their network. A participating app rewards a user with virtual currency for installing your app. If that user purchases your app, then the developer whose app delivered that new sale to you gets 50 percent of your 70 percent App Store royalty. That leaves you with 20 percent of the revenue. Although that may seem like a large portion of profit to be giving away, you've gaining new customers and revenue that you would not have ordinarily gotten on your own.

Tapjoy reports that after integrating the Tapjoy SDK into its own TapWord app, the number of daily active users increased from an average of 1,000 to close to 90,000 within a week of starting the rewarded installs. Within days, the Pay Per Install program delivered tens of thousands of installs for TapWord in a risk-free way, and the increased visibility quickly made TapWord the top game in its category.

Although this program is open to both free and paid apps, it is obviously harder to justify the investment with free apps. For a paid app, the cost is simply deducted from your sales revenue, but the cost for free apps would come out of your own pocket as a marketing expense.

iVdopia

http://www.ivdopia.com/

This mobile ad network claims to be the first iPhone video ad platform. Built on a robust, scalable technology that's optimized for serving billions of mobile videos, iVdopia specializes in immersive, full-screen video ads with real-time analytics for both advertisers and iPhone developers. iVdopia video ads can be seen in some of SGN's apps, such as iBowl, iBasketball, and iBaseball.

VideoEgg

http://www.videoegg.com/

Like Quattro Wireless, VideoEgg participates in many of the mobile ad exchanges like AdWhirl and Mobclix, but it also provide its own iPhone SDK for directly embedding only VideoEgg ads into your app.

Its AdFrame format looks like a typical, small mobile banner ad at first glance. But then tap on it, and a full-screen, rich-media ad rolls into view within your app (see Figure 5–8). VideoEgg is different from the other ad networks in that it's focused on delivering user engagement for its advertisers. VideoEgg does not pay for ad impressions. Your app earns revenue when users interact with the video or media in the displayed ad. Because of this, VideoEgg attracts very big, well-known brands to advertise on their network.

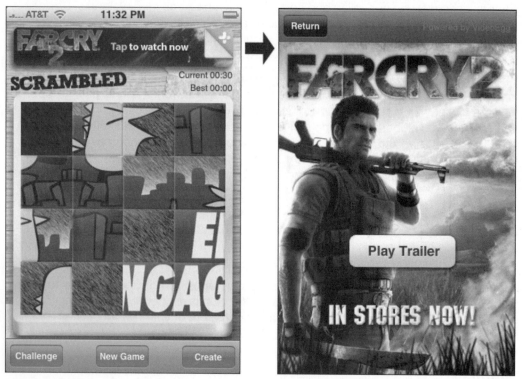

Figure 5–8. *With VideoEgg's in-app advertising, the revenue you earn depends on actual user engagement with its interactive ads, not page impressions.*

Building a Business with Ad-Supported iPhone Apps

Can iPhone developers make a living solely based on revenue earned from in-app advertising? Optime Software thinks so. It's a shining example of an iPhone app publisher that has found success in the App Store by offering beloved classic games as free, ad-supported apps. And this business model appears to be paying off for Optime Software because its free apps were downloaded more than 2 million times just in 2008. By constantly refining the user interfaces and utilizing smart cross-promotion tactics within its apps and across free advertising exchanges, many of its free apps continue to remain in the Top 100 charts even to this day.

While most iPhone app developers rely on revenue earned from paid app sales, Optime Software is a company built from the ground up on mobile ad revenue. Obviously, one major key to Optime Software's success is the fact that apps like Dots Free, Checkers Free, Chess Free, Tic Tac Toe Free, Four in a Row Free, and Crack the Code Free provide familiar game play that everyone already knows and loves. There's no learning curve. But with many other competitors offering similar free apps, I was curious about Optime Software's winning formula, so I set out to interview the founder and CEO, Jon Schlegel, to learn more about its in-app advertising strategy:

Can you talk about your experience working with the various ad networks?

"We started off by directly integrating AdMob into all of our free ad-supported applications. However, we quickly found that it's necessary to work with multiple ad networks if you want to make sure that all of your ad inventory gets filled at the best available rate. Therefore, we decided to integrate AdWhirl into our applications as a mediation layer. AdWhirl allows us to dynamically allocate our inventory across many different ad networks. Using AdWhirl, we've been able to achieve close to 100 percent fill rate and dramatically increase our eCPMs. AdWhirl was recently acquired by AdMob, so it will be interesting to see where they decide to take the platform."

Were its in-app advertising SDKs easy to use?

"Both AdMob and AdWhirl were very easy to integrate into our applications. I don't think the average developer would need more than an hour to complete the integration, and most could do it in considerably less time. Don't forget to disable the 'test ad' mode before you go live in the App Store. I know several developers who have forgotten to do that and have lost quite a bit of money as a result [from displaying test ads that don't earn revenue]. We trigger a compiler warning in all of our apps when the 'test ad' mode is enabled to make sure that we don't go live with the test ads."

Do you take advantage of advertising your own apps with AdMob's free Download Exchange? If so, does it generate enough click-throughs and downloads to warrant sacrificing some of your ad revenue inventory?

"Yes, we typically use the AdMob Download Exchange to promote new app releases. The extra download volume that comes from the download exchange can sometimes be enough to push an app into a more favorable position in the rankings. Apart from new app releases, we generally allocate all of our inventory to paid advertising and any remaining unfilled inventory to up-selling the premium versions of our applications. "

You recently started offering paid premium versions of your apps. Were you getting requests from people who wanted ad-free versions, or were you interested to see which version (ad-supported free app vs. paid app) would generate more revenue?

"Yes, we started offering premium versions of our applications in response to user requests. Many users outside of the United States don't have all-you-can-eat data plans and were concerned about the cost they were incurring due to ad downloads. The response we have received from users to the premium versions has been very favorable. Most users will buy the premium version of a game if they use it regularly."

Do you earn more revenue from your ad-supported free apps or from your paid premium apps?

"We earn significantly more from our ad-supported free apps than from our premium applications. The free apps also help drive visibility and create uplift for our premium apps. Many of our premium applications have made it onto the Top 100 lists for their categories entirely based on up-sell conversions from the free version of the app."

If a user is playing one of your free apps but is not connected online (such as an iPhone in Airplane Mode or an iPod touch with no WiFi access), what do you have set to be displayed in the banner ad space?

"Currently, the ad space is left blank if the device isn't connected online. We have considered inserting our own house ads locally on the device when the user doesn't have network connectivity. However, the value is somewhat limited because without network connectivity a user can't immediately take action on an ad. Down the road, we are hoping ad solutions will emerge that cache ads and deliver reporting data to the ad networks asynchronously in order to allow us to better utilize our disconnected ad inventory."

Strength in Numbers: Building Synergy with In-App Cross-Promotion

Another major factor that has contributed to the success of Optime Software's apps is its heavy use of in-app cross-promotion. Upon launching one of its free apps, there is a splash screen that briefly appears. While the user is waiting for the app to load, the splash screen not only promotes the premium version of the free app they're using but also promotes all of Optime's other free apps (see Figure 5–9). Each app listed is a live link. Tapping the app names will take you to its respective page in the App Store so that you can learn more about the app and download it.

Figure 5–9. *The splash screens in Optime Software's free apps effectively cross-promote their other apps.*

While Optime Software has seen sales increase four to five times from cross-promoting its apps across the AdWhirl network, doing its own in-app cross-promotion has also proven to be a valuable method for boosting awareness for all of its free apps to existing users. The more downloads it receives, the more the company eventually earns from ad revenue and premium app sales.

"Splash-screen cross-promotion has been a very effective tool for us," says Schlegel. "We track the click-through rates from our splash-screen advertising, but not the conversion rates. We've seen click-through rates as high as 10 percent for some of our splash-screen ads. Click-through rates for the splash-screen ads tend to decline over time though as regular users become acclimated to the ads and start to ignore them. We're looking into ways to make the splash-screen advertising more dynamic in order to increase its effectiveness."

Even though Apple's iPhone Human Interface Guidelines frowns upon splash screens, they seem to be prevalent in countless applications in the App Store. But upon submitting your app via iTunes Connect, if it gets rejected because of a splash screen, then you'll know you went too far with the concept. If you do utilize a splash screen in your app, then before submitting it, make sure it doesn't linger on-screen for too many seconds and especially doesn't go over the top with a blatant "hard sell." Since splash screens fall into that mysterious gray area of the approval process, just take great care that when designing it as a cross-promotional tool, it remains visually effective without calling too much attention to it.

Circumventing the splash-screen approach, many game publishers include a More Games button on their app's main screen. Selecting More Games often launches the publisher's web site in Mobile Safari, but that ultimately takes the user away from the game they were playing, which is never optimal.

Setting Up Shop

In a move to keep users engaged within the app, NimbleBit opted to embed its own custom "app store" into their games. Tapping the More Games button in its apps displays the NimbleStore screen, which cross-promotes all of its available apps (see Figure 5–10). The nice thing about the NimbleStore is that when tapping an app icon, instead of redirecting the user to the respective page in the App Store, the NimbleStore displays an embedded, custom app page, which allows NimbleBit to tailor its own enhanced sales pitch. Although it offers the usual array of screenshots and detailed app description, it also spotlights a few of its best reviews and a video trailer for the app—something the App Store sorely lacks.

Figure 5–10. *Tapping the More Games button in one of NimbleBit's games displays its embedded NimbleStore, which cross-promotes its catalog of apps with video trailers and more.*

The beauty of the embedded NimbleStore is that it is a remote mini-site displayed in a UIWebView. Not only does this allow NimbleBit to modify the NimbleStore pages at http://m.nimblebit.com/ without requiring updates to the iPhone games themselves, but it also allows the company to utilize Google Analytics to track which store pages are being accessed by users. According to NimbleBit's statistics, approximately 85 percent of the people who visit the NimbleStore within their apps go on to further explore one of the specific game pages. In only the first nine months, the NimbleStore received a little more than 1.6 million page views and has been responsible for 13,170 game sales!

Having the NimbleStore remotely hosted enables NimbleBit to dynamically alter pricing based on regions and limited-time sale offers. Apple tends to reject apps that display pricing, so I'm not sure how NimbleBit escaped that particular restriction (unless having the pages hosted remotely makes the difference), but just to play it safe, you probably should not list prices in your own cross-promotion efforts.

If someone chooses to buy an app from the NimbleStore, the button sends the user to the iTunes App Store to make the purchase. As any smart iPhone developers should be doing, all redirects to the App Store are iTunes affiliate links, so any time a user purchases one of the games listed in the NimbleStore, NimbleBit makes an affiliate commission. The iTunes Affiliate Program also enables NimbleBit to track the commissions earned, which tells them how many total games are being purchased from NimbleStore leads.

The We Play games listed in the NimbleStore (such as Harbor Master) are not NimbleBit games, so although those specific purchases won't net NimbleBit an App Store royalty, they will earn the company affiliate commissions. So if you don't have enough apps to fill your own embedded mini-store, you can always list some of your favorites apps from other publishers. You'll be supporting your fellow iPhone developers, as well as making a little money yourself from the referrals. I'll be talking more about the iTunes Affiliate Program in Chapter 6.

If you have only a few apps and would rather limit your cross-promotion efforts to your lite version's Info screen where you're currently up-selling the paid version, just be careful not to dilute your marketing message too much. If encouraging users to upgrade to the paid version is your priority, then make sure that any mention of your other apps on that same screen does not upstage the sales pitch for the paid version.

United We Prosper

If you like the idea of integrating your own mini-store within your app to cross-promote your other app offerings but you don't have enough apps to fill it, then you should consider partnering with a select few of your developer peers. With several developers integrating a shared "community" store in all their apps, you'll benefit from having a populated storefront and the increased synergy of cross-promoting your apps not only within your own apps but also across all the other apps in this community network. It's a win-win for all the developers involved.

This strategy is exactly what five independent iPhone game developers set out to achieve when they banded together to form App Treasures. Accessible from the More Games button within all the participating games, App Treasures is an embedded view that spotlights apps from all five developers (see Figure 5–11).

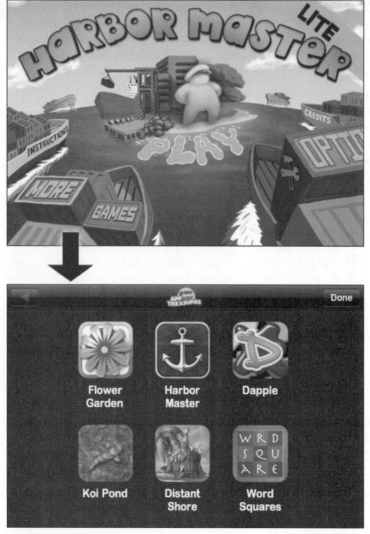

Figure 5–11. *Tap the More Games button in any of the participating developers' apps to access the cross-promotional App Treasures screen.*

The developers involved in App Treasures are The Blimp Pilots (Koi Pond), Imangi Studios (Harbor Master), Snappy Touch (Flower Garden), Streaming Colour Studios (Dapple), and Veiled Games (Up There). They have positioned the App Treasures label as a seal of quality that consumers can trust—if they liked one of the games, they'll most likely enjoy other games in the App Treasures family.

With the App Store's games category so often dominated by the big game publishers such as Electronic Arts and Gameloft, the feeling was that it was more difficult for smaller, independent developers to gain the same level of visibility. Keith Shepherd, CEO of Imangi Studios, said that App Treasures "is our way of combining resources to become a bigger player, while retaining our independence and without any of the drawbacks and strings attached that come from working with a publisher."

What makes this kind of shared, cross-promotional network especially valuable is that when one partner's app becomes successful, the other partners benefit from the heightened exposure. When Harbor Master skyrocketed into the App Store's Top 25, the embedded App Treasures screen was receiving as many as 10,000 views a day, which resulted in a sales surge for the other App Treasures games listed there.

Independent iPhone game developers interested in participating in App Treasures are welcome to contact their web site—http://www.apptreasures.com/—but only a few select applicants may be hand-picked to protect the high-quality reputation that App Treasures strives to maintain.

Rolling Your Own Solution

David Smith, owner and principal engineer of Traveling Classics, has found cross-promotion to be a very effective revenue-generating strategy for his audiobook apps. Traveling Classics offers dozens of paid applications in the App Store, each one containing a classic audiobook with an easy-to-use, custom-player interface. To promote the paid versions, a free Audiobooks app is also available.

Audiobooks, which features streaming access to more than 1,800 audiobooks from LibriVox, has been downloaded by hundreds of thousands of users and enjoys a seemingly perennial spot in the book category's Top 25 free apps. With Audiobooks installed on so many iPhones and iPod touches, David Smith wanted to see whether he could leverage all of those eyeballs to help promote other apps.

In July 2009, he began experimenting with in-app advertising in Audiobooks, limiting the advertisers to only iPhone developers. Since he wanted to control the ad links in order to earn the maximum commissions through the iTunes Affiliate Program, he opted not to use existing cross-promotion ad platforms like AdMob's Download Exchange. Instead, he set up his own ad server and began offering "boutique advertising" directly to iPhone app developers—http://www.travelingclassics.com/ads.

After one month, he found the advertising experiment to be much more beneficial in cross-promoting apps (including his own paid apps) than it was in selling actual ad space. And with the iTunes Affiliate Program, if users tap an ad, clicking through to the App Store, even if those users don't buy that specific app but end up buying other apps, Traveling Classics still earns affiliate commissions on those purchases.

Based on the sales statistics from the App Store and the iTunes Affiliate Program, David Smith estimates that before this experiment, one of his paid apps was selling two to three per day. When promoted in an ad within Audiobooks, that same paid app was selling 25 to 30 a day. And if a free app was promoted in Audiobooks, it would see an increase of up to five times the number of usual downloads. Since there's no monetary barrier to try free apps, this kind of cross-promotion tends to be very successful for lite versions. Once downloaded, the lite versions act as gateways to purchasing the premium versions.

Enthusiasm Is Contagious: Get Your Users Talking with Third-Party Social Platforms

If you're a game developer, you're most likely familiar with the various social gaming platforms available for the iPhone, such as OpenFeint and Scoreloop. The obvious benefit to using one of these platforms is that they provide ready-to-use hosted services such as high-score leaderboards, multiplayer connectivity, and social challenges, which alleviates the need for you to code this complex functionality yourself. By integrating a third-party social platform into your iPhone game, you're potentially saving hundreds of hours of programming time. This seems like a no-brainer, especially since most of these platforms are free to use.

What many people don't realize is that these social gaming platforms also provide powerful environments for increased app discovery. The more games that use the same social platform, the more they all benefit from that platform's inherent cross-promotional synergy. Beyond the fact that most of them include Twitter and Facebook support, some of them also offer "virtual lobbies" where users can see what other people are playing and what games are connected with that platform. The sheer influence of what's currently popular in these arenas helps drive new app sales because interested users want to get in on the action.

"If a friend tells you to watch a movie or listen to a song, it's pretty likely you're going to buy that movie or song based on your friend's recommendation. This is why Facebook's App Platform has been so successful and is one of the basic principles upon which OpenFeint is built," says Jason Citron, founder and CEO of Aurora Feint. "OpenFeint provides Xbox Live–style hosted game services such as multiplayer, leaderboards, challenges, chat, achievements, etc., that create cross-promotion events when players interact with them. So, for example, by adding achievements and leaderboards to your game with OpenFeint, you will sell more games. It's important to mention that this isn't some dry sales pitch—we see this happening today with millions of players across more than 100 games. As ridiculous as it sounds, you do less work, your players have more fun, you sell more games, and Apple pays us affiliate fees so you don't have to."

In fact, app discovery is such a strong component in these social environments that the companies that run these free platforms are monetizing their services by collecting iTunes affiliate fees.

Although each social gaming platform initially launched with a unique set of features, most of them have eventually anted up their offerings so that they now provide similar functionality to remain competitive. OpenFeint is often seen as more social since it offers extensive chat features (see Figure 5–12). Scoreloop offers a distinctive virtual coins system for rewarding challenge winners and users who activate new games. Geocade has positioned itself as a location-aware platform. Many of them even support customizable skins so that their embedded interfaces can be modified to match the same look and feel of your own game! They all offer easy-to-use SDKs for iPhone developers, and their services are free with the exception of ByteClub. There's no current standard, so even though it's impossible at this early stage to know which one will end up the market leader, that should not stop you from taking advantage of their community-building services.

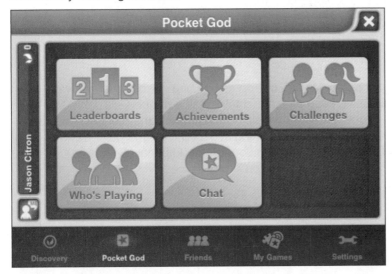

Figure 5–12. *Beyond its many social features, OpenFeint's free platform provides appealing cross-promotion opportunities for game developers. Notice the Discovery tab, which enables users to see what other people are playing and even purchase the listed games to join in the fun.*

So, which one is right for your game? When choosing a social platform, there are two major factors to consider. First, the platform that is being adopted by more of the high-profile bestsellers will attract a larger audience. More players congregating in one online community equals more exposure for your app. For example, OpenFeint is currently the platform of choice for the wildly popular Pocket God and Stick Wars, while Scoreloop is integrated into the acclaimed Parachute Panic. And the successful publisher, Freeverse, has exclusively chosen Plus+ for its many games, such as Flick Fishing. Second, although app discovery is definitely a vital component, your number-one priority should be to choose the platform that works best for your app's specific game play. It needs to make your game more fun, not more complicated or frustrating. If your players are having a great time, then that enthusiasm will show in the online social community, which will in turn drive additional sales.

Listing all the specific services offered by these social gaming platforms would require far too many pages, so I won't go into any further details here, but if you're an iPhone game developer, I highly recommend exploring all of their web sites and SDKs to find the one that best fits your specific development and marketing needs.

- OpenFeint: `http://openfeint.com/`
- Scoreloop: `http://scoreloop.com/`
- AGON Online: `http://developer.agon-online.com/`
- ngmoco's Plus+: `http://plusplus.com/`
- Chillingo's Crystal SDK: `http://www.crystalsdk.com/`

- Geocade: http://www.geocade.com/

- ByteClub Multiplayer Gaming Platform:
  http://byteclub.com/platform

Shifting Gears

Ready for more? Traditional app sales and in-app advertising are not the only ways to make money in the mobile universe. It's time to think outside the box. With In-App Purchase (introduced in iPhone SDK 3.0), developers can now construct new business models within their iPhone apps such as providing subscriptions and purchasing add-on content and services. In Chapter 6, you'll learn about the additional revenue opportunities of In-App Purchase and affiliate programs.

Chapter 6

Exploring New Business Models with In-App Purchase and Affiliate Programs

In-App Purchase was one of the more exciting and highly anticipated features introduced in iPhone SDK 3.0. The option to integrate e-commerce within both free and paid iPhone apps opens up a brand new frontier for developers to create additional revenue opportunities beyond just traditional app sales. In-App Purchase enables you to sell subscriptions, services, virtual goods, and add-on content, such as new features or additional game levels—all within your app.

And don't forget about affiliate programs. If your app currently links to an external web site that offers an affiliate program, you should be benefitting from the traffic you're sending their way. Got a music app that includes links to buy selected songs in the iTunes Store? Or maybe your app includes web links to books on Amazon.com or products listed on eBay? If your app took advantage of affiliate links, then you could be earning commissions on all sales you drive to those respective web sites.

With average iPhone app prices being so low with free updates, it's important for you to embrace new business models to help monetize continued development costs. It's time to get creative! In this chapter, we'll be exploring the power of In-App Purchase and affiliate programs as a way for app developers to help sustain their businesses for the long run.

Loyalty Pays: Existing Users Make the Best Customers

In the world of desktop software, customers who are happy using your application are more likely to purchase subsequent upgrades, especially if they use your product frequently. Their motivation to stay up-to-date with the latest version is usually driven by either satisfaction with the user experience or dependence on the unique features your software provides (or both if you're lucky).

This is why software developers spend so much time strengthening the relationship with their customers. Sure, finding new customers is crucial, but selling upgrades to existing customers is what supports continued development on a particular application. Developers can afford to offer products at low introductory rates (or even free) to entice new customers, knowing they'll be able to sell additional upgrades to those users in the future.

And beyond that, loyal customers are already sold on the product quality, so they'll be more inclined to buy other applications from you than new users who are unfamiliar with your offerings.

Up-selling new products and upgrades is the lifeblood of the software industry. And developers are already translating this model to mobile platforms on a smaller scale. Microtransactions are the key to the mobile economy. The App Store takes that model to the next level by combining microtransactions with an extremely powerful software platform. But the App Store has its own unique buying culture—one that introduces a new set of challenges that developers must overcome to sustain a long-term business.

Supporting the Long Tail: Monetizing Continued Development

The App Store is no stranger to "the Long Tail," a concept described by acclaimed author Chris Anderson, where new products experience an initial sales spike and then, after they've plateaued or reached saturation, their sales gradually drop off. This eventual downward slide of sales, or the *long tail* (as it looks on a graph), is where app developers start to scramble to figure out ways to either increase sales or find alternative methods to monetize app development.

Because of how the App Store was initially set up, once a user purchased an app, any updates were required to be free. Unlike traditional desktop software, there was no way to charge existing iPhone app customers for an upgraded version. This was a great value for users, especially if the app only cost 99 cents, but financially difficult for developers, who were expected to frequently update their apps without a way to monetize those development efforts.

Some game developers worked around this limitation by releasing new versions as completely separate apps. As a follow-up to its successful Rolando game, ngmoco spent a lot of time and money developing version 2. Rather than releasing it as a free update, ngmoco made the wise decision to launch Rolando 2 as a separate stand-alone app, enabling the company to charge a fee for this worthy sequel.

In the case of Bolt Creative's wildly popular Pocket God game, a big factor in its success has been the near weekly free updates of new game play the company has delivered to customers. Each episode includes a massive amount of fresh content, which not only helps attract new customers but also sustains user engagement with every updated adventure. At only 99 cents (which includes all released episodes), it remains one of the best values in the App Store. As long as Pocket God continues to rank in the App Store's Top 25, the sheer volume of sales appears to support the accelerated development pace. However, with so many new games flooding the App Store, Bolt Creative's Dave Castlenuovo knows this can't last forever. In an interview with PocketGamer.biz, he mentioned that Pocket God updates are not delivering quite the same sales spike they used to, so the game may be reaching a saturation point, eventually heading into the long tail of sales. Granted, this particular long tail may still be much more lucrative than the peak sales of most apps, but those indie developers probably don't have the same overhead production costs as Bolt Creative either.

To continue releasing the same level of new updates, Bolt Creative will begin experimenting with In-App Purchase to help offset development costs. Although new updates of Pocket God will always be free, customers will have the ability to customize their adventure by purchasing skin packs and other add-on items. With Pocket God, users accustomed to receiving so much new content for free, Castlenuovo admits the primary challenge will be in properly communicating that the addition of microtransactions is not an act of greed but merely the means to help fund the continued free updates of new episodes.

The Challenge of Changing User Perception

Since the App Store infrastructure has bred a shopping culture where iPhone users expect to receive a lifetime of free updates for the apps they've purchased, shifting their mind-set to accept in-app microtransactions may take a little time. With In-App Purchase being a relatively new SDK feature for developers, the concept of paying for new content within an app that users have already purchased or downloaded for free is still a new business model that consumers have yet to widely embrace.

The million-selling Enigmo puzzler was one of the first games to offer In-App Purchase when the iPhone SDK 3.0 was initially released. Since the iPhone OS 3.0 was a paid upgrade for iPod touch owners, the adoption of 3.0 was slow for those game-centric devices in the first few months, which did affect games requiring the new 3.0 OS. But even with that said, Pangea's Brian Greenstone remarked to PocketGamer.biz that he was surprised at how few in-app purchases Enigmo was receiving for the expansion Kid Packs. The best-selling game was only generating an average of 25 in-app purchases a day, but considering how big its customer base is, Greenstone had expected more.

But this will change. As more and more high-profile apps begin to offer In-App Purchase items, balancing out the ratio of free updates to paid add-on content, consumers will eventually acclimate to the new model. Of course, developers will undoubtedly see an initial backlash from some customers who resent the new a la carte pricing structure, but I'm guessing it's the same vocal minority of users who complain about having to pay more than 99 cents for a full-featured game that would cost 50 times as much on Xbox or Playstation. In time, this pushback will subside, especially if the add-on items represent exciting features that users are eager to buy. Right now, only a few dozen apps are utilizing In-App Purchase, so the scales have not yet tipped. But as soon as thousands of apps are offering In-App Purchase items, the concept of in-app microtransactions will become commonplace in the App Store, forcing consumers to adapt if they want the latest features and game levels.

Freeverse is already seeing a change in attitude. Its popular Flick Fishing game began offering a new, full-featured Private Beach pack as an in-app purchase (see Figure 6–1), and in just the first few months that followed, they've already sold tens of thousands of the In-App Purchase item to existing Flick Fishing customers. By continuing to provide free updates alongside their In-App Purchase offerings, they've been successful in properly communicating to users the distinct difference between free enhancements to the core game functionality vs. the new content available as in-app purchases.

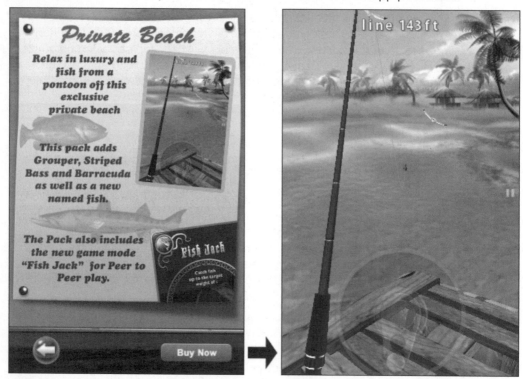

Figure 6–1. *Freeverse has found a successful formula for adding In-App Purchase to its best-selling Flick Fishing game with the Private Beach expansion pack.*

Even free apps are finding ways to monetize development through In-App Purchase. Apple is very particular about how In-App Purchase is utilized, so even though free apps are now allowed to offer In-App Purchases, it's important to note that this ecommerce

API can't be used to create trialware. As I mentioned in Chapter 5, In-App Purchase is not intended for unlocking previously crippled features, since Apple still prohibits iPhone apps from presenting features as disabled. The current implementation of In-App Purchase enables developers to provide *additional* features that are not currently included in the app, such as subscription services, new content, and add-on game levels. ngmoco has found success with this model in its popular Eliminate Pro app, which is offered for free, and additional game play, weapons, and armor can be bought via In-App Purchase.

With this in mind, it's never too early to look at ways your app could benefit from In-App Purchase. Loyalty pays! In the long run, even if your app eventually attracts fewer and fewer new customers, your satisfied users could continue to support you through In-App Purchases!

When and How to Use In-App Purchase

So, you're ready to tackle In-App Purchase in your application, but what can it be used for? Unlocking additional game levels is an obvious choice, but what if you're not developing a game? The best way to approach this is to take a good look at your app's current functionality and future road map of features to see whether In-App Purchase can help extend its product life span and sales potential.

Apple currently supports four types of In-App Purchase items:

- Content
- Functionality
- Services
- Subscriptions

Cool, right? Did that give you any ideas for use within your own app? I thought it might. But before you start planning your next major masterpiece with In-App Purchase, there are a few strict rules to follow:

- In-App Purchase items must be digital elements that can be delivered within your app. You cannot use it to sell physical products and services outside of your app. For example, you can't use In-App Purchase to sell a printed book, but you could definitely sell an e-book, as long as it can be delivered within your app immediately after purchase confirmation.

- In-App Purchase items are not allowed to contain prohibited content, such as pornography or hate speech.

- In-App Purchase items cannot represent virtual money. For example, you cannot sell virtual currency or credits that are used to buy other objects within your app or across other apps.

- And most important, you cannot facilitate a complete payment transaction inside your app without using In-App Purchase. For those of you who are looking to side-step the iTunes App Store, you'll need to link to a checkout page on an external web site (displayed in Mobile Safari), similar to how Amazon Kindle for iPhone redirects users to the Amazon.com site for web-based purchases. Implementing your own homemade version of In-App Purchase within your app is guaranteed to earn you a rejection notice from Apple's app review team.

In-App Purchase isn't suitable for every application. It's a great way to generate additional revenue streams and support continued development, but don't try to force this functionality into your app if you don't have a good reason to do it. It should not be treated as a solution in search of a need. You certainly won't want to wear out your goodwill with loyal customers by "nickel and diming" them to death for core features they expected to get as part of the original purchase price.

The Power of Simplicity

The best part about In-App Purchase is that beyond the handful of guidelines, it does not impose any kind of predefined business model. The Store Kit framework that powers In-App Purchase is nothing more than a secure payment collection gateway. It does not include a prefabricated storefront like the App Store, which gives you the ultimate creative flexibility to integrate In-App Purchase in any manner that best suits your app's current user interface. This is especially helpful if your app offers only one In-App Purchase item. Displaying an entire store window to list only a single item is not an effective use of screen space. With only one or two In-App Purchase items, you can easily implement those buy buttons seamlessly into your existing user interface. This may sound like it leaves a lot for you to program yourself, but truthfully, In-App Purchase is really quite simple, requiring a lot less code than you might think. I'll walk through the steps of adding In-App Purchase to an Xcode project later in this chapter.

Since all In-App Purchase transactions are done through the App Store, they retain the same business terms as purchasing standard apps within the store. You, the developer, receive 70 percent of the In-App Purchase price, and Apple keeps 30 percent as a service fee. Although some developers may cringe at giving up 30 percent of in-app purchases, you need to remember that not only does this cover credit card fees, fraud protection, and refund-related chargeback fees, but it also provides an elegant microtransaction model in the secure, trusted environment of the App Store. There's no need to maintain your own customer account and ecommerce system. The Store Kit framework makes the transaction process seamless for your customers, enabling them to use their existing iTunes login account for a quick and painless purchase experience.

Every item that you want to sell via In-App Purchase needs to be configured in iTunes Connect as its own In-App Purchase product, similar to how standard iPhone apps are submitted. Each In-App Purchase item is assigned to its related parent app so that the iTunes App Store knows the relationship between the products. Just like regular apps, each In-App Purchase item needs to be approved by Apple's app review team before it can be made available within your app. This entire setup process is described in detail later in this chapter.

So, what does a typical In-App Purchase look like to the consumer? One of my favorite apps, Comics by ComiXology, serves as a great example. Comics is a digital comics reader with an innovative viewing engine for easily reading comics on the iPhone screen. The free app includes access to 50 free digital comics from dozens of publishers, such as Image Comics. Most of the free comics are the first issues of popular series, providing a great entry point for new readers. By supplying so much free content, Comics not only gives customers a lot of immediate value, but the free comics also get people hooked on various series. If they want more, that's where In-App Purchase comes into play. Within the app is a very easy-to-use store catalog of available comics, ranging from free to 99 cents to $1.99 each. All of the pay comics were configured in iTunes Connect as individual In-App Purchase items. If you decide to purchase a specific comic book issue, the App Store displays a default dialog box asking you to confirm your purchase request for this item (see Figure 6–2).

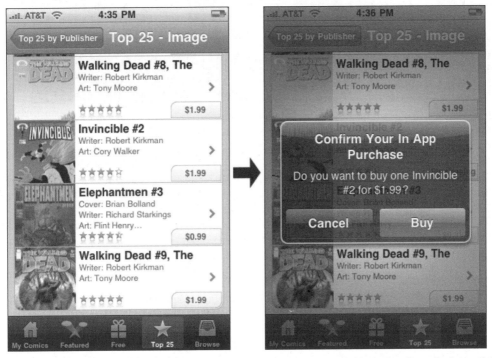

Figure 6–2. *When purchasing a digital comic book within the Comics app (left), the App Store displays a default dialog requesting confirmation of your In-App Purchase request for this item (right).*

If you tap the dialog box's Buy button, you're then asked to enter your iTunes login, just like any other purchase through the iTunes Store. Once the login is confirmed, the secure transaction is completed using your existing iTunes account's billing information, and your purchased item immediately begins to download into the Comics app (see Figure 6–3). And that's it! No tedious order forms to contend with. Just a drop-dead simple purchase process, requiring only a few finger taps.

Figure 6–3. *After confirming your purchase and your iTunes login (left), the transaction is completed, and your purchased digital comic immediately begins to download into the Comics app (right).*

Although the Comics catalog list looks similar to the App Store in appearance, you have the flexibility to design your in-app storefront to emulate your own custom user interface design. Smule's I Am T-Pain takes advantage of this, extending the same UI design theme throughout every screen, including its in-app store. I Am T-Pain provides users with the ability to sing and record Auto-Tune-enabled songs with backing music tracks. The $2.99 app price includes a collection of popular tracks, and if you want more, additional tracks are available via In-App Purchase (see Figure 6–4).

Most people assume that games and entertainment titles will be the dominant champions of In-App Purchase since selling new game levels, music, additional characters and ammunition, and other virtual-world components seem like such a natural fit for microtransactions. But the truth is that with a little creativity, In-App Purchase can be an effective revenue vehicle for almost any category genre. Case in point: *Men's Health Magazine*. Similar in strategy to Smule's I Am T-Pain, the magazine's fitness app, Men's Health Workouts, includes an extensive collection of workouts and exercises for the initial $1.99 app price. But it also provides additional workout packs that can be purchased in-app (see Figure 6–5). There's a smart play here in that one free add-on workout is uploaded each week (accessible within the app), which not only encourages continued user engagement from week to week but also helps promote the other add-ons available for sale.

Figure 6–4. *Within Smule's I Am T-Pain, In-App Purchase items are listed with the app's included free tracks. The Store Kit framework gives you complete flexibility to customize how those items are displayed.*

Figure 6–5. *Not just for games! Apps like Men's Health Workouts prove that In-App Purchase can be just as powerful in other category genres.*

We've looked at several examples of downloadable content, but what about services and subscriptions? Polar Bear Farm's Tweet Push is a great example of both, using an in-app subscription model for its Twitter-based push notifications service. The free app includes 14 days of service. After that, you'll need to renew your subscription in-app to continue using the service (see Figure 6–6).

An important factor to remember with subscriptions is that the Store Kit framework does not include any functions for checking a user's current subscription expiration date or automatic renewal billing. It's up to your app to self-monitor customer subscriptions. Tweet Push simply keeps track of user expiration dates, displaying a countdown of days left in their subscriptions. Since customers need to supply their iTunes login to confirm In-App Purchases, there's no way to automatically bill a user behind the scenes to prevent their subscription from expiring. By showing users how many days are left until expiration, Tweet Push puts the responsibility on its users to renew their own subscriptions. This also provides users with the security of knowing they won't ever be charged for anything without their prior consent.

Figure 6–6. *Tweet Push uses In-App Purchase to sell subscriptions for its Twitter-based push notifications service.*

Tweet Push offers only three subscription options, so displaying them as dialog buttons works fine in this specific case, but depending on your app's subject matter, you should consider spending the time to design an attractive visual interface component for your In-App Purchase items.

Presentation Is the Key to Success

How do you get users to buy your In-App Purchase products? The same way you got them to buy your app in the first place: by offering an appealing package that they'll want. Beyond creating great add-on content, you have to communicate to your customer base why they need to buy it.

Looking back at the Flick Fishing example referenced earlier in this chapter (see Figure 6–1), you'll notice that Freeverse used an entire screen to pitch its Private Beach add-on pack. It includes a full description of what it is, tells what you get, and even shows a small screenshot of the beach scene. In fact, it looks very similar to the promotional "What's in the Full Version" screens from the free Lite app examples in Chapter 5. Since In-App Purchase items are essentially their own products, this is your sales pitch within the app. Your visual presentation of these items is just as important as the presentation for promoting the parent app itself.

When crafting descriptions for both the App Store and within your app, you need to be very clear about what people will get with each purchase. Ambiguous descriptions often result in frustrated users, who then post negative customer reviews complaining that the purchased app was not what they had expected. Add multiple In-App Purchase items into the mix, and suddenly the situation gets quite a bit more complex. Communication is vital in preventing confusion.

Customers like knowing up front how much an item costs before tapping the buy button, so you should always include pricing within your in-app storefront whenever possible. You can dynamically list the prices of available In-App Purchase items within your app, which is especially helpful when localizing your app across several regions (and I'll show you how to do this later in this chapter), but this is not possible within your App Store description. In fact, since the App Store localizes prices for different country currencies, Apple strongly dislikes the inclusion of static prices in your App Store description. Yes, I know that listing the available In-App Purchase items and their prices would make your App Store description much more explanatory in a very concise and simple way. Luckily for you, Apple fixed this issue with the introduction of iTunes 9. Now when visiting the App Store within the desktop version of iTunes, your app's product page displays a "Top In-App Purchases" list. This feature was also added to the iPhone's built-in App Store, with the "Top In-App Purchases" list displayed in a prime location near the top of the screen (see Figure 6–7). Tap it to see In-App Purchase items and their related prices for that app.

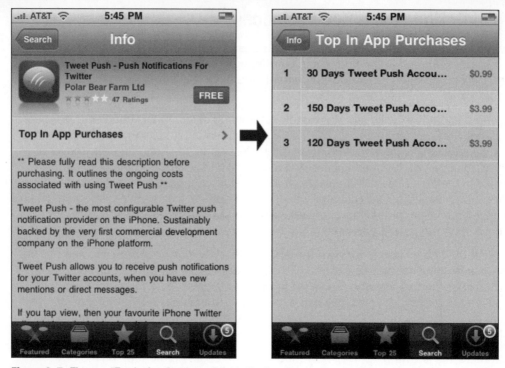

Figure 6–7. *The new "Top In-App Purchases" list in the App Store helps promote and clarify the available In-App Purchase items and prices for the related app.*

Finding the Sweet Spot

Beyond communication, having the right mix of ingredients in your product is also crucial. For a paid app, it's important to know which features your customers consider to be the app's primary draw. Those are the features that should be included in your app's price. Additional features that enhance the core offering are the ones better suited as potential In-App Purchase items. What you don't want happening is to charge an in-app fee for a feature that users believe should be part of the original app price—some core functionality that they thought they were getting right out of the box.

Networks In Motion ran into this problem when it first released its GPS navigation app, Gokivo. At only 99 cents, it included a lot of features, such as Yahoo! Local Search, maps, traffic, and favorites. But to unlock the turn-by-turn, full GPS navigation service, an additional $9.99 monthly subscription fee via In-App Purchase was required. Consumers perceived the turn-by-turn GPS feature as core functionality that should be included with the app. Although the other features were nice, the turn-by-turn navigation service was the primary reason they bought the app in the first place. But then to discover they had to shell out another $9.99 a month to get the feature they assumed they had already purchased (regardless of the fact that the app was only 99 cents), many of them felt duped.

Networks in Motion went to great lengths to explicitly clarify their pricing structure in their App Store description, but somehow the message was not getting through to some of their customers. Many people were not taking the time to thoroughly read the description before purchasing the app.

The company's eventual solution to the issue was to raise the price of the app to $9.99 and include a 30-day subscription to their turn-by-turn navigation service. This way, customers are now able to access the core feature they wanted immediately after purchasing the app. And after 30 days, they can renew their subscription for another month via In-App Purchase.

Even though we're talking about the same amount of money in both scenarios, the perception is vastly different. It comes down to the principle of the purchase and satisfying user expectations.

Although your app's core functionality will be the primary attraction that brings in new customers, your In-App Purchase strategy will succeed only if you're offering enticing add-on content at a reasonable price that makes sense to consumers. This gets back to the problematic state of "race to the bottom" pricing in the App Store. Even though iPhone users are accustomed to getting full-featured games and apps for as low as 99 cents, Apple currently enforces a 99-cent minimum for in-app purchases. It's OK if your In-App Purchase items are priced the same or even higher than the related parent app as long as the inherent value is apparent to your customers.

Configuring In-App Purchase in iTunes Connect

Before diving into the programming of an In-App Purchase example in Xcode, the first steps that need to take place are the creation of an In-App Purchase Test User account and your In-App Purchase items, both of which are done online in iTunes Connect. As previously mentioned, In-App Purchase items are added to iTunes Connect as individual products, so they need to be created before you can test the in-app purchase of them.

Setting Up an In-App Purchase Test User Account

Why the need for a test user account? Since you'll want to test your application's In-App Purchase functionality extensively before submitting it to the App Store, using a test user account will enable you to perform test purchases without actually getting billed for them. Whew! That's definitely good news. Now you can do all the In-App Purchase testing you want without worrying about draining your pocketbook in the process.

- Log into iTunes Connect: `https://itunesconnect.apple.com/`

On the main iTunes Connect page, click the Manage Users link, and then select the user type In-App Purchase Test User (see Figure 6–8). On the Manage In-App Purchase Test Users page, click the Add New User button.

When completing the required form fields, be sure to use an email address that is valid but is *not* associated with any existing iTunes accounts. This is very important. Using an email address that is already assigned to an iTunes Connect or iTunes Store account will invalidate your test user account. Plus, you don't want your test purchases to accidentally get charged to an existing credit card–enabled iTunes account.

After creating the new In-App Purchase Test User account, you can view or delete it from within the Manage Users section of iTunes Connect (see Figure 6–8). There does not appear to be a way to edit an existing user account, so if you want to modify the email address or password, you'll need to delete that test user account and then create a new one to replace it.

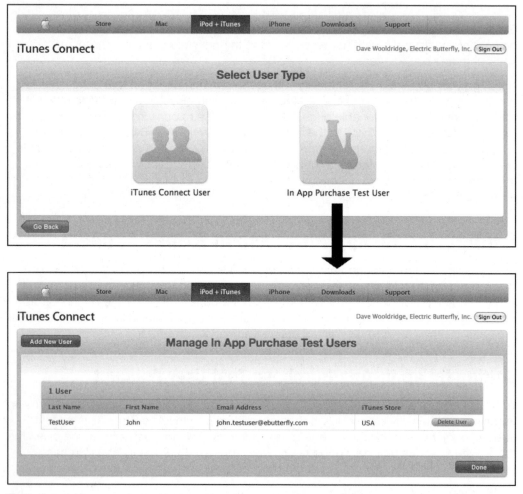

Figure 6–8. *Adding a new In-App Purchase Test User account within the Manage Users section of iTunes Connect.*

Creating In-App Purchase Items

Now that you have a test user account in place, the next step is to add your In-App Purchase item as its own individual product to iTunes Connect.

It is important to note that iTunes Connect will only allow you to add a new In-App Purchase item if you already have an app listed in iTunes Connect. This way, when you're creating the In-App Purchase item, you can properly assign the listed application as its parent app.

You can create an In-App Purchase item within either the Manage Your Applications section or the Manage Your In-App Purchases section of iTunes Connect. If Manage Your In-App Purchases is not listed in your iTunes Connect, then you probably have not yet submitted an app or your Paid Applications Contract to iTunes Connect—both of which are required in order to create an In-App Purchase item.

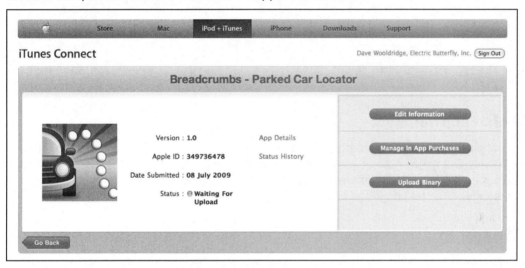

Figure 6–9. *Select your app from within the Manage Your Applications section of iTunes Connect, and then click the Manage In-App Purchases button to create a new In-App Purchase item.*

Within the Manage Your Applications section, click the Manage In-App Purchases button of the listed app you want to create In-App Purchase items for (see Figure 6–9). Then click the Create New button and assign the new item to your parent app's bundle ID.

After assigning the new In-App Purchase item to your parent app's bundle ID, you'll be required to complete the following fields on the online form that's displayed.

To select your parent app's bundle ID during the creation of a new In-App Purchase item, you must first upload an application binary for your parent app. For apps that are already live in the App Store, this is not an issue, but for new apps that have not yet been submitted for review, this seems like a problematic request. Why would you want to submit your app for review if it's not yet finished? I know this sounds like a ridiculous requirement just to test your In-App Purchase items, but you can easily work around Apple's odd system with minimal hassle. So, go ahead and upload an unfinished application binary to iTunes Connect and submit your app for review. The important trick during the app submission process is to choose an availability date that is very far in the future so that your unfinished app does not accidentally appear in the App Store (in the off chance Apple approves it). While the app is in active review, you can proceed to create new In-App Purchase items in iTunes Connect and test them within your app. Once you've completed testing, simply log back into iTunes Connect and reject the app, removing it from review. When your app is eventually finished and ready for the App Store, simply resubmit it via iTunes Connect with an adjusted availability date. For complete details on the app submission process, please see Chapter 9.

Reference Name

This field is fairly self-explanatory. It is the name of your In-App Purchase item in iTunes Connect, but it may not necessarily be the name that is displayed in the App Store (if a customer's device has a different language setting than your iTunes Connect default language). See the Language field description for your item's actual display name.

Product ID

Every product in iTunes Connect requires a unique ID, and In-App Purchase items are no exception. Any UTF-8 string can be used to indentify this product, but it's recommended to use a common ID system across all of your products. Many iPhone developers use "com.company.appname" as the naming scheme for all application SKU numbers, and related In-App Purchase product IDs could use an extension of that, such as "com.company.appname.productid." So if we used our fictional Breadcrumbs app as an example, its application SKU number would probably be "com.electricbutterfly.breadcrumbs." If we added a related In-App Purchase item for a 30-day subscription, its product ID could be "com.electricbutterfly.breadcrumbs.sub30days" to visually reference its relationship to the parent app. This simple system gives you an easy and consistent naming scheme across all your own products, as well as unique IDs that no one else would be using. This is a significant factor since iTunes Connect does not allow any two products to have the same ID.

Type

The most important field to understand before submitting this form is Type, especially since it cannot be edited after you've saved your new In-App Purchase item in iTunes Connect. Type defines what kind of In-App Purchase item you're creating. Currently, there are three types: Non-consumable, Consumable, and Subscriptions. It's essential that you understand the differences between these Types since it affects how you handle this purchased item within your app.

Non-consumable is the default type. This would be an item that is purchased only once and should always remain available within the app on all devices associated with the customer's iTunes account. So if it's a new game level that was purchased within a game on Johnny's iPhone, not only should that new level be persistent every time Johnny runs the game on his iPhone, but it should also be made available within the same game installed on Johnny's iPod touch. The Store Kit framework provides support for querying the App Store for purchased items so that your app can be programmed to restore those items on a specific device, even if it was initially purchased and installed on another device owned by the same customer. I'll talk more about this when we walk through an Xcode project example later in this chapter.

Consumable is an item type that can be used up or depleted and then purchased again multiple times. A good example of a Consumable item would be weapon ammunition in a game. Once the customer depletes the stock of ammunition that was purchased, it cannot be retrieved again. To continue using that weapon, the customer would need to buy another round of ammunition. Because of the disposable quality of this type, Consumable items are not required to be available across all of a customer's related devices. If you do choose this type for your In-App Purchase item, you should always state in very clear language within your app that it is consumable, explaining that once used up, it's gone, but a new one can be purchased.

Subscriptions are much like Consumables in that a Subscription can be purchased several times. If the customer bought a 30-day subscription to a service within your app, when the subscription expires, the customer can renew it by buying another 30-day subscription. The big difference between Subscriptions and Consumables is that Subscriptions must always be made available within the same app on all devices associated with the customer's iTunes account. So if Johnny has your app installed on both his iPhone and iPod touch, the subscription he purchased should be persistent within the app on both devices.

Price Tier

This drop-down menu provides a list of available pricing tiers for assigning a specific price to your In-App Purchase item. As I've mentioned before, give this a lot of consideration before deciding upon a price. Your in-app item can certainly be set at a higher price than the related parent app, but just make sure it's an appropriate price for what customers will be receiving. For your In-App Purchase strategy to be successful, the right price needs to be matched with the level of demand for the add-on content. For example, Comixology's Comics app is free, but many of the digital comics available via In-App Purchase are priced at $1.99. If I'm hooked on a particular series, then $1.99 per issue seems like a fair price to me. But if the digital comics were ever priced higher than a physical comic book, then that would be enough of a deterrent to prevent me from buying.

On the flip side, many developers want to offer lower In-App Purchase prices than Apple's current 99-cent minimum. Their argument is that for microtransactions to really take off, lower price points are needed. With many iPhone games costing only 99 cents, some developers think a 99-cent add-on must include just as much content as the game itself. Although I do not necessarily agree with that theory, I do believe that being able to choose tiers that are less than 99 cents would provide the flexibility to create a broader spectrum of in-app business models.

You can modify the price of In-App Purchase items to hold a special promotional sale, but they can never be offered for free—not even for a limited time. In-App Purchase items must include a price. To offer free downloadable content within your app, you'll need to implement your own system for retrieving those items from your server, outside of the App Store.

Cleared for Sale

If this check box is left unchecked, then your In-App Purchase item will not be available for listing within your app. But even if you select this box, that doesn't mean your In-App Purchase item can be publicly purchased. As individual products, all In-App Purchase items need to be reviewed and approved by Apple before they are made available in the App Store. But for testing purposes (as well as when you're ready to go live), you definitely want this box to be selected.

Language

This is where you choose the languages you want to support. For each language selected, you'll input a localized name and description for your In-App Purchase item. Type carefully, since the In-App Purchase item name and description you submit here is what the App Store displays to customers when they attempt to buy it within your application. Your In-App Purchase item must support at least one language. If you only have one language listed, then make sure it is the same as the language set for the related parent app.

Screenshot

This is for review purposes only and will never be displayed in the App Store. When first creating a new In-App Purchase item, you'll leave this field empty. After you've extensively tested In-App Purchase within your app, you'll need to take a screenshot of that purchase process in action. Upload the 320 × 480 or 480 × 320 image to this Screenshot section. This image will aid Apple during the review process of your In-App

Purchase item, so only upload a screenshot *after* the item has successfully passed your own testing and is ready for submission.

Managing Your In-App Purchase Items

After saving your new In-App Purchase item within iTunes Connect, you can make changes to it later by accessing it via the Manage Your In-App Purchases section. Until you submit it to Apple for review, the item's status will be Pending Developer Approval, and you can freely edit or delete it. But once you click the Approve button, the status will change to Waiting for Review or In Review, and you will not be able to make any further changes while it's being reviewed.

After clicking that Approve button, you'll be prompted to choose one of two options: Submit Now or Submit with Binary. If your existing iPhone app is already supporting In-App Purchase and you're merely adding yet another In-App Purchase item to an existing list of offerings, then selecting Submit Now will send it directly to the review queue. If your In-App Purchase item requires an updated version of your iPhone application, then you'll want to select Submit with Binary to ensure that both products are reviewed together and go live in the App Store at the same time.

After your In-App Purchase item has been rejected or approved by Apple, any additional modifications you make will require it to be reviewed again. If it gets rejected, then Apple requires you to re-create it as a new In-App Purchase item before resubmitting for review. Also keep in mind that the rating you choose for your parent application needs to reflect the content of all related In-App Purchase items as well.

You can create up to 1,000 In-App Purchase items per parent application. If you delete an In-App Purchase item from iTunes Connect, that unique product ID can never be used again for another item. Even if you're replacing the deleted item with a similar In-App Purchase item, you'll be required to use a different product ID for it.

Preparing Your Test Device

I can hear you groaning. Yes, this part is required. I know testing your apps on a device can sometimes be a little tedious, but unfortunately, the iPhone Simulator does not support In-App Purchase. To properly test an In-App Purchase transaction, you'll need to run through it on an iPhone OS device using your new In-App Purchase Test User account.

To avoid account issues, you must log out of any existing iTunes accounts on your test device. To do this, simply launch the device's Settings app, and tap on Store. On the Store screen, tap the Sign Out button to log out of the iTunes Store (see Figure 6–10). I cannot stress enough how important this step is. Clearing out existing accounts from the device's Store settings will prevent a nontest account from accidentally being used during your In-App Purchase test transactions. Just leave the Store setting empty. Do *not* log in here with your In-App Purchase Test User account. Doing so may invalidate it as a test account.

In the Restrictions section of your test device's General Settings, make sure the In-App Purchases feature is switched on under Allowed Content (see Figure 6–10).

Figure 6–10. *You must sign out of your iTunes account on your test device before testing In-App Purchase (left). You'll also need In-App Purchases turned on in your test device's Allowed Content settings (right).*

Now that your device is ready, simply connect it to your development computer. To compile and test your project on your device, make sure you select Device as the Active SDK in Xcode's drop-down menu.

When running an Xcode debug build of your application on your test device, the Store Kit framework communicates with a special test environment instead of the App Store. If an In-App Purchase request is made, the Store Kit will prompt you to confirm the purchase. Then Store Kit will display an iTunes sign-in screen. Select Existing Account, and log in with your In-App Purchase Test User account. In this special test environment, successfully completing a transaction will return an order receipt, but no money is transferred, and no invoice is generated.

Never use your In-App Purchase Test User account in a live production environment. Your test account should be used only when debugging your app in Xcode's test environment. Doing otherwise will invalidate your account credentials.

Tapping into the Store Kit Framework

Time to start programming! Fire up Xcode, and create a new iPhone project, selecting the View-based Application template and naming the example project InAppPurchase. Before we write any code, the required StoreKit.framework has to be added to the Xcode project. To do this, Control-click the project's Frameworks folder, and from the contextual menu that appears, select Add ➤ Existing Frameworks... (see Figure 6–11). Select the StoreKit.framework, which can be located in the Xcode tools' parent Developer folder at the following path:

Developer ➤ Platforms ➤ iPhoneOS.platform ➤ developer ➤ SDKs ➤ iPhoneOS3.0.sdk ➤ System ➤ Library ➤ Frameworks ➤ StoreKit.framework

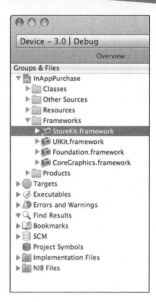

Figure 6–11. *Add the StoreKit.framework (left) for inclusion in your Xcode project (right).*

Since In-App Purchase is not supported in the iPhone Simulator, select Device as the Active SDK in the top left drop-down menu (see Figure 6–11) to reflect your connected test device.

The example project we're about to build should not be viewed as a functional, self-standing app. For it to work, you'll need to plug in your own In-App Purchase items and information in various places in the code. So, this project should really be treated like a very basic template, outlining the steps needed to complete an example in-app purchase. It should merely serve as a good jumping point to get you started, enabling you to extend this code and customize it for your purposes.

Setting Up the Basics

First, you'll need to add a new class to the project, so select the Classes folder in the Groups & Files column, and then choose New File… from the File Menu. Next, in the New File dialog box that appears, select the Objective-C Class template from the Cocoa Touch Class category, and configure the Subclass drop-down menu to make it a subclass of `NSObject`. Click the Next button, and have Xcode create both the `.h` and `.m` files, naming them both `InAppPurchaseObserver`. You don't have to touch this new class yet. We'll come back to it later to add some code, so I'll explain its purpose then.

For now, let's move on to the `InAppPurchaseViewController` class. You'll want to design your own storefront UI, especially if you're offering several In-App Purchase products within your app, but for the purposes of this basic example, you'll use a simple `UIButton` for a single In-App Purchase item.

Open the InAppPurchaseViewController.h header file, and modify the code as follows:

```
#import <UIKit/UIKit.h>
#import <StoreKit/StoreKit.h>
#import "InAppPurchaseObserver.h"

@interface InAppPurchaseViewController : UIViewController <SKProductsRequestDelegate> {
    InAppPurchaseObserver *inappObserver;
    UIButton *inappButton;
}

@property (nonatomic, retain) InAppPurchaseObserver *inappObserver;
@property (nonatomic, retain) IBOutlet UIButton *inappButton;
-(IBAction)buyInApp:(id)sender;

@end
```

The code highlighted in bold represent new additions. The Store Kit framework has been imported, and a new UIButton and buyInApp function are referenced. This enables you to modify the button's properties via code, and it'll call the buyInApp function when the button gets tapped.

You'll also notice the assignment of the SKProductsRequestDelegate. This allows the InAppPurchaseViewController to receive responses from the Store Kit framework, which will come into play later when you start adding Store Kit code to the project.

The new InAppPurchaseObserver class has also been imported and can be referenced via the inappObserver property. This will enable the InAppPurchaseViewController to send Store Kit transaction responses to the InAppPurchaseObserver class. I'll talk about that more later in this chapter.

Save those changes; now open the InAppPurchaseViewController.m implementation file, and add the following bolded code to complete your setup of the inappObserver property, UIButton, and the buyInApp function:

```
#import "InAppPurchaseViewController.h"

@implementation InAppPurchaseViewController
@synthesize inappObserver;
@synthesize inappButton;

// Implement viewDidLoad to do additional setup after loading the view, typically from a
nib.
- (void)viewDidLoad {
    [super viewDidLoad];
}

// When the buy button is clicked, start In-App Purchase process.
-(IBAction)buyInApp:(id)sender {
    // Interact with StoreKit here.
}

- (void)didReceiveMemoryWarning {
    // Releases the view if it doesn't have a superview.
    [super didReceiveMemoryWarning];
```

```
        // Release any cached data, images, etc that aren't in use.
    }

    - (void)viewDidUnload {
        // Release any retained subviews of the main view.
        // e.g. self.myOutlet = nil;
    }

    - (void)dealloc {
        [inappButton release];
        [inappObserver release];
        [super dealloc];
    }

    @end
```

After saving those changes, you can now launch InAppPurchaseViewController.xib in Interface Builder. Add a Rounded Rectangle Button to the View, and wire up its Touch Up Inside connector to the File Owner's buyInApp connector. Then wire the File Owner's inappButton outlet to the Rounded Rectangle Button. I also added a Label with Purchase Add-On Game Content as the Text and changed the button's default Title to read None Available (see Figure 6–12). Make sure to disable the button by unchecking the Enabled property. This will all make sense when we start interacting with Store Kit.

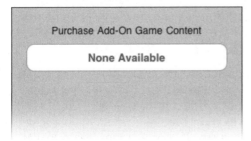

Figure 6–12. *Setting up our simple example in Interface Builder. Uncheck the button's Enabled property.*

Now that we're done building and wiring up our basic user interface, it's time to have some fun with Store Kit. In only five steps, you'll have In-App Purchase up and running in your application!

Step 1: Does the Consumer Allow In-App Purchase?

Since users can disable the In-App Purchase feature in their device settings, you'll want to check that an in-app purchase can be made before doing anything else. After you've saved your changes in Interface Builder, go back to Xcode, and open the InAppPurchaseViewController.m implementation file again, and add the following new code to viewDidLoad:

```
    - (void)viewDidLoad {

        if ([SKPaymentQueue canMakePayments]) {
```

```
        // Yes, In-App Purchase is enabled on this device!
        // Proceed to fetch available In-App Purchase items.

    } else {
        // Notify user that In-App Purchase is disabled via button text.
        [inappButton setTitle:@"In-App Purchase is Disabled"
forState:UIControlStateNormal];
        inappButton.enabled = NO;
    }

    [super viewDidLoad];
}
```

What's happening here is that a quick call is being made to the canMakePayments method
in Store Kit's SKPaymentQueue class. If a "Yes" boolean is returned, then the In-App
Purchase feature is allowed on that device and the App Store is accessible. If a "No" is
returned, then you can notify the users that they have In-App Purchase disabled via the
button's Title label. Remember that initial state of the button was set to disabled in
Interface Builder, so just leave it disabled for now, simply using it to communicate
information to the user.

Step 2: Fetch Available In-App Purchase Items

With the In-App Purchase feature accessible, you can now check the App Store for the
availability of your item. It is important to note that your application needs to already
know the related In-App Purchase product ID before performing this check.

If you are offering only one or two In-App Purchase items with no plans on adding more,
then the easiest thing to do is store your In-App Purchase product IDs within your app.
Of course, any time you add a new In-App Purchase product ID to your app, you'll need
to make it available to customers as an update, which will require submitting your app
again for review/approval. Since iTunes Connect requires In-App Purchase product IDs
to be unique, don't preassign nonexistent IDs in your parent app with plans to later
create those IDs in iTunes Connect at some point in the future. That strategy could
backfire on you if some other developer takes ownership of that product ID before you
get a chance to create it in iTunes Connect. Of course, you could plan ahead by creating
all your known In-App Purchase items in iTunes Connect now and simply mark them as
"Not Ready for Sale." That way, you'll know the product IDs to include in your
application binary, and when you're ready to make those future In-App Purchase items
available to consumers, you can submit them for approval.

If you want the flexibility to add new In-App Purchase items without requiring a new
build of your app, then you'll need to set up a mechanism on a remote server, where
your app can fetch all related product IDs from your server. Store Kit does not provide
any infrastructure for this, so it would be your responsibility to configure the app to talk
to your server. Although this requires extra work on your part, it is the recommended
method for retrieving product IDs, especially if you're constantly adding new In-App
Purchase items. Apple's approval process is too time-consuming to continuously submit
a new app update every time you release new purchasable add-on content.

The related In-App Purchase items will need to be approved and ready for sale in the App Store before customers can purchase them within your application. Before they are approved, they are available only to your In-App Purchase Test User account within your parent app's development build.

Once your app has retrieved the In-App Purchase Product ID—in this example, you're using only one—proceed to request that product from the App Store to ensure that it's currently available for purchase.

```
- (void)viewDidLoad {

    if ([SKPaymentQueue canMakePayments]) {
        // Yes, In-App Purchase is enabled on this device!
        // Proceed to fetch available In-App Purchase items.

        // Replace "Your IAP Product ID" with your actual In-App Purchase Product ID,
        // fetched from either a remote server or stored locally within your app.
        SKProductsRequest *prodRequest= [[SKProductsRequest alloc]
initWithProductIdentifiers: [NSSet setWithObject: @"Your IAP Product ID"]];
        prodRequest.delegate = self;
        [prodRequest start];

    } else {
        // Notify user that In-App Purchase is disabled via button text.
        [inappButton setTitle:@"In-App Purchase is Disabled"
forState:UIControlStateNormal];
        inappButton.enabled = NO;
    }

    [super viewDidLoad];
}
```

Of the new code added (in bold) to `InAppPurchaseViewController.m`'s `viewDidLoad`, you'll need to replace the placeholder string "Your IAP Product ID" with your own actual In-App Purchase product ID.

And remember that `SKProductsRequestDelegate` code you added to the header file a while back? By assigning `InAppPurchaseViewController` as the `SKProductsRequest` delegate, you can simply state "self" for the Delegate property. The Store Kit will then return a response to this delegate. To receive that response, add the following code to the `InAppPurchaseViewController.m` file:

```
// StoreKit returns a response from an SKProductsRequest.
- (void)productsRequest:(SKProductsRequest *)request
didReceiveResponse:(SKProductsResponse *)response {

    // Populate the inappBuy button with the received product info.
    SKProduct *validProduct = nil;
    int count = [response.products count];
    if (count>0) {
        validProduct = [response.products objectAtIndex:0];
    }
    if (!validProduct) {
        [inappButton setTitle:@"No Products Available" forState:UIControlStateNormal];
        inappButton.enabled = NO;
        return;
```

```
    }

    NSString *buttonText = [[NSString alloc] initWithFormat:@"%@ - Buy %@",
validProduct.localizedTitle, validProduct.price];
    [inappButton setTitle:buttonText forState:UIControlStateNormal];
    inappButton.enabled = YES;
    [buttonText release];
}
```

Store Kit responds with an array of available In-App Purchase products. Since you have only one here, you populate the inappBuy button with the product's localized Title and Price (see Figure 6–13). If you're interested in also displaying the localized description, then that can be accessed via the localizedDescription property. Don't forget to enable the button via code now that it's displaying a valid In-App Purchase item.

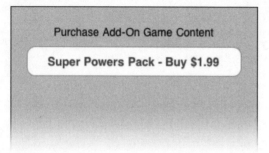

Figure 6–13. *The Store Kit replies to the product request with information on the available In-App Purchase item. The example code then populates the button with the item's localized title and price.*

Why bother checking for the In-App Purchase item through the Store Kit if you already know the product ID? This vital step ensures that your application does not try to sell an item that is not currently available in the App Store. For example, what if you submitted both your application and an In-App Purchase item for review at the same time, but only your iPhone app was approved? By forcing your application to first check for the availability of the In-App Purchase item before listing it will prevent potential customer purchase issues. Never assume. Always perform this check before displaying any items for sale within your app.

If you successfully set up an In-App Purchase item in iTunes Connect and yet your app encounters problems retrieving that item data as a valid product, make sure your application's Bundle Identifier in its Info.plist file matches the parent app Bundle ID assigned to your In-App Purchase item in iTunes Connect.

Do not discard that In-App Purchase Product ID after using it for the product request. It'll come in handy again soon. If the user taps the buy button, you'll need that Product ID to submit a purchase request to Store Kit.

To retrieve valid product data from the App Store and successfully test In-App Purchase within your app, remember that your app must be either live in the App Store or in active review in iTunes Connect. As previously mentioned, if your app is currently unfinished, you can work around Apple's odd requirement by uploading an unfinished application binary to iTunes Connect and submitting your app for review. The important trick during the app submission process is to choose an availability date that is very far in the future so that your unfinished app does not accidentally appear in the App Store (in the off chance Apple approves it). While the app is in active review, you can proceed to test In-App Purchase within your app. Once you've completed testing, simply log back into iTunes Connect and reject the app, removing it from review. When your app is eventually finished and ready for the App Store, simply resubmit it via iTunes Connect with an adjusted availability date. For complete details on the app submission process, please see Chapter 9.

Step 3: Requesting a Purchase

If the user taps the buy button in the example, that will fire the `buyInApp` action in the `InAppPurchaseViewController.m` file. So, the next step is to handle that action by sending a payment request to Store Kit.

```
// When the buy button is clicked, start In-App Purchase process.
-(IBAction)buyInApp:(id)sender {

    // Replace "Your IAP Product ID" with your actual In-App Purchase Product ID.
    SKPayment *paymentRequest = [SKPayment paymentWithProductIdentifier: @"Your IAP
Product ID"];

    // Assign an Observer class to the SKPaymentTransactionObserver,
    // so that it can monitor the transaction status.
    [[SKPaymentQueue defaultQueue] addTransactionObserver:inappObserver];

    // Request a purchase of the selected item.
    [[SKPaymentQueue defaultQueue] addPayment:paymentRequest];
}
```

After creating an `SKPayment` instance with the In-App Purchase product ID of the item the user wants to buy, you'll need to assign an observer class to the `SKPaymentQueue`'s transaction observer. This is where your `InAppPurchaseObserver` class comes into play. Remember how the `inappObserver` property was created to reference that class? By assigning `inappObserver` as the `SKPaymentTransactionObserver`, your project's `InAppPurchaseObserver` class can monitor the transaction status of the `SKPaymentQueue` after a payment request has been sent to it.

Since payment transactions are not lost when the app quits, you may want to assign your observer to the payment queue when your app launches so that any existing transactions can resume being monitored and processed the next time your app is run. Why would this be important? One possible scenario is the user receives a phone call in the middle of an in-app purchase. After the call, when the user returns to your app, the transaction can be resumed.

When the payment request is delivered, the App Store prompts the user to confirm the purchase and then enter an iTunes account login. When testing your own app, this is where you select Existing Account and enter your In-App Purchase Test User email address and password.

Step 4: Receiving Payment Status

After the user either cancels or confirms the purchase, the transaction status is then sent back to your InAppPurchaseObserver class. Now it's time to add code to that class to handle this job. Open the InAppPurchaseObserver.h header file, and update the code as follows:

```
#import <Foundation/Foundation.h>
#import <StoreKit/StoreKit.h>

@interface InAppPurchaseObserver : NSObject <SKPaymentTransactionObserver> {

}

- (void)paymentQueue:(SKPaymentQueue *)queue updatedTransactions:(NSArray
*)transactions;

@end
```

As you'll notice, the bold code imports the Store Kit framework and assigns this NSObject subclass to be an SKPaymentTransactionObserver. With that in place, along with a reference to paymentQueue, save and close that header file. To receive payment transaction status updates, your InAppPurchaseObserver.m implementation file should include the following code:

```
#import "InAppPurchaseObserver.h"
#import "InAppPurchaseViewController.h"

@implementation InAppPurchaseObserver

// The transaction status of the SKPaymentQueue is sent here.
- (void)paymentQueue:(SKPaymentQueue *)queue updatedTransactions:(NSArray *)transactions
{
    for(SKPaymentTransaction *transaction in transactions) {
        switch (transaction.transactionState) {

            case SKPaymentTransactionStatePurchasing:
                // Item is still in the process of being purchased.
                break;

            case SKPaymentTransactionStatePurchased:
                // Item was successfully purchased!
                break;

            case SKPaymentTransactionStateRestored:
                // Verified that user has already paid for this item.
```

```
            // Ideal for restoring item across all devices of this customer.
            break;

        case SKPaymentTransactionStateFailed:
            // Purchase was either cancelled by user or an error occurred.

            if (transaction.error.code != SKErrorPaymentCancelled) {
                // A transaction error occurred, so notify user.
            }
            break;
        }
    }
}
```

@end

Within this paymentQueue status receiver, you can check the current state of the transaction. As noted in the previous code, SKPaymentTransactionStatePurchasing means the purchase is still in progress, so there's nothing for you to do yet. You'll want to pay close attention to the return of SKPaymentTransactionStatePurchased or SKPaymentTransactionStateRestored, since that will signal the need for your app to unlock or download the purchased content.

SKPaymentTransactionStateFailed is returned if either the purchase was canceled by the user or a transaction error occurred. If the user tapped the Cancel button (as indicated by SKErrorPaymentCancelled), the aborted purchase can be safely ignored. But if the transaction failed for some other reason, you should let the user know that their purchase was not completed.

Step 5: Providing Access to the Purchased Content

If the transaction status received proves to be SKPaymentTransactionStatePurchased, then this confirms that the user's in-app purchase was successful. This is the point where you should reward the customer by immediately providing access to the purchased content. You have the option to either unlock the item within your app or download the content from a remote server. I'll explore the pros and cons of both methods in a moment. For now, let's finish the task at hand. After the purchased content has been successfully delivered to the user, the last thing you'll need to do is remove the transaction from the payment queue by calling finishTransaction:

```
- (void)paymentQueue:(SKPaymentQueue *)queue updatedTransactions:(NSArray *)transactions
{
    for(SKPaymentTransaction *transaction in transactions) {
        switch (transaction.transactionState) {

        case SKPaymentTransactionStatePurchasing:
            // Item is still in the process of being purchased.
            break;

        case SKPaymentTransactionStatePurchased:
            // Item was successfully purchased!

            // --- UNLOCK FEATURE OR DOWNLOAD CONTENT HERE ---
```

```
                        // The purchased item ID is accessible via
                        // transaction.payment.productIdentifier

                        // After customer has successfully received purchased content,
                        // remove the finished transaction from the payment queue.
                        [[SKPaymentQueue defaultQueue] finishTransaction: transaction];
                        break;

                    case SKPaymentTransactionStateRestored:
                        // Verified that user has already paid for this item.
                        // Ideal for restoring item across all devices of this customer.

                        // --- UNLOCK FEATURE OR DOWNLOAD CONTENT HERE ---
                        // The purchased item ID is accessible via
                        // transaction.payment.productIdentifier

                        // After customer has restored purchased content on this device,
                        // remove the finished transaction from the payment queue.
                        [[SKPaymentQueue defaultQueue] finishTransaction: transaction];
                        break;

                    case SKPaymentTransactionStateFailed:
                        // Purchase was either cancelled by user or an error occurred.

                        if (transaction.error.code != SKErrorPaymentCancelled) {
                            // A transaction error occurred, so notify user.
                        }
                        // Finished transactions should be removed from the payment queue.
                        [[SKPaymentQueue defaultQueue] finishTransaction: transaction];
                        break;
                }
            }
        }
```

Since transactions are persistent, removing the finished transaction from the payment queue is very important. You'll notice from the highlighted code that this is done not only after a successful transaction but also after a failed transaction. But only do this after you're done retrieving the information you need from the transaction.

In the case of a successful transaction, you'll want to capture the ID of the purchased item via `transaction.payment.productIdentifier` before removing the transaction. This will tell you the specific In-App Purchase product that should be provided to the user, which is especially useful if your application offers multiple in-app items for sale. You should store this ID somewhere in your app (such as in a plist file) so that it can keep track of customer purchases. For Non-consumables and valid Subscriptions, your customers should have access to their purchased items every time they run your app.

If purchased content is downloaded from your server, then you'll also want to grab the `transaction.transactionReceipt` before removing the transaction from the payment queue. Your server will need to receive this receipt data so that it can verify its authenticity with the App Store before authorizing the download request from your app. Keep reading because I'll later explain the server model in detail and how this verification process is a vital security measure.

Last, but not least, is the transaction status for `SKPaymentTransactionStateRestored`. This is usually returned when a restore request has been sent to the payment queue.

Restoring Paid Content

At first glance, ensuring that in-app purchases are accessible on all compatible devices owned by a customer may sound like a fairly daunting task, but the Store Kit provides support for automating much of this for you. For Non-consumable In-App Purchase items, you can send a restore request to the payment queue by calling the following:

`[[SKPaymentQueue defaultQueue] restoreCompletedTransactions];`

The result is returned as `SKPaymentTransactionStateRestored` to the `paymentQueue` receiver in your transaction observer class. In the example project, the `paymentQueue` is located in the `InAppPurchaseObserver.m` file. Just like a normal in-app purchase, you can check the product IDs in the restored transaction record and then provide the customer with access to these paid items. The main difference with restored transactions is that the user is not billed again. The items are already paid for, so this method is simply identifying which in-app items your application should make available to the user. Likewise, if customers accidentally attempt to purchase a Non-consumable item that they've already bought, then the result is returned as `SKPaymentTransactionStatePurchased`, but there is no charge for the transaction. After you've provided access to the user's purchased items, you should remove the transaction from the payment queue.

Unfortunately, Subscriptions and Consumable item transactions are not restored by Store Kit. To restore those types, you'll need to keep records of the original purchase transactions on your own server and have that server orchestrate the restoration of those items to your customer's devices.

No matter what you have to do on the back end to support this, you should make the restoration process as convenient and simple as possible for your users. Many apps accomplish this by including a Restore Purchased Content button.

Delivering and Managing In-App Purchases

As mentioned throughout this chapter, either In-App Purchase items can be built into your application and then unlocked after purchase or they can be downloaded from a remote server. Which method you choose will depend on what kind of content you're delivering and the extensibility your app requires.

Unlocking Built-in Content

This method is by far the easiest route, requiring far fewer steps that can all be done from within your app. There's no need to maintain a server, and you don't have to worry about security issues when communicating between your app and server. Just a few interactions with the App Store and then purchased content is unlocked from within your app (see Figure 6–14).

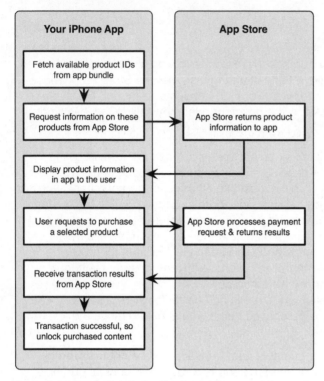

Figure 6–14. *The built-in In-App Purchase delivery model*

Using this model requires all your related In-App Purchase content to already be embedded into the app, hidden away from users. When a customer purchases a particular item, your app simply unlocks access to it. This works great for providing integrated content such as new levels in a game or additional features in a productivity app or for activating subscription-based functionality.

Store Kit does not support any way to "patch" your app binary with a downloaded update from a remote server. If your app requires the purchased content to be integrated within the app bundle, then you should include it in your application before submitting it to the App Store. Then after a customer purchase, your app can simply unlock this content.

The easiest way for your app to record and remember unlocked content is to store the information in your app's preferences, which get backed up when users sync their devices with their computer via iTunes. Having the app's preferences backed up will help prevent purchases from being lost, even if the app gets deleted on a user's device. Your app needs to remember which items have already been purchased so that the next time the user runs your app, the purchased content is still readily accessible.

The one major drawback to using this built-in unlocking model is that if you decide to make additional In-App Purchase items available in the future, you'll need to submit a new, updated application binary to the App Store that includes the new content.

Downloading Content from Your Server

If you're constantly adding new In-App Purchase items for your application, then using the server download approach is the recommended route. This requires quite a few more steps and saddles you with a lot of server management responsibilities, but this model provides the most flexibility and future growth possibilities for your app (see Figure 6–15).

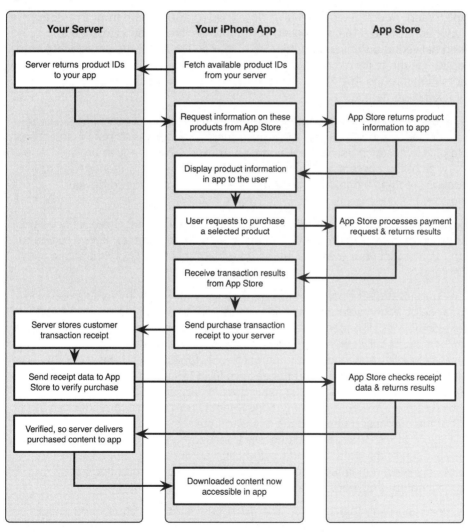

Figure 6–15. *The server-based In-App Purchase delivery model*

The Comics app by ComiXology (showcased earlier in this chapter) is a perfect example of this model. The app fetches the latest list of product IDs for available digital comics from the server. When a user purchases a specific digital comic book, the app then downloads the file from the server. The app can open and view any selected digital comic file from the user's downloaded collection of purchased issues.

This approach enables new digital comics to be made available every week as In-App Purchase items without requiring any updates to the actual Comics application. New In-App Purchase items are submitted for review through iTunes Connect, and when they're approved, ComiXology simply adds their product IDs to the database on their server. Then the next time the Comics app checks for new items, it retrieves the latest list of new digital comics from the ComiXology server.

You cannot "patch" your app binary with a downloaded app update from a remote server. If your app requires the purchased content to be integrated within the app bundle, then delivering purchased content from your server is not the appropriate path. You'll need to use the built-in model of embedding the content in your application before submitting it to the App Store. Then after a customer purchase, your app can simply unlock this content.

Ever plan on delivering the same content to more than just iPhone users? The server-based model is recommended if you allow customers to access their purchased content on multiple platforms, such as via the iPhone, an Android phone, a web browser, and so on. This way, all of the content and customer records can be easily managed in one central location (such as a database on your server) with all supported devices connecting to it.

The big drawback to delivering content from a remote server is that Store Kit does not provide any kind of infrastructure for communicating with your server. It's up to you to develop and implement your own custom server-side applications for interacting with your iPhone app.

The only thing the Store Kit does offer is a method for your server to verify a received transaction receipt. When your iPhone app notifies your server that a purchase was successfully completed, it needs to send a transaction receipt to the server. As you may remember, I mentioned that when an In-App Purchase transaction is finished, the App Store returns valuable transaction information to your application's transaction observer class. Before removing the completed transaction from the payment queue, you should first capture the `transaction.payment.productIdentifier` and the `transaction.transactionReceipt`. The `productIdentifier` property provides the product ID of the purchased item and the `transactionReceipt` property includes an encrypted receipt of the order. By sending this transaction receipt to your server, you've now given your server the data needed to verify and authorize the purchase. Without a valid receipt, this prevents hackers from tricking your server into granting free downloads of content that were never legitimately purchased.

Of course, you can't send this raw data in a URL query string, so you'll need to first Base64-encode the transaction receipt before sending it to your server. As I mentioned in Chapter 5, The iPhone SDK does not include Base64 encoding and decoding, but several third-party Objective-C libraries are available that provide Base64 support for iPhone, such as Google Toolbox for Mac (`http://code.google.com/p/google-toolbox-for-mac/`).

So, how does this verification process work? When your server receives the Base64-encoded string from your iPhone app, it should then submit the receipt data as a JavaScript Object Notation (JSON) dictionary directly to the App Store via an HTTP POST request:

```
https://buy.itunes.apple.com/verifyReceipt
```

If you're testing your app and server prior to public release, then receipt data should instead be sent to the App Store's test environment here:

```
https://sandbox.itunes.apple.com/verifyReceipt
```

If you're unfamiliar with JSON syntax, here's an example of how your post should be formatted:

```
{
        "receipt-data" : "Your receipt data goes here"
}
```

The App Store will respond by returning a JSON dictionary to your server:

```
{
        "status" : 0
        "receipt" : { …Includes a list of keys with purchased product details… }
}
```

If the "status" key has a value of 0, then your receipt has been validated as a real App Store purchase. Now that the authenticity of the transaction has been confirmed, your server can safely authorize the download. The list of keys returned in the "receipt" key contains details about the purchased product, which your server can use to determine which specific content to deliver to your iPhone app.

This added verification layer is a good security mechanism to help prevent piracy. Although In-App Purchase makes it a little more difficult for hackers to crack the paid content within your app, nothing is bullet-proof. It's only a matter of time until they figure out how to bypass Apple's In-App Purchase verification scheme. If you produce popular software products, then unfortunately piracy will always be part of the equation. It's good to do what you can to prevent casual hackers, but it's really not worth obsessing over too much. If hackers want to crack your app, they'll find a way to do it. Even though a select handful of iPhone developers have reported dismal app piracy rates as high as 80 percent, that's not all money lost. A large percentage of those people using a cracked version would never have paid for your app anyway. Your time and energy is best invested in keeping your paying customers happy.

For the descriptions and syntax of those JSON-based receipt keys, please see Apple's Store Kit documentation in the iPhone SDK. To learn more about using JSON with various server-side languages, such as PHP or Ruby on Rails, check out the official JSON web site at `http://www.json.org/`.

If you're not an experienced web developer, then the prospect of creating custom web applications and server-side infrastructure for communicating with your iPhone app can seem overwhelming, to say the least. This server-based model also puts the burden of reliable scalability and security on your shoulders. If your app enjoys a large customer base, testing your server to withstand a lot of traffic and potential security threats is essential. Server-related problems affect not only the perceived performance quality of your iPhone app but also your business reputation (and liability).

Finding Help in the Cloud

Most of us are software programmers, feeling most comfortable when coding Objective-C in Xcode. If just the idea of spending countless hours learning, developing, and maintaining web applications and expensive server systems makes you break out in a sweat, then rest easy. If you need to employ a server-based download model for your In-App Purchases, then there are a few third-party services out there offering comprehensive In-App Purchase support:

- Push.IO: `http://push.io/`

- Urban Airship: `http://urbanairship.com/`

- iLime:Purchase: `http://www.ilime.com/in-app-purchase/`

- Dodaii: `http://dodaii.com/`

The benefit to using one of these third-party services is that they take care of the related server management hassles such as scalability, security, performance monitoring, App Store receipt verification, content delivery, and even app integration. And since this elastic cloud architecture is hosted on their servers, you'll save a ton of money in the process, paying only for the services you use vs. the expensive fixed monthly costs of maintaining your own server.

In the case of Urban Airship, they even supply you with a convenient, ready-to-use storefront UI and the ability to deliver free downloads within your app, both of which are currently not offered through Apple's Store Kit framework.

In talking with Joe Pezzillo of Push.IO, it's evident he's very excited about the new business models that In-App Purchase provides for iPhone developers.

"The In-App Purchase functionality introduced with iPhone OS 3.0 is a major game changer. We're helping companies take advantage of this opportunity with a platform of integrated tools that helps manage mobile customers," says Pezzillo. "Indie developers can certainly relate to this challenge, and many of them likely would rather not have to manage their own server infrastructure for their apps. The same issue confronts businesses deploying iPhone applications for their customers and internal needs. Push.IO's platform makes it possible for companies to take advantage of the iPhone's unique capabilities such as In-App Purchase and Push Notifications and do so in a way that integrates more easily with traditional customer relationship management and content management services."

Pezzillo goes on to add, "We started Push.IO because we saw a particular opportunity to build 'picks and shovels' for the iPhone gold rush, having worked for a Fortune 100 financial services company and seeing the challenges they faced trying to adapt to the modern era of smartphones, combined with seeing what kinds of applications customers are paying to have developed and the ways in which those apps would benefit from a comprehensive suite of infrastructure services."

Unless you have some compelling reason to host, troubleshoot, and maintain the server yourself, letting the experts handle this back-end architecture will save you time and money (and help alleviate those stress-induced headaches) and allow you to stay focused on what you love doing most: creating iPhone apps.

Mining Additional Revenue with Affiliate Programs

In Chapter 5's coverage of cross-promotional efforts, I briefly mentioned the use of iTunes affiliate links when sending users to the iTunes Store. For those of you unfamiliar with affiliate programs, the way it works is quite simple. Participating companies want to encourage software and web site owners to send traffic to their retail sites. As an incentive to do so, a small commission fee is earned for sales that are generated. This is tracked by using special URLs that include unique affiliate IDs. The commissions earned by an affiliate are based on a percentage of the sales that were derived by customers who came from that affiliate's links.

Most bloggers and web site owners are very familiar with Amazon.com Associates, one of the oldest and most popular affiliate programs online. If your site visitors follow your affiliate link to Amazon.com and purchase products there, then you'll earn a commission on that sale (typically 4 percent or higher, depending on the products).

Although there are thousands of affiliate programs out there, the one you should be most interested in is Apple's iTunes Affiliate Program. With the iTunes Store and the App Store built into every iPhone and iPod touch, it's so easy for apps to link to the store pages of music, movies, TV shows, audiobooks, and even other applications. Free Lite apps do it all the time, redirecting users to the full Paid version in the App Store, in the hopes they'll buy it.

So, there's no lack of links here. Thousands of iPhone apps and their related web sites are chock full of links back to the iTunes Store and the App Store. What I find odd is that a large percentage of those links are not affiliate links. I'm constantly surprised by just how many iPhone developers still do not take advantage of this free revenue generating opportunity.

Earning a 5 percent commission on digital items that may only be priced at 99 cents does not sound like a windfall of money, but just like low-priced app sales, this business model is all about volume. If you're sending app users or site visitors to the iTunes Store and Apple's making money from your links, why shouldn't you be compensated for the sales you're generating for them? It's hard enough to make money in the App Store if you're not in the Top 200, so why would you ignore an easy option to earn some extra cash? As a software business owner, you should be looking for any and all possible revenue streams that your iPhone app and web site can deliver for you (legitimately, of course). And in this case, all it requires you to do is sign up for the free affiliate program and modify your existing URLs.

Not yet convinced that it's worth the effort? Here's a little tidbit that might pique your interest…

Pandora is one of the most beloved Internet radio services available online, and its Pandora iPhone app is a perennial favorite, resting atop the iTunes Top Free Music Apps chart for the last several months. Listeners who like the currently playing song can easily purchase that track by tapping the Buy from iTunes button (see Figure 6–16). The button uses an affiliate link to send the user to the related song page in iTunes. If the track gets purchased by that user, then Pandora earns a commission fee.

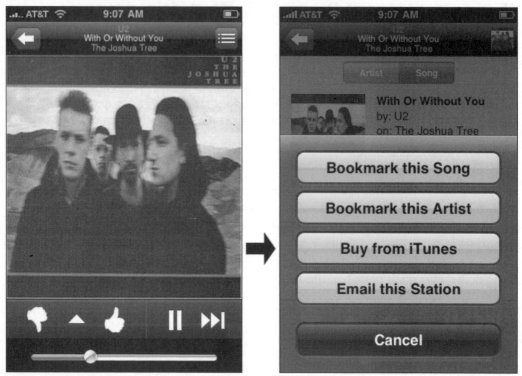

Figure 6–16. *The Pandora Internet radio app includes affiliate links to the iPhone's embedded iTunes Store, enabling listeners to easily buy the currently playing song.*

Pandora's CTO, Tom Conrad, revealed that between Pandora's web site and iPhone app, Pandora listeners are buying approximately 1 million songs a month through their affiliate links! And of those song sales, Pandora's iPhone app is responsible for a whopping 20 percent of that!

It's not difficult to see how a large customer base can generate substantial traffic to the iTunes Store, turning those affiliate links into a major revenue stream. The commissions earned from iTunes affiliate links are one of the primary sources of income for many of the social gaming platforms, such as OpenFeint (see Chapter 5), which is why they're able to provide those feature-rich gaming services for free to iPhone developers.

The great thing about the iTunes Affiliate Program is that when users follow your affiliate link to the iTunes Store, you'll earn a 5 percent commission on everything they buy within a 24-hour session or until they click another affiliate link. Pandora has seen many of their listeners not only buy the song from the affiliate link they followed but also go on to purchase a few other songs as well, which just adds more commissions to Pandora's earnings.

Granted, your iPhone app may not have as many users as Pandora (not many apps can match that level of popularity), so let's examine a more realistic scenario. Let's say your app drives only 50,000 people to the iTunes Store every month. Even if only half of them end up buying one or two 99-cent digital items, at a 5 percent affiliate commission, you'd be earning $1,250 to $2,500 per month. That's a lot of money for doing nothing but a one-time URL change to your embedded iTunes Store links.

To sign up, head over to the iTunes Affiliate Program web page:

```
http://www.apple.com/itunes/affiliates/
```

Click the Apply to be an Affiliate link, which will take you to LinkShare's sign-up form. LinkShare is the official affiliate network for iTunes, so if you already have a LinkShare account, then simply log in at `http://www.linkshare.com/`.

Once you've completed the sign-up process and logged into your LinkShare account, there's still one more step to tackle. LinkShare is the affiliate network for hundreds of retailers, so within your LinkShare account, you're required to apply for the individual affiliate programs you're interested in joining. Perform a search of their advertiser network for the keywords *Apple iTunes* and the iTunes Affiliate Program will be displayed in the listed results (see Figure 6–17).

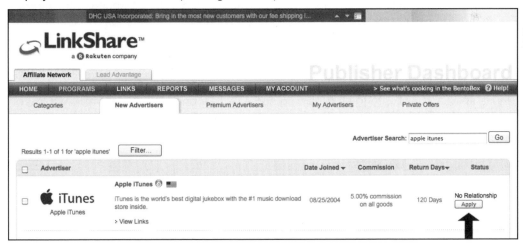

Figure 6–17. *After signing up for LinkShare, you'll then need to apply for the iTunes Affiliate Program within your LinkShare account. Search for* **Apple iTunes**, *then click the Apply button.*

Click the Apply button, and agree to Apple's terms and conditions. Since Apple manually approves all of its affiliates, you'll need to wait until you receive approval confirmation (via email) before you can create any affiliate links.

Figure 6–18. *To generate affiliate links for items in the iTunes Store, you'll need to use Apple's special Link Maker Tool.*

Once approved by Apple as an official iTunes affiliate, log back into your LinkShare account, and navigate your way over to the iTunes Affiliate Program page. You should now see a blue "iTunes: Create Links" banner with a row of buttons underneath (see Figure 6–18). To generate iTunes affiliate links for use in your iPhone apps and web site, be sure to click the Link Maker Tool button. Do not use LinkShare's Link Builder feature. Apple's Link Maker Tool is very easy to use, allowing you to easily search for a specific product and then copy the custom affiliate link that the online tool provides. And that's it! It's really that simple. Use those special links (which include your affiliate ID) in your iPhone apps and web site to start earning some extra money for all that traffic you're sending to the iTunes Store.

Digging for Gold

Between the in-app advertising opportunities discussed in Chapter 5 and the new business models explored in this chapter with In-App Purchase and affiliate programs, there are many ways to make money on the iPhone beyond just traditional app sales.

This chapter has provided you with a good starting point for understanding and using In-App Purchase within your applications. For an in-depth look at the entire Store Kit API, I highly recommend reading the related iPhone SDK 3 documentation. Log into the iPhone Developer Program, and then visit these links:

■ In-App Purchase Programming Guide:
  http://developer.apple.com/iphone/library/documentation/Network
  ingInternet/Conceptual/StoreKitGuide/

■ Store Kit Framework Reference:
  http://developer.apple.com/iphone/library/documentation/StoreKi
  t/Reference/StoreKit_Collection/

Chapter 7

Testing and Usability: Putting Your Best Foot Forward

As I've discussed various techniques for improving your app's marketability from within the app itself, you've probably noticed a running theme throughout this book. Your app needs to rock! Having a great app idea is not enough. So, what sells? Beautiful, intuitive interfaces that are easy to use with functionality that works as intended sell. No amount of marketing and publicity will help a poorly conceived app. Buggy performance and rough edges in usability can quickly ruin your app's reputation, prompting negative word-of-mouth, bad reviews, and disastrous customer ratings in the App Store.

Before any release, especially your initial 1.0 launch, implementing a thorough testing process should be a key step in your development cycle. This chapter will also touch upon the merits of beta testing, providing in-app help, and tracking usage through app analytics.

Preventing the Majority of One-Star Reviews

On the surface, many of the negative customer ratings in the App Store appear to be complaining about nothing more than pricing. There are countless reviews stating that after purchasing the app, the user felt it was not worth the price. Those kinds of comments seem quite petty if the app costs only a few dollars or less, but it's important to understand why those customers feel cheated. Sure, there are always going to be those unique individuals who shout from the rooftops about pricing, no matter how good of an app you delivered, but for a large portion of those disgruntled customers, there is an underlying principle in effect. For them, it's not really about the money—their morning latte from Starbucks costs more than the app—but it has everything to do with their purchase satisfaction. After reading the App Store description and browsing the screenshots, they downloaded the app with specific expectations in mind. Whether right or wrong, if those expectations are not met, frustration sets in…even if the app was free! Obviously, some expectations are bound to be unreasonable, and you won't be able to make everyone happy, but there are steps you can take to minimize the number of unsatisfied customers.

Avoiding Common Pitfalls

These are the two biggest factors that contribute to user frustration:

- Poor performance
- Lack of usability

The good news is that those two showstoppers are in your control to fix before unleashing your app into the wild. Of course, no one *wants* to release buggy software that's hard to use, so although avoiding those two issues may seem plainly obvious to you, it's amazing just how many apps are live in the App Store that fall victim to those very problems. So, how does this happen? It's easier than you might think if you're working in an isolated bubble where you're the sole developer and the only tester.

Unfortunately, way too many developers don't take the time to extensively test their apps across multiple devices and users before submitting them to the App Store. An app may run fine in your iPhone Simulator, but how about on an actual iPhone and iPod touch? A number of performance, memory, and usability issues can only be discovered by testing your app on the device itself. In the iPhone Simulator, your app may run fast on your mighty Mac with high-speed broadband Internet connectivity, but the real performance test is running on the slower wireless network and processor of a real iPhone.

And don't forget that the iPhone Simulator has a much larger display size than the device's compact screen. On a big 72 dpi Mac monitor, an app's 320 × 480 pixel interface design can look deceptively large but then shrinks dramatically on the tiny, dense 160 dpi iPhone screen. UI elements may appear quite functional in the iPhone Simulator, but then when tested on the iPhone's small screen, developers often find that custom buttons are too small and close together, making accurate finger taps extremely difficult.

Apple rejects almost 60 percent of app submissions at least once. The handful of high-profile rejections that you've read about in the various tech blogs have become news fodder because of vague or ridiculous rejection reasons, but most of the daily rejections that don't make headlines are simply apps that don't work or fall prey to bugs and crashes while being reviewed. It is the single most common reason for rejection from the App Store, so it's important that you take the time to test your app not only in the iPhone Simulator but also on as many devices as possible. If you're a solo, independent developer, you may not have access to all the iPhone OS-powered hardware models, such as the Edge, 3G, 3GS, and iPod touch, but it's a worthy investment to have more than one testing device at your disposal. As for myself, I test apps on an iPod touch, as well as an original iPhone. To accommodate the broadest possible audience, you should consider targeting the lowest common denominator. If an app's Internet-related functionality performs well on the original iPhone's slower Edge network, then it can only be that much faster on the newer 3G and 3GS. For memory-intensive apps, it's recommended to test on the original iPhone since it has the least amount of available RAM. And if you plan on making your app backward compatible with older versions of the iPhone OS, then I recommend using test devices with those OS versions installed, such as a few different iPod touch models.

Have you let anyone else test-drive your app? If not, then it's imperative that you do! Recruiting beta testers to evaluate your app is one of the most effective ways to unearth hard-to-find bugs and other critical issues. As the app's creator, you've lived with this app through months of laborious designing and development. Its completion is your pride and joy. You're too close to it, so either you won't be able to see glaring problems that others will see or subconsciously you might not want to find any faults since that will mean delaying the release to fix the app. But when it comes to the harsh frenzy of the App Store, ignorance is not bliss.

Beta testing is not only about squashing bugs. Everyone approaches an app with a unique mind-set and varying expectations. You know your own app inside and out, so naturally, its design seems intuitive to you, but to others who are unfamiliar with it, figuring out how to use it may prove much more elusive. Also, the way someone else uses your app may be vastly different from how you intended it to be used. This is important knowledge that will help you fill usability holes and also reveal new target markets for your app that you had not previously considered. For example, a once generic note-taking app may evolve into a more clearly defined journal-writing tool after discovering the specific needs expressed by beta testers.

If you're new to device testing or beta testing, then keep reading because both topics are covered in greater detail later in this chapter.

Soliciting Direct Feedback

Including an in-app mechanism for customers to easily send you feedback directly can help alleviate many of those negative app store postings. Remember how we integrated In-App Email into an example project in Chapter 4? Even though that was for providing users with a Tell A Friend feature, that same In-App Email functionality can be employed for soliciting direct feedback from customers.

Giving users a dedicated channel for emailing you from within your app provides a huge level of convenience for your customers. Don't assume that users will take the time to hunt down the support page on your web site, especially if they are using their iPhone or iPod touch (away from their computer). The most convenient avenue to express their opinion is to simply post it as a review on the App Store...unless you give them an easier and quicker method directly within your app!

ComiXology's ultra cool Comics app, which I spotlighted in Chapter 6's coverage of In-App Purchase, also includes a nice example of an in-app feedback form. It appears to be the same feedback form as the one in their ComiXology iPhone app, which is why the form's dark blue style looks more like the ComiXology interface design than the UI theme of Comics. But regardless of its appearance, by making this form accessible from the main My Comics tab, the developers have made it remarkably easy for customers to submit direct feedback from within the app itself (see Figure 7–1).

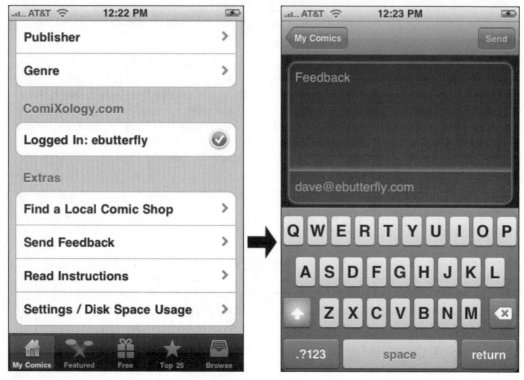

Figure 7–1. *ComiXology's Comics app provides an easily accessible in-app feedback form.*

So, you're interested in adding similar functionality into your own app, but where do you start? Check out Chapter 4's Tell A Friend example project. It should be easy enough to modify that In-App Email code for use as an in-app feedback form.

If you also offer a free lite version of your paid app, it's just as important (if not more important) to add this in-app feedback form to the lite version as well. With no barrier to entry for lite apps, their availability as free downloads invites a much broader audience of users, most of which are simply curious to kick the tires. Without a vested interest in the app like paid customers have, lite users tend to be harsher critics, with lite apps generally receiving lower App Store ratings than their paid-version counterparts. Don't forget that upon deleting an app from an iPhone device, Apple prompts the user to rate the app in the App Store. With this in mind, your goal is to get them to submit their feedback directly to you within the app before they're given the opportunity to publicly post their thoughts online in the App Store.

By providing an in-app feedback form, you're letting users know that their voice matters to you. If given the choice to either communicate directly with the app developer or just wait and hope the developer sees their App Store review, odds are, they will choose the in-app feedback form if they are seriously interested in seeing the app improve and evolve. This won't stop that minority of loud users who simply like to complain about everything from their online soapbox in the App Store, but it will help deter the number of negative App Store reviews that are nothing more than feature requests and support questions.

But won't an in-app email form also accidentally funnel positive feedback directly to you instead of posted publicly on the App Store where it can help promote sales? Sure, you may find a little of that happening, but you can always reply to those customers via email, politely thanking them and asking whether they'd be willing to post their positive comments in the App Store. If they love your app, more often than not, they'll be flattered by the request and help you out. Establishing a direct connection with your customers is always a win-win for everyone involved. If a customer is rooting for your personal success as an independent developer, there's a stronger likelihood that they'll evangelize your app in their own interactions online with friends via Twitter, Facebook, and so on.

Preventing User Frustration with In-App Help

A major cause of user frustration is the inability to figure out how your app works. In a desktop computer world, people have grown accustomed over the years to massive, complex software applications that require bible-sized manuals, which is not necessarily a good thing in my opinion. But in a mobile environment where apps are often operated with one free hand (and sometimes only a single thumb), users expect those apps to have intuitive interfaces that can be quickly learned at a glance. The iPhone SDK helps in that regard by providing a universal set of native UI controls for common functions. If you've used a navigation controller in one app, then you'll automatically know how to use it in all other iPhone apps.

For most mobile apps, if a manual is required to explain how to use even the most basic functions, then you should seriously consider rethinking your current interface design. Users should be able to download your app and immediately begin playing with the core functionality without being told how to use it. If not, then your interface design has failed, and it may earn you plenty of scathing reviews in the App Store.

Obviously, there are specific cases where a game may need to explain how to activate various controls and commands or a productivity app may need to reveal advanced tips and tricks for power users. In these situations, it's important to make this information easily accessible within your app. Don't just post it on your web site or support site, assuming users will find their way there. If customers have gotten to that point, then they're already frustrated from searching high and low for the instructions you seem to be keeping well hidden from them. Also keep in mind that your app may be used on an airplane or away from a wireless connection, so including any and all documentation within your app will prove much more convenient for your users.

This will also help reduce the amount of time you spend on customer support, which in turn saves you money (and countless headaches). If users can easily find the answers to their questions within your app, then there'll be fewer support requests for you to deal with. And if you're an independent developer, you know that the less time you have to spend fielding customer support queries, the more time you have to do actual programming.

There are four common types of in-app help that you can employ in your iPhone application: on-screen tips, instructional videos, integrated demos, and HTML-based help. I'll discuss the pros and cons of each approach so that you can decide which type best suits your app.

Planting Knowledge Seeds with On-Screen Tips

Let's say your app is easy to use and does not require a dedicated help screen or tutorial, but there are some advanced power features you want users to be aware of. Displaying on-screen tips in a `UIAlertView` pop-up is a great way to quickly educate users. Upon launch, the popular ebook reader app, Stanza, displays a helpful tip (see Figure 7–2). The app automatically chooses a random tip each time the app launches. A user can opt to see more tips by tapping the Show Next Tip button or choose Dismiss to begin enjoying the app.

Figure 7–2. *Upon launch, the Stanza ebook reader displays helpful on-screen tips for using the app. There are convenient options to either disable tips or show more tips.*

Notice that there is also a Disable Tips button. This is a critical option so that power users who are already familiar with all of the tips can easily deactivate that start-up alert before it becomes annoying. The tips feature can be turned on and off in the app's Settings panel, but why make the user search for that? By allowing users to quickly disable tips with a simple tap will prevent them from becoming frustrated with something that is supposed to be nothing but helpful.

Instructional Videos: The Double-Edged Sword

For many games, a video showing the actual game in action is often the easiest way to explain how to play it. Although this is highly effective, there are some drawbacks. Because of the typical file size of a video clip, you won't want to include it in your app's download for fear of bloating your mobile app to an unreasonable size. This means your only options are to either upload it to a video-sharing site like YouTube or host the video on your own web server. One option is vastly more effective than the other.

Since many game developers upload trailers and instructional clips to video-sharing sites to help promote their app, an easy solution would be to simply link to one of those "how to play" videos from a button in the iPhone game. There are a couple problems with this approach. First, most video-sharing sites utilize Flash Video, which the iPhone does not currently support. Second, even if you use YouTube because its videos are dynamically converted from Flash Video into the iPhone-compatible H.264 video format, it still forces your app to quit to load the video in either the YouTube app or the Mobile Safari browser. Such is the case with Panaku's fun Light Bike game, which includes a Demonstration Movie button on its main screen. Tapping it launches their YouTube video in the iPhone's built-in YouTube app (see Figure 7–3). When the user is finished watching the video, they are left on the video's info screen within the YouTube app. Since users were not aware they had left the game to begin with, they may not understand why they are not returned to the game after viewing the video.

Although it is good to have that video available on YouTube for promotional reasons, I don't recommend repurposing that same link for use within your app. Yes, I know that directing all traffic to that YouTube video page will increase the number of viewings and your YouTube ranking, but in this case, user experience should trump your online social marketing efforts.

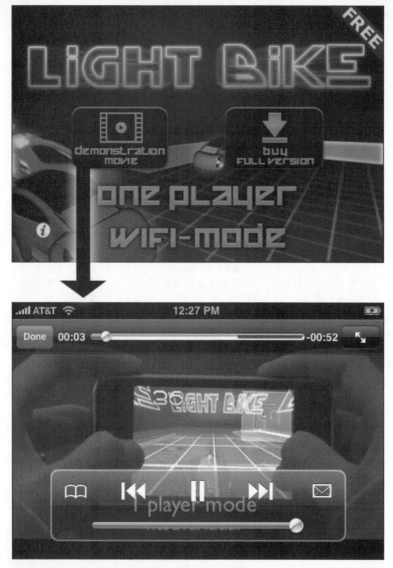

Figure 7–3. *In Panaku's addictive Light Bike, the YouTube-hosted demo movie launches the YouTube app, so users are not automatically returned to the game afterward.*

For best results, you can place that same video in QuickTime format on your web server. If your web hosting package does not include unlimited monthly data transfers and you're worried about bandwidth costs, then you may want to investigate leasing some cheap server space from one of the many cloud-based services like Amazon S3 (Simple Storage Service). Then your app can remotely play the video file within a `UIWebView`. As an alternative option, you may even want to experiment with embedding your YouTube video's HTML markup in the `UIWebView`. Loading the movie will open it in the iPhone's built-in video player. But here's the major distinction with this scenario:

when the user taps the player's Done button, they are returned to your game. This provides a seamless transition, enabling them to instantly begin playing the game after watching the "how-to" video.

Of course, producing an instructional video requires some digital filmmaking chops, but if you're a game developer, then it's practically a marketing requirement these days. It seems like every iPhone game has a slick video trailer for promotional purposes, so creating another video that explains how to play it may prove equally important.

Show, Don't Tell, with Integrated Demos

You know the old saying "a picture is worth a thousand words." It rings just as true when teaching people how to use your app. Although a video is great, an interactive demo is even better. Unlike passive video, an integrated demo can immerse users in the app, getting them to actively touch and try features as they learn.

I know I keep mentioning ComiXology's Comics app, but the developers have done so many things right, making the app a worthy example on many fronts. Within the main My Comics tab (right below the Send Feedback feature from Figure 7–1), if you tap Read Instructions, the interactive demo loads into the app's comics viewer. With the demo being a digital comic book itself, it is the perfect vehicle for showing users how to read digital comics in the Comics app (see Figure 7–4).

Figure 7–4. *ComiXology's Comics app uses an actual digital comic book to teach customers how to read digital comics within the app.*

The popular Convertbot app boasts a beautiful and unique interface, but since it doesn't use familiar UIKit controls, it may not be apparent at first glance how to use it. The developers, Tapbots, solve this issue by asking users upon first launch if they would like to view a quick demo. If the prompt is dismissed, the demo can always be accessed again at any time through the Info panel. Convertbot has one of the best demos I've seen in an iPhone app. Instead of loading the demo into a different view, the actual app's main interface is shown full-screen, performing actions on autopilot with pop-up balloons describing how the different UI elements work and what steps to take to perform specific unit conversions (see Figure 7–5).

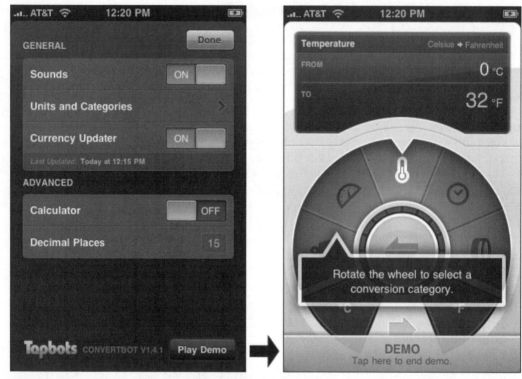

Figure 7–5. *Convertbot includes a very effective demo, placing the main interface on autopilot, showing you how to use the unique UI elements with pop-up balloon descriptions.*

The only drawback to this approach is that it requires you to spend the time and energy to construct an effective in-app demo. But believe me, when done right, it can result in a richer, satisfying user experience. It does not have to be a video but could just as easily consist of a series of modified screenshots with instructional annotations. You could write a very simple slide show view controller to run through the PNG screenshots. If you have an app that would benefit from an embedded demo, then it's well worth the effort.

In-App Web Help: A Little HTML Goes a Long Way

Even if you don't have the resources to produce a tutorial video or demo, if your application needs a little documentation for revealing extras such as advanced features, then create your own in-app help by providing the information in a help screen. A dedicated help view is extremely easy to set up with every little work and should be made accessible from your app's Settings or Info panel. But don't settle for plain text. Present the information in an appealing format. By using a UIWebView, you can utilize HTML to display stylized text and images!

The beauty of HTML is that it's easy to create and maintain. Just add a UIWebView to your Help View Controller and have it load the HTML page or HTML string you want displayed. You can even include the HTML help page within your compiled app so that there's nothing to fetch remotely—perfect for devices that are not connected to the Net, such as an iPod touch without WiFi or an iPhone in airplane mode. And during development, modifying the documentation only requires a few simple text changes to the HTML—no need to fiddle with Objective-C code.

But what if you're building a sophisticated productivity app that requires multiple pages of information? If you really feel that extensive documentation is needed, then just remember that your target is a mobile handheld device, so the primary objective should always be simplicity and ease of use. With many users navigating your in-app help with single thumb taps, take great care to keep the help content tightly organized.

Most developers groan at the thought of writing documentation of any kind, and if there's a lack of web design skills, then having to create an HTML set of pages makes matters even worse. But not to worry, there are some amazing third-party iPhone web kit frameworks that you can use to streamline this process. Here a just a few:

- iUI, an iPhone UI web framework: `http://code.google.com/p/iui/`
- jQTouch, a jQuery plug-in for iPhone web development: `http://www.jqtouch.com/`
- iWebKit, an iPhone web site toolkit: `http://iwebkit.net/`
- WebApp.Net, an iPhone web development framework:: `http://webapp-net.com/`
- Magic Framework, an iPhone HTML5 framework: `http://www.jeffmcfadden.com/projects/Magic Framework/`
- SaFire, an iPhone web app framework: `http://code.rememberthisguy.com/safire/`
- UiUIKit, a universal iPhone UI kit: `http://code.google.com/p/iphone-universal/`

Not only are these toolkits specifically optimized for the iPhone screen size, but they also provide timesaving templates that mimic native iPhone UI controls and behavior. This is beneficial for two major reasons: first, the web design looks like an iPhone interface, so it blends well with the rest of your app, and second, the UI is familiar, so there's absolutely no learning curve for the user. An instant help system that works like an iPhone app! All you have to do is write the text.

So, which one should you use? They all have their own unique benefits and strengths, so check out all the web sites listed to see which offering best suits your specific needs. All of the frameworks include full source code and are available as free downloads. If you're a fan of the jQuery JavaScript library, then you'll love David Kaneda's jQTouch. iWebKit, WebApp.Net, and Magic Framework are also impressive. These four toolkits are offered as donationware, so if you end up using one of them, please consider supporting their hard work by sending a PayPal donation. And just as worthy of your attention are the open source solutions: iUI, SaFire, and UiUIKit.

The popular iUI, which was originally created by the well-respected iPhone and web app developer, Joe Hewitt, is one of my favorites. Most of you know Joe for his work on Firefox, Firebug, and the Facebook iPhone app.

To show you how easy it is to add in-app web help to your iPhone application, let's run through a quick little example project. Open the InAppHelp Xcode project, located in this book's companion examples folder. If you don't have those files, you can download them from the book's web site at http://www.iphonebusinessbook.com/

The InAppHelp example is a modified version of Xcode's Utility Application template. I simply changed all of the FlipsideView and FlipsideViewController references to HelpView and HelpViewController, respectively. I also deleted the default Info button, which will soon be replaced with a Rounded Rectangle Button with the title In-App Help. Next, I added a line of code to the MainViewController.h header file for the button's IBAction:

```
#import "HelpViewController.h"

@interface MainViewController : UIViewController <HelpViewControllerDelegate> {
}

- (IBAction)showHelp;

@end
```

Then I inserted the code for that showHelp function in the MainViewController.m implementation file:

```
#import "MainViewController.h"
#import "MainView.h"

@implementation MainViewController

- (id)initWithNibName:(NSString *)nibNameOrNil bundle:(NSBundle *)nibBundleOrNil {
    if (self = [super initWithNibName:nibNameOrNil bundle:nibBundleOrNil]) {
        // Custom initialization
    }
    return self;
}

- (void)helpViewControllerDidFinish:(HelpViewController *)controller {
```

```
    [self dismissModalViewControllerAnimated:YES];
}

- (IBAction)showHelp {
    // The Help button was tapped, so display the Help View.
    HelpViewController *controller = [[HelpViewController alloc]
initWithNibName:@"HelpView" bundle:nil];
    controller.delegate = self;
    controller.modalTransitionStyle = UIModalTransitionStyleCoverVertical;
    [self presentModalViewController:controller animated:YES];
    [controller release];
}

- (void)didReceiveMemoryWarning {
    // Releases the view if it doesn't have a superview.
    [super didReceiveMemoryWarning];
    // Release any cached data, images, etc that aren't in use.
}

- (void)viewDidUnload {
    // Release any retained subviews of the main view.
    // e.g. self.myOutlet = nil;
}

- (void)dealloc {
    [super dealloc];
}

@end
```

The Utility Application template uses a default animation that flips the view horizontally to the Info panel by setting the controller's modalTransitionStyle to UIModalTransitionStyleFlipHorizontal. For in-app help, I wanted the help view to slide up from the bottom, so I changed that setting to UIModalTransitionStyleCoverVertical.

Now that the button's code was in place, the next step was to launch MainView.xib in Interface Builder, add the In-App Help Rounded Rectangle Button, and then wire up the button's Touch Up Inside connector to the File Owner's showHelp connector.

Switching back to Xcode, I added @interface and @property references for UIWebView, as well as IBAction code for done and contactSupport to the HelpViewController.h header file (see highlighted code):

```
@protocol HelpViewControllerDelegate;

@interface HelpViewController : UIViewController {
    id <HelpViewControllerDelegate> delegate;
    UIWebView *webView;
}

@property (nonatomic, assign) id <HelpViewControllerDelegate> delegate;
@property (nonatomic, retain) IBOutlet UIWebView *webView;
- (IBAction)done;
- (IBAction)contactSupport;

@end
```

```
@protocol HelpViewControllerDelegate
- (void)helpViewControllerDidFinish:(HelpViewController *)controller;
@end
```

Then I moved to the `HelpViewController.m` implementation file and added a `@synthesize` reference for `webView`, inserted the done and `contactSupport` functions, and released `webView` when `dealloc` is called (see the bold code):

```
#import "HelpViewController.h"

@implementation HelpViewController

@synthesize delegate;
@synthesize webView;

- (void)viewDidLoad {
    [super viewDidLoad];
}

- (IBAction)done {
    // The Done button was tapped, so close Help View.
    [self.delegate helpViewControllerDidFinish:self];
}

- (IBAction)contactSupport {
    // The Contact Support button was tapped, so go to
    // the online customer support web site in Mobile Safari.
    NSURL *url = [NSURL URLWithString:@"http://www.apress.com/"];
    [[UIApplication sharedApplication] openURL:url];

    // An alternative option is to implement In-App Email instead,
    // enabling the user to send feedback directly to you via email.
}

- (void)didReceiveMemoryWarning {
    // Releases the view if it doesn't have a superview.
    [super didReceiveMemoryWarning];
    // Release any cached data, images, etc that aren't in use.
}

- (void)viewDidUnload {
    // Release any retained subviews of the main view.
    // e.g. self.myOutlet = nil;
}

- (void)dealloc {
    [webView release];
    [super dealloc];
}

@end
```

The done function merely performs the same action as the one in the default Utility Application template. When the Done button is tapped on the Help View (see Figure 7–6), the panel will revert to the Main View. Since I had changed the transition style to roll up from the bottom, when dismissed, the Help View will slide back down off the screen.

The contactSupport function is a new addition. If users can't find the answer they're looking for from your help content, don't let them vent their frustration in the App Store. Instead, give them convenient access to contacting you directly by providing a Contact Support button at the bottom of your Help View (next to the Done button).

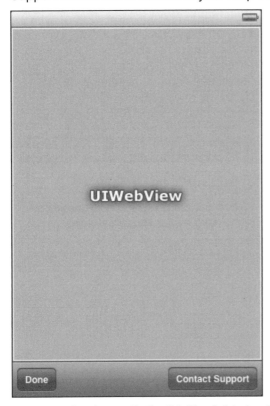

Figure 7–6. *Creating an effective Help View in Interface Builder, using only a toolbar, two buttons, and a UIWebView*

Open the project's HelpView.xib in Interface Builder, and you'll see the simple help viewer panel. Across the bottom is a standard toolbar with the Done button and the Customer Support button. As you would expect, the Done button is wired to the File Owner's done connector, and the Customer Support button is wired to the File Owner's customerSupport connector.

When run, if the Customer Support button is tapped, the current code in the customerSupport function simply launches a designated URL in Mobile Safari. This should be your online support page with a web form for requesting assistance. You could just as easily replace this code with your own implementation of In-App Email, enabling users to submit support queries directly from within your app. If this appeals to you, you could grab the relevant code from Chapter 4's Tell A Friend In-App Email example project.

The last thing added to the Help View window was the UIWebView. Since it is being used only to display read-only HTML content with no interaction with the app itself, there was no need to assign a UIWebView delegate. The only required task was wiring the UIWebView to the File Owner's webView connector.

But what shall you display in the UIWebView? For the purposes of this example, I opted to use the open source iUI as the framework for my help content. The iUI download includes several templates, so I cobbled together the elements I liked to suit my needs. By modifying the existing templates, I was able to simplify my documentation into a basic list of topics. Tap on a topic row to read the related content. And because I'm using the iUI framework, its built-in system emulates the interface and animations of native UIKit controls for a seamless user experience within the app (see Figure 7–7).

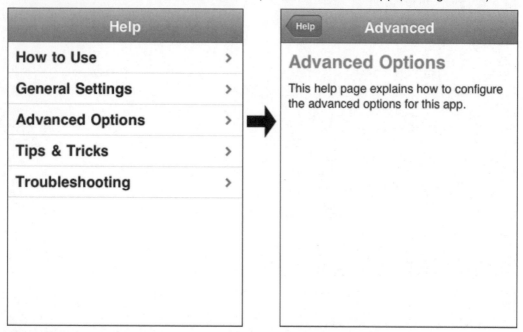

Figure 7–7. *The open source iUI web framework presents the HTML-based help content to look and feel like native iPhone interface components.*

That's not a real UINavigationBar or UITableView in Figure 7–7. Everything you see in that screenshot is powered by iUI's framework of sophisticated CSS and JavaScript code. All I had to do was insert my help text into a single HTML file, using specific iUI-centric HTML tags. Here's what my help content looks like within the HTML body:

```
<div class="toolbar">
    <h1 id="pageTitle"></h1>
    <a id="backButton" class="button" href="#"></a>
</div>
<ul id="home" title="Help" selected="true">
```

```
    <li><a href="#howtouse">How to Use</a></li>
    <li><a href="#general">General Settings</a></li>
    <li><a href="#advanced">Advanced Options</a></li>
    <li><a href="#tipstricks">Tips &amp; Tricks</a></li>
    <li><a href="#troubleshoot">Troubleshooting</a></li>
</ul>
<div id="howtouse" title="How to Use">
    <h2>How to Use</h2>
    <p>This help page explains the basics of how to use this app.</p>
</div>
<div id="general" title="Settings">
    <h2>General Settings</h2>
    <p>This help page explains how to configure the general settings for this app.</p>
</div>
<div id="advanced" title="Advanced">
    <h2>Advanced Options</h2>
    <p>This help page explains how to configure the advanced options for this app.</p>
</div>
<div id="tipstricks" title="Tips &amp; Tricks">
    <h2>Tips &amp; Tricks</h2>
    <p>This help page reveals all of the app's cool tips and tricks.</p>
</div>
<div id="troubleshoot" title="Troubleshoot">
    <h2>Troubleshooting</h2>
    <p>Having problems with this app? This help page includes troubleshooting tips for
resolving common issues.</p>
</div>
```

At a glance, you can immediately see that each "page" is contained within its own <div> tag, and the Table View list is nothing more than a simple HTML List. Since I'll be including the HTML and related image files within my Xcode project, the one worry is that relative path hyperlinks may break after compiling the app. There's a distinct advantage to storing all your help content within a single HTML file to avoid that potential issue. In fact, I even went so far as to remove all dependencies on links to external JavaScript and CSS files. I copied and pasted all of the required code directly into my one HTML file.

After finishing the modifications, I tested my help system in the Mac OS X version of the Safari browser, since it uses the same WebKit engine as the iPhone. Happy with the result, I then added it to my project by dragging the HTML file and related images onto the main Xcode window, placing them in the Resources folder (see Figure 7–8).

Figure 7–8. *Adding the HTML help page and related image files to your Xcode project's Resources folder*

You're almost done. The last step is to program the app to load the HTML help page within the UIWebView. In the HelpViewController.m implementation file, I added the following code to the viewDidLoad event:

```
- (void)viewDidLoad {
    // Load the htmlHelp.html file into the UIWebView.
    NSString *path = [[NSBundle mainBundle] pathForResource:@"htmlHelp" ofType:@"html"];
    NSURL *url = [NSURL fileURLWithPath:path];
    NSURLRequest *request = [NSURLRequest requestWithURL:url];
    [self.webView loadRequest:request];

    [super viewDidLoad];
}
```

In a nutshell, this new code fetches the HTML page from within the app bundle and loads it as a local URL into the UIWebView (see Figure 7–9).

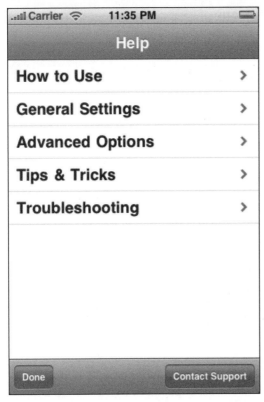

Figure 7–9. *Loading the HTML page into the UIWebView via code in HelpViewController.m*

Surprised at how good it looks? I was too. If you hadn't known it was an HTML page, you might have assumed you were looking at a native `UINavigationBar` and `UITableView`. You're probably wondering: why go to all the trouble of embedding HTML-based help if you're simply going to mimic native `UIKit` controls? Sure, I could have built the same thing in Interface Builder, but by using the open source iUI web framework, I was able to construct a custom Help View for my app in very little time and with much less code.

Another powerful advantage is that it gives me the option to host the help content remotely on a web server if desired. For apps that require a constant Internet connection for their core functionality, the Help panel's `UIWebView` could just as easily load an URL of an external web site. This gives you the flexibility to update your help content without needing to modify or recompile the actual iPhone app.

Remotely hosting the help content is especially useful if you receive a lot of feedback from users. You can continuously update your help page with additional answers to frequently asked questions, improving the support within your existing iPhone app. This also allows you to maintain a single source of help content on your web server that gets accessed by multiple platforms. On the iPhone, the help is fetched and displayed within the iUI framework or a similar toolkit. A different set of CSS styles are employed when that same help content is rendered in a web browser on a desktop computer.

Whichever method you choose, including some form of in-app help can only improve your application's overall user experience.

Provisioning: Setting Up a Development Device

When you need to test features that are not supported in the iPhone Simulator, such as the Accelerometer, multi-touch gestures, and In-App Purchase, you should run your app on an actual iPhone or iPod touch.

For preliminary testing during development, Vimov's ingenious iSimulate iPhone app and SDK can wirelessly send the GPS location and multi-touch, accelerometer, and compass events to the iPhone Simulator from an iPhone or iPod touch on the same WiFi network. This can greatly reduce the amount of time spent on testing since running apps in the iPhone Simulator is a much faster process than installing apps on a test device.

- iSimulate: `http://www.vimov.com/isimulate/`

Even if you don't utilize the specific features that require running on an actual mobile device, it's highly recommended to test and debug your app on several iPhone and iPod touch devices to ensure that everything works as intended *before* submission to the App Store. But before you can do that, you'll need to set up a developer certificate and provisioning profile to authorize your device.

Thoroughly testing your project on actual mobile hardware is such an important factor in the potential success of your application, and yet many developers avoid this task because Apple's provisioning process is so incredibly complicated. Perform a quick search through the popular iPhone development forums, and you'll find dozens (if not hundreds) of frustrated posts from programmers who have been unable to get this working correctly.

If you're never done this before, setting up a test device can be quite daunting, so here's a step-by-step walk-through to help demystify the process.

Step 1: Establishing Your Test Device in Xcode Organizer

Before we dive into generating certificates and provisioning profiles, the first thing you'll need to do is assign an iPhone or iPod touch as a test device within Xcode Organizer. Using the 30-pin USB cable that came with the device, plug it into your Mac. This action will typically cause iTunes to launch. If iTunes' preferences are configured to automatically sync the device upon connection, then simply wait for the syncing to finish. Once completed, open Xcode and choose Window ➤ Organizer.

When the Xcode Organizer window appears, you should see your connected device listed in the left pane. Select that device and in the main pane's Summary tab, and you should see device-related information listed. To designate the selected device for testing in Xcode, click the Use for Development button (see Figure 7–10).

Figure 7–10. *Designate the selected device for testing in Xcode Organizer by clicking the Use for Development button.*

It's perfectly fine to use your primary iPhone as a development device. Even after clicking the Use for Development button, that device will still operate like a normal iPhone. Just remember to always back up the device's data when syncing in iTunes. That way, if anything does go wrong during testing, you can always restore the device's OS, applications, and settings in iTunes with the last saved backup. If you're paranoid like I am, then you may want to purchase a second device, dedicated for testing purposes, such as an iPod touch.

After finishing this step, do not quit Xcode Organizer, since we'll be referring to it again later in the provisioning process. One essential bit of information that will be needed is the 40-character Device Identifier, which is listed there in the device's Summary tab.

Step 2: Verify That Apple's WWDR Certificate Is Installed

When you initially signed up for the iPhone Developer Program online, one of the first things you might have done was download and install Apple's Worldwide Developer Relations certificate. If so, then you can skip ahead to step 3.

If you don't yet have Apple's WWDR certificate in your Mac's Keychain, then you'll need to take care of that right now. Using your iPhone Developer ID and password, log into the iPhone Dev Center:

```
http://developer.apple.com/iphone/
```

Once logged in, click the iPhone Developer Program Portal link in the top-right corner of the page, and then within the main Program Portal page, select Certificates in the left pane. On the Development certificates tab, look for the text "If you do not have the WWDR intermediate certificate installed, click here to download now." And then click that link. When prompted, choose to save the `AppleWWDRCA.cer` file to your desktop.

Now double-click that downloaded .cer file. A dialog will appear asking if you'd like to add this certificate to your Mac's Keychain. Make sure the login keychain is selected, and then click the Add button.

Step 3: Launch the Online Development Provisioning Assistant

If you closed your browser session from step 2 or skipped step 2 altogether (with the WWDR certificate already installed), then using your iPhone Developer ID and password, log back into the iPhone Dev Center:

```
http://developer.apple.com/iphone/
```

After logging in, click the iPhone Developer Program Portal link in the top-right corner of the page. On the main Program Portal home page, you'll notice the recent addition of a Development Provisioning Assistant (see Figure 7–11). Although the proper sequence of events in generating and installing certificates and provisioning profiles has always been somewhat confusing, to say the least, Apple's new online assistant greatly simplifies this once laborious task by walking you through each and every required step. To get started, click the Launch Assistant button, and follow the instructions provided.

Figure 7–11. *Within the main iPhone Developer Program Portal page, click the Launch Assistant button.*

The first thing you'll be asked to do is create an App ID description. This is a unique identifier that labels the app you're assigning to your provisioning profile. It does not need to be the actual name of your application or Xcode project since this online assistant is creating a convenient "wildcard" App ID that can be used to test multiple apps. I'll talk more about "wildcard" IDs vs. app-specific IDs later in this chapter. Just use an easily identifiable name for your own reference within the Program Portal. For this example, I used the generic name TestApp (see Figure 7–12).

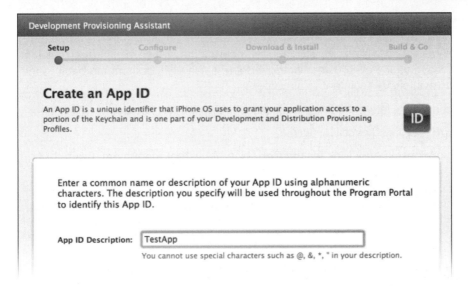

Figure 7–12. *For your own reference within the Program Portal, use an easily identifiable, unique name for the App ID description.*

Continuing to the next screen, you'll need to enter the device description and ID of your test device. The Device Description can be any name you want. I opted to call mine "Dave iPod touch" to differentiate it from my iPhone device. Referring to your selected device in Xcode Organizer, copy the 40-character device identifier, and paste it into the assistant's Device ID field (see Figure 7–13).

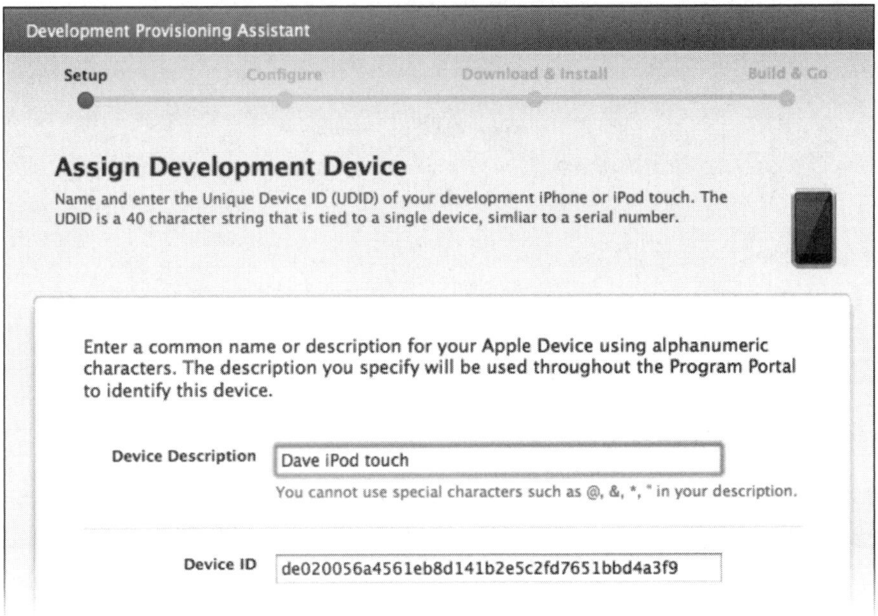

Figure 7–13. *The device ID should be your test device's 40-character device identifier listed in Xcode Organizer.*

Step 4: Request a Development Certificate

Next, the online assistant will ask you to request a certificate, which you'll need to do on your Mac. But leave your web browser window open, since we'll be jumping back to the Development Provisioning Assistant in a moment.

To request a certificate, launch the Keychain Access application, located on your Mac:

```
/Applications/Utilities/Keychain Access
```

In the Keychain Access menu, look for the Certificate Assistant menu item. From that submenu, select Request a Certificate from a Certificate Authority. In the Certificate Assistant window that appears, enter your iPhone Developer Program email address and a name for your certificate (see Figure 7–14). In this example, I simply used my full name but could have just as easily used a more descriptive label like Dave Dev Key. The "Request is" option should be set to "Saved to disk." Upon clicking the Continue button, Keychain Access will generate and save your certificate request file to your hard drive. If you chose your desktop as the location, you should see a new file there called CertificateSigningRequest.certSigningRequest.

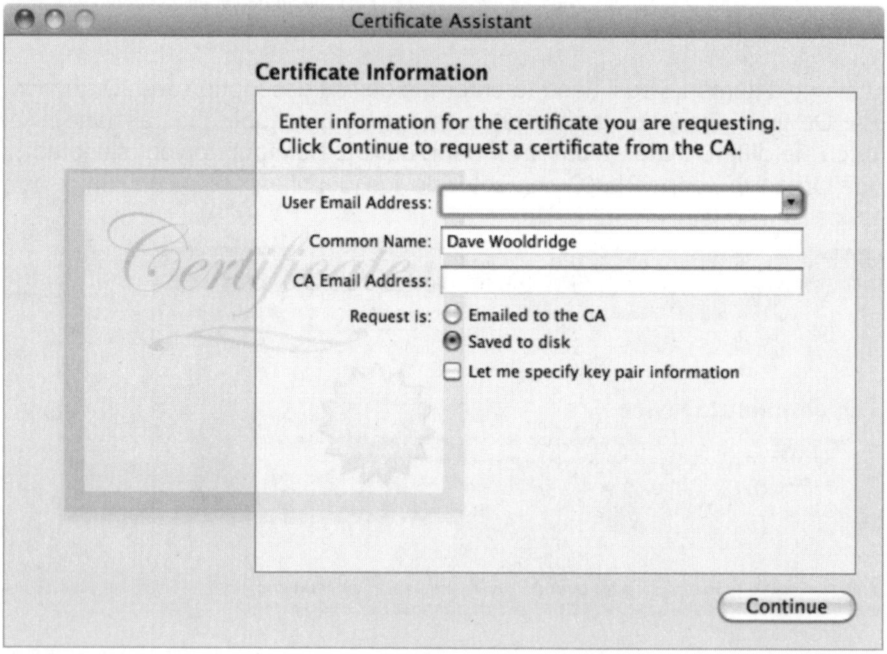

Figure 7–14. *Generate a certificate-signing request file from the Keychain Access application on your Mac.*

Go back to the online Development Provisioning Assistant in your web browser, click the Continue button to arrive at the screen that asks you to submit your certificate-signing request. Using the web form, upload your CertitificateSigningRequest.certSigningRequest file to the online assistant (see Figure 7–15).

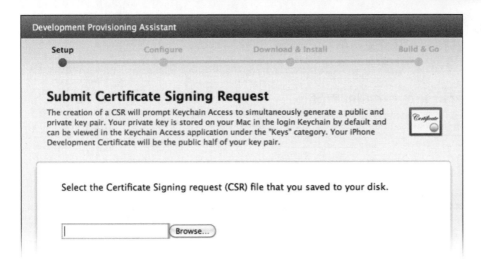

Figure 7–15. *Upload your certificate-signing request file to Apple's online assistant.*

Step 5: Generate and Install Your Provisioning Profile

With your certificate-signing request uploaded, the online Development Provisioning Assistant will next ask you to name the provisioning profile you're about to create (see Figure 7–16). If you've done everything correctly up to this point, you should also see the names of your App ID, test device, and uploaded certificate request listed there. The profile description you enter will be the profile name reflected within the Program Portal. For this example, I used the name Dave Dev Profile. With a name in place, click the Generate button. The online assistant may take a few moments to finish generating your provisioning profile.

Figure 7–16. *Using the online Development Provisioning Assistant to generate your provisioning profile.*

When your provisioning profile has been generated, you'll be prompted to download it (see Figure 7–17). Download the `.mobileprovision` file to your Mac desktop.

Figure 7–17. *Download your new provisioning profile to your Mac desktop.*

With your test device still connected to your Mac, drag the .mobileprovision file from the desktop onto the Xcode icon in your Dock. Xcode will automatically install that provisioning profile in the proper location. If imported correctly, you should now see your provisioning profile listed in Xcode Organizer on your test device's Summary tab (see Figure 7–18).

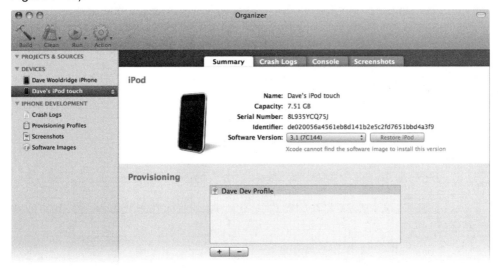

Figure 7–18. *If your provisioning profile was installed successfully, you should see it listed in Xcode Organizer on your test device's Summary tab.*

Step 6: Download and Install Your Development Certificate

With your provisioning profile securely in place, now the online assistant will prompt you to download your development certificate. Download the developer_identity.cer file to your Mac desktop (see Figure 7–19).

Figure 7–19. *Download your iPhone development certificate to your Mac desktop.*

Double-click that downloaded .cer file, which will launch the Keychain Access application (if it's not already open). Keychain Access will display a dialog window, asking if you'd like to add the certificate to a keychain. Make sure the dialog's keychain menu is set to login, and then click the Add button. In the Keys category of the main Keychain Access window, verify that your private and public keys are now paired together with your Development Certificate to ensure it is properly configured on your Mac. In this example, my "Dave Wooldridge" key (which was created when I generated a certificate-signing request under the same name) is now paired with my imported iPhone Development Certificate (see Figure 7–20).

Figure 7–20. *Verify that your imported iPhone Development Certificate has been paired with your developer key in Keychain Access.*

Step 7: Run Your Xcode Project on Your Test Device

Now that you have the proper provisioning profile and certificates in place, you can finally start testing your app on the connected device. For example purposes, I simply opened the InAppHelp Xcode project that was created earlier in this chapter. In the top-left corner of the Xcode project window, select Device | Debug from the drop-down menu (see Figure 7–21).

Figure 7–21. *Select Device | Debug from the top-left drop-down menu in the Xcode project window.*

When you click the Build and Run button, Xcode will compile the app and send it via USB to the test device, where it will get installed and run. The first time you attempt this, you'll be prompted by a code signing dialog, requesting to use your developer key (see Figure 7–22). Click the Always Allow button to proceed.

Figure 7–22. *The first time you attempt to run an app on your test device, you'll be prompted by a code-signing request, so click the Always Allow button to proceed.*

And we have lift-off! The InAppHelp project is now successfully running on my iPod touch! And if I quit the app, I see it installed on the device's home screen; however, without an assigned icon, the app is displayed with a blank white icon (see Figure 7–23).

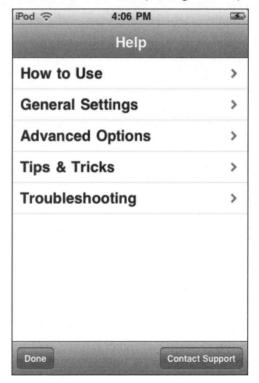

Figure 7–23. *Success! The InAppHelp example project is now installed and running on the test device.*

By default, Apple's Development Provisioning Assistant creates a wildcard App ID, which means your generated provisioning profile can be used to test any iPhone application. Since building and installing provisioning profiles is a rather tedious process, using a single wildcard App ID can be incredibly convenient for heavy testing needs, but it does have significant limitations that are worth noting.

The Limitations of Wildcard App IDs

As convenient as wild-card App IDs are, they cannot be used to test Push Notifications or In-App Purchase functionality on your device. Those two major features can be tested only with application-specific App IDs. What does that mean? Essentially, a wildcard App ID is assigned an asterisk (*) as its bundle identifier, which is what allows it be used with any Xcode project. If you navigate to the App IDs section of the online iPhone Developer Program Portal in your web browser, you'll notice that the wildcard App ID created by the Development Provisioning Assistant includes an asterisk as the bundle identifier that's attached to the unique ten-character bundle seed ID (see Figure 7–24).

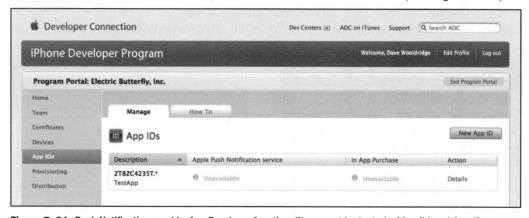

Figure 7–24. *Push Notifications and In-App Purchase functionality cannot be tested with wildcard App IDs.*

As you can see from Figure 7–24, the configuration options for Push Notifications and In-App Purchase are grayed out since they cannot be tested with wildcard App IDs. If you need to test one of those features in your application, then create a new App ID, specifying your Xcode project's reverse-domain name bundle ID as the bundle identifier. For example, I have an Xcode project called IAPTestApp that utilizes In-App Purchase, so I'll set com.ebutterfly.IAPTestApp as the App ID's bundle identifier (see Figure 7–25).

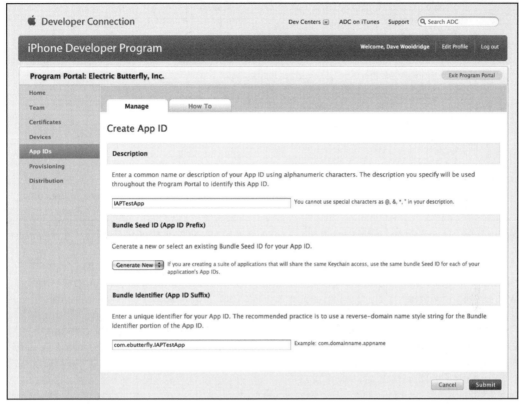

Figure 7–25. *To test Push Notifications or In-App Purchase, you'll need to create a new App ID with an app-specific bundle identifier.*

With the new application-specific App ID saved in the Program Portal, you'll notice that its Push Notifications and In-App Purchase options are configurable (see Figure 7–26). For my example IAPTestApp App ID, I'll need to configure it for use with my In-App Purchase settings. This requires that I've already created an In-App Purchase Test User account online, as well as In-App Purchase items assigned to this application. For details on setting up these elements in iTunes Connect, please see the In-App Purchase section in Chapter 6.

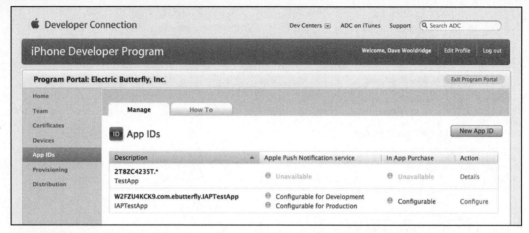

Figure 7–26. *An application-specific App ID can be configured for testing Push Notifications and In-App Purchase.*

But wait, you're not done! Xcode does not yet know about your new App ID. Your provisioning profile in Xcode Organizer still refers to the original wildcard App ID that was previously created by the Development Provisioning Assistant. To resolve this, you'll need to modify your existing provisioning profile settings in the online iPhone Developer Program Portal. In the Provisioning section's Development tab, choose to Edit > Modify your existing profile. The only property you'll want to change is the App ID setting. In my example, I'll select the new IAPTestApp from the App ID dropdown menu (see Figure 7–27).

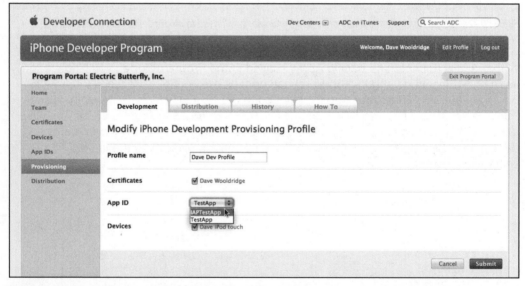

Figure 7–27. *To use the new App ID, you'll need to modify and regenerate your provisioning profile, then download and reinstall it in Xcode Organizer.*

After updating the provisioning profile settings online, regenerate the provisioning profile, and download it to your Mac desktop. Since you'll be replacing your original provisioning profile with a new updated one with the same name, you should first delete the old one from your test device's Summary tab in Xcode Organizer. Just to be safe, you might also want to delete the provisioning profile from the test device itself, which can be located in the Settings app at General ➤ Provisioning.

With your test device still connected to your Mac, drag the new `.mobileprovision` file from the desktop onto the Xcode icon in your Dock. Xcode will automatically install that provisioning profile and will list it in the Organizer on your test device's Summary tab.

Managing Multiple Provisioning Profiles

What if you don't want to replace your existing provisioning profile but would rather create and install multiple provisioning profiles for testing different apps? This is easy enough to do but requires several extra steps:

- In the Provisioning section's Development tab of the online iPhone Developer Program Portal, create a new provisioning profile. Assign the same certificate and device that you've already established on your Mac. Enter a unique profile name, and select the appropriate App ID.

- After generating this new provisioning profile, download the file to your desktop.

- Make sure your test device is still connected to your Mac and that its Summary tab is selected in Xcode Organizer. Then drag your new provisioning profile from the Desktop into Xcode Organizer's Provisioning file list.

- With your additional provisioning profile now successfully installed in both Xcode and on your connected device, proceed to open your Xcode project, and choose Device | Debug from the top-left drop-down menu.

- Before you can run your project, you'll also have to modify the Target's Info settings. In the left pane of the Xcode project window, select the project Target, and click the blue Info button in the toolbar menu. In the Target Info window that appears, choose the Build tab, and find the Any iPhone OS Device listing under Code Signing Identity. Select your desired provisioning profile from the Any iPhone OS Device pop-up menu (see Figure 7–28).

- Now you can go back to the main Xcode project window and click the Build and Run button to test your app on your connected device!

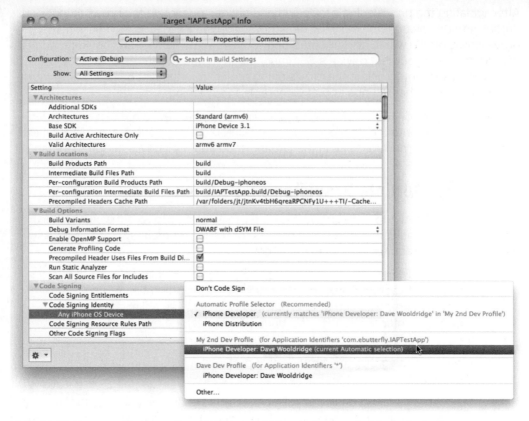

Figure 7–28. *You can assign a specific provisioning profile to your Xcode project for device testing.*

For this to work, the provisioning profile you assign to your Xcode project must reflect either an App ID bundle identifier that matches your project's identifier or a wildcard App ID that is compatible with any project. In Figure 7–28, my example IAPTestApp Xcode project's identifier matches my second provisioning profile's App ID bundle identifier so that provisioning profile is selectable in the target Info settings.

Beta Testing: Navigating the Complexities of Ad Hoc Distribution

Even more important than your own testing in the iPhone Simulator and on an actual device is having multiple people test your app. After performing extensive tests of your own, it's highly recommended that you round up a group of volunteers who are willing to beta-test your application before release in the App Store. Avoid recruiting your close friends and family since their feedback will not be as objective as you'd like. More often than not, they'll give only positive comments instead of the harsh truth you need at this juncture. By having a group of strangers play with the app for a dedicated amount of time, not only will they discover new bugs that you've never encountered, but they'll also stumble upon usability issues that may not be apparent to you, the creator.

Don't just get fellow developers to test your app. Also recruit a fresh set of nontechnical eyes to run the app through its paces. People who are not familiar with programming offer a very valuable, objective viewpoint, and they will most likely be a closer representation of your app's target audience. Just be prepared to ask a lot of questions to extract the pertinent bits. Often, nontechnical users will know when they don't like something, but they may not initially understand why it bothers them. It may take a great deal of patience on your part to get them to properly communicate their reasoning behind a reported issue. On the flip side, developers speak your language, so they can easily describe problems on a very technical level and may even suggest ways to fix them. But since developers are attuned to navigating through even the most nonintuitive interfaces, they may not recognize usability issues that would trouble a newbie. Your best bet is to gather a diverse group of beta testers that's comprised of developers, power users, and nontechnical, casual users.

Since quality beta testing requires a fair amount of dedicated time from a participant, you should offer some form of payment as an incentive for providing a satisfactory amount of feedback. It does not have to be cash. For developers on a shoestring budget, the reward can be a free copy of the app they're testing or a free license to another related product you sell. Just make sure to carefully outline exactly what a beta tester is required to complete to earn the free software. A good barter system will be a win-win situation for everyone involved. You get valuable feedback and the testers get free swag and software.

So, beyond your own pool of developer friends, where can you find additional beta testers? Imangi Studios (creators of Harbor Master) and other popular game developers recruit many of its beta testers from popular gaming sites, such as the Touch Arcade forums. It's not uncommon to see online postings from companies looking for beta-test volunteers. If you're looking for quite a few testers but need some help managing them, then it's definitely worthwhile to check out third-party services like iBetaTest.com, one of the largest iPhone and iPod touch beta tester groups (`http://ibetatest.com/`).

Now that you're familiar with the concept of certificates and provisioning profiles for testing on your own iPhone OS device (as discussed earlier in this chapter), many of the steps required to set up ad hoc distribution for multiple beta testers will seem quite similar with a few exceptions. But make no mistake, configuring your app for ad hoc distribution includes some very subtle, yet important, extra tasks that must be followed in order for the process to work smoothly. This is yet another stumbling block for many new iPhone developers, so let's take our time walking through each and every step.

Step 1: Acquire the Device IDs of Your Beta Testers

Remember when using the Development Provisioning Assistant to create your development provisioning profile, you needed to input your test device's 40-character UDID into the Device Identifier field? The same holds true when creating a distribution provisioning profile, so before you can do that, you'll need to add the UDID of every beta tester as a new device ID in the online iPhone Developer Program Portal.

The one major drawback to Apple's current system is that your iPhone Developer Program account is limited to only 100 devices per membership year. That may seem like a lot, but in reality, if you're developing several applications and each one has its own group of beta testers, it's actually pretty easy to max out your device ID allotment. You do have the option to delete old unused device IDs from the Portal, but they'll still count toward your device ID total within that membership year. So with that said, take care to use your device ID assignments wisely. Whenever possible, only register the device IDs of beta testers you know will provide quality feedback.

Unfortunately, you should know who all of your beta testers are before you generate your distribution provisioning profile, since every beta tester's device ID must be tied to that profile. If you need to insert additional device IDs later, then that will require you to generate a new distribution provisioning profile and then redistribute the updated profile and app. It's a very laborious, time-consuming process, so it would be best not to have to go through that more than once.

Most users won't know where to locate the UDID on their iPhone or iPod touch, so there's two easy ways to acquire that information from them:

- Have the user sync their device with iTunes. Select the device's Summary tab to display its properties. If the serial number is listed, then click it to toggle the listing to show the identifier (UDID). Now choose Copy from the Edit menu to copy that 40-character UDID to the clipboard, which can be pasted into an email and delivered to you, the developer.

- If that's too complicated, then simply have the user download Erica Sadun's free Ad Hoc Helper app or SPECTROsoftware's free BetaHelper app from the App Store. Once installed on the test device, running either of those apps generates an email containing the device's UDID, which the user can send to you.

After receiving all your beta testers' UDIDs, now it's time to log into the iPhone Dev Center with your iPhone Developer ID and password:

`http://developer.apple.com/iphone/`

Once logged in, click the iPhone Developer Program Portal link in the top-right corner of the page, and then within the main Program Portal page, select Devices in the left pane. Add a new device ID for each and every one of your beta testers, giving each device listing a unique name and 40-character UDID.

Many developers employ a naming scheme to help keep their devices list organized. For example, instead of just the beta tester's first and last name, you may also want to consider adding an abbreviated name of the app they will be testing or the kind of device, such as " Joe Smith iPhone 3G" or "Jane Walker iPod touch."

Step 2: Request a Distribution Certificate

After inputting all your beta testers as new device IDs online, leave your web browser window open since we'll be coming back to the Program Portal in a moment.

Launch the Keychain Access application, located on your Mac at the following location:

`/Applications/Utilities/Keychain Access`

First, open the Keychain Access Preferences, and select the Certificates tab. Set both the Online Certificate Status Protocol (OSCP) and Certificate Revocation List (CRL) to Off.

Then, in the Keychain Access menu, look for the Certificate Assistant menu item. From that submenu, select Request a Certificate from a Certificate Authority. In the Certificate Assistant window that appears, enter the email address and exact name listed for you in your iPhone Developer Program account (see Figure 7–29). Since this request is for your official distribution certificate, which will be used for both ad hoc distribution and App Store distribution, the email and name must match up identically to your iPhone Developer Program credentials. For example, my company "Electric Butterfly, Inc." is the official name in my account, so that's what I used for this form. The "Request is" option should be set to "Saved to disk."

There's one more thing that makes this request different from the one previously made during the development provisioning process. Make sure "Let me specify key pair information" is checked. When clicking the Continue button, that checked box will prompt the Certificate Assistant to ask you to assign the key size and algorithm, which should be set to 2048 bits and RSA, respectively.

Click the Continue button yet again, and Keychain Access will generate and save the new `CertificateSigningRequest.certSigningRequest` file to your hard drive.

Moving back to your web browser, navigate to the Certificates section of the Program Portal. Select the Distribution tab, and then click the Request Certificate button. Upload your new `CertificateSigningRequest.certSigningRequest` file. Once submitted, the certificate request must be approved by the account agent. If you're the only admin managing the iPhone Developer Program account, then you're probably the team agent, so click the Approve button (see Figure 7–30). Once approved, a download button will be displayed, allowing you to save the generated distribution certificate to your Mac desktop.

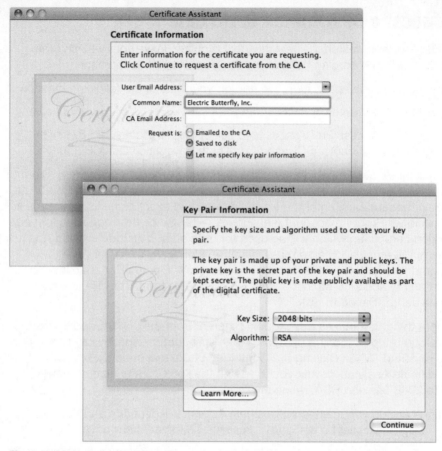

Figure 7–29. *Your distribution certificate request must include the same name and email address as assigned to your iPhone Developer Program account. You must specify the Key Size and Algorithm settings as 2048 bits and RSA, respectively.*

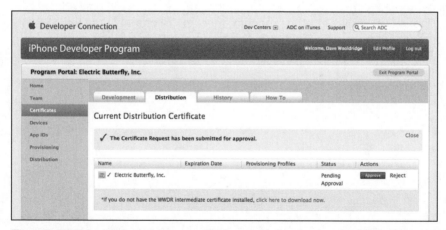

Figure 7–30. *Upload and approve your certificate request. Once approved, you'll be able to download and install the generated distribution certificate.*

Step 3: Install and Backup Your Distribution Certificate

Double-click the downloaded distribution_identity.cer file, which will launch the Keychain Access application (if it's not already open). Keychain Access will display a dialog window, asking if you'd like to add the certificate to a keychain. Make sure the dialog's keychain menu is set to login, and then click the Add button. In the Keys category of the main Keychain Access window, verify that your private and public keys are now paired together with your Distribution Certificate to ensure it is properly configured on your Mac. In this example, my "Electric Butterfly, Inc." key (which was created when I generated a certificate-signing request under the same name) is now paired with my imported iPhone distribution certificate (see Figure 7–31).

Figure 7–31. *Verify that your imported iPhone distribution certificate has been paired with the correct private key in Keychain Access.*

Do not install distribution certificates for multiple iPhone Developer Program accounts into the same Keychain. Doing so will cause problems in Xcode. If you're compiling and submitting iPhone apps for clients, then create a separate Mac OS X user account for each distribution certificate you need to install. You can do all your development within your primary Mac user account, but to compile for distribution, you should switch to the user account that has that client's distribution certificate installed.

IMPORTANT NOTE: Export your iPhone distribution private key for safekeeping. This step may very well be the most important one in this entire process, so please do not skip ahead. This private key is required by Xcode to sign compiled app binaries. Without the proper code signing, the application cannot be uploaded to the App Store, nor will it work with ad hoc testing. This private key cannot be reproduced, so it is imperative that you export it and save the file in a special place, just in case you need to restore it at a later date when switching to a new Mac or reinstalling the operating system.

To export your Distribution private key, select it from the Keys section of Keychain Access. In the Figure 7–31 example, my Distribution private key is selected. Then from the File menu, choose Export Items. Save the file in Personal Information Exchange (.p12) format, which requires you to assign a password.

If you ever need to reinstall this private key, simply double-click the exported .p12 file and enter your password. Keychain Access will take care of the rest.

Step 4: Generate and Install an Ad Hoc Distribution Provisioning Profile

Jumping back to the iPhone Developer Program Portal in your web browser, select the Distribution tab within the Provisioning section. Click the New Profile button. In the form that's presented, be sure to choose Ad Hoc as the distribution method. Select the appropriate App ID for your application, and verify that the distribution certificate is assigned correctly. Enter a profile name that reflects the nature of this provisioning profile. When testing multiple applications, developers have found that including the name of the app along with a reference to the testing stage (alpha or beta) in the Profile Name area helps keep the collection of profiles organized.

Last, but not least, you'll need to select all the beta tester device IDs that should be included in this provisioning profile (see Figure 7–32). If a specific beta tester's device ID is not embedded in the provisioning profile, then that person will not be able to install and run the app on their device. Any accidental omissions will force you to create and install a new, updated provisioning profile, so carefully review the selected devices before clicking the Submit button.

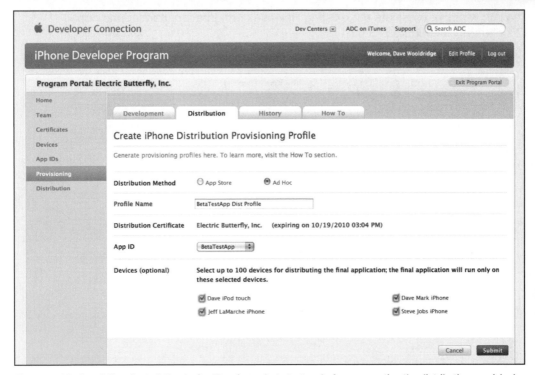

Figure 7–32. *Carefully select all the device IDs of your beta testers before generating the distribution provisioning profile.*

When your distribution provisioning profile has been generated, click the download button to save the .mobileprovision file to your hard drive. With your test device still connected to your Mac, drag the .mobileprovision file onto the Xcode icon in your Dock. Xcode will automatically install that provisioning profile in the proper location.

Save a copy of that distribution provisioning profile that you saved on your hard drive. You'll need to include that .mobileprovision file with the compiled app you deliver to your beta testers.

Step 5: Configure Your App for Ad Hoc Distribution

Now that you have the distribution certificate and provisioning profile in place, the last part of this equation is to configure your Xcode project for ad hoc distribution. Fire up your project in Xcode, but before you do anything, first ensure that you've added a 57 × 57 pixel icon.png file to the project. Beyond the fact that you may encounter distribution build errors without one, visual impressions count even in the beta testing stage, so including a beautiful app icon is important.

In the main Xcode project window, select the project name at the top of the Groups & Files pane, and then click the Info button in the toolbar. Within the Configurations tab of the Info window, duplicate the existing Release configuration, naming the copy Distribution (see Figure 7–33).

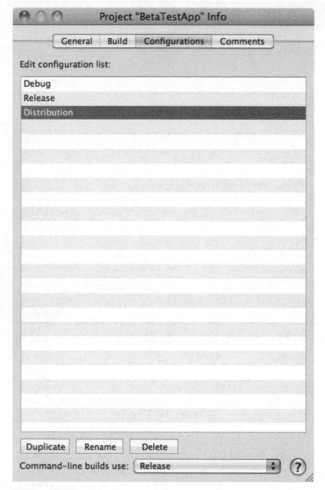

Figure 7–33. *Within the Xcode Project's Info window, duplicate the Release configuration and name it Distribution.*

Close the project's Info window. Now select the Target app within the Groups & Files pane, and click the toolbar's Info button again. In the new Target Info window that appears, navigate to the Build tab, and choose Distribution from the Configuration drop-down menu. Scroll down to Any iPhone OS Device field below the Code Signing Identity row, and assign it to your new distribution provisioning profile (see Figure 7–34). Even though your development provisioning profile may also be listed in the pop-up menu, it's critical that the distribution provisioning profile is selected since that is the only one that will work with ad hoc distribution.

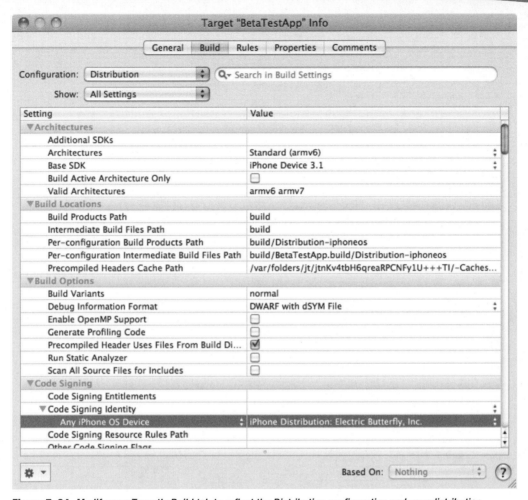

Figure 7–34. *Modify your Target's Build tab to reflect the Distribution configuration and your distribution provisioning profile.*

Switch over to the Properties tab, and enter your App ID's bundle identifier in the Identifier field. For the example in Figure 7–35, the App ID bundle identifier for BetaTestApp is com.ebutterfly.BetaTestApp and is also listed as such in my Xcode project's Info .plist file.

Target "BetaTestApp" Info

General   Build   Rules   Properties   Comments

Executable: ${EXECUTABLE_NAME}

Identifier: com.ebutterfly.BetaTestApp

Type: APPL   Creator: ????

Icon File: icon.png

Version: 1.0

Principal Class:

Main Nib File: MainWindow

Document Types:

Name	UTI	Extensions	MIME Types	OS Types

+ −   Open Info.plist as File   ?

Figure 7–35. *Input your App ID's Bundle Identifier in the Target Properties tab's Identifier field.*

With all of that completed, go back to the main Xcode project window. From the drop-down menu in the top left corner, select Distribution as the Active Configuration and Device as the Active SDK (see Figure 7–36).

Figure 7–36. *On the main Xcode project window, select Distribution as the Active Configuration and Device as the Active SDK in the top left dropdown menu.*

Step 6: Create the Entitlements File

Before you can compile your application for ad hoc distribution, you need to add a special code-signing Entitlements file to your project. From Xcode's File Menu, choose New File, and then select Entitlements from the iPhone OS ➤ Code Signing category in the window that appears (see Figure 7–37).

Figure 7–37. *Add a special code-signing Entitlements file to your Xcode project.*

Name the new file `Entitlements.plist`, and save it in the top level of your project. With it selected in Xcode, make sure the `get-task-allow` Boolean is set to False (unchecked), and then resave the file if needed (see Figure 7–38).

Figure 7–38. *The get-task-allow property must be unchecked in your Entitlements.plist file.*

Finally, re-open the Target Info window, and enter the `Entitlements.plist` filename in the Code Signing Entitlements field of the Build tab (see Figure 7–39).

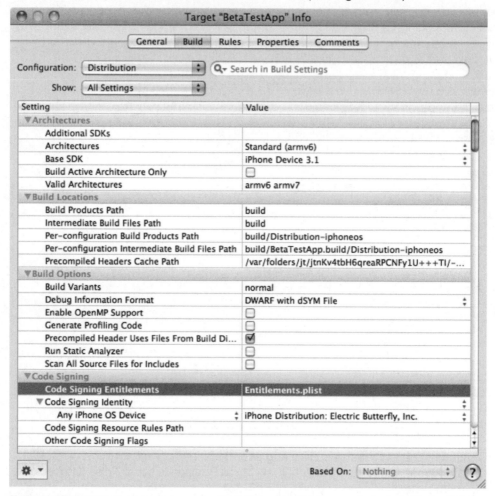

Figure 7–39. *In the Target Info window, enter the Entitlements.plist filename in the Code Signing Entitlements field of the Build tab.*

Step 7: Compile Your iPhone App

After making all the described changes to your project, save it and click Build (from either the toolbar or Build menu). If you've configured everything correctly, then your app should compile successfully. The first time you build the app with your distribution provisioning profile, a CodeSign dialog will appear, asking you to grant code-signing permission. Simply click the Always Allow button.

If build errors arise that are related to the project settings, retrace your steps to ensure that you've followed every single task outlined in these instructions, no matter how insignificant it may seem. Build errors can often be caused by the smallest mistakes, such as a misspelled bundle identifier or a mismarked checkbox. If problems persist and you've ruled out code bugs and faulty configuration settings, then clean out your project's build directory, re-open the project in Xcode, and try another build attempt.

Once you've successfully compiled your app, take a moment to revel in the accomplishment. Preparing your application for ad hoc distribution is a long and tedious process, so making it this far deserves a pat on the back.

To verify that your distribution provisioning profile was properly embedded in the binary and that the app was securely signed by your iPhone distribution certificate, access the Build Results window in Xcode's Build menu, and search for the presence of "embedded.mobileprovision" and "CodeSign" in the build log.

Step 8: Distribute Your App to the Beta Testers

Now you're ready to send the app to your beta testers! In the Groups & Files pane of the main Xcode project window, select the compiled `.app` file in the Products folder. From either the contextual menu (Control-click) or the Action menu, choose Reveal in Finder to locate the compiled binary on your Mac.

The recommended method for packaging up your application is to compress the `.app` file into a zip archive. This will prevent the app bundle from possible file corruption when delivered as an email attachment. If you create the zip archive using the Mac's built-in Compress feature, then the resulting zip archive may prove problematic for Windows users, since it may contain a Mac resource fork directory that's visible on Windows. Although those resource fork files won't hurt your `.app` file, the additional files may confuse Windows users. For best results, be sure to use a zip utility that ignores Mac resource forks, creating proper cross-platform zip archives.

Your beta testers will require two items: the app binary (in a zip archive) and your distribution provisioning profile (the `.mobileprovision` file).

For beta testers to install your app, their device should already be mounted in iTunes (connected via USB). They'll need to decompress the zip archive and then drag *both* the `.app` file and the `.mobileprovision` file into iTunes. Mac users can simply drag the two files onto the iTunes icon in the Dock, although Windows users should drag the files into the Library or Applications in the main iTunes window. If they perform a sync, your app and related provisioning profile should appear on their device, ready to run. Let the beta testing begin!

Knowledge Is Power: Tracking App Usage Through Analytics

Have you added an analytics system to your iPhone application? I'm really hoping your answer is "yes." If not, then before submitting your application to the App Store, and maybe even before performing beta testing, you should *seriously* consider using one of the many third-party iPhone analytics services available.

Any successful web developer understands the immense value of tracking web site traffic statistics with tools like Google Analytics or Site Meter. Mobile applications are no different. Which devices and OS versions are they currently running? How much time do they spend using your app? Which features are popular, and which ones are rarely accessed? The more you know about your users' demographics and their usage patterns will help you make better development and marketing decisions. Having this kind of knowledge at your fingertips will empower you with the ability to improve your app's user experience and sales potential.

I could talk for days about the importance of app analytics for iPhone developers, but instead, I thought you might like to hear from two of the experts themselves.

Answers from the Source

I had the opportunity to interview Pinch Media's cofounder and CEO, Greg Yardley, and TapMetrics' cofounder and CEO, Christopher Brown, who shed light on not only their own services but also the overall value of analytics for iPhone developers.

Let's start off with the most basic question: why should an iPhone developer care about analytics?

Chris Brown: Analytics are installed by developers for a number of reasons. They provide important information about your user demographic that may help you tailor the experience to their particular device or country or OS. For instance, if 85 percent of your users are iPod touch/OS 2.2.1 users, you're not going to stop support for it. With the iPod touch being marketed as a gaming device, there are a lot of developers who should consider that user base during development. Others use it to find the faults in their design by comparing the statistics of user engagement with a certain feature against other parts of the app. This works well for seeing how difficult a level in a game is or how many people use the photo section of your social networking app.

Greg Yardley: iPhone development is a business—potentially a very lucrative business—and every successful business needs to be constantly improving. Developers should be setting goals for their applications depending on their business model—for example, free-to-paid conversion rates, in-application purchases per user, or advertising performance. Even stand-alone paid applications should set goals for user retention over time, since many application sales result from user-to-user referrals. Whatever goals you set, analytics can help you measure your progress toward them and gauge the effect of the changes you make to your application over time.

Some critics seem to have the misconception that the "phone home" nature of app analytics borders on spyware. What do you say to educate them and dispel privacy concerns?

Greg Yardley: Pinch Media's analytics never collect anything personally identifiable, and the analytics themselves are always aggregated—application developers can discover that 50 percent of their users are between 18 and 24, that 25 percent of their users are in the United Kingdom, and that 5,100 different devices ran their application yesterday for an average of four minutes each, but not that 23-year-old Susie Q. of Roxbury Lane ran their application for 76 seconds at 3:49 pm. No one's privacy is violated by aggregated information from thousands of different devices. For developers who are particularly concerned, Pinch Media makes it easy to add a user opt-out to their application.

Chris Brown: The data that is collected is anonymous and aggregate. Developers can't see personal information about their users or statistics on any particular user. Additionally, any customer who licenses an application from the iTunes Store agrees that information can be collected to help improve the app. My response to anyone that presents the "spyware" argument is that websites collect much more information about a user than iPhone apps. Additionally, they should be more concerned about giving away their Social Security number on a form or their address to a store clerk. And I think most iPhone developers are savvy enough to know what the analytics are really doing.

What about tracking offline usage, such as an iPod touch temporarily away from a WiFi connection?

Greg Yardley: Most analytics software for iPhone applications uses caching, including Pinch Media's. If a connection is not available when an application is run, the data will stay resident in the local storage of the application and be sent the next time the application runs.

Chris Brown: A device that is offline logs the data and stores it until it reconnects to a network and can send it. The amount of data is very small and won't substantially affect memory on a device.

Greg, you wrote a great blog post about tracking iPhone app piracy through analytics.

Greg Yardley: Piracy affects most paid applications, and opinions on whether it's worth it to implement antipiracy measures vary widely—after all, the time spent implementing antipiracy code is time that could've been spent improving your application. However, understanding the extent of piracy is completely necessary when your application has costs that vary with usage—for instance, if you're operating a server to support a feature of your application. Here pirates can quickly cut into your profit margin and in sufficient numbers can cause your business to operate at a loss.

Pinch Media offers several unique features no other analytics provider does, including jail-broken phone and pirate application reporting, demographic reporting, and action timers for the measurement of individual feature usage. We also don't impose artificial limits on the number of actions tracked by our product. But I like to think the primary thing separating Pinch Media from its competitors is our customer service.

TapMetrics seems to focus not just on in-app analytics but also on tracking global app sales and crash reports.

Chris Brown: We designed TapMetrics to be a one-stop site for app publishers. Beyond the usage analytics, this means processing the sales reports Apple gives you to see how many actual sales you are making. Ultimately, I think the two are tied together and should be able to be viewed alongside each other. A number of other factors can affect sales and usage: iTunes Store reviews, blogger reviews, social media. We bring those together so developers can have access to qualitative feedback from the users. Many feature requests lie in the reviews, but it doesn't help if a developer only has access to one iTunes Store. Our approach is to use all these different inputs to help a developer improve the app and ultimately increase sales.

We created our Mac OS X app, TapMini, as a way to download the sales reports from iTunes Connect. If you forget to download them every seven days, or go away for a bit, you can't download them later. So our app automatically downloads them when they are available and saves them to your hard drive. If you have a TapMetrics account, it will also upload them to your account and you can view the stats.

Apple provides crash reports, but it only shows a snapshot in time. We provide statistics about the number of crashes over time, and those figures in comparison to the number of sessions will tell you if an app is really buggy or if it just has a glitch occasionally. It shows if a publisher should rush an update or if bug fixes can wait until the next development cycle.

For many developers, being discovered is the next challenge. Finding the right place to market your app, which can vary widely based on who it is made for, is the key. We plan to introduce some tools for developers to get the word out about their apps.

Evaluating the Players

Pinch Media and TapMetrics are not the only games in town. Several other worthy analytics options are available. Here's a snapshot of third-party services to consider:

- Flurry: http://www.flurry.com/

- Mobclix: http://www.mobclix.com/

- Pinch Media: http://www.pinchmedia.com/

- TapMetrics: http://www.tapmetrics.com/

- Google Analytics for Mobile Apps:
  http://code.google.com/p/gaformobileapps/

- Motally: http://www.motally.com/

- Medialytics: http://www.medialets.com/

- Mobilytics: http://www.mobilytics.net/

All these iPhone-related services provide easy-to-use SDKs with simple tutorials. Adding analytics support into your Xcode project often requires nothing more than importing a small library and writing only a few lines of code. Designed specifically for mobile applications, these analytics packages typically leave a tiny footprint and require very little memory.

Although all of these third-party services capture basic usage data, some of them offer unique features that may appeal to more specific needs, so it's definitely in your best interest to evaluate all of them before choosing one. For example, Mobclix includes an extensive analytics service within the same SDK as its mobile advertising platform, so if you're currently using Mobclix for in-app advertising, then you already have access to its comprehensive analytics. If your iPhone app utilizes a custom, back-end web service, then you might find it convenient to have all of your web server and mobile application analytics data tracked by one central provider such as Google Analytics. And just before this book went to press, Pinch Media and Flurry announced plans to merge, so it'll be interesting to see how their combined forces reshape the mobile analytics landscape in the near future.

Optime Software, the creators of Dots, Crack the Code, and several other popular iPhone apps, have found in-app analytics to be an indispensable resource for its business. Founder and CEO Jon Schlegel remarked, "We currently use Flurry for usage tracking and analytics. We've found their service to be quite good. Flurry helps us keep an eye on macro trends like the number of unique users using our applications and the average amount of time they spend using it each session. We've also instrumented our applications with a variety of custom events, which allow us to track which features users are using so that we can focus our development effort. It takes about five minutes to complete the initial integration of an analytics solution like Flurry, and it's definitely worth it."

Sitting Pretty

This was, by far, one of the more instruction-heavy chapters in the book. Since both provisioning and ad hoc distribution have proven to be such challenging topics for many new iPhone developers, I hope the thorough explanations helped clarify the process for anyone struggling with these two tasks.

It won't matter how brilliant your app idea is if it's poorly executed. I can't emphasize enough the importance of your app's overall user experience as one of the primary factors in its potential success. On-device testing and group-managed beta testing should be mandatory steps in every application's development cycle.

Chapter 8

Get the Party Started! Creating a Prerelease Buzz

Development completed? Check. Testing Completed? Check. Ready for the App Store? Almost.

After months of hard work to finish your application, I know you're eager to release it to the world, but don't jump the gun just yet. You still need to accomplish a few very important tasks first.

Before submitting your iPhone app to the App Store, it's time to start generating some prerelease buzz through a carefully crafted online presence. This chapter will explore the best ways to stir up some excitement and anticipation for your app by promoting it on your web site, blogs, and social networking sites, such as Twitter and Facebook.

The Final Countdown: Preparing for Lift-Off

I know what you're thinking…why can't you simply take care of building your app's web site and prerelease buzz while the app is being reviewed by Apple? Since the App Store submission process often takes weeks to approve or reject an application, that should give you enough time, right? Don't count on it. Even if your app review takes longer than the average 14-day turnaround, that's still not enough time to cultivate a large online following and effective web presence.

Just your luck, when you actually rely on Apple's app review team to take a long time, that will undoubtedly be the one rare occasion your app sails through to approval within only a few days, leaving you unprepared without your app's web site and social marketing plan in place.

Marketing Requires an Audience, So Invest the Time to Find Yours

Even though developing an attractive web site always takes longer than you think it will, if you were really pressed for time, you could probably construct a decent site in only a matter of days with a little web design expertise. But what does require a much longer gestation period is the time-consuming job of growing your online audience. This audience usually consists of not only influential bloggers and journalists but also your own Twitter followers, Facebook friends, Linked In connections, blog readers, and email newsletter subscribers. To a social media newbie, this may all seem a little overwhelming, but don't worry. Later in this chapter, I'll be explaining how to take advantage of these powerful tools and relationships in extensive detail.

If you don't yet have a Twitter account, a Facebook fan page, or a good rapport with high-profile bloggers and journalists, then it's never too soon to get the ball rolling. How early should you start? It usually takes a few months to acquire a decent number of followers on Twitter and Facebook, so you should dive into the social media sea at least three months before you plan on submitting your app to the App Store. Some developers start tweeting about their forthcoming iPhone app while it's still in development. The goal here is to amass your own social information network for easily distributing news about your iPhone applications, so the earlier, the better.

Just be careful not to give away too much information during this prerelease campaign. You don't want to prematurely expose your poker hand to your competitors (yes, they are watching). Also, if you inundate your online audience with a blitz of over-hyped marketing messages long before your app is released, you risk losing a large portion of your followers before launch day. No one likes an over-zealous, aggressive salesperson who clutters their Twitter streams and email inboxes with too much marketing noise. It's all about gently stoking the fire, building anticipation and interest. Simply whet their appetite, leaving them wanting for more…be a tease!

Crafting Your Elevator Pitch

To effectively explain the features and benefits of your forthcoming iPhone app in a quick and concise manner, you should write several versions of your application description. Each variation should be limited to a specific length for different uses. Don't mistake this exercise as writing a full-blown press release. You'll have plenty of time to do that later for your app's actual release. For now, think much shorter.

I typically write three versions at this stage: a one-sentence description, a single-paragraph description, and then one that's a few paragraphs long. Not only does that provide me with an app description size that's appropriate for almost any need, but it also helps me fine-tune my marketing message. When forced to explain your app in only a few sentences, it requires you to cut out "the fat," leaving only the key selling points that would appeal to potential customers.

The old term, *elevator pitch*, refers to the ability to sell someone on an idea in the short amount of time it takes to ride an elevator. This concept applies to almost every industry. When pitching a movie treatment, a screenwriter may have no more than a brief moment to convince a studio executive of its merits. A publisher may discard a book submission if it fails to captivate them in the first few pages. In a radio commercial, an advertiser may have only 15 seconds to grab the listener's attention. Promoting an iPhone app in the fast-paced, ADD-riddled world of technology is no different.

Often you have only a minute or two to describe your app to an influential journalist. Hot tech blogs are flooded with press releases and queries about new iPhone apps every day, so what makes yours so special? Whether it's read in an email or quickly explained at a conference, after only a few sentences, you want that journalist to instantly "get it" and want to write about it.

To start off, think of an effective caption that describes your app in only a few words. For our fictional Breadcrumbs app example, we've established the caption: Parked Car Locator. Sure, it's basic, but in only three words you already know what the app does. And with the 140-character limit imposed by Twitter, short is sweet. Now with the general functionality covered by the caption, the Breadcrumbs description can focus on the primary features and benefits, as well as the key differentiator that sets this app apart from its competition.

Remember our discussion of determining your application's differentiator in Chapter 2? Here's where it starts to pay dividends for you. Not only will it help attract customers, but it will also help capture the attention of the media in this prerelease stage. When describing your app to journalists and bloggers, you never want them to ask why. With the many existing parked-car locators in the App Store, why should anyone care about your app? If you've crafted your pitch successfully, you've already answered that question, describing how your app is the first parked-car locator to implement augmented reality using the iPhone's built-in camera. Augmented reality in mobile apps has been a recent hot topic in the news, so that's the hook. And the media loves a good hook.

Just make sure that any claim you make is true before including it in your pitch. You don't want to announce your app as the first augmented reality-based parked car locator if there's an existing iPhone app that's already staked that claim. As always, do your homework first with plenty of research online and in the App Store.

Ad-supported blogs and news sites need to continuously draw in readers to satisfy sponsors, and in order to do that, there's an insatiable demand to publish fascinating, topical stories. If your pitch fails to interest the press, you'll want to rethink your strategy. Later in this chapter, I'll touch upon when and how to communicate with the press to establish important relationships and jump-start some prerelease publicity.

Another advantage to crafting your elevator pitch now is that it will help you write a better App Store description when you're eventually ready to submit your iPhone app to Apple. I've seen so many long-winded App Store descriptions that scroll for days to explain a simple game concept. Those lengthy descriptions actually do the apps a disservice since no one will spend the time reading them. Like your elevator pitch, your

App Store description should be brief and concise with bulleted key features and a few highlighted testimonial quotes (and even award mentions). It should quickly tell the reader what your app does and why the user should buy it. Anything more is just noise that gets in the way of your sales pitch.

Additional Prerelease Marketing Materials

Beyond having short and long text descriptions of your app, you should also have the following items prepared for use in your marketing campaigns (both pre- and post-release). These items will come in handy for not only your own web site and social media efforts but also for the press if requested by journalists and bloggers.

Company Logo (High-Resolution)

No matter what kind of products you develop, you should always have a high-resolution version of your logo available, just in case the press request it. Many companies actually include a "press room" page on their web site or a download link to a press kit so that their company information and logo are always available 24/7. Technology is a global industry, so reporters and bloggers from various time zones may be interested in writing about your company or product. They may be on a tight deadline and can't wait until you read your email in the morning. Providing a press kit or company logo download on your web site will help make their job easier!

Although most media coverage may be online, don't discount the needs of print magazines and newspapers. Make sure your company logo is a scalable, vector-based image and saved as an EPS file. Or at the very least, it's a large 300 dots per inch (dpi) bitmap image saved as an uncompressed such as PNG or TIF. That will ensure maximum flexibility for any use.

If you're a publisher who partnered with a third-party development company to create the application, you'll also want to have their logos available. This would be a good time to check your contracts to see whether they also require their logos and/or names included in all press coverage about your iPhone app.

App Icon and Logo (High-Resolution)

Like your company logo, you should also have a high-resolution icon and logo for your iPhone app. Ideally, you took my advice in Chapter 4 to design your app icon at such a high-resolution for various press and marketing purposes. Scalable, vector-based EPS files are always nice, but large 300 dpi bitmap files (like PNG or TIF) can also work just as well. If saving as a PNG file, ensure that the background is transparent. If saving as a TIF or high-quality JPEG, use a default white background.

Since most of your media coverage and marketing efforts will focus primarily on your iPhone app and not necessarily your company itself, the 300 dpi print-ready versions of your app's icon and logo will prove much more important than any of your other logos. You'll also find high-resolution app branding graphics useful when designing other related elements, such as your app's web site and the background image for your Twitter profile. And in the off-chance that Apple were to ever ask you for an ultra-large app icon for inclusion in its print advertisements or WWDC wall banner, you'll have one ready at your fingertips (and you can thank me later).

Screenshots

Having a few good screenshots of your app in action may seem fairly obvious, but it's amazing just how many bad screenshots I've encountered in the App Store and online at various developer web sites and app review blogs. Don't just run your app and take some random screenshots of the main views. The screenshots you unveil to the world should be stellar examples of your app, showing off just how much fun or productive it is to use it. If your app is a notebook-style writing tool, don't show me an empty, unused list. And don't show me a few test notes with generic titles like "Note 1" or "Example 1." If I'm a writer looking for a tool like that, I want to see it being utilized to its full potential. Create some authentic-looking documents inside your app's notes list, like "My Novel Outline," "Research for Tech Article," and "Tuesday Meeting Notes." The app needs to look valuable and worthy of my purchase.

In the real estate market, there is a term called *staging*. Many prospective buyers have trouble envisioning what an empty house would look like with their own furniture in it, so they often walk away, believing it's not really a good fit for their needs. Staging is the act of filling that house with appealing furniture and interior design nuances to help those people better visualize the possibilities. "See, this is what your house could look like! Nice, right?" In recent years, staging has become a very popular and effective way to sell homes faster.

You need to take the same "staging" approach with your iPhone app screenshots. This does not mean faking your screenshots in any way. Just spend some time actively using the app yourself, setting up a scenario within your app that would make for a visually enticing screenshot. This "in-action" screen should help potential buyers immediately see the value in purchasing your app. Although this applies well to productivity and utility apps, it's also a good rule of thumb for all other types of apps, such as games. Don't just show any example of game play. If it's a first-person shooter, show the player in the middle of heavy combat, racking up a high score. Showcase the fun!

Optional Video Trailer

Producing an engaging video trailer for your app is something every iPhone developer should seriously consider. Some apps are hard to describe through static images alone. Providing an actual video walk-through of the app in a slick, movie-style video trailer, complete with title treatments, visual effects, and music is a very powerful marketing tool. Captivating video trailers on YouTube have helped hundreds of iPhone games become best-sellers.

Depending on the kind of app you've developed, producing a trailer now may be a tad premature for your prerelease marketing efforts. Since you haven't submitted your app to Apple's review team, you have no idea if you'll be required to change major portions of your app in order to receive an approval. With that in mind, you may not want a video trailer floating out there on YouTube and other video-sharing sites that is not representative of the actual final application that will be in the App Store.

However, if you do plan on creating a video trailer for your app, then I definitely recommend completing it before your app is released so that it can help boost awareness from the very beginning. Two compelling reasons to produce your own video trailer are control and convenience. Without a video trailer, some app review sites may choose to shoot their own video walk-through, which may not show your app in its best light. By providing them with your own video trailer, you retain control of how your app will be presented visually. And by alleviating the need for reviewers to shoot a video, you've just made it that much more convenient for them to write a review of your app.

Using a video camera to film the app running on your iPhone is a huge undertaking that often produces poor results if not done properly. There are many potential headaches when taking this approach such as capturing the right lighting, ensuring the iPhone screen is always in focus, and keeping your hands from shaking—all of which are much harder to achieve than you might think. Unless you're a professional filmmaker or have access to one, this is not the ideal path.

Most iPhone developers rely on screen capture software to record video of their apps running in the iPhone Simulator. This provides a high-quality solution that is easy to implement.

To enhance the look and capabilities of the iPhone Simulator, there are a few third-party software products that are worth exploring. If you need to emulate support for GPS location, multi-touch gestures, the accelerometer, and the compass, then check out Vimov's clever iSimulate iPhone app and SDK, which wirelessly sends those events to the iPhone Simulator from an iPhone or iPod touch device on the same WiFi network. To customize the look of the iPhone Simulator's home screen and improve the visibility of the cursor with a translucent white dot, atebits offers its SimFinger utility as donationware. And if you'd rather use an actual finger image as a cursor replacement in the iPhone Simulator, Wonder Warp Software's PhoneFinger is also available as donationware.

- iSimulate: http://www.vimov.com/isimulate/
- SimFinger: http://blog.atebits.com/2009/03/not-your-average-iphone-screencast/
- PhoneFinger: http://www.wonderwarp.com/phonefinger/

Once you have the iPhone Simulator optimized, you'll need to choose a screen-capture utility for recording the video. Some popular choices among iPhone developers are Telestream's ScreenFlow, Ambrosia Software's Snapz Pro X, shinywhitebox's free iShowU, and even Apple's QuickTime X Player in Mac OS X 10.6 Snow Leopard. The benefit of ScreenFlow is that it's a comprehensive screencasting solution that includes video- and audio-editing features, as well as on-screen annotation tools. The other mentioned utilities do a great job of recording the screen as digital video (such as an

MPEG or MOV file), but they require a third-party editor like Apple's iMovie or Final Cut Pro to turn the footage into a polished video trailer.

- ScreenFlow: http://www.telestream.net/screen-flow/
- Snapz Pro X: http://www.ambrosiasw.com/utilities/snapzprox/
- iShowU: http://www.shinywhitebox.com/home/home.html
- QuickTime X: http://www.apple.com/macosx/technology/#quicktimex

It's up to you to create a compelling video trailer, so take the time to not only plan the recorded walk-through of your app in the iPhone Simulator but also to script any audio voice-over tracks as well. Don't forget to add some music to set the tone, although make sure to use licensed or royalty-free music. Since the trailer may be played on various video sharing sites and app review sites, always incorporate your app's icon and logo within the video to help reinforce its brand identity. If producing a video trailer falls far outside your comfort zone, then don't think twice about hiring a professional editor. An amateurish video can definitely taint consumer perception of your app's quality, so when possible, don't cut corners on production value.

If an image is worth a thousand words, the impact of video can be even more effective in building anticipation for your forthcoming iPhone app or game. Just be careful not to release the video trailer too far in advance of your app's release. Since Apple's app review process can often take longer than expected, you don't want to over-hype your app prematurely only to lose that momentum long before the app becomes available in the App Store.

Dedicated Web Presence

Last, but not least, you need a web site or dedicated web page for your app. Providing a central online destination for both consumers and the press to access additional information is a powerful tool that every software developer should embrace. Let's take a look at what constitutes a good web site for promoting an iPhone app.

Your iPhone App Deserves a Well-Designed Web Site

You'll need a web site and online support up and running for your app before it becomes available in the App Store, so why not take advantage of its promotional power while drumming up excitement during the prerelease phase? Since your application is not in the App Store yet, your site should be the primary URL where all interested parties are directed. And even after your app is released, a custom-designed web site (when done right) can be a much more effective sales tool than the limited content found in App Store product pages.

Having a strong web presence should be mandatory for every iPhone developer, regardless of the fact that the App Store is a closed system. The App Store includes direct external links to a developer's web site and support site from an app's product page, so consumers interested in your application will most likely visit your web site before making a purchase decision, looking for additional information, a video trailer, or animated tutorial, and maybe even check to see whether you're a legitimate business that offers customer support. When people buy your app, in a small sense it's an investment in your company, so they like to know you're going to be around awhile.

Establishing a Web Site Infrastructure

You don't want any technical glitches or missed opportunities to ruin the heightened exposure that surrounds your app's actual release in the App Store. By getting all of your "ducks in a row" now, you'll be able to navigate through any web issues that may arise long before your app's debut.

If you don't yet have a web site, the first step is to set up an account with one of the many web hosting companies available. Just do a quick Google search for *web hosting*, and you'll see there's no shortage of companies. Most of them offer very affordable hosting packages, but the real trick is to find one that meets your specific needs. Ask fellow developers who they recommend for web hosting. It's important to inquire about their experiences with server uptime and customer service. Does their site ever go offline for long periods of time? Do they offer 24/7 support and resolve server issues quickly?

Format Wars: Blogs vs. Custom Sites

Once you have web hosting established, the next question that arises is, should I create a traditional web site or use a blog instead? Although a blog is certainly easier to update and maintain, there are distinct disadvantages to the blog format as your primary site in this particular situation. Every developer should have a blog to easily announce updates and news, but it should be connected to static web pages that you can custom design to promote your app without being limited to the blog post structure.

If you're comfortable building web sites, then I recommend creating a custom site for your app. If web development is not your thing and you'd rather use a blog (such as WordPress), then be sure it supports the addition of static pages so that your app can have its own set of permanent pages for screenshots, videos, support, and other typical marketing elements.

Most of the successful iPhone developers have dedicated web sites for their apps, and if they also have blogs, their respective sites link to them. One of the rare exceptions is Bolt Creative's Pocket God site, which consists entirely of a blog, hosted free on Blogger at `http://pocketgod.blogspot.com/`. In the unique case of Pocket God, the developers are updating the app with new episodes so frequently that the blog format works well for them, allowing them to easily post new information for fans every few days. For most apps and games, updates are much less frequent, so a blog should be secondary to a primary application web site.

Domain Name Benefits

In Chapter 2, I mentioned the importance of registering a domain name for your iPhone app web site, so you've already done that, right? I won't rehash that prior discussion, but I will reveal one more reason why a unique domain name for your app can be very valuable.

The length of your web site URL may not appear relevant in the desktop version of iTunes since the actual URL is hidden behind a text-based link. For example, the URL for the popular Bejeweled 2 by PopCap Games, Inc., is `http://www.popcap.com/promos/iphonebejeweled2/`, but on the Bejeweled 2 App Store page, all you see is an active link titled PopCap Games, Inc. Web Site (see Figure 8–1).

The problem lies in how Apple lists the same web site link in the iPhone version of the App Store, in which the actual URL is displayed. On such a narrow mobile screen, a long URL is truncated. And since the URL is merely listed and not provided as an active link, the user may have a difficult time guessing what the URL should be. This may seem like a minor nitpick, but according to AdMob, more than 90 percent of iPhone users browse and purchase from the App Store on their mobile devices, so the ability to easily access your web site in Mobile Safari is a lot more important than many developers realize.

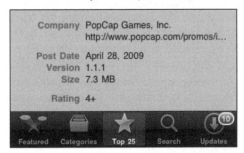

Figure 8–1. *Long URLs don't matter in the desktop version of iTunes (left), but truncation issues arise when displayed in the iPhone version of the App Store (right).*

If you already have an existing web site for your company or you currently maintain one central site for all your software products, most likely you've organized your site to assign each app to its own directory. For example, Streaming Color Studios has its iPhone games categorized this way. The Dapple game's web page is located at `http://www.streamingcolour.com/games/dapple/`. Although that URL seems simple enough, it would definitely display truncated in the iPhone version of the App Store. To avoid that issue, the developer Owen Goss registered the domain name `http://www.dapplegame.com/`. Not only does this shorter domain name fit nicely when displayed in the iPhone's App Store (see Figure 8–2), but it's also a much easier URL for users to remember when they see it listed in marketing materials and advertisements.

Company	Streaming Colour Studios
	http://www.dapplegame.com
Post Date	September 18, 2009
Version	1.3.1 (iPhone OS 3.0 Tested)
Size	9.3 MB
Rating	4+

Figure 8–2. *Instead of using the long company URL of its official Dapple web page, Streaming Color Studios opted to use a much shorter app-specific domain name.*

Don't worry, this does not require you to maintain two separate sites and hosting bills, one for your company and one for your app. Most domain registrars offer web forwarding services so that you can easily set your iPhone app URL to redirect to any directory or page within your existing company web site. That's what Streaming Color Studios does. The domain `http://www.dapplegame.com/` simply redirects to the actual Dapple web page at `http://www.streamingcolour.com/games/dapple/`.

Another option is to use subdomains. Instead of using nested directories within its site at `http://www.smule.com/`, Smule uses a unique subdomain for each of its products. For example, the Ocarina app's web page is located at `http://ocarina.smule.com/`, and the I Am T-Pain web page is at `http://iamtpain.smule.com/`. This enables Smule to display short, easy-to-remember app URLs while maintaining only one central company web site, all without the expense of registering additional domain names and web forwarding fees.

SEO Tactics

Search engine optimization (SEO) is a vast topic, one that has birthed a cottage industry of SEO consultants, seminars, and books. Suffice it to say that I don't have enough space here to cover everything on this subject, but let's tackle the basics you should know.

`<title>` Tag

This tag, which is located within the `<head>` tag in your HTML code, displays the title of the page in the web browser's top title bar. Although that may seem fairly useless, it is actually quite an important tag when it comes to search engines and social media. The `<title>` tag is the primary link headline displayed in search engine results. Let's use the fictional Breadcrumbs app as an example:

```
<title>Breadcrumbs - Parked Car Locator App for the iPhone</title>
```

Notice how I incorporated not only the app's name and caption but also that it's an iPhone app. It's important to use strategic keywords in your title to help improve your ranking in the search results. When that page is listed in Google's search engine results, users will immediately know what it is by the link headline alone.

If you take advantage of one of the many free sharing services available, such as AddThis, ShareThis, and TweetMeme, to enable site visitors to share that web page with their friends, their JavaScript code that you've pasted into your HTML simply grabs that page's `<title>` tag on the fly as part of the message that's being sent along with the page's URL. With this mind, it's always a good idea to keep the character count well below 140 characters to promote easy retweeting on Twitter.

description and keywords <meta> Tags

Although these meta tags are not required, they should never been seen as optional. Also located within the HTML `<head>` tag, they are important elements that most search engines analyze when crawling your site. Although the keywords `<meta>` tag helps provide context as to the subject of your web page, the `description` `<meta>` tag is often used as the text description that is displayed directly below the title link headline in search engine results. Here's an example of the syntax:

```
<meta name="description" content="Easily find your car in crowded parking lots with
Breadcrumbs, now available in the iPhone App Store">
<meta name="keywords" content="iPhone, App Store, GPS, car finder, car locator, mobile,
augmented reality, map, directions, lost car, parking">
```

For your description, to prevent it from displaying truncated in search engine results, try to limit its length to no more than 25 to 30 words. You can include a lot more than that in your keywords `<meta>` tag, but be very careful to only include keywords that are relevant to that web page. Don't try to "game" the system by including popular search terms that are unrelated in the hopes of getting broader exposure. That's so 1998. These days, modern search engines utilize extremely sophisticated algorithms that compare your meta keywords with the keywords in your main body text. Any discrepancies found will penalize your current search engine page ranking.

Not sure what keywords to use for optimal results? Try using Google's AdWords keyword tool at `https://adwords.google.com/select/KeywordToolExternal`. Although it was designed to help advertisers refine their ad campaign keywords, it can also help you determine the value of search keywords so that your keywords `<meta>` tag is loaded with the most optimized words. Another valuable resource is Google's Search-based Keyword Tool at `http://www.google.com/sktool/`.

Keyword-Rich Text

Like the keywords `<meta>` tag, make sure the visible text within the main body of your web page contains optimized keywords to help improve your search engine rankings. If your app currently has several competitors, check out their web sites to see what keywords they're using and how they rank in the search engines. Your goal is to place just as high, if not better than them, in the search engine results for similar keywords.

For all web images, make sure they include the `alt` text parameter so that search engines can still read their intended description. It's also a good idea to appropriately name your image files. For example, an SEO-optimized buy button might look like this:

```
<img src="images/buy.jpg" alt="Buy Now at the App Store" width="200" height="60"
border="0">
```

Try to avoid using Adobe Flash on your web site whenever possible. Although it's a great web technology, it poses two serious problems for iPhone app developers. First, the iPhone OS' native browser, Mobile Safari, does not currently support Flash; it renders Flash objects as broken when viewed on an iPhone or iPod touch. And second, search engines have trouble properly searching Flash-based SWF files, so embedded text keywords may not get indexed. If you want to use the popular Flash Video format on your site, I'll talk more about how to best work with Flash in the section "Why Site Compatibility with Mobile Safari Is So Important."

Keyword-Friendly URLs

Following the theme of strategically named image files, if your app-specific domain name redirects to your existing company web site, you should also try to use strategically named directories and files in your URLs. For example, using a web site naming structure like this:

```
http://www.mywebsite.com/iphone/breadcrumbs/
```

will help your site rank much higher in search results than a nondescript URL like this:

```
http://www.mywebsite.com/sw/0901/page01.html
```

Maintaining Valid Links

Make sure to place default index pages within all subdirectories to prevent both users and search engine spiders from encountering 404 errors or "forbidden directory" warnings. Broken URLs can dramatically affect how your site is indexed in the major search engines.

XML Sitemap

This is a standard introduced by Google several years ago that enables you to submit an XML Sitemap file to Google, Yahoo!, and Microsoft Bing. The XML listing includes entries for all of the web page URLs in your site that you want indexed by these search engines. Within the XML, you can specify the priority (importance) of each page, the last date it was modified, and the frequency rate of changes. This sitemap helps Google, Yahoo!, and Bing discover pages on your web site that their search bots may not have found during their crawling process. And if you add or delete pages from your site, simply update the XML Sitemap file and resubmit it to Google and others for indexing.

To get started, visit Google's free Webmaster Tools site to learn how to create and submit your own XML Sitemap file: `http://www.google.com/webmasters/tools/`. Google even provides helpful reports on any crawling issues found, as well as identifies any `<meta>` tag issues.

Never seen an XML Sitemap before? Here's a short example:

```
<?xml version="1.0" encoding="UTF-8"?><urlset
xmlns="http://www.sitemaps.org/schemas/sitemap/0.9">
    <url><loc>http://www.ebutterfly.com/</loc><lastmod>2009-9-
30</lastmod><changefreq>weekly</changefreq><priority>1.0</priority></url>
    <url><loc>http://www.ebutterfly.com/books/devsketchbook/</loc><lastmod>2009-9-
30</lastmod><changefreq>monthly</changefreq><priority>0.9</priority></url>
    <url><loc>http://www.ebutterfly.com/books/iphonebusiness/</loc><lastmod>2009-9-
30</lastmod><changefreq>monthly</changefreq><priority>0.9</priority></url>
    <url><loc>http://www.ebutterfly.com/iphoneinsights/</loc><lastmod>2009-9-
30</lastmod><changefreq>weekly</changefreq><priority>0.9</priority></url>
    <url><loc>http://www.ebutterfly.com/helplogic/</loc><lastmod>2009-4-
6</lastmod><changefreq>monthly</changefreq><priority>0.9</priority></url>
    <url><loc>http://www.ebutterfly.com/company/</loc><lastmod>2009-9-
30</lastmod><changefreq>monthly</changefreq><priority>0.6</priority></url>
</urlset>
```

See how simple the syntax is? Within the main parent `urlset` tag, each child `<url>` tag contains the information for a different, unique URL in my web site (although keep in mind that my real XML Sitemap file is actually much larger).

If you're not comfortable crafting your own XML code within a text editor, you may prefer to use a sitemap automation tool. Here are a few:

- XML Sitemap (Web): `http://xmlsitemap.com/`

- XML-Sitemaps.com (Web): `http://www.xml-sitemaps.com/`

- RAGE Sitemap Automator (Mac OS X): `http://www.ragesw.com/products/googlesitemap.html`

After creating your Sitemap, submit it to the major search engines that support this standard:

- Google: `http://www.google.com/webmasters/tools/`

- Yahoo!: `http://siteexplorer.search.yahoo.com/submit`

- Bing: `http://www.bing.com/webmaster/`

If you're looking to learn more about search engine optimization, check out the free SEO Starter Guide from Google: `http://googlewebmastercentral.blogspot.com/2008/11/googles-seo-starter-guide.html`.

Tracking Web Site Traffic

In Chapter 7, I expressed how important it is to track iPhone app usage via third-party app analytics, such as Flurry. And it is equally beneficial to do the same with your web site. Tracking site traffic can shed light on where visitors are originating from, the browser versions they're using, when and how many people are viewing your site, which web pages and links are the most popular, and much more.

By monitoring when peak traffic hours occur for your site, combined with which days of the week generate the most downloads for your app in the App Store, you can best determine the optimal times to announce limited sale offers and related app news. On the flip side, site traffic statistics can also help pinpoint design weaknesses by listing which pages are responsible for the most visitor exits (leaving your site).

Since English is a globally accepted language, your English-based app can achieve success in Apple's various regional App Stores. But if you're interested in producing localized versions of your app to increase sales in countries outside of your own, which languages should you target first? Good web site traffic statistics can tell you which countries your visitors are from. Beyond the United States, are a large percentage of your site visitors coming from Italy, France, or Germany? Or maybe Japan and China? The combination of your international App Store downloads/sales reports and web site traffic statistics can help you determine which countries to focus your translation efforts on.

Most web hosting companies offer traffic tracking as part of their package, but if your web host does not include traffic statistics (or if their bundled solution lacks robust features), then several third-party analytics services are available, and many of them are either free or very low cost. Here are a few of the popular offerings:

- Google Analytics: http://www.google.com/analytics/

- SiteMeter: http://www.sitemeter.com/

- Mint: http://haveamint.com/

If you're already using Google Analytics for Mobile Apps within your iPhone application, then utilizing the free Google Analytics for your web site should be a no-brainer! Being able to monitor both your web site and iPhone app usage statistics within the same web-based dashboard is a highly convenient and powerful solution.

Anatomy of an iPhone App Web Site

Now you're ready to design your application's web page, but what elements should you include? Here's a list of common ingredients to consider:

- Consistent brand identity, displaying your app icon and name/logo

- Caption and/or "quick pitch" description

- Apple's App Store identity badge

- Buy button

- Pricing

- Screenshots and video

- Additional details such as features, benefits, requirements, testimonials, and reviews

- Sharing URL with others via social media, such as Twitter, Facebook, and Digg

- Building a community with a blog, RSS, and email newsletter

- Customer support and contact information

- Company identity

- Links to cross-promote your other products

- Download extras (optional)

If you've evaluated the web sites for your favorite iPhone apps and games, you've seen many (if not all) of these items already. Although that may seem like a long list of elements, the really effective sites present the information in a very clean, simple layout that is easy for visitors to read. Figure 8–3 provides a conceptual mock-up of how all these components can be integrated into a single web page. After evaluating several leading iPhone app web sites, this example outline will appear quite familiar.

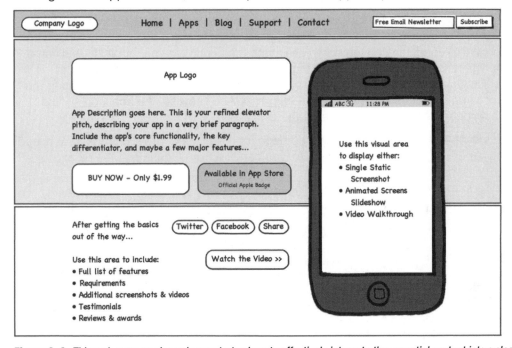

Figure 8–3. *This web page mock-up demonstrates how to effectively integrate the essential content into a clean, easy-to-read layout (designed with Balsamiq Mockups,* `http://www.balsamiq.com/products/mockups/`*)*

Unlike printed pages, a web page can scroll vertically, containing a lot more content. The trick is to avoid overwhelming the user with too much information all at once. This is achieved by placing only the most important "quick pitch" data front and center at the top of the screen. For those users interested in reading more, they can scroll down the page for additional details. This enables you to space out the content so that the design can "breathe" on the page.

If the top portion of your page is overcrowded, it will appear cluttered, making it difficult to read. By keeping the design simple, the page is much easier for the human eye to quickly scan and process. A product-based web site is little more than an online marketing brochure, so it must convey its message quickly and efficiently. The Web is a very visual medium, so don't weigh down the page with too much text. Of course, you want to include enough rich, related keywords to successfully describe the app to both consumers and search engines, but it's very important to draw in visitors with appealing imagery.

Let's take a closer look at each of these listed elements.

App Brand Identity

The bare-bones mock-up shown in Figure 8–3 could serve as the layout for almost any iPhone app or game. What will make it unique to your application will be the visuals you incorporate. The web imagery should directly reflect your application's icon and interface theme. Brand consistency is key.

Always, always, always display your app's icon! The icon visually represents your product in the App Store, so you need to reinforce that same imagery on your web site. The goal is to condition consumers to associate that icon with your application's name and functionality. Whenever they see that icon in the App Store, you want them to immediately recognize it. It's for this very reason that I recommended incorporating the app icon into the overall logo design in Chapter 4. And likewise, the app icon should also be a prominent part of your web page design.

As an example, I've designed a fake web page for the fictional Breadcrumbs app, based on the generic layout from Figure 8–3. As you can see from Figure 8–4, the page structure is identical to the mock-up outline, but what sets it apart is the unique branding in the underlying design theme.

Figure 8–4. *Based on the mock-up shown in Figure 8–3, this Breadcrumbs web page example reinforces the app's brand identity.*

Notice how the app's icon is an integrated part of the Breadcrumbs logo in Figure 8–4. The branding is further supported by using the icon's blue sky horizon as the web page's background image.

The nice thing about the Internet is that its accessibility truly equalizes the playing field for developers. You may not have the massive marketing budgets of the big publishers, but if you're skilled at using Adobe Photoshop and a web page editor, you can make your site look just as impressive.

Don't worry if your graphics experience is limited. You can design an amazing site with only a few key visuals. Just look at the web page for Shiny Development's Balloons! app at `http://balloonsapp.com/` (see Figure 8–5). Although the page design is fairly minimal with black text on a solid white background, the app's primary art of floating balloons is very bold and eye-catching. It's the only imagery on the page, yet the simplicity of it strongly reinforces the established brand identity and nonverbally communicates ease of use, both of which are vital to the success of a social media app.

Figure 8–5. *You don't have to be a Photoshop guru to build an attractive web site. With only one central image in the background, the simplicity of Shiny Development's web site for its Balloons! app is eye-catching and effective.*

Even though the Balloons! app icon is not displayed next to the logo, it is integrated into the Get Balloons! buy button. If you click the button, that red balloon is the same one you'll see in the icon listed in the App Store.

As with the design of your app's interface, the look and feel of the corresponding web site should be just as appealing. If you hired a professional designer to create your app's icon and logo, then you should consider contracting that same person to also generate visuals for your web site and all other promotional needs so that your branding remains consistent across all of your marketing materials.

The Quick Pitch: What Is It and Why Should I Care?

Remember when I talked about crafting your elevator pitch earlier in this chapter? You'll want to place this at the top of your web page, typically below your app name. This will quickly inform visitors what your app does and how it can benefit them. Your app may be packed with tons of great features, but don't overwhelm the reader by listing it all at once. That will only make the page feel cluttered and top-heavy.

In Figure 8–5, only a short caption and a few sentences are displayed within the main Balloons! visual. Within seconds, you have a broad grasp of what this app does and the potential fun you could have using it. That's the "hook" that draws you in, motivating you to keep reading. To learn more, simply scroll down the page for a comprehensive list of features.

App Store Identity Badge

The most common element you'll see on most iPhone app-related web sites is the official App Store identity badge that shows a little iPhone icon with the words "Available on the App Store." To obtain this graphic, you'll need to log into the iPhone Dev Center at `http://developer.apple.com/iphone/` and then navigate your way to the iPhone Developer Program Portal. Within the Portal site, click Distribution in the left menu, and then select the App Store tab (see Figure 8–6). You'll see the identity badge displayed under the "Available on the iPhone App Store logo license program" heading. Click the "To become an authorized licensee" link for complete instructions.

In a nutshell, you'll need to download and sign the iPhone App Store Artwork License Agreement form and mail it back to Apple. Although the identity badge and iPhone graphics download link is already provided there, before using any of those images, be sure to download and read the "App Store Identity Guidelines for Developers" PDF. This document explains the rules for how to properly use the App Store identity badge and the authorized iPhone image. Since Apple reserves the right to revoke permission to use the supplied graphics if you fail to follow the guidelines, it's in your best interest to thoroughly read that document so you understand how to remain compliant.

The graphics download includes both web and print resolutions of the badge, as well as several different versions of iPhone and iPod touch images in layered Photoshop PSD files. This gives you the flexibility to utilize these graphics within all your marketing materials.

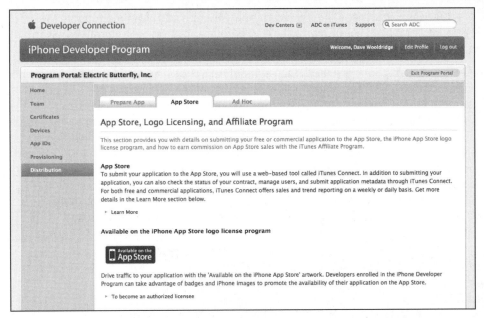

Figure 8–6. *Sign up for Apple's iPhone App Store logo license program in the iPhone Developer Program Portal site.*

Buy Button

Although the App Store identity badge is typically linked from your web site to your app's product page in the App Store, don't rely on it as your sole buy button. Some people may see it only as an official badge, not understanding that it actually links to the App Store. Since the primary goal of your web site is to sell more units of your app, you should also include a dedicated buy button to help drive traffic to the App Store.

In our fictional Breadcrumbs web page example (see Figure 8–4), the large Buy Now button uses the same high-contrast red color as the icon's red car so that it really "pops" as a prominent, eye-catching element. And any time you're linking to the App Store, don't forget to use an iTunes affiliate link so that you can earn extra revenue from all the sales you're sending Apple's way. You did join the free iTunes Affiliate Program after reading Chapter 6, right?

Pricing

Including the app's price on your web site seems to be a highly debated topic among iPhone developers. Some believe that stating the price may deter people from clicking through to the App Store, while others believe the price can actually help drive sales. Although there are valid points to both arguments, I think stating the price in all your marketing materials, including your site, will help sales more than it could possibly hurt. If you're constantly experimenting with different price points to improve your app's position in the App Store's top sales charts, then I can understand your reluctance to display the fluctuating price on your web site. But this is a venture you're attempting to grow into a successful business, so it's worth every minute of extra time it takes to frequently update pricing on your web site. And if your app is on sale, surely you want the world to know about it.

If you're selling your app in more than one regional App Store, try to be conscientious of the currency in those countries. Many app-related web sites display the price in both U.S. dollars and in euros to accommodate the majority of their target audience. FutureTap took this idea one step further. Since its Where To? app is available in several languages, it has localized its web site with pricing and text descriptions translated for every major region their app supports. If you visit `http://www.futuretap.com/home/whereto-en/`, you'll see tabs along the left side of the screen, each one representing a different country flag. Click a flag icon to display the translated product page and pricing for that country. In Figure 8–7, the English product page displays the price in U.S. dollars, and the French product page shows the equivalent price in euros.

Figure 8–7. *FutureTap's web site for its WhereTo? app displays the price in the appropriate currency for each localized product page, such as U.S. dollars for the English description and euros for the French description.*

For best results, display your app's price either within the buy button (as shown in the Figure 8–4 Breadcrumbs example) or near the iPhone image on your web page (like FutureTap does in Figure 8–7). Do not include the price on or within the App Store identity badge because Apple's guidelines specifically prohibit modifying that logo.

Screenshots and Video

Besides designing the web page to emulate your app's brand identity, the other crucial visuals are screenshots and video of your app in action. To make a purchase decision, people need to see what your application looks like and how it works. Outside of a free trial version of the software, the best way to do that is through screenshots and video simulations.

Although most developers display their app's primary screenshot within a large iPhone image on their web pages, the more effective sites actually embed video or an animated slide show of screenshots within the iPhone image. This is very engaging and gives the user a much more immersive representation of your app's functionality or game play.

The iPhone displayed on the Traveling Classics web site at `http://www.travelingclassics.com/` links to a QuickTime video for AudioBookShelf (see Figure 8–8). It has also included a few screenshots. Since it's an audio-based application, the addition of a pair of earbuds to the displayed iPhone is a nice touch.

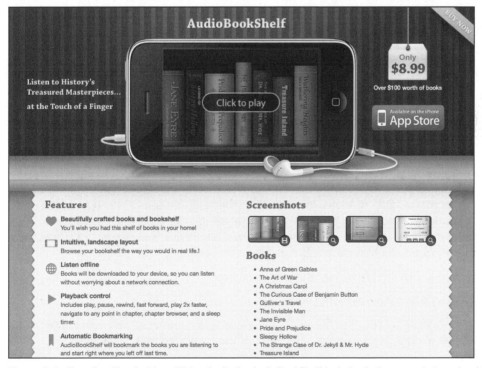

Figure 8–8. *Traveling Classics' beautiful web site for AudioBookShelf includes both screenshots and a video walk-through of the app.*

While the Click to Play button within the AudioBookShelf iPhone image links to a much larger video screen, Tapbots embedded the QuickTime video simulation of Convertbot within the iPhone image at `http://tapbots.com/convertbot/`. The Balloons app does the same thing on its web page (see Figure 8–5). This eye-catching technique creates the illusion that the iPhone graphic is running the app live within your web browser. To maintain that illusion, set the HTML QuickTime code's `controller` parameter to `false` to ensure that the playback controller bar is invisible. You should also set the `bgcolor` parameter to #000000 (black) to avoid any unsightly borders around the video frame. Here's an HTML QuickTime object code example:

```
<object width="200" height="300" classid="clsid:02BF25D5-8C17-4B23-BC80-D3488ABDDC6B"
codebase="http://www.apple.com/qtactivex/qtplugin.cab">
<param name="src" value="http://www.breadcrumbsapp.com/appdemo.mov" />
<param name="controller" value="false" />
<param name="autoplay" value="true" />
<param name="loop" value="true" />
<param name="bgcolor" value="#000000" />
<param name="pluginspage" value="http://www.apple.com/quicktime/download/" />
<embed src="http://www.breadcrumbsapp.com/appdemo.mov" width="200" height="300"
controller="false" autoplay="true" loop="true" bgcolor="#000000"
pluginspage="http://www.apple.com/quicktime/download/"></embed>
</object>
```

This example also sets the `autoplay` and `loop` parameters to `true` so that the video beings playing immediately when the web page loads and continues to loop endlessly. To learn about the dozens of other QuickTime parameters for customizing video playback, check out Apple's official list of supported tag attributes at `http://www.apple.com/quicktime/tutorials/embed2.html`.

Interested bloggers and journalists may pull content from your site when writing a review, so it's always a good idea to include both video and screenshots whenever possible. If you have not yet finished producing your app's video trailer, then at the very least include some quality screenshots.

Another effective technique is to use JavaScript code to run through a slide show of static screenshots within the iPhone frame. FutureTap does this on its Where To? web site (see Figure 8–7). Every few seconds, a different screenshot fades into view within the displayed iPhone. If you want to go back to a particular screen, it has even included iPhone-centric page "dot" markers for manually stepping to a specific image. Not a JavaScript guru? No problem. Plenty of great image slide show scripts are available online, many of which are free. Just search the Web for *JavaScript image slideshow*, or check out the nice collection of JavaScript solutions here:

- Dynamic Drive: `http://www.dynamicdrive.com/`

- Hot Scripts: `http://www.hotscripts.com/`

Some of the slide show scripts offer such smooth transition effects between images that the slide show almost plays like a movie, without the overhead of a large video download.

If you have produced a video trailer for your app, you'll want to upload it to the major video-sharing sites like YouTube to benefit from the additional exposure of their massive audiences and social media sharing features. But don't be a lazy web designer and simply link directly to your video page on YouTube or Vimeo. It may be tempting to do this in the hopes of increasing your video's view count (and popularity ranking), but that would pull visitors away from your site. Your goal should be to keep users engaged within your site so that your buy button is always only a click away. You can achieve this by simply embedding the video in your own web page. Even if your video trailer plays more like a commercial than pure simulation and would not make sense framed within a large iPhone graphic, it still should be viewable within your own site. For example, in the top-right corner of your YouTube video page, there is an Embed field that contains a short snippet of code. Copy and paste that into one of your own web pages, and you'll see something that looks similar to this:

```
<object width="425" height="344">
<param name="movie" value="http://www.youtube.com/v/hw4yU74SMJI&hl=en&fs=1&" />
<param name="allowFullScreen" value="true" />
<param name="allowscriptaccess" value="always" />
<embed src="http://www.youtube.com/v/hw4yU74SMJI&hl=en&fs=1&" type="application/x-
shockwave-flash" allowscriptaccess="always" allowfullscreen="true" width="425"
height="344"></embed>
</object>
```

This HTML code embeds the assigned Flash movie object within your web page. This allows you to keep visitors on your web site longer, and it also gives you control over the displayed content. As you may know, Flash is not supported on the iPhone or iPod touch, so if a consumer views your web site in Mobile Safari, Flash content will not load, displaying a nasty broken plug-in symbol instead. Since the view count, popularity, and sharing features of YouTube may be important to maintain for your Mac and Windows site visitors, you can use JavaScript, PHP, or other web scripting languages to first check the user's browser agent. If they are viewing your video page from a desktop computer, your code can show them the embedded YouTube Flash video, and if they're accessing the page from their iPhone or iPod touch, your code can load an embedded QuickTime video instead. But you'll only be able to properly control this if you're playing the video from within your own web site. Check out the section "Why Site Compatibility with Mobile Safari Is So Important" later in this chapter for complete details and code examples.

Additional Details

The lower half of the page is an ideal area to include additional text such as a comprehensive list of features, benefits, requirements, and even quotes from testimonials and reviews. Most people lead very busy lives with increasingly short attention spans, so don't expect anyone to take the time to read long, dense paragraphs of information. Organize the data into easy-to-read bullet points, such as demonstrated in Figure 8–8 (AudioBookShelf) and some of the other web site examples I've shown you.

Social Media

I'll be talking at length about growing your social media presence later in this chapter, but one major way to draw new followers to your social network identities is to heavily promote them on your web site. Looking at the blogs and web sites for most iPhone developers, you'll notice that a vast majority of them display button links to their Twitter and Facebook pages in the hopes you'll follow them there.

Social media is obviously an important factor in Guided Ways Technologies' marketing strategy for its 2Do app since the Twitter and Facebook buttons at http://www.2doapp.com/ (see Figure 8–9) are actually bigger than the buy button! The icons for both of those social media titans are very well known, so you could opt to display only their linked icons if you prefer a more subtle, space-saving approach, as shown in my fictional Breadcrumbs web page (Figure 8–4).

Figure 8–9. *Based on the prominent placement and size of the Facebook and Twitter web buttons, social media appears to be an important online marketing factor for Guided Ways Technologies' elegantly designed 2Do app.*

Another icon button you may have noticed in Figure 8–4 (Breadcrumbs) is the little green sharing emblem. You don't just want people to follow you, but you also want them to share your web site URL with their friends and family. Word-of-mouth is one of the most powerful marketing forces that social media provides. People trust their friends, so recommendations that come to them via word-of-mouth are a much more powerful sales tool than any advertising or self-promotion you do yourself.

In previous chapters, I've shown you how to build support for Twitter, Facebook, and Tell A Friend functionality within your iPhone app. Your web site should also offer those same features, but thanks to some wonderful third-party services, you won't have to write a single line of code! These services provide custom "share" widgets that can be easily installed on your web pages by copying and pasting their supplied code snippet, which typically consists of only a few lines of JavaScript. Here are a few of these services, which you may recognize from their use on millions of web sites:

- AddThis: http://www.addthis.com/

- ShareThis: http://sharethis.com/

- AddToAny: http://www.addtoany.com/

The beauty of these share buttons is that they give your site visitors the ability to bookmark or share a specific URL with dozens of popular social media sites, such as Twitter, Facebook, Digg, Delicious, StumbleUpon, LinkedIn, MySpace, Slashdot, Reddit, Technorati, and the list goes on…. You can even "tell a friend" via email. Their share buttons are designed small and compact for easy placement anywhere on your web pages. Simply mouse over the button, and a drop-down menu appears with sharing options (see Figure 8–10).

Figure 8–10. *The default button offerings from ShareThis.com (Left) and AddThis.com (Right) provide comprehensive drop-down menus for convenient URL sharing.*

Don't like their default button choices? No problem. Some of these sharing services even let you use your own custom button image. This enables you to better integrate their service into your site's existing design, such as in Figure 8–4 (Breadcrumbs) where the share icon was modified to match the same dimensions as the accompanying Twitter and Facebook icons for visual consistency.

You can easily grab the needed code from these sharing services and be on your way, but if you want to track the performance of your share buttons, I recommend signing up for a free account with them. Like web site analytics, you'll be able to log into your AddThis or ShareThis account to monitor which of your web pages are being bookmarked and shared the most and what social media sites they are sharing with. This is very valuable information to have. Knowing which social networking sites your visitors use regularly can help you determine where to focus your own online marketing efforts.

If the majority of your web audience is using a specific social media site, such as Facebook, then you may be interested in targeting your share button to that site, rather than the "everything but the kitchen sink" approach of third-party share services like AddThis.com. If you read a lot of blogs, then you've undoubtedly seen the popular TweetMeme, Facebook Share, and Digg buttons (see Figure 8–11).

Figure 8–11. *Targeted sharing buttons provided by TweetMeme, Facebook Share, and Digg dramatically increase URL sharing, but visible counters can also reveal unpopular web pages.*

These high-profile buttons reduce the sharing task down to a single targeted click, which results in a greater number of URLs shared. The easier you make sharing for your site visitors, the more they'll do it. And if your web page is popular and racks up a nice large number in the share counter, as shown in Figure 8–11's TweetMeme button (on the far left), then that makes your content look that much more attractive to new visitors, who in turn are eager to share the page as well. But on the flip side is the inevitable disadvantage that visible counter will have for new or rarely visited sites. Clocking in at an excruciatingly low number of retweets is frustrating enough, but to have it advertised to everyone who visits your web page is just downright embarrassing. And no one likes to hang around the unpopular kids.

If your site is still struggling to increase traffic, then you may want to use all-in-one sharing aggregators like ShareThis.com until you're able to drum up higher numbers. But if your web site already enjoys a healthy stream of traffic, then these high-impact, targeted share buttons are worthy additions. Here are a few, all of which are easily installed on your web page or blog by copying and pasting a small snippet of JavaScript code:

- TweetMeme (Twitter): http://tweetmeme.com/about/retweet_button

- Topsy (Twitter): http://labs.topsy.com/widgets/

- Facebook Share: `http://www.facebook.com/facebook-widgets/share.php`

- Digg: `http://digg.com/tools/integrate`

Whichever share button options you decide to utilize, just be sure your web pages have HTML `<title>` tags that are short enough to easily retweet. If your site visitors are forced to edit your title text in order to share it via Twitter, then odds are they'll abandon the URL share attempt, not wanting to be bothered with the extra effort required. So, what's an appropriate title length? Twitter limits tweets to no more than 140 characters, but even that's too long for your title, since your retweet will need to also include your Twitter ID and web page's URL. Let's subtract the known elements to see how many characters remain for the actual title text.

For the sake of this example, let's pretend to construct a viable web page title for the fictional Breadcrumbs app that is easily retweetable. My Twitter handle is @ebutterfly, which consumes 11 characters. The web site URL of `http://www.breadcrumbsapp.com/` can be reduced to fewer characters by using a URL-shortener service like Bit.ly. So, combine all of that into a single string of text with the usual retweet syntax and spaces, and we have this:

`RT @ebutterfly: http://bit.ly/3EmvfN`

We're now weighing in at 36 characters, which leaves us with 104 characters to avoid exceeding Twitter's 140-character limit. To safely account for any excess spaces, let's craft a title that's 100 characters or less.

"Breadcrumbs for iPhone - Never misplace your car again with this new parked car locator app!" is only 92 characters, so that'll work! The web page's HTML Title tag now reads as follows:

`<title>Breadcrumbs for iPhone - Never misplace your car again with this new parked car locator app!</title>`

This produces the following 129-character retweet when the TweetMeme share button is clicked:

`RT @ebutterfly: Breadcrumbs for iPhone - Never misplace your car again with this new parked car locator app! http://bit.ly/3EmvfN`

Perfect! Our web page's `<title>` tag includes important keyword phrases like *iPhone app* and *car locator* for proper search engine positioning, yet it's short enough to promote URL sharing across the popular social networking sites. This may all seem like a lot of attention paid to trivial minutiae, but it's this level of detail that can turn an ordinary web site into a powerful marketing tool.

Your Blog, RSS Feed, and Email Mailing List

Most of you already maintain a blog for posting news about software releases and development updates. And if you don't, then you really should! It's a great way to grow a readership, drawing users to your site. Don't have much to say? That's OK, because you don't have to utilize it like a daily journal. A blog establishes a direct connection between you and your customers, where readers can stay on top of your latest news and post comments. For those of you new to blogs, I'll be discussing the community-building power of blogs later in this chapter.

For now, if you do maintain a blog for discussing software development or iPhone news, just make sure that your app-related web site includes a direct link to it. Beyond Twitter and Facebook, you want site visitors to know that your blog is yet one more available resource for staying informed about your iPhone app.

Since most blog software, such as WordPress, automatically generates RSS feeds for the latest blog entries, many bloggers aren't placing much emphasis on their feed beyond offering the obligatory link for interested subscribers. Although hot new platforms like Twitter have seemingly cooled the popularity of this XML-based standard, RSS is still a very powerful mechanism for distributing information. To really leverage RSS for your own marketing needs, I highly recommend signing up for Google's free FeedBurner service.

- Google FeedBurner: http://www.feedburner.com/

At first glance, FeedBurner may only appear to be a glorified analytics service, tracking who's subscribing to your RSS feed and which browsers or client apps are being used to read it. Although RSS statistics monitoring is very useful, FeedBurner is really so much more than that. One of the included features is FeedFlare, which inserts social media links within your feed so that with a single click, RSS subscribers can actually share individual posts on Digg, Delicious, Facebook, and other social networking sites. On top of that, FeedBurner will automatically send ping notifications to all major feed aggregators and search engines when you've posted a new blog entry. The service also provides JavaScript widgets for easily publishing feed content in HTML form on any web site, which is perfect for third-party sites interested in syndicating your blog content without the hassles of parsing XML. Although some bloggers may be wary of who repurposes their content, you're using your blog and RSS feed to market your iPhone app, so the more locations your feed is syndicated, the more exposure your iPhone app receives. It's a win-win for you since your primary goal is to drive as much traffic as possible to your product page in the App Store.

But the most valuable feature by far is FeedBurner's free Email Subscriptions service. This enables your site visitors to receive your blog posts via email. Think about that for a moment. Instead of installing and maintaining complicated mailing list software on your own server for managing subscribers and sending out broadcast emails, FeedBurner does all of that for you. And you don't even have to waste time configuring a SQL database and constructing email templates. Just post a blog entry. It gets added to your RSS feed, which in turn gets sent out via email to your email subscribers. And did I already mention it's free? You can even customize the emails with your own logo and font styles. And with the simple copy-and-paste Email Subscription HTML form code that FeedBurner provides, people can easily subscribe from within your own web site.

But what if you don't want every single blog post to be sent out to your mailing list? What if you need more control over the design of the emails? And how about importing existing mailing lists from previous marketing campaigns? To solve those needs, you'll need a more robust email marketing solution. If you're like me, you may not want to be bothered with monkeying with your own mailing list software and the maintenance headaches to come with aggressive spam filters, SQL database security to keep out hackers, and other time-consuming nuisances. Fortunately, some easy-to-use yet affordable third-party email marketing services can take care of all the heavy lifting. They maintain your mailing list databases and email campaigns on their secure servers, support custom HTML emails, list imports and exports, provide extensive web-based admin sites with comprehensive analytics reports for each campaign, and even produce custom HTML form code for you to copy and paste into your own web site for visitors to easily subscribe. These services have "whitelist" agreements with the major ISPs and email vendors to help prevent your campaigns from getting eaten by server-side spam filters—this alone makes these third-party services a better option than installing your own PHP/MySQL solution. Hundreds of email marketing companies exist, but here's a select group that have proven popular with software developers:

- Campaign Monitor: `http://www.campaignmonitor.com/`

- MailChimp: `http://www.mailchimp.com/`

- Constant Contact: `http://www.constantcontact.com/`

- iContact: `http://www.icontact.com/`

- StreamSend: `http://www.streamsend.com/`

- Vertical Response: `http://www.verticalresponse.com/`

I've had the most experience with Campaign Monitor, which offers complete design control over the look and feel of your email blasts. The thing I like best about Campaign Monitor is that you only pay per email campaign. There's no monthly fee, so if I don't send out an email campaign this month, then I pay nothing. And then when I do send out a campaign, their rate is very affordable. This is a great solution for developers with large mailing lists who send out very few emails.

If your mailing list has fewer than 500 subscribers, then MailChimp offers its service free for low-volume accounts with the ability to upgrade to larger-capacity plans as your subscriber base grows. If you have a large mailing list with high-volume email needs, then a flat monthly fee from some of the other listed companies may be your best bet.

Whether you choose the free FeedBurner Email Subscriptions or a more comprehensive email marketing solution, let your site visitors know that unsubscribe links are located at the bottom of every email newsletter for their convenience. It's also important to include a link to a privacy policy somewhere on your web site. People are tired of dealing with spam, so they've become very wary of giving out their email address to anyone. A simple privacy policy statement can reassure site visitors that you won't be selling or sharing their email addresses with anyone. Not sure how to word it? Perform an online search for *privacy policy*, and you'll find hundreds of samples to refer to. Just be sure to adhere to whatever privacy policy you set to avoid liability issues. Beyond the fact that most countries now have strict antispam laws in effect, the wrath of negative word-of-mouth from angry subscribers can be even more damaging to your business.

Why bother with email newsletters at all if it's so troublesome? With overly aggressive spam filters, is it still an effective delivery mechanism? True, a fair percentage of your recipients may never see your emails because of hungry junk mail filters, but email is still a very powerful pipeline to communicate news. Although you may be tempted to only post announcements on Twitter, Facebook, or your blog, you're reliant on users to follow you there and religiously monitor your latest news. That places the responsibility on your audience, and although you may be vigilant about reading every tweet and Facebook update, most people are not. Why risk the possibility of your important posts being overlooked? There are still a lot of consumers who prefer a more passive approach where requested information is delivered directly to them, rather than being forced to go find it for themselves. It's all about providing as many communications options as possible on your web site so that anyone interested in your iPhone app can receive related news in the format or platform of their choice.

Customer Support and Contact Information

Even though I'll be talking more about customer support options in Chapter 9, I will mention that you should always link to your support page from your app's main web site. At the very least, give site visitors some way to contact you, whether by email or an HTML form. Even though the desktop version of iTunes supplies a dedicated active link to your support site from your product's App Store page, that's not the case in the mobile version of the App Store. As referenced in the previously shown Figure 8–1, the App Store in the iPhone OS only lists the web site URL for a selected application. And with more than 90 percent of all iPhone and iPod touch users browsing and downloading apps directly from their device, if they encounter a support issue, they'll look up your web site in Mobile Safari in the hopes of finding online assistance. So, make life easier for both you and your customers by making your support page easily accessible from your app's web site.

Company Identity

This may seem obvious if your app's web page is part of your existing company site, but for those independent developers who decide to build a stand-alone web site for just their iPhone app, don't forget to include your own business name and an About page. If you're only building a cheap $0.99 novelty app that will soon be forgotten three months from now, then establishing a company identity may not matter (and if that were the case, you probably wouldn't be reading this book either). But if you've developed a rock-solid, niche application that sells for more than the average app price (such as $3.99 or higher), then consumers will want to know you're a serious developer with plans to support the app for the long haul before making their purchase decision. When people buy a higher-priced app, especially one that they've come to rely on daily, they're really investing in the product's future. You want your web site to exude a prosperous and confident professionalism. Seeing your business logo and reading your company/developer bio online can help give them that peace of mind.

Cross-Promote Your Other Products

Trying to sell multiple software applications? If you're driving traffic to your web site to promote a new iPhone app, take advantage of this opportunity to also spotlight some of your other products, especially if they're iPhone apps that would appeal to this same audience. That's what Tap Tap Tap does at http://www.taptaptap.com/. Its web site was designed with cross-promotion as a central factor. Using a clever sushi theme, app icons for all of the products sit on a virtual wood table. Select an app, and its icon slides forward, revealing a full description, screenshots, video demos, and other related information. But the other app icons remain visible on the left. Click another, and the current app icon slides back into place, while the new selection slides forward (see Figure 8–12). This is all done within the same screen. It's an elegant, animated design that was achieved with a sophisticated mix of CSS and JavaScript—no Flash.

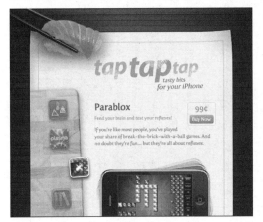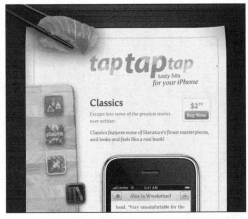

Figure 8–12. *Tap Tap Tap utilizes a clever web site design that cross-promotes all of its iPhone apps within a single screen.*

You can also cross-promote other products and services. Even though people came to your site interested in an iPhone app, they surely have other interests as well for books, desktop software, related consulting services, and so on. But be very careful not to over-promote those other items, or else you run the risk of appearing too ad-centric, pimping out your iPhone app as bait. Also keep in mind that you don't want to distract site visitors from your primary goal: convincing them to buy your iPhone application in the App Store!

Downloadable Extras

People love freebies! And offering up fun downloads on your web site such as Twitter avatar images, desktop backgrounds, and iPhone wallpaper are easy ways to promote your app. But just because you create it does not necessarily mean your site visitors will want it. Since these freebies are essentially digital advertisements for your product, you need to make them visually compelling enough for people to look at every time they turn on their computer or mobile device. People don't want to stare at interface components or company logos, so if you're promoting a productivity app, then these kinds of image-based freebies may not be a good fit. But if your app is a game with cool scenery and characters, then the game's visuals may lend itself quite well to promotional downloads like iPhone wallpaper.

To build anticipation for the ngmoco releases of Rolando and Rolando 2, the developers, Hand Circus, created several iPhone wallpapers based on the beloved Rolando characters and offered them as free downloads on `http://www.handcircus.com/`. These 320 × 480 pixel PNG files did not include any corporate logos or copyright lines, just fun graphics with a single reference to either Rolando or Rolando 2 (see Figure 8–13).

Figure 8–13. *Hand Circus offered free 320 × 480 iPhone wallpaper downloads to promote its Rolando games.*

Notice that the Rolando characters and the comic-style dialogue bubble in Figure 8–13's iPhone wallpaper are perfectly centered so that their heads and the "Rolando 2" words are not cut off or hidden behind the visible iPhone OS interface elements. If you decide to create iPhone wallpaper images to promote your own app or game, you'll want to keep those same design considerations in mind for best results.

Don't just throw up a download link on your web site and assume consumers will know how to save the image as their iPhone wallpaper. Make it easy for them by providing simple instructions:

1. In Mobile Safari, hold the image with your finger, and choose Save Image to save it to your photo library.

2. Open the Photos app, and select the image.

3. From the image's Action menu, select Use as Wallpaper.

When installed, every time those users turn on their iPhone or iPod touch, they'll be greeted by a unique graphic, reminding them that your app or game is coming soon.

Before Selling, Start Collecting

Your iPhone application is not yet live in the App Store, so including a buy button and App Store identity badge on your site is a tad premature (as shown in the Figure 8–4 Breadcrumbs example). Although it is good to have those two images designed and ready to go, you'll want to leave them off your web page for now.

During this prerelease stage, use your web site to grow your online audience. You could keep it simple and just ask people to follow you on Twitter or become a Facebook fan to stay informed on the latest news about your forthcoming iPhone app. But if you're not yet a known developer, then there may not be a compelling reason for people to follow you. They may just decide to check your site later, but in time, memory fades, and they may not remember to come back. By placing the ball in their court, you're risking the loss of those potential app sales.

Here's where offering that free email newsletter can really benefit your prerelease marketing efforts. Interested site visitors can subscribe, and then a month later after they've forgotten about your app, you can send them an email announcing its availability in the App Store! Don't rely on the small subscription link located in your navigation menu or in another section of the site. Replacing the buy button and App Store identity badge, position the subscription form front and center on your app's web page with an invitation to visitors to submit their email address to be the first notified when your iPhone application becomes available in the App Store (see Figure 8–14).

The convenient thing about this strategy is that nothing else on the web page was moved or modified. Once your app is live in the App Store, you can easily swap out that prominent "Notify Me..." email form, adding back the buy button and App Store identity badge (as previously shown in Figure 8–4).

Figure 8–14. *During the prerelease stage, replace the buy button and App Store identity badge with a "Notify Me When It's Available" email subscription form.*

Why Site Compatibility with Mobile Safari Is So Important

As previously mentioned, AdMob reported that a whopping 93 percent of iPhone users browse and purchase apps directly from the App Store on their mobile devices, while only a meager 7 percent do so from the desktop version of iTunes. Since it's highly possible that consumers may check out your app's official site before making a purchase decision, it's in your best interest to make sure your web site is compatible with iPhone's Mobile Safari browser.

Since Mobile Safari utilizes the powerful WebKit engine under the hood, it has extensive support for JavaScript, CSS, and other modern web standards, so most sites actually render quite well in Mobile Safari. But you should be aware of a few optimization tricks to make your site more enjoyable for iPhone users:

- Controlling page scale with the `viewport` meta tag
- Detecting the platform from the browser's user agent
- Working around Mobile Safari's lack of Flash support
- Enhancing home screen bookmarking

"I'm Ready for My Close-up, Mr. Viewport"

The majority of web developers design page layouts based on average desktop screen dimensions, so to accommodate the typical widths of most web sites, Mobile Safari's default zoom is set at a screen width of 980 pixels. This enables all web sites to fit nicely within the Mobile Safari browser window when initially loaded. In Portrait mode, the browser window is only 320 pixels wide, so the pages are scaled down quite a bit, making the text practically illegible. To read the content and tap text links, users are forced to finger pinch the screen to zoom in closer.

But what if you want to design your web site to accommodate the unique dimensions of the Mobile Safari browser, alleviating the need to manually pinch zoom? As previously seen in Figure 8–12, Tap Tap Tap's web page layout is only a little wider than 600 pixels, designed to display well in both the wide-screen format of desktop computer browsers and the narrow Portrait mode of Mobile Safari. Yet Mobile Safari's default screen scale of 980 pixels wide would still render the page's main content as a tiny object centered in the screen with a large unused margin of black background color on both sides. The solution is an HTML tag called `viewport`. Within the `<head>` tag of Tap Tap Tap's web page at `http://www.taptaptap.com/` is the following meta tag:

```
<meta name="viewport" content="width=device-width" />
```

The `viewport` tag is acknowledged by Mobile Safari but is ignored by all other browsers, so it will affect your site display only on the iPhone and iPod touch. Assigning the content parameter to `width = device-width` tells Mobile Safari to appropriately scale the page content's width to match the browser's width, which makes Tap Tap Tap's web site appear iPhone-optimized and easy to read (see Figure 8–15). This only affects the amount of zoom and page positioning that's applied. The web page's original aspect ratio remains unaltered.

There are actually several other `viewport` properties that can be assigned to affect the scaling and a user's zoom capabilities, all of which are documented by Apple online here:

`http://developer.apple.com/safari/library/documentation/appleapplications/reference/safarihtmlref/Articles/MetaTags.html`

But if you're simply looking for greater control over the viewport's width than the `device-width` value, then set the `width` property to a specific number of pixels. Why would this come in handy? Let's say your page's background imagery is an integrated part of the overall design. With the `viewport` tag set to `width = device-width`, the foreground web content will fill the screen with little to no margin space remaining to see the background image. If your main content is 400 pixels wide (and centered on the page) and you'd like to see at least 50 pixels of background image on both the left and right sides of the screen, then set your `viewport` tag to the following:

```
<meta name="viewport" content="width=500">
```

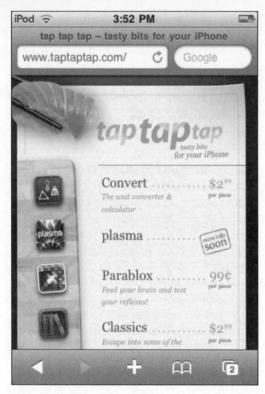

Figure 8–15. *Tap Tap Tap set the* `viewport` *tag's width to match the device width, which enhances its web site's appearance and readability within Mobile Safari.*

On a side note, I did notice that Tap Tap Tap's cool JavaScript-driven app icon animations don't slide as well in Mobile Safari, but they're flawlessly smooth in the Mac OS X version of Safari. I'm not knocking the beautiful page design but rather pointing out a common problem that plagues quite a few iPhone-related web sites. Even though both browsers utilize WebKit, there are subtle differences in JavaScript and CSS support. When using complex scripts or third-party web frameworks in your site, be sure to always test your code in Mobile Safari to ensure that the viewing experience is similar on both desktop computers and mobile devices.

If you need help debugging your web page within Mobile Safari, turn on the Debug Console located in Safari's Developer panel within the iPhone's Settings app. Mobile Safari's Debug Console is a huge time-saver, pinpointing errors and recommending optimization tips.

Using Browser Detection to Deliver Targeted Content

For software publishers who develop apps and games for several different platforms, it may not be appropriate to modify their main web site to accommodate just one of them. A perfect example of this is PopCap Games, which produces games for Mac, PC, Web, Nintendo, Xbox, PlayStation, and even various mobile devices such as the iPhone. To promote all its latest games and supported platforms within a single site, it's essential to take advantage of the wide-screen real estate of desktop web browsers, which probably accounts for the majority of their site traffic.

As you can see from the screenshot on the left in Figure 8–16, the main PopCaps.com home page would be quite difficult to navigate and read when scaled down to fit within the Mobile Safari browser window. Instead of trying to dynamically alter the existing site design on the fly based on the browser accessing it, PopCap instead uses a simple redirect to send Mobile Safari users to a special iPhone-optimized web site that showcases only its iPhone games. Within Mobile Safari, visiting `http://www.popcap.com/` will automatically redirect you to `http://www.popcap.com/iphone/` (see the screenshot on the right in Figure 8–16).

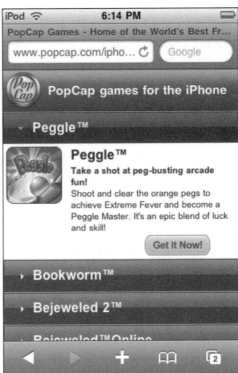

Figure 8–16. *PopCap Games' main home page caters to several platforms and would be hard to read on a small mobile screen (left), so Mobile Safari users are automatically redirected to a special iPhone-centric site (right).*

This simple redirect trick is achieved by first detecting the browser's user agent. Here's what Mobile Safari's user agent looks like from an iPhone running OS 3.1:

```
Mozilla/5.0 (iPhone; U; CPU iPhone OS 3_1 like Mac OS X; en-us) AppleWebKit/528.18
(KHTML, like Gecko) Version/4.0 Mobile/7C144 Safari/528.16
```

And here's Mobile Safari's user agent from an iPod touch running OS 3.1:

```
Mozilla/5.0 (iPod; U; CPU iPhone OS 3_1 like Mac OS X; en-us) AppleWebKit/528.18 (KHTML,
like Gecko) Version/4.0 Mobile/7C144 Safari/528.16
```

The browser's user agent can be accessed from any modern web scripting language. If the user agent description reveals the user's browser is from the iPhone or iPod touch, your web code can send the user to a different URL. If the user agent is from any other platform, then do nothing, remaining on the current web page. Let's take a look at how to easily program this in JavaScript and PHP with only a few lines of code.

JavaScript

Place the following code within the <head> tag in your HTML page. This will cause the redirect to happen for Mobile Safari users before the rest of the page finishes loading, which will make the transition fast and seamless.

```
<script type="text/javascript">
<!--
var os = navigator.userAgent.toLowerCase();
if (os.indexOf('iphone')!=-1) {
    window.location.href = "http://www.mywebsite.com/iphone/";
}
// -->
</script>
```

In JavaScript, the user agent is accessed via navigator.userAgent. Although Mobile Safari's current user agent references iPhone, it's best to convert the entire string to all-lowercase letters using JavaScript's toLowerCase() function to ensure this code will always work, regardless if Apple ever switches the case in the future. Once you have the user agent string in lowercase format, use the indexOf() function to search for *iphone* since *iPhone OS* is listed by both the iPhone and iPod touch. An integer position of the first occurrence of that word is returned. If that search term is not found, then -1 is returned. But if any other number is returned, that signals a match for Mobile Safari, so the JavaScript code redirects the browser to the URL location of your iPhone-optimized web page.

PHP

For this example, you must place the following PHP code at the very top of the HTML page, before even the <html> tag. This PHP code needs to run before any HTML code is executed.

```
<?
$os = $_SERVER['HTTP_USER_AGENT'];
if (stristr($os, 'iphone')) {
    header("Location: http://www.mywebsite.com/iphone/");
    exit;
}
?>
```

In PHP, the user agent is retrieved from the HTTP_USER_AGENT property in the $_SERVER array. Similar to how the JavaScript version works, this PHP code uses the case-insensitive stristr() function to search the user agent string for an occurrence of *iphone*. If the search term is not found, then stristr() returns False, and the rest of the web page continues to load. But if the word *iphone* is found, then the PHP redirects the identified Mobile Safari browser to your dedicated iPhone site URL. After calling the redirect via the header() function, you should include the exit() function, which will prevent the rest of that HTML page from loading while the redirect is being processed.

Dynamically Replacing Flash with iPhone-Compatible Content

What if you don't need to redirect to a separate iPhone-centric site but merely need to replace a single web element—such as a Flash video—for your web page to be iPhone compliant? You can also apply the browser user agent detection technique here.

As I've mentioned, Flash is not yet supported in Mobile Safari, but for people visiting your site from a desktop computer, having them view your iPhone app demo trailer as an embedded YouTube or Vimeo video may benefit its popularity and viewer count on those respective video-sharing sites. Since the Flash Video format won't play in Mobile Safari, you'll want to provide an alternative QuickTime-compatible video for viewing on iPhone and iPod touch.

This content swap can easily be done dynamically on your web page with only minor tweaks to the JavaScript and PHP browser detection examples.

JavaScript

Place the following JavaScript code anywhere in your web page where you need to switch between two content formats based on the browser model. Just like in the previous JavaScript example, retrieve the user agent and check it for the presence of *iphone*. If that word is found, then the page is being viewed with Mobile Safari, so display an iPhone-compatible video format like QuickTime MOV. If some other web browser is being used from a computer, then it's safe to load a Flash Video file instead, such as an embedded YouTube video.

```
<script type="text/javascript">
<!--
var os = navigator.userAgent.toLowerCase();
if (os.indexOf('iphone')!=-1) {

    // Yes, viewed by Mobile Safari, so show QuickTime video!
    document.write("Place QuickTime HTML Object/Embed code here");
}
else {
    // No, some other browser, so show Flash Video instead.
    document.write("Place Flash Video HTML Object/Embed code here");
}
// -->
</script>
```

PHP

Likewise, you can place the following PHP code anywhere in your web page where you need to swap content based on the browser being used. If the PHP determines the user agent is from Mobile Safari, then display an iPhone-compatible QuickTime video. If the user agent reveals some other web browser, then you can display Flash Video.

```
<?
$os = $_SERVER['HTTP_USER_AGENT'];
if (stristr($os, 'iphone')) {
?>
    <!-- Yes, viewed by Mobile Safari, so place QuickTime HTML Object/Embed code here! -
->
<?
}
else {
?>
    <!-- No, some other browser, so place Flash Video HTML Object/Embed code here. -->
<?
}
?>
```

Of course, if you don't have a specific need to use Flash on your web site, the easiest solution is to simply use the QuickTime format for all your web-based videos. Anyone who has an iPhone or iPod touch is required to have the desktop version of iTunes on their computer for device syncing. Since QuickTime is installed with iTunes, even Windows users will be able to watch your web site's QuickTime videos.

Home Screen Bookmarking Made Beautiful

For loyal fans who visit your site frequently, make it easy for them to add a web site bookmark to their iPhone home screens. When bookmarking a URL in Mobile Safari, one of the options is Add to Home Screen, which saves the bookmark as an app icon in your iPhone or iPod touch home screen. Tap the icon, and it displays that web site in Mobile Safari. By default, a thumbnail snapshot of your web page is displayed as the app icon, but at only 57 × 57 pixels, that shrunken thumbnail is so small that the site is probably unrecognizable.

Fortunately, you don't have to settle for that. You can create your own custom image for display as a home screen bookmark icon. Just like an iPhone app icon, do not add rounded corners or the glossy bevel, since the iPhone OS will automatically add those effects to the icon. Just upload a square 57 × 57 image in PNG format—named apple-touch-icon.png—to your web site's root directory. Then in your web page HTML, add the following line of code within the <head> tag:

```
<link rel="apple-touch-icon" href="apple-touch-icon.png" />
```

If the URL points to a dedicated web site for your iPhone app, then don't use your application's existing icon, since that might prove confusing to customers who have both icons on their home screen. Instead, use an alternate image so that users can easily differentiate between your app icon and your web site bookmark icon. If the URL points to your company site that showcases several apps, then assigning your company logo as the bookmark icon is a good branding choice.

Let's Make Some Noise: The Power of Blogs, Twitter, and Social Networks

Now that your web site is ready, you finally have an online destination for promoting the forthcoming release of your iPhone app. But the only way anyone will know about your new web site is if you get out there and start building your online audience.

Although important, submitting your web site URL and XML site map to the major search engines is not enough. Don't wait for the masses to find you. Go out and find them. You want to start conversations and get people talking about your new iPhone app. By focusing your initial marketing efforts on Twitter, Facebook, and other popular social networks, the goal is to leverage their word-of-mouth power to drive interested consumers to your web site. Since your app is not yet available in the App Store, this prerelease stage is all about building awareness and anticipation for the product.

I will warn you in advance that diving into the world of social media can be very time-consuming. If you already actively use Twitter or Facebook, then you already know what I'm talking about. Be prepared to dedicate at least one hour every day to online marketing. If done right, your interactions should feel less like business and more like community building, establishing meaningful connections with a global audience. Carving out an hour or more each day for online marketing can seem like an overwhelming concept, especially if you're as busy as I am, but to succeed in the App Store, it's worth every second. And the punch line is that this is all free grassroots advertising. There's no cost to join any of these social networks, so the only investment is your time.

It's important to remember that the only way any of this works is if you treat your audience with respect. If you only tweet and blog about press releases and sales pitches, then no one will want to follow you. To grow your audience requires posting about things that people want to read.

The top three social media sites are Facebook, MySpace, and Twitter. Facebook boasts more than 300 million members, and although Twitter has not revealed the size of their user base, eMarketer estimates that there will be more than 18 million Twitter accounts by the end of 2009. With third-party iPhone APIs available for Twitter and Facebook Connect, it should come as no surprise that these are the two most widely embraced social networks within the iPhone community, so that's where you'll want to concentrate most of your energy.

Blogging

As I've already mentioned, maintaining a blog is an essential element in driving traffic back to your web site. Your iPhone app's main web page probably won't change often since it primarily serves to educate people on what it is and why they should buy it.

Your blog, on the other hand, is the central online engine for posting all your announcements and news updates. You just posted a new video trailer or screenshots? Blog about it. Your app has been submitted to the App Store review team? Blog about it. Your app won an award or has been reviewed by another site? Blog about it. Have an interesting story to share about your development experience? Yes, you guessed right...blog about it.

Syndicating Your Blog Content

Every time you publish a new blog entry, the related RSS feed gets updated, along with feed reader subscribers and any site that syndicates your blog content. You should also post a link to the new blog entry on Twitter, Facebook, Digg, Delicious, and all other major social media sites that could push web traffic your way and increase awareness for your iPhone app. Don't assume everyone who visits your site will subscribe to your blog's RSS feed or email alerts (see the "Anatomy of an iPhone App Web Site" section for details on FeedBurner's email subscriptions). Some people prefer to receive news through other services such as Twitter.

If the thought of having to manually post your blog update on each and every one of your social network accounts sounds like a tedious, time-consuming job, you can use one of the free blog services that can automate this task.

You can configure Posterous.com, Tumblr.com, and TypePad.com to automatically syndicate your blog entries to your Twitter and Facebook accounts, as well as several other sites. And you can even set Tumblr to autopost your tweets on your blog, retrieved from your Twitter RSS feed.

If you currently have a blog with a different service, such as WordPress.com, Blogger.com, LiveJournal.com, or MovableType.com, then you can still automate the posting of your blog entries into Facebook. Keep reading because I'll later explain how to easily syndicate your blog's RSS feed into your Facebook account.

Inviting Comments

The one feature that really makes a blog come alive is the inclusion of commenting. By giving your readers a voice, it turns your blog from a read-only article into a vibrant two-way conversation. By encouraging interaction, your blog readers will become much more loyal and supportive. Even if they disagree with one of your posts, they're still talking about it and linking to it. When building a community, not everyone is going to have the same opinion, which is fine—that's what keeps the conversation interesting.

Unfortunately, the amount of spam that ends up clogging up the comments section of many blogs can be quite annoying. To help eliminate spam that comes from automated bots, make sure to use a blog service with CAPTCHA web forms and spam filters to ensure that posted comments are from actual humans. You may also want to monitor posted comments frequently and remove questionable ones via the blog's admin dashboard, which can be time-consuming but ultimately worth it to offer a true blogging environment.

Although some people opt to hold their conversations on a Facebook Page to avoid anonymous spam, the convenience of blog comments is that no account is required. There's no barrier to entry. If I want to comment on a TechCrunch.com article, I don't need to join a social network or log into any system. I just fill out the comment form and click the submit button.

Host Your Own Blog or Use a Third-Party Blog Service?

If you're comfortable with installing and modifying blog software on your own web server, such as the open source download from WordPress.org, then you'll have the power to customize every aspect of the blog to suit your specific needs. But if you'd rather not deal with configuring MySQL databases, installing security update patches, and editing PHP files, then you may want to consider using one of the many free blog services previously mentioned. They automatically update the blog software on their servers and offer state-of-the-art antispam tools for managing comments. You can also customize the look and feel of your blog to match your web site's existing page design if desired. For example, I use Blogger.com to remotely host my company blog, but the template was customized to mimic the same design as my Electric Butterfly web site for a seamless transition between the two.

Twitter

Since a large percentage of iPhone and iPod touch users are on Twitter, that's one social network you really can't afford to avoid. If you don't already have a presence on Twitter, then before we go any further, do yourself a favor and sign up for a free account now!

- Twitter: http://twitter.com/

Although you can easily access Twitter from a web browser on both your computer and mobile device, you may prefer using a dedicated client app for staying on top of your Twitter world. Popular favorites are Tweetie, Twitterrific, and TweetDeck, but to explore all the available options for Mac, Windows, and iPhone, check out the comprehensive Twitter apps directory here:

- oneforty: http://oneforty.com/

Twitter's microblogging/messaging is not only a great way to communicate with your customers in real time on everything from support issues to feature requests, but it's also a very accepted platform for promoting your iPhone apps and games. And on top of that, many of the major app review sites and iPhone news bloggers keep tabs on related trends and topics within the Twittersphere, so your tweets may attract additional press coverage for your iPhone apps!

According to the recent report "Winning iPhone Strategies," written by Kisky Netmedia and supported by Northwest Vision and Media, the fourth most influential method of app discovery for iPhone users was recommendations on Twitter, just below the top three:

word-of-mouth, online reviews, and browsing the App Store. This reinforces the importance of Twitter as a powerful marketing tool for iPhone developers.

Gaining Followers

When establishing your existence on Twitter, you should decide how you want to use the service. Some developers create a Twitter account for themselves and then a separate account for their iPhone app. This allows them to use the app-focused account for posting related news and fielding support queries, while their own personal account is utilized for tweeting about other products or miscellaneous, nonbusiness items. Another common practice in managing multiple accounts is where one is dedicated to company news and others are assigned to each employee of the company. These two approaches work well if your venture is comprised of more than one developer or if you want to reserve one Twitter account for only personal use.

If you're a solo developer, you may find it much easier to consolidate your efforts into a single Twitter account. And with a few iPhone apps under your belt, cross-promoting them within a single Twitter feed can be very beneficial, especially if one of your apps becomes popular and brings you a lot of Twitter followers, providing you with a large audience that would be eager to hear about any other products you release.

For the uninitiated, followers are those users who choose to follow your Twitter stream, which means your tweets will show up in their timelines: a stream of posts from the people they follow. The more followers you accrue, the larger your audience becomes. And since growing your audience is the main marketing objective here, how does one get more followers?

Ah, that is probably the most frequently asked question on Twitter. Sure, lots of third-party services promise to boost your number of followers if you agree to follow the people they request, but that's the wrong avenue to take. It's not about getting just anybody and everybody to follow you in exchange for following them. True, your audience will grow exponentially with that kind of tactic, but quantity does not necessarily equal quality. Typically, those people only care about one thing: increasing their own follower count. You're just a number to them. Most (if not all) of them don't really care what you have to say and may not even own an iPhone or iPod touch.

Don't worry about how many people follow you. Focus on growing a quality audience, one genuinely interested in iPhone apps. Here are a few steps you can take to make that happen:

- **Who you follow matters.** Building an audience starts with you. Search Twitter for the people who influence you most—your favorite iPhone developers, publishers, bloggers, journalists, friends, and peers. Whenever they post something of value related to your views, then retweet it. They may notice your occasional retweets and reply to you. There's absolutely nothing wrong with being on the radar of influential people! Who knows, they may even follow you back. And even if they don't, who you follow says a lot about you. People who stumble upon your Twitter profile may look at who you follow before deciding whether to follow you themselves.

- **Follow your fans.** Create a connection with loyal followers by showing them a little love in return. Nothing is more complimentary than reciprocity in following. Now that doesn't mean you have to follow everyone who follows you, but if their tweets interest you, then it is the ultimate gesture of thanks.

- **Engage your community.** If people reach out to you on Twitter with comments or questions, always answer them. Twitter is not about talking *at* people. It's about talking *to* people. Having public conversations on Twitter can not only draw others into the discussion, but it also shows a personal touch, proving you're not an automated spam-bot that only spews out marketing messages. If you feel that your Twitter stream is becoming dominated by a single conversation, you may want to follow the person and continue the discussion via direct messages, so as not to alienate any of your other followers. If someone is being rude, then you do have the option to block them, but that should always be a last resort. More often than not, people just want to be heard. By following you, they've agreed to listen to your voice, so it's only fair that you listen to theirs as well.

- **Quality content is king!** Don't just tweet about your app nonstop with an endless barrage of links to reviews and announcements. No one will follow if you only post marketing spam 24/7. And that's probably a surefire way to lose whatever followers you do have. Give people a reason to follow you. Your tweets should portray a genuine voice that's entertaining and informative. Like a blog, your Twitter posts should reflect your personality and even your opinions (as long as they are not offensive or counterproductive to your marketing mission). And if you publish a blog post, then tweet about it with a link! Followers will evangelize and retweet people, not corporate entities, so let them see the person behind the product.

- **Stay true to your voice.** To retain your followers, it's important to stay on topic. If you're known for tweeting about iPhone game development, then spending a solid month talking about nothing but house renovations will quickly decimate your follower count. They followed you to learn from your valued game programming expertise, not to trudge through hundreds of tweets about laying new tile in the bathroom. It's good to share personal events in your life, especially if your audience has similar interests, but those posts should be sprinkled among your primary topic tweets. Staying focused on only one or two themes will also help attract new followers. If someone is searching Twitter for *iPhone dev* to learn and network with fellow programmers and they stumble upon one of your tweets, they'll most likely follow you only if the majority of your other posts are also related to iPhone development.

- **Retweet!** If someone posts something that you feel your audience would enjoy, then retweet it. Twitter is built on the spirit of karma. What goes around comes around. Spend the time promoting other people's tweets more than you promote yourself, and you'll cultivate a deeper bond with your followers. They may even retweet *your* posts more often to return the favor. Remember, this isn't about finding people you can merely talk at but rather building synergy within the community. And if someone does retweet you or promotes one of your links, take a moment to thank them. It's small gesture, but it goes a long way. If your followers know their support is appreciated, they're more likely to retweet your posts again in the future.

- **Timing your tweets.** Very few people monitor Twitter all day long. And then there's that damn sleep thing that gets in the way every night. Unless your followers are using a client app like Tweetie that keeps track of their current reading position in the timeline, they may miss some of your posts. Of course, it's always that perfect tweet you spent 10 minutes crafting or the all-important product announcement that you've been planning for weeks. We all live in different time zones with different schedules, so your timing is essential. Sending out a tweet at 7 a.m. from Los Angeles would cover quite a few territories during daylight hours. For example, it would be 10 a.m. in Chicago, 11 a.m. in New York, 4 p.m. in London, and 5 p.m. in Paris, Berlin, and Rome. Twitter allows you to repeat a tweet every eight hours, so if the same message was sent out again at 5 p.m. from Los Angeles, it would be 8 a.m. in Hong Kong, 9 a.m. in Tokyo, and 11 a.m. in Sydney, Australia. Since some of your followers will see *all* your tweets, don't make a habit of repeating posts multiple times. If it starts smelling like spam, you're liable to lose followers. But a rare repeated tweet every once in awhile for special announcements is tolerable and can be very effective in reaching more people.

Customizing Your Profile

Twitter offers a nice selection of background images and colors to beautify your account pages. Although the colors are easy enough to modify, don't settle for the same default themes seen on countless profiles. Be unique and personalize your page with your own custom background image and avatar picture. Take advantage of this free marketing opportunity to visually showcase your iPhone app and brand identity!

Regarding your avatar picture, if you maintain two Twitter accounts—one for your company and one for your own personal use—then you'll most likely want to differentiate the two by using a corporate logo for the company profile and a photo of yourself for the personal profile. For an independent developer using a single Twitter account, I highly recommend using a photo of yourself as the profile picture. Even though you'll be tweeting about your software products and iPhone news, a photo adds a personal touch. People like to see who they're following.

When I first joined Twitter, I listed Electric Butterfly as the profile name and uploaded my company logo as the avatar picture. I didn't tweet that much, and in return, few people followed me. After a couple months of seeing how other people operated on Twitter, I decided to follow their lead and switched the profile name to Dave Wooldridge and replaced the avatar with my photo. By providing a human face and name to my Twitter presence, along with a conscious effort to tweet more frequently, my followers count began to rapidly increase.

The next item to tackle is your profile's background image. In the "Design" section of Twitter's Settings page, you can upload your own custom image file. Although all Twitter clients support the display of avatar pictures, a person's background image is seen only when visiting the profile page on Twitter.com, but that does not minimize the importance of it. On the contrary. Most people will check out your profile page on the Twitter web site before deciding whether to follow you. This is yet another case where the first impression is key.

Since this is a valuable piece of screen real estate, the background should be designed to effectively promote your company or iPhone app without being hidden by the main Twitter content centered within the browser. To accommodate most common screen dimensions, this requires a design theme that's planted in the top-left corner and extends outward to the right and down. Take a look at several custom backgrounds. Check out the great collection from real Twitter accounts at the fun site `http://twitterbackgroundsgallery.com/`, and you'll see what I mean.

With large monitors with high resolutions of 1280 × 800, 1900 × 1200, or even higher, it's recommended that your background image be at least 1600 pixels wide. Since web browsers are not usually maximized full width on such large screens, that size should work fine. But web pages scroll down, so the chances are greater that a web browser's height may span from top to bottom on the screen. For best results, set your image height to a minimum of 1300 pixels.

If your image fades to the same solid color as the background color, then the image can be much shorter. By ensuring that Twitter's "tile background" setting is left unchecked, the background color will show through where the image ends, but with the color the same, it will appear seamless to the viewer. This is the approach used in the example background image designed to promote the fictional Breadcrumbs app (see Figure 8–17). The background image is only 700 pixels tall, yet because the background color is set to the same brown as the ground beneath the car, it creates the illusion that the ground continues far below it.

Figure 8–17. *A Twitter background image design for the fictional Breadcrumbs app, leaving plenty of empty space for the main Twitter page content that will be centered on the screen.*

Looking at Figure 8–17, you'll notice that the iPhone app graphics are positioned in the far top left, leaving the rest of the image fairly empty with nothing but the simple horizon line and the navigational breadcrumbs leading off the screen. This was done intentionally so that there is ample room for the main Twitter page content that will be displayed in the center of the browser screen. The trick is to create something unique and compelling without being visually overpowering. The space behind the Twitter logo and navigation bar is best left a solid color or subtle texture to prevent the page from looking cluttered.

Based on average screen sizes, I recommend limiting your primary design elements to 180 pixels wide by 660 pixels tall in the top-left corner of the background image. By confining your main graphics to that safe area, this ensures your background visual will never be obscured by the Twitter page content, even on smaller screens (see Figure 8–18).

For those of you who think the inclusion of the iPhone app's site URL in the background is a little too much, let me be the first to say it really is quite effective. Not because everyone seems to be doing it (they are), but because it actually works! After changing my own Twitter background image to promote a few of my Electric Butterfly products with web site domain names listed, I began receiving a lot more tweets asking about those products. I also saw a significant increase in traffic to those URLs. I was surprised by this since you can't add active hyperlinks to a Twitter background image, so a person is forced to manually type that URL into their browser to visit that site. But if someone is curious enough, they'll do it, especially if the URL is short and easy to remember—yet another reason for registering a dedicated domain name for your app's web site.

Figure 8–18. *By limiting your primary graphics to 180 pixels wide by 660 pixels tall in the top-left corner, it ensures that imagery won't be obscured by the main Twitter content when viewed on smaller screens.*

Keywords and Hash Tags

Before you dash off your next tweet, it's important to know that the wording of your message can greatly impact its success in reaching the right audience. You want to use words that are quickly identified by readers scanning the timeline and searching Twitter for specific keywords. For example, if you're talking about your iPhone app in a tweet, don't refer to it as a generic "app." You know it's an iPhone app, but for those new to you via a retweet or Twitter search, they may not know what platform you're referring to. Most people will search for *iPhone* or *iPhone app*, so always include the term *iPhone* in product-related tweets.

Don't assume everyone knows what your app does. If you're tweeting the iTunes App Store link of your application, don't just post the app name and URL. I know the limit is 140 characters, but I'm sure you have a few more characters to spare (especially when using a URL-shortener service like Bit.ly). Don't be vague. Oh, it's a parked-car locator for the iPhone? Ah, I could use one of those. And you were kind enough to state "(iTunes)" after the URL, warning me that the link will launch iTunes on my computer. Very convenient and respectful.

Besides crafting your tweet with appropriate keywords, hashtags can also be included. *Hashtags* are keywords that are preceded with a number (#) symbol. What makes them special is that Twitter and most third-party clients display hashtags as active text links. Click a hashtag, and a group of recent tweets that include that same hashtag are listed.

It's a great way to increase the discoverability of your tweets by including them in popular hashtag groups. People who don't follow you or even know your Twitter ID can stumble upon your tweets from a hashtag list. Just be careful not to overuse hashtags. Don't insert a hashtag in every tweet, and certainly don't #pollute a #single #tweet with #multiple #hashtags, or else your posts will be hard to read and look like spam.

For those select few tweets that are important enough to warrant a little extra exposure, convert one of the keywords into a hashtag. If none of your words is a popular tag, then tack on the desired hashtag to the end of your tweet. For example, when I post valuable links that would benefit fellow iPhone developers, I often add the known hashtag #iphonedev. To help pinpoint existing hashtags and popular search keywords, check out these handy resources:

- Twitter Search: `http://search.twitter.com/`

- #Hashtags: `http://hashtags.org/`

- What the Trend?: `http://www.whatthetrend.com/`

Retweet Appeal

Similar to making your web site HTML title tags easily retweetable via URL-sharing buttons like TweetMeme, you'll want to do the same thing with anything you manually post on Twitter yourself. The objective is to publish messages that anyone can retweet with a single click. When retweeting, the `RT @username` syntax is typically added to the front of your message, so if it all exceeds the 140-character limit, the user is then forced to edit your text in order to retweet it. Because of this inconvenience, the longer your message, the fewer retweets you'll receive. Or you run the risk of your text being crudely edited in a way that invalidates your message or link, rendering the retweet much less effective.

Let's say our original text with URL-shortened Bit.ly link is 92 characters long:

```
Breadcrumbs for iPhone - Never misplace your car again with this new parked car locator
app! http://bit.ly/3EmvfN
```

Since Twitter allows ID handles to be a maximum of 15 characters long, a possible retweet could add as much as 20 characters to the message. My `@ebutterfly` ID is purposely short at only 10 characters to conserve space:

```
RT @ebutterfly: Breadcrumbs for iPhone - Never misplace your car again with this new
parked car locator app! http://bit.ly/3EmvfN
```

This puts a retweet at 129 characters. Although this is definitely within the 140-character limit, there are still three flaws with this example. First, that leaves only 11 characters for someone to add their own comment when retweeting. It would be good to give them a little breathing room to say more, especially if they have to something nice to say! Second, what if someone else retweets a retweet? You'll need as much as 20 free characters to accommodate someone's tacked-on Twitter ID. And third, the message is still a little on the long side, not really optimized for quick reading as followers scan their timelines for eye-catching news. Let's try consolidating the message:

```
RT @ebutterfly: new Breadcrumbs iPhone app! Never misplace your parked car again.
http://bit.ly/3EmvfN
```

Now the potential retweet weighs in at only 102 characters. That leaves a whooping 38 extra characters for followers to add their own comments and retweets to your retweet:

```
Wow, cool app! RT @fifteencharname: RT @ebutterfly: new Breadcrumbs iPhone app! Never
misplace your parked car again. http://bit.ly/3EmvfN
```

The previous retweet has again been retweeted and even includes a comment—all within the 140-character limit! By leaving enough spare characters for followers to retweet among their own followers and personalize with their own comments, positive retweets can serve as powerful testimonials and recommendations for purchasing your iPhone app! There's nothing more effective than good old-fashioned word-of-mouth.

And remember, if you want your followers to retweet your posts, then be sure to retweet their posts that you like. What goes around comes around.

Twitter Lists

Lists are a relatively new Twitter feature and represent yet one more reason why the number of followers you have isn't as important as it once was. Within your account on Twitter.com, you can create a new list and give it a unique name. Since Twitter assigns a domain name to it—such as http://twitter.com/ebutterfly/iphonedev—it's best to use a name without spaces. The beauty of lists is that it provides a way to organize people into groups, making it easier to follow particular topics. The reason it chips away the importance of followers is that you can follow a list without following all the people in the list. And you can create a list of people you don't follow.

Some app developers have created lists of their favorite iPhone-related Twitterers, including fellow developers, review sites, and bloggers. It's a great way to see a daily snapshot of the iPhone developer community, so a lot of developers follow the iPhone lists of other developers as a way to connect with the major influencers. Creating your own lists can bring new followers to it, so make sure you include yourself in your own lists, something many people tend to forget to do. If you've compiled a great list and submitted to the major Twitter list directories like Listorious.com, newcomers will possibly follow your list and maybe also your own Twitter account. It's yet another way to get discovered on Twitter and reach a larger audience with your tweets.

Don't just create iPhone-related lists. If your app is related to a specific subject such as music or writing, then create lists for those topics as a way to draw new followers to you who are interested in those subjects. If they own an iPhone, then your tweets within those lists will expose your app to people who may not have known about it.

Managing your own lists and following dozens of other people's lists can become overwhelming—and you thought staying on top of your own timeline was time-consuming! Instead of reading every single tweet, you could use a service like Listiti.com to monitor the lists you choose for specific keywords. If keywords surface in related tweets, Listiti.com sends you an email alert with the tweet links you're interested in.

If someone adds you to their list, it means they think your tweets provide enough value to warrant being part of a select group. Be sure to thank them for the kind gesture. And likewise, if someone follows your list, thank them for it. In such an impersonal online world, you'd be surprised how much good will can be exchanged with a simple "thank you."

Managing the Pipeline

Everything you post on Twitter (not counting retweets) should drive traffic back to your web site. That includes any photos or videos you tweet. It's true that many of the Twitter client apps make it extremely easy to upload photos from your iPhone camera to media-sharing sites like Flickr.com, TwitPic.com, and yfrog.com, but that's not an optimal use of your tweets. If people are interested enough to check out cool screenshots or video play from your app, you should be hosting those media files on your own web site, within web pages that provide additional information about your product. Even if you're showing very early alpha screenshots that you don't want published on your main web site, just link to a stand-alone page on your server that serves as a sneak preview for your tweets. This way, you get to control the message and content on the page. Plus, it can be designed to reflect your app's visual branding, rather than the generic pages of third-party media sharing sites.

You should track the click-throughs and retweets of the URL-shortened links you post on Twitter. Many of the URL-shortener services like Bit.ly offer very nice traffic statistics. Don't use the default URL-shortener feature of most Twitter client apps since you won't have access to those logs. Instead, sign up for a free account at Bit.ly so that every link you create under your account will be tracked. To check your link statistics, simply log into your Bit.ly account online. If you experiment with two different ways to word a tweet about your iPhone app, use two different Bit.ly URLs so that you can track which word phrasing was more successful in click-throughs and retweets. This will help you refine your marketing messages as effective, eye-catching tweets!

For those of you ready to dive deeper into the Twitterverse with advanced management tools, check out oneforty.com's vast directory of third-party applications and services for tracking unfollows, Twitter marketing campaigns, follower locations, spam filters, and much more. With too many to list here, there really is quite an amazing cottage industry of businesses out there based on Twitter. Some of them are less useful than others, so tread carefully.

Facebook

The Facebook Connect SDK is widely used in the iPhone development world. Facebook Connect logins are almost as common as Twitter in today's iPhone apps and games. Although Facebook has made it extremely easy to interface with its API from within an iPhone project, your marketing efforts within the social networking site itself need to be formulated a little differently than Twitter. Since it's all about growing your audience, all of the same rules of etiquette discussed for Twitter also apply to Facebook. The difference here is that while you can mix personal and business tweets within a single

Twitter account, it's recommended to separate the two in Facebook. If you don't have a Facebook account already, you'll want to sign up for one and use that for personal interactions with friends and colleagues:

- Facebook: `http://www.facebook.com/`

With Twitter, you can choose not to follow everyone who follows you, but not so with Facebook. If someone adds you as a friend in Facebook and you approve the request, they are automatically added to your friends list as well. For this reason, you'll want to create a Facebook Page for your business. For those people interested in following your iPhone app news and updates, they can become a fan of your Facebook Page. This provides you with a way to grow your audience without being forced to add each and every one of them to your own personal friends list, since those followers are instead added to your Facebook Page's list of fans.

Creating a Facebook Page

Setting up a Facebook Page for your product or business is a great way to connect with people on the world's most popular social networking site. Unlike Twitter, members are not able to search for keywords in posts. Facebook's search engine is limited to searching for member names. With only a personal Facebook account under your own name, you won't be listed in Facebook searches for your iPhone app name or business name. But with a Facebook Page for your iPhone app or company, related Facebook searches will find it by name.

To create a Facebook Page, you must have a personal Facebook account since that is the account assigned as the Page's administrator. If you plan on creating more than one iPhone app, then I recommend building a fan base under one company Facebook Page, rather than several separate accounts for each iPhone app. One centralized page will not only be easier to manage but will also allow you to cross-promote your products to the same fan audience.

Sign into your personal Facebook account, and then visit the following link:

- Create New Facebook Page:
  `http://www.facebook.com/pages/create.php`

In the online form provided, select Technology Product/Service under Brand, Product, or Organization in order to assign the correct categorization to your new page (see Figure 8–19).

The only requirement is that you must be the owner or official representative of the business reflected in the page you're creating. Once the new Facebook Page is built, add your company description to the Info tab and logo to the page's icon/picture.

Figure 8–19. *Creating a new Facebook Page for your iPhone app business*

Connecting with Fans

Now that your Facebook Page is up and running, it's time to spread the word about it, encouraging people to become a fan! To get one of those cool Facebook domain names assigned to your page—such as `http://www.facebook.com/iTunes`—you must have at least 25 fans.

There's absolutely nothing wrong with appealing to your existing blog and Twitter audience. Let them know you have a new dedicated Facebook Page, and invite them to show support by becoming a fan. As expected, Facebook even provides an affordable way to advertise your page throughout their network to gain new fans.

When communicating with your fans, most of your posts should be shared via standard status updates, which appear on your Facebook Page. Occasionally, you may have a need to broadcast an important announcement to the inbox of every fan, which can be done by clicking the Send an Update to Fans link. No one likes to receive a barrage of inbox updates, so to retain your fans, try not to abuse that direct message feature.

Import Blog, Output Twitter

By extending your marketing reach across more and more social networks, the first concern is time. Posting the same content across multiple sites, such as your blog, Twitter, and Facebook, can be very time-consuming. Fortunately, a recent trend in social media is the ability to syndicate content across networks to make publishing more convenient. Post your news in one place, and it gets published on multiple sites. As I already mentioned, several blog sites like Tumblr.com and Posterous.com enable users to autoupdate Twitter and Facebook with links to their new blog posts. Facebook also offers a way to do this with its own Import a Blog feature.

Want your new blog posts to automatically be published on your FaceBook Page? Just follow these steps. From your Facebook Page's profile, select the Notes tab. On the right side of the screen, you should see the gray Notes Settings box, as shown in Figure 8–20. If Notes Settings is not visible, then you may need to post at least one note on your page for that Notes Settings box to appear.

Figure 8–20. *Select the Notes tab on your Facebook Page, and then click the Import a Blog link in the Notes Settings box in the right column.*

Under Notes Settings, click the Import a Blog link. You'll be prompted to enter your blog's RSS feed URL (see Figure 8–21). Once submitted, Facebook will automatically post your new blog entries to your Facebook Page's notes. Although you can easily remove any imported notes, you won't be able to edit them. If you want the flexibility to edit a particular note, you should manually post that note to Facebook yourself to retain editing access.

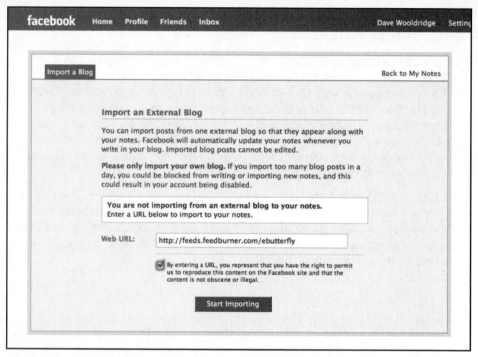

Figure 8–21. *Submit your blog's RSS feed URL to autoimport blog posts into Facebook as notes.*

If you want your Facebook status updates to be automatically posted on Twitter, Facebook now offers support for that (see Figure 8–22). Since tracking the click-through statistics of your links is always important, if you activate that feature, be sure to still generate your own shortened URLs from your Bit.ly account for the external links to your web site or the iTunes App Store included in your status updates.

In reverse, you can also publish your tweets as status updates on your Facebook Page by installing Andy Young's handy Facebook application Selective Twitter Status at http://www.facebook.com/selectivetwitter. This application is much more powerful than importing your Twitter RSS feed as a blog because it allows you to choose which specific tweets get posted on your Facebook Page by marking them with the special #fb hashtag. This prevents nonbusiness tweets from accidentally sneaking into your company's Facebook Page. For the Selective Twitter Status application to work, your Facebook Page updates must not be protected.

Figure 8–22. *Facebook provides support for autoposting your page's status updates to your Twitter account.*

Other Social Networks and Bookmarking Sites

Obviously, Twitter and Facebook aren't the only social media giants in town. Depending on the kind of app or game you've developed, some of the other sites may offer a more targeted demographic.

Although MySpace may have been dethroned by the current king, Facebook, MySpace.com is still the second most popular social networking site and a very powerful force in the music community. Countless new artists have been discovered via MySpace, moving on to lucrative record deals and high-profile music careers. If your iPhone app is music-related, then the MySpace music crowd may just be the perfect audience for you to reach. Time to unveil your own MySpace profile page to network with other music lovers and promote your iPhone app!

If your app appeals to businesses, then you'll definitely want to get connected on LinkedIn.com. Besides including a link to your iPhone app's web site on your LinkedIn profile, the popular business network hosts thousands of active discussion groups. Pick the groups that best match your app's target audience, and promote it by posting your press releases and links to related blog articles. This is a great way to reach business executives who may not have found your iPhone app on their own in the crowded App Store.

LinkedIn also makes it easy to publish your Twitter posts on your LinkedIn page. Activate your Twitter account on your LinkedIn profile and then append either the #in or #li hashtags to your tweets for those select messages to also be published as LinkedIn status updates.

And for additional exposure, don't forget to submit your blog posts and published web articles to sites like Digg.com, Delicious.com, Technorati.com, Reddit.com, and StumbleUpon.com that specialize in sharing news and social bookmarking.

Commenting on Forums, Groups, and Blogs

Do a little research to find online forums, message boards, and blogs related to your iPhone app's target audience. If it's a music app, explore the most popular music forums and groups. If it's a writing app, then investigate which sites are the most popular hangouts for authors. Since you developed an app for a particular niche market, it's a safe assumption you know a little something about it. Put your knowledge to good use by offering help on related special-interest forums or posting comments on blogs.

Yes, I'm creating extra work for you, but there's a method to the madness. Don't ever post anonymously on those sites. Most forums, groups, and even blogs support member logins to make frequent posting more convenient and secure. When requested, sign up as a free member and enter all the profile information so that your presence on those sites is visibly identifiable with a name, URL link, and photo. Some blogs utilize third-party avatar systems like Gravatar.com, so it's worth having a Gravatar profile already registered and ready to use. If signatures are supported, then use that small bit of HTML-savvy space to promote your iPhone app and web site.

See where I'm going with this? Every time you post a comment to a forum thread or blog article, your photo, your name, your web site link, and a subtle iPhone app reference are always represented. As long as you don't ever abuse your presence by spamming blatant sales pitches for your app, it's a win-win for everyone. In helping others, you're also increasing awareness for your forthcoming iPhone app simply by referencing it in your member URL and signature.

But Not Too Much Noise: Maintaining a Professional Reputation

Because of the high volume of informal conversations that occurs on social media sites like Twitter and Facebook, it's often easy to forget that the things you say are not just between you and the participants but can be read by literally everyone within your network. And in the case of Twitter, anyone can visit your profile page and read your tweets, whether they follow you or not. Your online actions play out on a very public, global stage.

While being personable is encouraged, you're still representing your product and/or company, so your online behavior should be respectful, knowing that the things you say and link to make lasting impressions with potential customers worldwide. If you feel this advice is painfully obvious and shouldn't warrant a mention, then you're one step ahead of the game. You may have enough business savvy to recognize this, but you'd be surprised at just how many professional developers are oblivious to the overall image they project.

Over the years, I've seen developer web sites that promote their software products alongside their online shrines to pro wrestling stars and the sexy cylon babes from *Battlestar Galactica*! Yeah, you know who you are. It's fine if you're still in college and operate your software business out of the garage, but the world does not need to know this. In fact, you want your web site and your social media accounts to project a professional image that instills confidence in consumers. They want to know that by purchasing your iPhone app, they're investing in a developer who will continue to update and support the product. If they suspect it's nothing more than a hobby for you, then you run the risk of missing out on those potential sales. Without faith in you, how can they have faith in your product?

Here are a few guidelines to consider:

- **Perception.** Always portray a professional image of how you want to be seen. It doesn't matter if you're 18 or 68, fresh out of high school, or recently retired. The Internet equalizes the playing field. The visual design of your web site, the kind of content it offers, and the way you present yourself to others via email, tweets, and blog posts—it all paints a vivid picture of you and how you do business. It's not about projecting a false illusion but rather showcasing your true self in a professional light.

- **NSFW? Not appropriate to post!** If you're using your blog and social media accounts to promote your iPhone app and business, don't curse or post jokes, funny photos, and videos that others might find offensive. Just because you tack on the warning "NSFW" (not suitable for work) doesn't make it acceptable. Living in a liberal big city, sometimes it's easy to forget that there are parts of the world (even large populations within the country you live) that are far more conservative than you. What you find funny, others may find wildly offensive. And those are potential sales you just lost. I hate to be a killjoy. We all want to have fun, and there's lots of it to be had online, but the goal is to sell more iPhone apps, right?

- **Don't mix business with politics or religion.** The two topics that elicit the strongest reactions from people are politics and religion. Whatever your viewpoint is, there is always someone just as passionate on the opposing side. It's a conversation you can't win. If you're using social networks like Twitter and Facebook to promote your forthcoming iPhone app, taking advantage of your audience by preaching your own political or religious agendas is the quickest way to alienate potential customers.

- **Keep your emotions in check.** Don't ever tweet, comment, or post blog entries in anger. Even though you can usually delete most items after the fact, copies of them linger on the Web to haunt you for years to come. You may have deleted that nasty blog post, but all of your blog's email subscribers still have it sitting in their inboxes. And don't forget the elephant memory of Google's cache. Your online rants can live on indefinitely in Google's search databases.

- **Two wrongs don't make a right.** Just because someone says something negative about your iPhone app or your blog posts, don't lash back with venom. Talking trash about someone—especially online where everything is logged, cached, and archived—can win you a defamation lawsuit. You laugh, but it's happened before. Protect your reputation and your personal assets by taking the high road.

- **Customers come first.** The customer may not always be right, but they should always be given your utmost respect and attention. Reply to every email and tweet you receive in a prompt and courteous manner. There's no such thing as a stupid question, only stupid answers. OK, so maybe there are stupid questions and some customers may get on your nerves, but if you embarrass them in any way with sarcastic public replies on Twitter, then that's not only a lost customer, but someone who may warn friends and family to avoid your products. Be willing to go out of your way to make your customers happy. If they feel important, they'll reward you with their loyalty.

Everyone Loves a Winner: Collecting Prerelease Press and Testimonials

Although growing the prerelease buzz via social media is important, you should also start reaching out to influential journalists and bloggers who you hope will cover your app's forthcoming launch announcement and publish a review. As I've said before, if you don't have the patience or time to dedicate to prerelease publicity, then it may be worth hiring a third-party firm that specializes in iPhone app marketing. After searching Google for *iPhone app marketing*, you'll see there are many agencies to choose from, so if you do go that route, do your homework and talk to several of them to find the one that can meet your needs and budget.

Preparing a Hit List

Whether you hire a third-party publicist or do it yourself, you'll need to have a few marketing materials ready at your fingertips. Luckily, these are elements I've already discussed earlier in this book, so you should already have them prepared:

- Company logo

- Your iPhone app's icon and logo

- The app description—the quick elevator pitch and full list of features

- A few stunning screenshots that best represent your app

- A dedicated web page for your app

- Optional video trailer

Most tech journalists will be publishing coverage online, but in the event that your app attracts interest from a print magazine or newspaper, be sure to have high-resolution images ready of your company logo and iPhone app icon/logo. Getting your app's web site completed before you reach out to the press is vital since journalists will ask for your web site URL. Additionally, if you produced a video trailer, be sure to upload it to a video-sharing site like YouTube so that online publications can easily embed the video in their news articles.

It's time to do a little research online. To receive news coverage from the most influential press sources, you need to know which tech sites and journalists would be interested in writing about your particular iPhone app. Prepare a hit list of people you should contact. Take note of their target audience and what they specialize in writing about. There's no point spending valuable time pitching your app to an iPhone games site if it's not a game. If they've never covered productivity apps in the past, they're probably not looking to start now. It's best to conserve your efforts and focus only on those select people who will be interested in your app's category.

Establishing Relationships

When performing competitive research in Chapter 2, several iPhone app review sites were listed. Those sites will prove important once again when you want them to review your application once it becomes available in the App Store. And don't forget about the various tech sites and magazines that cover iPhone news. Even the ones that don't post press releases may be interested in writing about your app if it provides a unique feature or service that is either deemed newsworthy or would directly benefit their readers.

I'll discuss acquiring media news exposure and reviews for your iPhone app extensively in Chapter 10, so for now, I'll simply mention that if you don't have an existing relationship with any prominent tech journalists and bloggers, then now is the time to introduce yourself. You don't want to cold call them when your app is released. That's too late, wasting valuable time with introductions when your marketing engine should be moving at full speed.

During this prerelease stage, establish a connection with the people on your press hit list. Target the most important ones first, gradually making your way through the list. Although their phone numbers may be listed on their respective web sites, don't call them first. Introduce yourself initially through email so that they can read about your company and your forthcoming iPhone app at their convenience. Remember that most journalists are under deadline to write several articles each day, so their time is very limited. Don't expect an instantaneous response. It may take them several days or even a week to reply to your email, so patience is key here. Yet another reason to begin this process a good month or so before your application goes live in the App Store.

Even if some journalists ignore your queries, do not under any circumstances bombard their voice mail or email inboxes with an onslaught of repeated messages. With more than 100,000 apps in the App Store, you're not the only iPhone developer looking for press coverage. There's nothing wrong with being persistent, but no ones like being spammed either.

Another good way to make journalists and influential bloggers aware of you is to follow them on Twitter. Since Twitter has become a major news source for the press, your tweets will not only increase awareness of your iPhone app with potential customers but may also attract the attention of the press, generating requests for interviews and app reviews. Follow your favorite tech journalists, and they may just follow you back!

One of the reasons it's so crucial that your app's web site and screenshots are stunning visuals is so that you can stand out from the overwhelming pile of queries from other developers. An eye-catching web site linked from a tweet and a killer screenshot posted on a popular iPhone forum have been known to kick-start a good dose of press coverage and word-of-mouth.

The tech press deals with thousands of developers and publishers of applications and games for several different platforms, so for those journalists who have reported on your products in the past, don't assume they'll remember you when you send out a new press release. Reintroduce yourself before then, thanking them for their previous coverage as a reminder before mentioning your impending new iPhone app.

Be conscious of their busy writing schedules and deadlines by asking about editorial calendars and how much advance notice they need in order to run a review during a given time period. This is especially important when dealing with the print world. Online bloggers can usually turn around articles within days, but print magazines typically have a three-month lead time.

Offering Exclusives and Advance Ad Hoc Builds to Secure Coverage

If you have something new and exciting to offer, journalists will want to be the first to break the news. They'll have more interest in covering your story if it's an exclusive. Obviously, you can't offer everyone an exclusive, so if you do provide a special sneak preview of your app in the form of a video clip, a screenshot, or even an early beta version, make sure it's with a major publication that pulls in a large audience.

Having a few key bloggers play with your app before its release can work in your favor. If they enjoy your app, they're more likely to talk about it. If they love your app, they may even become an unofficial evangelist for it, providing you with amazing quotes that you can include in your press release and on your web site (see Figure 8–23).

Figure 8–23. *Having testimonials in place from respected tech sites can help kick-start sales when your iPhone app becomes available in the App Store. Shown here: Spiffing Apps' web site proudly displays glowing press quotes for its Put Things Off app.*

Most iPhone reviewers and bloggers are accustomed to receiving apps via ad hoc distribution, so when beta-testing your app, don't forget to reserve a few of your allotted device slots for prerelease press coverage. Many iPhone-savvy journalists even include their device's UDID in their contact vCard or online bio. This is handy since you'll need to set up a device ID for them in your iPhone Developer Program account. Yes, configuring and providing ad hoc builds of your app for a select group of influential press members can be a hassle, but the potential publicity is well worth it. If you're sending a beta version, then be sure to make them aware of that fact so that they don't judge it as the final app release.

Even though the app may change or encounter unexpected delays during Apple's review process, some tech sites don't respect embargoes, so even if you stress the importance of holding back the publication of their app review until its release in the App Store, your wishes may not always be granted. Since you can't always control when reviews are published, it's vital that you don't send out ad hoc builds to tech sites too far in advance. You certainly don't want to over-saturate the market with tons of press coverage long before the actual release since that's simply a waste of publicity that would be of greater benefit post-release. People generally have short memories when it comes to software products, so the majority of your publicity should take place when it can do you the most good—when consumers can instantly buy the app they just read about.

With that said, it's always nice to have some winning testimonials in place from respected tech sites before your application is released. This way, when your app goes live in the App Store, it won't seem like such an unknown entity. Based on the prerelease buzz and the endorsements plastered on your web site, your new iPhone app will appear that much more appealing to consumers. Everybody loves a winner.

Passing the Baton

With your prerelease marketing efforts in full swing, it's now time to place your iPhone application in the good hands of Apple's app review team. Next up, I'll walk through the dreaded app submission process. You've read the horror stories posted online from fellow iPhone developers of long review times and disheartening rejections, but don't let that discourage you. Like quickly ripping off a Band-Aid to minimize the pain, let's not waste another minute! The sooner you work through Apple's app review process and get approved, the sooner you can start selling in the App Store. So, take a deep breath, and turn the page.

Chapter 9

Keys to the Kingdom: The App Store Submission Process

After months of extensive planning, development, and testing, you're finally ready to submit your iPhone application to the App Store! Congratulations on all your hard work! Your beta testers love your app, but will Apple's app review team give it a thumbs-up?

If you're a Mac or Windows software developer, you're accustomed to controlling the deployment method of your products, distributing them as digital downloads from your web site. Need to quickly fix a bug or push out a new release on a specific date? No problem. You have complete control over uploading software updates to your web site at any time.

With the App Store, Apple controls the deployment and distribution gateway, requiring every new app version and update to be reviewed and approved before being released. For desktop software developers, this is a foreign concept that takes quite a bit of time to get used to. The Internet is full of stories from frustrated iPhone developers about long review times and inconsistent rejections, making the app submission process the most dreaded step in the road to the App Store. But don't be discouraged. Although many developers see this as an annoying bottleneck that makes it difficult to provide quick bug fixes and impossible to plan exact release dates, it is nonetheless the rules of the game. Apple's App Store is the hottest mobile software market out there, making it extremely easy for iPhone and iPod touch users to buy apps—nothing yet has come close to the App Store's level of sales success. If you want to play in this popular arena, then dealing with Apple's guidelines is simply the price of admission.

Fortunately, just in the short time I've been writing this book, Apple has made several improvements to the app submission process, providing a little more transparency to review status, rejection criteria, availability to request priority bug fix app reviews, and more. Many of the items I had planned to include in this chapter are now nonissues. I have no doubt that Apple will continue to enhance iTunes Connect and the iPhone Developer Program Portal to address many of the concerns that currently worry developers.

If you've followed Apple's guidelines, chances are good that your app submission will go smoothly. Just remember, more than 100,000 apps have already been approved, far outweighing the number of rejected apps. Before submitting your application in iTunes Connect, there are a few elements you'll need to have ready for the online submission form. It's worth taking the time to craft a quality app description, screenshots, and a keywords list *before* logging into iTunes Connect, since those items will influence not only Apple's app review team but also your product's marketability in the App Store.

The Politics of Pricing

One of the most important things you'll need to determine before submitting your app is the selling price. With most of the apps in the App Store's Top 25 priced at only 99 cents, don't assume that's the magic price point for your app. There are actually quite a few factors to consider before settling on a price.

Analyzing Similar Apps

Having already researched your competition in Chapter 2, you should already know the prices and feature sets of similar apps. Although keeping your price below that of competitive apps may seem like the obvious move, don't sell yourself short just yet.

If your app does not offer an attractive differentiator, such as an enhanced user interface or killer feature, then you may be forced to price your app below similar apps, especially if they already enjoy a successful run of sales and positive customer reviews. But if you did your competitive homework, then this shouldn't be an issue, right?

If your app *does* bring a much desired feature that sets it apart from the competition, you may be able to do quite well in the App Store with the same price or even a higher price. If you feel similar apps selling at $1.99 will quickly copy your unique killer feature, then maintaining the same $1.99 price point might be the answer, but if you think the feature may remain exclusive to your app—for whatever reason, such as technical difficulty or licensing deals—then you may be able to charge $2.99 or a slighter higher price.

If you've stumbled upon an untapped market where your app does not currently have any competitors, then it really comes down to determining how much your product is worth to potential customers. Usually the more niche market it serves, the higher price threshold it can bear. For example, apps that cater to scientists, doctors, or sales reps are often priced at the higher end of the spectrum, ranging anywhere from $6.99 to $99. You'll want to research the particular field your app specializes in to help calculate how much potential customers would be willing to spend on such a mobile application, based on the benefits it provides. You certainly don't want to gouge your customers, but at the same time, you don't want to leave money behind on the table either.

Room to Maneuver

Productivity apps experience a longer life span than fly-by-night, hit-driven apps, so pricing can be a little easier to determine. But for games and novelty apps that don't benefit from that same longevity, ranking high in the App Store charts immediately after launch is usually the goal. Although most of those hit-driven apps debut at the rock bottom price of 99 cents in the hopes of propelling them into the Top 100, you should think twice before employing this same pricing strategy.

Setting the price at 99 cents upon release is a nice impulse-buy incentive, but what happens when the initial sales boost from your launch publicity efforts eventually taper off? When awareness and sales later drop (and at some point, they will), that's when you'll want to rejuvenate your presence in the App Store with a limited-time sale offer, but with your app already priced at the minimum 99 cents, you have no room to maneuver. But with an app price of $1.99 or higher, then you'll have room to offer a special discount sales when needed to keep your momentum going in the App Store. Games often receive complaints from consumers when released with a price tag higher than 99 cents, but don't let the vocal few sway you. If you've built a quality game, then complaints aside, your profits will benefit from the higher price. Although most higher-priced games are from big publishers like Electronic Arts and Gameloft, many small, independent developers have also found success as well, such as Semi Secret Software's Canabalt at $2.99.

At only 99 cents, you have to sell a lot of apps to make any decent money, especially after Apple takes its 30 percent cut. This usually requires ranking in the Top 25, with your business model relying on the boosted sales volume. And if you can get there, the visible exposure of the Top 25 can increase your sales exponentially, making the low 99–cent price worthwhile. *If you can rank high...* That's the gamble. Since there's no guarantee your app will make it to the Top 25 or even the Top 100, pricing it at 99 cents is very risky if you end up selling fewer copies than expected. With an app price of $1.99 or higher, you don't have to sell as many units to make just as much money, which in turn makes the App Store ranking less vital to your app's profitability.

Let's say your app manages to sell only 10,000 units over the course of several months:

- 10,000 × $0.99 = $9,900 – $2,970 (Apple's 30%) = $6,930
- 10,000 × $1.99 = $19,900 – $5,970 (Apple's 30%) = $13,930

With disappointing overall sales, a $1.99 or higher price can still provide respectable sales numbers and may even recoup the product's initial development costs, but a 99–cent price drastically reduces your profit margin by half!

Sustaining a Long-Term Business

Since you've purchased this book, then it's probably a safe bet that you're looking to make money from your iPhone app development. And you're not just looking to bank on a single iPhone app but ideally build a profitable business producing several iPhone apps. To accomplish this, you must price your apps not only to be competitive with other similar apps but also to provide enough revenue to pay for the actual development costs of each app and run your business. To help determine your pricing, you should first figure out what your business needs to earn each year to survive.

As a fledging business, your operating overhead may appear to be very low. Like many independent developers, you could be starting out working from home and doing all of the design, programming, marketing, accounting, and other business tasks yourself. This is a common formula that has worked for many iPhone app developers, but when calculating your financial needs, don't focus on only immediate expenses such as advertising, web hosting, Internet access, telephone lines, health insurance, food, and your mortgage/rent. It's important to also place a value on your time as well. You don't want to merely "get by." Your plan should be to profit from all your hard work, earning enough money to not only fund your next iPhone app project but also reward your efforts with a little luxury.

For example purposes, let's say your iPhone app will cost $5,000 to develop. To put food on the table and pay all of your bills, let's assume your monthly overhead is $4,000. If you plan on producing three apps within a year, your total development budget and annual living expenses would be approximately $63,000. To give yourself a little breathing room in case of additional expenses and expected emergencies, let's round up to $70,000.

- $70,000 / $0.69 ($0.99 – Apple's 30%) = 101,449 apps sold

- $70,000 / $1.39 ($1.99 – Apple's 30%) = 50,360 apps sold

- $70,000 / $2.09 ($2.99 – Apple's 30%) = 33,493 apps sold

To generate $70,000 in annual revenue, your three 99–cent apps would have to sell a staggering 101,449 copies before the year's end! Easy enough if your three apps are best-sellers, sitting comfortably within the App Store's Top 25, but if they're ranked outside of the Top 100, then charging only 99 cents per app is not going to get you anywhere close to your annual $70,000 revenue goal.

And if you're coming from the world of desktop software development and consulting, you're probably used to making quite a bit more than that per year, so just do the math, and you'll quickly see how selling apps for only 99 cents requires them to be best-sellers with no margin for failure. Are the development costs for your iPhone app project more than $5,000? Looking to support your business with an annual revenue stream of $100,000?

- $100,000 / $0.69 ($0.99 – Apple's 30%) = 144,928 apps sold

- $100,000 / $1.39 ($1.99 – Apple's 30%) = 71,942 apps sold

- $100,000 / $2.09 ($2.99 – Apple's 30%) = 47,847 apps sold

That's a lot of apps you'll need to sell per year at only 99 cents each! You'll either need a bona fide hit or work that much harder to release a larger collection of apps that can be generating revenue. Just remember, the more apps you produce, the more money you spend on development, which in turn raises your overhead.

Perceived Value and Consumer Resistance

Starting to understand the great risk involved with the 99–cent price point? Your revenue earnings are not the only potential victim if your app does not sell well. There also seems to be a direct correlation between price and ratings, but not in the direction you'd expect. The lower your price, the lower your customer ratings may sink.

It's true that if your app is priced too high, consumers will lash out with negative ratings in the App Store. So, the cheaper your app is, then the better the reviews, right? Not necessarily. A lower price brings a broader audience of customers, many of whom acquired it as an impulse buy. At 99 cents, you wouldn't think anyone would complain, but complain they do. There are quite a few users out there with unreasonably high expectations for only 99 cents. Many of them have been spoiled by the wealth of great 99 cent games like the ever-evolving Pocket God phenomenon. With many developers dropping app prices to only 99 cents in an attempt to boost volume sales and ranker higher on the App Store charts, their strategy seems to have cultivated a distorted perception of app worth among consumers.

In August 2009, Hog Bay Software's Jesse Grosjean decided to experiment with the pricing of his acclaimed WriteRoom for iPhone, dropping from the regular $4.99 price down to free (for a weekend) and then 99 cents. The test was to see whether the limited free offer and then the later subtle increase to 99 cents would spur enough of a boost in overall sales volume to make up for the decreased profit per sale. Although sales did increase, they eventually tapered off again—proof that for the longevity of the app, the higher price ultimately generated more revenue in the long haul. Jesse Grosjean blogged that he had planned to end up at a lower price point such as $1.99 or $2.99, but during the sales experiment, he watched WriteRoom's App Store star ratings "go from mostly fours and fives to evenly distributed between five and one star." Even though the cheaper pricing did increase the number of new users, it also yielded a perception that users were overall less satisfied. The experiment revealed a lot about App Store behavior, but after the sale ended, he opted to return to his original $4.99 price tag.

At a higher price, you may attract fewer customers, but they bought your app because they genuinely wanted it. They have a vested interest in the app's survival and success, so their posted App Store ratings tend to reflect a more positive tone. A higher price can also give your app a greater perceived value. Psychologically, many people relate price to quality, believing that you get what you pay for.

So if 99 cents is too low for a large percentage of apps, then what price is too high? It is generally believed that apps ranging from $0.99 to $1.99 are perceived as impulse buys. $2.99 seems to be the threshold that causes people to think and evaluate the app with a higher degree of scrutiny before making a purchase decision. Real resistance kicks in at $4.99 and higher, which requires a really high-quality game or app with strong features. There are a handful of best-in-class apps that have prospered at the higher end of the price spectrum, such as The Omni Group's OmniFocus at $19.99, Culture Code's Things at $9.99, and Illusion Labs Touchgrind at $4.99.

One of my favorite games, Firemint's Real Racing, was originally launched at $9.99 to great fanfare, and to sustain continued sales after several months of release, Firemint eventually dropped the price to $6.99 and then again to $4.99. This has enabled Firemint to extend the product's life span and remain competitive among the new releases in the App Store without sacrificing too much revenue. Real Racing is *not* one of those games that can be developed for only a few thousand dollars. It's a state-of-the-art virtual racing game that required a large development budget and many months of programming, and should be priced accordingly, reinforcing the perceived value. At the reduced price of $4.99, it seems like a steal for those consumers who were hesitant to buy it at $9.99, yet it still retains a profitable price tag to help support continued development of updates and new games.

Just keep in mind that once your app has been released in the App Store, it's much easier to later reduce your price than to increase your price. After a few weeks of sales, if you're experiencing a lot of push back from consumers over your app price, you can always experiment with sale prices or permanent price drops. But if you already established a set low price, then raising the price at a later date can often cause friction with consumers, angered by the increase.

Improving App Discovery: The Art of Keywords and Names

An app's description in the App Store used to be searchable, which allowed developers to fill their app descriptions with tons of optimized keywords and text phrases. It was also a source of abuse, because many developers tried to "game" the system by including competitor app names and irrelevant, popular keywords in their descriptions in the hopes of ranking better in search results. In the summer of 2009, Apple changed the iTunes search algorithm to prevent this kind of misuse. In its place, Apple introduced keywords, which developers can assign to their submitted applications.

Now, the only elements that are searchable in the App Store are your iPhone app's name, keywords, and company name. Because of this change, it's now more important than ever that your app's submitted name and keywords are search engine optimized to improve your app's visibility in related App Store searches.

Assigning Keywords

iTunes Connect limits the Keywords field to only 100 characters, so make every keyword count! When the Keywords feature was first unveiled, some references in Apple's Developer Center incorrectly listed the limit as 255 characters, but it is in fact only 100 characters. Keywords can be single words or multiword phrases, so for best results, Apple recommends separating multiple keywords with commas. Since your company name listed with your application is already searchable in the App Store, there is absolutely no need to include it in the Keywords field—doing so is only a waste of your precious 100 characters.

Although the Keywords feature may seem a lot more limiting than the lengthy text blocks of app descriptions, Apple has done you a small favor by making keywords hidden from public view. This prevents your competitors from easily copying all of your keywords! Of course, it's a double-edged sword in that you don't have easy access to their keywords either.

Since the keywords you select play such a crucial role in your app's discovery in the App Store, it's important to do a lot of search experiments of your own to find out which apps are included in the search results based on certain search queries. I mentioned this in Chapter 2 when discussing the benefits of researching your competition before developing your app. The goal is to build a list of keywords that you think would benefit your app's visibility in consumer searches. Sure, you'll want to include keywords that work for your competition, but you'll also want to use a thesaurus to figure out *all* the possible keywords related to your app's feature set that users might possibly search for. If you found a few keywords that seem like intuitive queries and are not used by your competition, those may be valuable keywords to include. The fewer similar apps that appear in a user's search results, the less competition you have when the user decides which listed items to explore.

Still not sure what keywords to use for optimal results? As previously mentioned in Chapter 8, Google's Search-based Keyword Tool (`http://www.google.com/sktool/`) and its AdWords keyword tool (`https://adwords.google.com/select/KeywordToolExternal`) can be helpful resources. Although Google designed these web tools to help people refine their SEO plans and ad campaigns, they can also help you pinpoint and compare the popularity of specific keywords. The data is not App Store related, but it does give you a good idea of what people are searching for online as it relates to your app's subject matter. For those of you having trouble pinpointing strategic keywords via App Store searches, these Google tools provide much better answers than simply making wild guesses on your own.

Stick to relevant keywords for best results. If you're selling a niche app such as a writing tool or parked-car locator, it might seem like a good idea to include popular terms such as *fart* or *bikini* in an attempt to push your app in front of broader audience, but that strategy won't help you in the App Store. Not only do unrelated keywords hurt your search relevancy—lowering your search ranking in your actual genre—but it also is a good way to get your app flagged by Apple during the review process.

> **APP REJECTION WARNING: Keywords cannot contain words or phrases that are irrelevant, offensive, or refer to other products, brands, and registered trademarks.** Don't try to be clever by including the names of competitive apps in your Keywords list. And be very careful not to include trademarked names or celebrity names that you do not have licensed permission to use. Doing so well will only get your app rejected! For example, if your app is an independent movie listings guide, including keywords like *Moviefone, Netflix, Fandango,* or even actor names could get your app booted from the App Store. Apple says that "improper use of keywords is the fourth most common reason for App Store rejections."

Also try to avoid overly common keywords, even if they are related. Common, generalized keywords will produce a huge list of search results, making it much more difficult for your app to be discovered. Honing in on more specific keywords that would produce fewer search results will not only improve your search relevancy but will also make it easier for your app to be included closer to the top of the search results list. For example, if your app is a flying game that requires users to navigate a spaceship through a three-dimensional maze of stars and planets, don't use general keywords like *game* or *fun*, which basically describes every game in the App Store. Narrow your keywords to more specific terms that game lovers might search for, such as *spaceship* and *mission*.

Since you're limited to only 100 characters, don't repeat the same words in both your app name and keywords since both are included in App Store searches. For example, if your app name includes the word *spaceship*, then there's no need to waste valuable characters by including *spaceship* in your keywords.

If you've localized your app to more than one language, then it's important to include localized keywords in the Localization page within iTunes Connect for *every* region your app supports. If you've decided to make your application available in both English and German App Stores, then you'll want to submit keywords in both English and German so that your app is searchable in those related, regional App Stores.

Take special care in crafting your list of keywords before submitting them in iTunes Connect, since you will only be able to edit them again upon uploading a new binary app version or if your app has been rejected and needs to be reviewed again. This precaution is done so that Apple can approve your keywords during the app review process. This prevents the keywords system from being "gamed" or abused by developers, but it also makes it vital that the keywords list submitted is perfectly optimized and free of typos, since you won't be able to go back and revise it until the next time your app is officially reviewed by Apple.

The Name Game

In Chapter 2, I stressed how important it is that your app name be short enough to display in its entirety on the iPhone's home screen without being truncated. Having a short app name also serves you well when displayed in search results in the iPhone version of the App Store. With a narrower screen width, a shorter app name ensures that the entire name is displayed without being truncated. Tap Tap Tap's Voices and Convert app names are very easy to read, leaving room to add a descriptive caption to the title (see Figure 9–1).

Figure 9–1. *With Voices and Convert, Tap Tap Tap kept its app names short for easy readability and added descriptive, keyword-rich captions to their name titles in the App Store.*

That's right, your application's name in the App Store does not have to be the same as the actual binary app name. It's perfectly acceptable to add a descriptive caption to the app name field, but be sure your app's name comes first, followed by any additional descriptive text, so that the actual name will always be visible when listed in search results. It's fine that the embedded caption shown in Figure 9–1's list is truncated, since it will be displayed in full on the app's product page (after tapping on the selection in the list). That added caption—usually separated from the preceding app name with a simple hyphen or colon—helps describe the application's core functionality. This eye-catching trick not only draws the viewer's attention but also lets the viewer know what your app does without having to first read the lengthy description. Since it would appear that not many people actually take the time to read long app descriptions anymore, this extended app title can really benefit your marketing efforts. The simple app names Convert and Voices are listed in the App Store as follows:

- Convert—the unit calculator

- Voices—fun voice morphing!

The other major benefit of this extended name technique is that it gives you the opportunity to fill the searchable app name field with related keywords! If a user searched the App Store for *convert*, then both Convert and the competitive app Convertbot by Tapbots are listed in the first 25 search results, because of both of them using that term in their app names. But if a user searched for *calculator* or *unit calculator*, then only Convert appears in the first twenty-five search results since its app title includes those terms as part of its extended name. Convertbot's keywords must not be optimized for *unit calculator* or *calculator* since it was not listed in those initial search results.

Keep in mind that the app name you choose for display within the App Store can be edited only when submitting a new app binary for review or if your app was rejected and requires resubmission. Like the Keywords feature, your app name is subject to Apple's review team to ensure that no one tries to abuse the opportunity with unlicensed trademarks or irrelevant and inappropriate words. So, all of the same rules apply here as they do for submitted keywords. Attempts to cheat the system will prevent your app from being approved.

Treat the app name title as a marketing extension of your related keywords. When your Keywords list and the app name are working together in unison with highly optimized words and phrases, you're increasing the chances of your product being discovered in the overcrowded App Store.

Perfecting the Sales Pitch of Your App Description

Although a product's App Store description is no longer searchable, it does still serve as a primary marketing tool for users who are interested in learning more about your application or game. Someone has gotten as far as viewing your product page in the App Store, so this is your one shot to convince them why their life is not complete until they've purchased your app! The three influential elements on your product page are the description, the screenshots, and the customer reviews. I'll be exploring all of these items in this chapter, but right now, let's tackle the anatomy of a good description. People read from top to bottom, and if your description is long, it may require some scrolling to read it in its entirety. Most people won't bother reading the complete block of text, especially if it's full of dense paragraphs, so it's important to break up the text into brief sections and bullet points for easy eye-scanning. Less is more!

What Is It?

If you're not using an extended app name (and you should) or if it's still not obvious what your app's primary function is, then the very first thing you should include in your description is a brief explanation of what it does and why people should buy it! Remember my Chapter 8 discussion of "the quick pitch" on your app's web site? This is no different. Just like your web site, visitors to your App Store product page will take only a few seconds to scan the description and screenshots to see whether the app captures their interest. Your job is to make sure you provide enough of a "sales hook" that they're motivated to continue reading.

With the new App Store page layout that Apple introduced in iTunes 9, it's more important than ever to really optimize your app summary into a brief couple of sentences that's placed at the very top of your description text. Although iTunes 8 displayed the full description as a long text column, the new iTunes 9 page layout includes only the first two to three lines of description text. To read the description in its entirety, users are required to click the More link to expand the display (see the screen on the right of Figure 9–2). But there's no guarantee that users will actually do that, so make sure those first few lines of visible text adequately explains what your app is. If that brief text summary interests users, then they can click the More link to view your complete list of features and benefits.

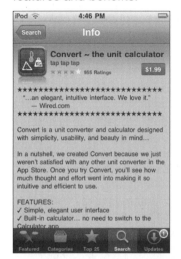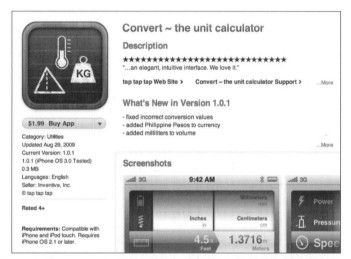

Figure 9–2. *Displayed in the iPhone's App Store (left), Tap Tap Tap's Convert description is brief and to the point with an eye-catching testimonial, an app summary, and a bullet list of features. With the new iTunes 9 page layout (right), make sure your app summary is in the first two to three lines of your description text to remain visible.*

Awards and Testimonials

Ideally, when you were generating a little prerelease buzz (Chapter 8), you managed to get a few prominent media reviewers to check out your app and provide you with some choice quotes. When your app is new in the App Store, you'll have very few (if any) customer reviews posted, so it's best to include a few winning testimonials in your app description to help convince consumers of the app's quality. And even when your app does receive a lot of customer ratings, there's nothing more influential than praise from respected bloggers and magazines! This is also a perfect place to mention any awards your app has won.

It may be tempting to place eye-catching awards and testimonials at the very top of your app description, but it is no longer an efficient strategy. Sure, it looks great in the iPhone's App Store (see the left screen of Figure 9–2), but it's not so effective in the desktop version of the iTunes App Store because of recent page layout changes (see the right screen of Figure 9–2), which truncates the description text after the first two to three lines.

With more than 90 percent of users downloading apps from the iPhone's App Store, optimizing the description text to also look good on the desktop iTunes may not seem that important. But before you ignore the desktop iTunes, just remember that 8 percent to 10 percent of more than 40 million iPhone OS users is nothing to sneeze at. That's still 4 million potential customers! Why would you not want to optimize your marketing message to include this massive audience? For best results across all the various versions of the App Store, place your brief app summary at the very top of your description text, followed by awards, testimonials, and additional features.

Did you notice in Figure 9–2 that special Unicode characters are supported? A clever use of stars draws the eye to the Wired.com quote and an effective check mark character is used when listing each feature.

Features and Benefits

Don't describe your app's features in paragraph form. Since you'll probably have a lot of items to mention, structure it as an easy-to-read bulleted list. Don't ramble on, listing every single last detail about the app. Again, less is more. Space and attention spans are limited, so consolidate your list to just the major features and benefits. This includes the core features that consumers are looking for, as well as the differentiating factors that set your app apart from the competition. If you think a specific feature is a key selling point, then it belongs in this list.

> **APP REJECTION WARNING: Do not include pricing in your app description, name, or icon.** The App Store caters to many regional languages and currencies, so displaying a static, text-based price is prohibited. If your English app description mentioned a price in U.S. dollars, then that could cause confusion among customers in the U.K. App Store since the dynamic buy button would list the app's price in British pounds. To avoid App Store rejection, you can promote limited-time sale offers in your app description without mentioning a specific currency. For example, if your $1.99 app is currently on sale for only $0.99, you could refer to the sale as "Half Off" or a "50% Discount."

Before submitting your app description, be sure to first proofread it using a good spell checker! I cannot stress this enough. Nothing says unprofessional like typos and misspellings! You want to compete with the big boys like Electronic Arts and Gameloft? Then you need to double-check everything you write *before* it gets uploaded into iTunes Connect. Afraid you'll miss something? Then have a few friends proofread it as well.

And beyond typos, you want to ensure that your description is easy to understand and does not in any way misrepresent your app's true functionality. Don't forget, this description is not only read by consumers in the App Store but is first read by an Apple reviewer. If something in your app description is ambiguous or misleading or if the reviewer couldn't locate one of your listed features in the short time the app is being reviewed, it could cause the approval process to be delayed or even result in a rejection, requesting further clarification. Remember, you can always modify your description with additional information after your app has been approved.

A Picture Is Worth a Thousand Words: The Importance of Screenshots

Since the iTunes App Store does not currently support the inclusion of video demos, the only way an interested consumer can immediately see what your app looks like is via the screenshots on your product page. Don't assume people will take the time to download your app just because you offer a free or lite version or that they'll jump to YouTube or your web site to view a video trailer. They're already browsing in the App Store, so they may not bother visiting other sites, especially if they're busy (and most people are). Your App Store product page needs to convince them to download the app, and probably the most influential element on that page will be your screenshots. With so much riding on the visuals, it's imperative that you upload screenshots that best promote your app's core functionality and quality. If it's a game, then your screenshots better scream fun and excitement! If it's a productivity app, then your screenshots need to emphasis just how much better someone's life is going to be when using this app. Your screenshots need to have impact!

Choosing the Primary Screenshot

The first screenshot that is shown is the most important. It may be the only screenshot consumers see if they opt not to tap/scroll through the rest of the screenshots. So, make sure this primary screenshot is the one that best describes your app visually. Someone viewing it should immediately understand the general concept without having read the description or loading the other screenshots. This *IS* the picture that's worth a thousand words!

Take some time to explore the App Store product pages of popular apps and games and analyze the first primary screenshot for each one, especially similar apps that will compete with yours. When you see a screenshot that catches your eye, try to determine what it is that makes it an effective graphic. On the surface, it may appear that the winning attributes are simply a stunning interface design, but look closer. Many of the best primary screenshots are ones that have been set up to look good! No, I don't mean Photoshop enhancements. I'm talking about showing the app in action! If it's a to-do list app, then don't show a new, empty list. Fill it with tasks that your target audience can relate to, demonstrating just how productive and timesaving it could be for them. If it's a space battle game, display the key fun factors like laser guns firing and alien crafts exploding! You want the reaction to be, "Wow, that looks exciting...I must buy it now!"

The goal is not necessarily about packing in as much action as possible into your screenshots. A compelling primary screenshot is one that instantly attracts your eye and successfully describes the core functionality in a single visual. The App Store product page for Streaming Colour Studios' Monkeys in Space: Escape to Banana Base Alpha displays a good example of an effective primary screenshot (see Figure 9–3). At first glance, the screen looks fairly empty with only a few monkey astronauts visible, but its simplicity communicates far more than the cluttered intensity of many other game screenshots in the App Store. Without reading the app description, this visual gives me a good idea what kind of game play it offers. It looks like pure fun without appearing too difficult for players of all ages to grasp the basics. After looking at that screenshot, who wouldn't want to help tether monkeys to space stations?

Figure 9–3. *Monkeys in Space: Escape to Banana Base Alpha by Streaming Colour Studios. Without reading the app description, this primary screenshot tells me quite a lot about the game play and looks like pure fun!*

Apple recommends removing the status bar from your screenshots, but looking around the App Store, it's apparent that advice is rarely heeded. Apple also recommends capturing screenshots directly from an iPhone or iPod touch, instead of the iPhone Simulator. To do this, when you're ready to take the shot, hold down the device's Home button and Power button at the same time. The screenshot is saved to the device's Photo Library. Although you could easily email the screenshot from the device's Photo Library to your desktop computer, that delivers it as an attached JPEG image. JPEGs typically include compression that lowers the image quality to reduce the file size. To avoid any loss of quality, it's best to sync the device with your desktop iTunes. With the device connected, launch the Mac's iPhoto application and import the saved screenshot. This will provide you with a pristine, high-quality PNG image. An alternative option is to capture screenshots from a connected device within the Screenshots tab of the Xcode Organizer window, which can then be dragged to the Mac desktop as PNG files.

When a Screenshot Is More Than a Screenshot

Even though Apple refers to them as screenshots, this feature is not limited to the literal definition. If your app's core functionality takes advantage of the accelerometer or special multi-touch gestures, then it's perfectly acceptable to show a photo of an actual person using the app on an iPhone device. Smule's Ocarina app, which turns your iPhone into a musical instrument, uses the primary screenshot to display a photo of how to "play" the app using the device's mic and multi-touch screen (see Figure 9–4). This photo does a much better job at describing the unique app than an actual screenshot would. Since the user's fingers obscure portions of the app's interface, Smule smartly included the Ocarina logo in the photo to reinforce the app name and branding.

Figure 9–4. *Because of the Smule Ocarina app's use of the iPhone's mic and multi-touch functionality, displaying a photo of a user in action is a much more effective primary image than an actual screenshot.*

What if you've built a productivity app that is so packed full of features that a simple screen capture simply does not do it justice? Not to worry, there's no rule forbidding the inclusion of text in your screenshots if it helps explain how your app works. A model example of this is the primary screenshot for 2Do from Guided Ways Technologies Ltd. (see the left screen of Figure 9–5). It complements the embedded interface view with additional text and icons to visually promote a vast array of key features.

The red banner at the bottom of the image (see left screen of Figure 9–5) even presents a clever call to action to Take the Guided Tour by prompting you to advance to the next screenshot. If you employ a visual trick like this, be very careful to avoid referencing actual iTunes App Store UI controls. Apple is continuously evolving the page layout of the App Store, so a specific UI element may change or move to a different location of the page in the future. The primary screenshot for 2Do was originally designed with the Take the Guided Tour arrow pointing at the Next button in iTunes 8 (see the top right screen of Figure 9–5). Fortunately, when Apple redesigned the App Store page layout in iTunes 9, replacing that navigation button with a horizontal scrollbar (see the middle right screen of Figure 9–5), that Take the Guided Tour arrow still makes sense.

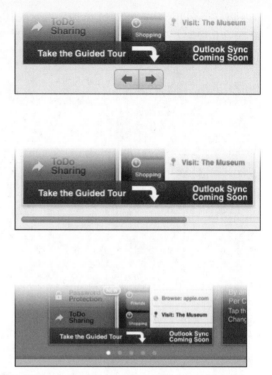

Figure 9–5. *The primary screenshot for 2Do by Guided Ways Technologies Ltd. uses text and icons to visually promote a vast array of key features (left). If you reference specific App Store UI controls, such as the clever Take the Guided Tour arrow, make sure it visually works across all platform versions: iTunes 8 (top right), iTunes 9 (middle right), and the iPhone App Store (bottom right).*

If you do include text in your screenshots and you offer localized versions of your app in multiple regional App Stores, then don't forget to also localize your screenshots accordingly. Before capturing the screenshots, first set the preferred language on the device, which can be located in the Settings app at General ➤ International ➤ Language. If you're creating a custom image such as the one shown in Figure 9–5, then be sure to translate the text correctly. Online web translator bots such as Google Translate can sometimes generate incorrect phrasing or syntax. To avoid confusion or even possibly offending someone with the wrong word, you might want to consult with a professional translator. When your localized screenshots are ready, simply upload them to the corresponding app language version in iTunes Connect.

Preparing Your Application Binary for the App Store

After learning the configuration process for ad hoc distribution (detailed in Chapter 7), you'll be happy to know that compiling your iPhone app for distribution in the App Store is almost the same process. The only difference is the provisioning profile you assign to your application in Xcode.

Finished beta-testing and tweaking your app? Ready to compile the master version for the App Store? Here's a rundown of the steps to prepare the application binary that you'll upload to iTunes Connect.

Step 1: Verify Your Distribution Certificate Is Still Installed

To compile your app for ad hoc distribution, you had to generate your distribution certificate from the iPhone Developer Program Portal and install it in your Mac's Keychain system. This distribution certificate is also used when compiling for App Store distribution, so take a moment to ensure that it is still installed properly on your Mac. Launch the Keychain Access application, located here:

/Applications/Utilities/Keychain Access

In the dialog box that's displayed, select "login" from the Keychains menu and Keys from the Category menu. In the list of keys, simply double-check that your private key is still paired with your distribution certificate. In the Figure 9–6 example, my "Electric Butterfly, Inc." key (which was previously created for ad hoc distribution) is paired with my imported iPhone distribution certificate. If your distribution certificate is not paired with the appropriate key in a similar manner, then revisit steps 1 through 3 of ad hoc distribution in Chapter 7 before continuing.

Figure 9–6. *Verify that your iPhone distribution certificate is still paired with the correct private key in Keychain Access.*

Step 2: Generate and Install an App Store Distribution Provisioning Profile

Log into the iPhone Dev Center with your iPhone Developer ID and password here:

`http://developer.apple.com/iphone/`

Once logged in, click the iPhone Developer Program Portal link in the top-right corner of the page, and then within the main Program Portal page, navigate to the Provisioning section. Select the Distribution tab, and click the New Profile button. In the form that's presented, be sure to choose App Store as the distribution method. Select the appropriate App ID for your application, and verify that the distribution certificate is assigned correctly.

Enter a profile name that reflects the nature of this provisioning profile. In Chapter 7, the example screenshots showed a project named BetaTestApp being configured for beta testing, and the ad hoc distribution provisioning profile had been named BetaTestApp Dist Profile. Now that you've finished beta testing and need to generate an App Store Distribution Provisioning Profile, let's differentiate this new profile name by calling it BetaTestApp Store Profile (see Figure 9–7).

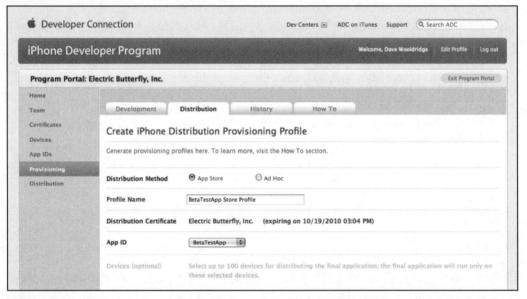

Figure 9–7. *Since you're done ad hoc beta testing the BetaTestApp project (from Chapter 7), it's now time to generate an App Store distribution provisioning profile in the online iPhone Developer Program Portal site.*

Choose Submit to generate your App Store distribution provisioning profile, then click the download button to save the `.mobileprovision` file to your hard drive. Drag the `.mobileprovision` file onto the Xcode icon in your Dock. Xcode will automatically install that provisioning profile in the proper location.

Step 3: Configure Your Xcode Project for App Store Distribution

Now with the proper provisioning profile in place, the next step is to open your project in Xcode and configure it for App Store distribution. In the main Xcode project window, select the project name at the top of the Groups & Files pane, and then click the Info button in the toolbar. Within the Configurations tab of the Info window, verify that you still have a Distribution configuration listed (which you should have already created during Chapter 7's ad hoc distribution stage). If you don't have one, then duplicate the existing Release configuration, naming the copy Distribution. Now close that Info window.

Now select the Target app within the Groups & Files pane, and click the toolbar's Info button again. In the new Target Info window that appears, navigate to the Build tab, and double-check the Configuration drop-down menu is set to Distribution. Scroll down to the Any iPhone OS Device field below the Code Signing Identity row, and assign it to your new App Store distribution provisioning profile. Even though your ad hoc distribution provisioning profile may also be listed in the pop-up menu, it's critical that your App Store distribution provisioning profile is selected (see Figure 9–8).

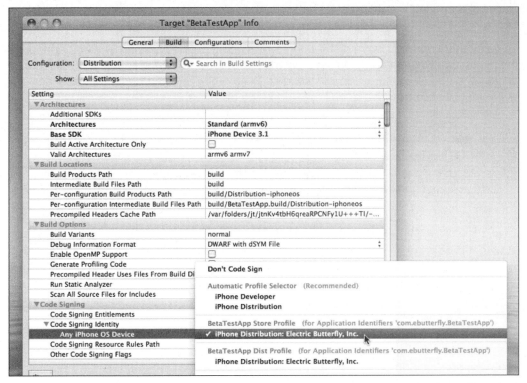

Figure 9–8. *Modify your Target's Build tab, assigning your new App Store distribution provisioning profile to the Any iPhone OS Device Code Signing Identity.*

Switch to the Properties tab, and verify that the correct App ID bundle identifier is in the Identifier field. For the example, for this BetaTestApp project, I had listed com.ebutterfly.BetaTestApp in this field, matching the bundle identifier property in my Xcode project's Info .plist file. With all of that completed, the last step is to navigate to the main Xcode project window and ensure that the drop-down menu in the top-left corner has Device and Distribution selected for the Active SDK and Active Configuration settings, respectively.

Step 4: Compile Your iPhone Application

Now you're ready to compile your Xcode project! App Store distribution does not require your project to include an entitlements file like ad hoc distribution, so save your project and then click Build (from either the toolbar or Build menu). If you've configured everything correctly, then your app should compile successfully.

If build errors arise that are related to the project settings, retrace your steps to ensure that you've followed every single task outlined here, no matter how insignificant it may seem. Build errors can often be caused by the smallest mistakes, such as a misspelled bundle identifier or a mismarked checkbox. If problems persist and you've ruled out code bugs and faulty configuration settings, then clean out your project's "build" directory, reopen the project in Xcode, and try another build attempt.

To verify that your App Store distribution provisioning profile was properly embedded in the binary and that the app was securely signed by your iPhone distribution certificate, access the Build Results window in Xcode's Build menu and search for the presence of *embedded.mobileprovision* and *CodeSign* in the build log.

> **APP REJECTION WARNING: Do not utilize undocumented private Apple APIs in your app.**
> Apple has rejected dozens of apps for tapping into private iPhone APIs that are not officially sanctioned for public use. Although one or two exceptions have been approved, such as the live video streaming Ustream app, Apple has otherwise been quite strict about this rule. The app review team is rumored to be using a static analyzer tool to ferret out calls to restricted, private APIs, so even if your app includes the code but doesn't execute it, it may still get flagged for the code presence alone. To avoid App Store rejection, it's recommended to stick with the authorized APIs.

Apple will only accept iPhone applications that were compiled with an App Store distribution provisioning profile. Unfortunately, an App Store distribution provisioning profile and an application compiled with that profile will not work on your test devices, so there's no way for you to test this version of the app before submitting it to Apple. With this in mind, it's important to do as much testing as possible—keeping a close eye on build logs and error messages—before configuring and compiling for App Store distribution.

Once compiled, select the .app file in the Projects folder, listed within the Groups & Files pane of the main Xcode project window. From either the contextual menu (Control-click) or the Action menu, choose Reveal in Finder to locate the compiled binary on your Mac. Control-click the .app file in the Finder, and from the contextual menu that appears, choose Compress to package the app into a zip archive. Apple recommends using the Finder's Compress option only because the command-line's zip method is known to create problems when uploading the zip archive to the App Store.

Are We There Yet? Submitting Your App in iTunes Connect

After months of development and testing, you probably can't believe that you've finally arrived at this point: ready to submit your application to the App Store. It's a moment filled with both excitement and trepidation, uncertain as to the fate of your product in the hands of Apple's app review team. But not to fear, you've planned your application very carefully, methodically following all of Apple's guidelines, so you should be in good shape. Don't let a few angry app rejection blog posts from disgruntled developers sway you from your journey to the App Store. Have some faith in your development efforts. You've crossed every *t* and dotted every *i*, so now you're ready to take the plunge.

Ensure Your Contracts and Payment Settings Have Been Processed by Apple

Before uploading your application, make sure all of Apple's required contracts, tax forms, and banking information have been properly submitted and processed. As I mentioned way back in Chapter 1, this process can often take a fair amount of time, so it's best to get all of this take care of while you're in the initial stages of development. That way, when you're ready to submit your application to the App Store, there's no lingering paperwork holding you back.

To check your current status, either log into the iPhone Dev Center and select the iTunes Connect button in the far-right column or log in directly to the iTunes Connect web site:

http://itunesconnect.apple.com/

On the main page of iTunes Connect, visit the section called Contracts, Tax, & Banking Information to view the contracts you currently have in effect. As discussed in Chapter 1, your should have the "Free Applications" contract already activated by default, which allows you to submit free iPhone apps to the App Store. To submit paid apps to the App Store, you should have already requested a "Paid Applications" contract and completed the related banking and tax forms. Without that information submitted, Apple is unable to pay you any revenue you earn from app sales and will instead hold your accrued earnings in trust until the required forms have been processed.

Like I've already said, this can be a fairly lengthy process, so I highly recommend completing the "Paid Applications" contract long before getting to this point since any pending contracts can also prevent your application from going live in the App Store.

Step 1: Add a New Application in iTunes Connect

With all of your contracts processed, take a deep breath and then head over to the Manage Your Applications section of iTunes Connect. If you're presently in a rush, then plan on submitting your app on a day when you have plenty of time to dedicate to this process. There are several screens of online forms to complete, so you'll want to patiently work through each screen at a relaxed pace to avoid making any careless mistakes or typos.

As a convenient safeguard, Apple provides a handy Application Loader tool, available as a free download link on the Manage Your Applications page (see Figure 9–9). The Mac-based Application Loader utility can analyze your iPhone app's zip file to verify that the required app icon, distribution certificate, code signing, and other required elements are properly embedded in the executable binary before uploading it to iTunes Connect.

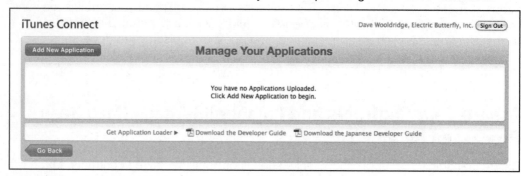

Figure 9–9. *In the Manage Your Applications section of iTunes Connect, click the Add New Application button to get started.*

Ready? Great, let's do this! Click the blue Add New Application button in the top-left corner of the Manage Your Applications page (see Figure 9–9). If this is your very first iPhone app submission, then the first screen will ask you to provide your official company name and your application's primary language (see Figure 9–10). *Please note that this information cannot be changed later, so do not make any mistakes on this page!*

The company name you submit should be the name you want listed in the App Store as the official developer of your application. Because of my own paranoia about proper code signing and App Store settings, *I recommend using the same company/developer name* across all of the following items to avoid any potential issues:

- Your iPhone Developer Program account
- Your iPhone distribution certificate
- Your iTunes Connect/App Store company name

I use my company name "Electric Butterfly, Inc." for all three of those items, making sure the spelling and punctuation are always consistent.

As for the primary language setting, this is the language that you'll use to enter all of your application data during this submission process. For example, if you choose

English from the drop-down menu, then the rest of the screen forms would require your information to be in English. Near the end of the new application submission process, you'll have an opportunity to add support for additional languages, such as French, German, Japanese, and so on.

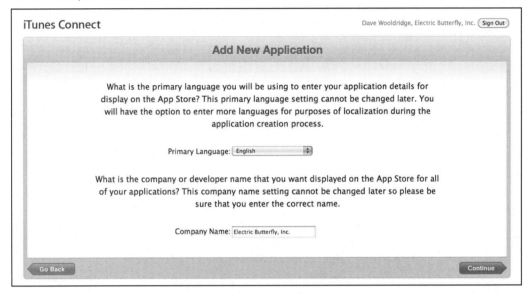

Figure 9–10. *When submitting your very first iPhone app, you'll be asked to provide your official company name and the app's primary language.*

Click Continue to move on to the next screen, Export Compliance. Because of current export laws, any products that contain encryption need to be authorized for export, so this screen presents a single question, "Does your product contain encryption?" If the answer is "No," then you can continue to the next screen. If the answer is "Yes," then three more encryption questions will appear, requiring answers before you can proceed.

Based on how you answer those additional questions, you may be asked to upload a copy of your Commodity Classification Automated Tracking System (CCATS) document. Since Export Compliance must review and approve your CCATS file before your application can be made available in the App Store, be prepared for a longer than normal app review period if a CCATS document is required. If you've never heard of CCAT before, then odds are good your app does not fall into this category.

Step 2: Submit Your App's Metadata

Of all the screen forms here, you'll probably spend the most time on this one: the Add New Application – Overview page. This is where you submit all of your application's metadata. Fortunately, many of the requested elements you should already have prepared, such as the app's name, description, keywords, and web site URL. As you can see from Figure 9–11, it's quite a long form, so let's take a closer look at each item.

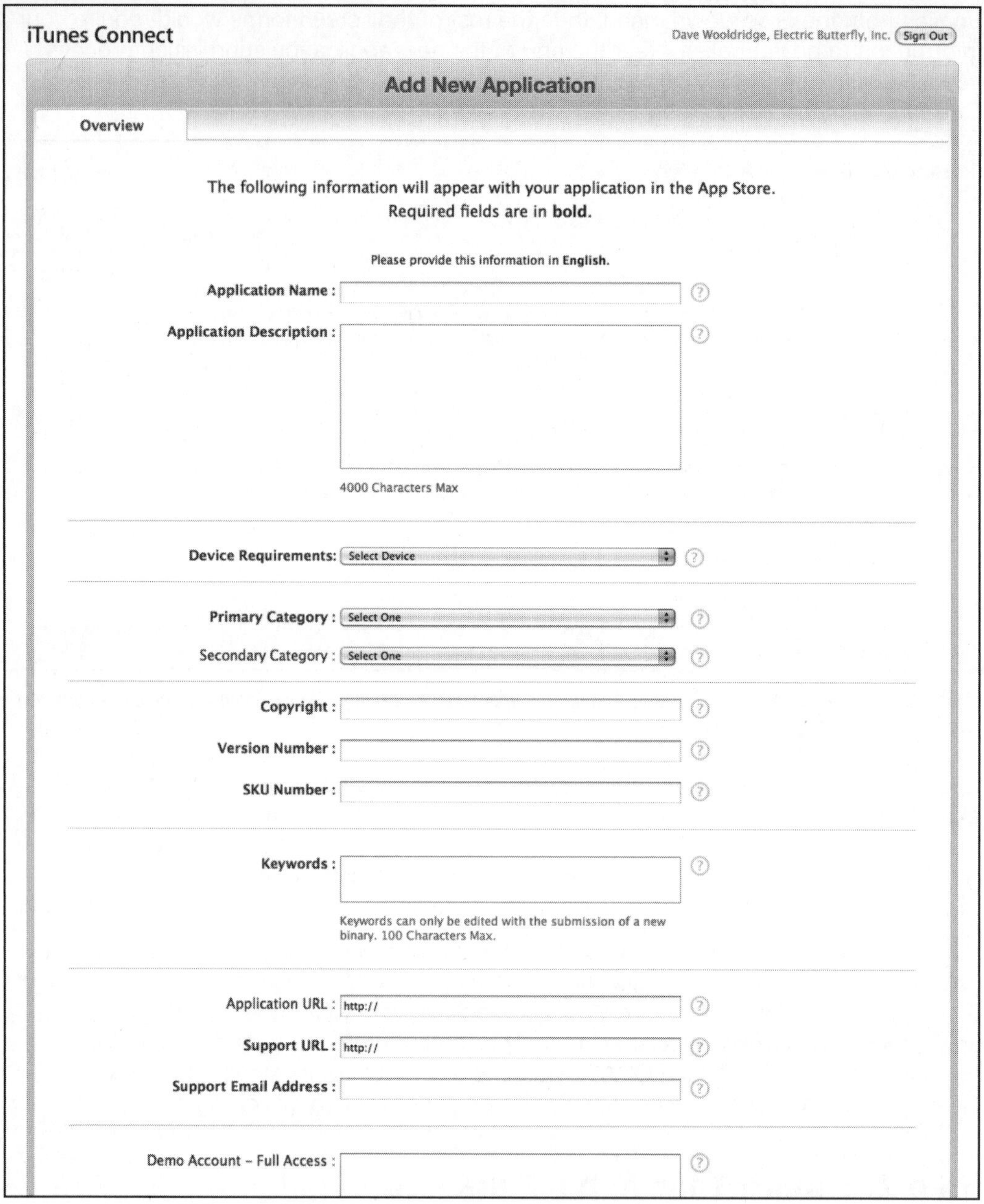

Figure 9–11. *Of all the screens in the submission process, the application metadata form is by far the longest, but fortunately, you should already have many of these items already prepared, such as the app's name, description, keywords, and web site URL.*

Application Name

As I discussed earlier in this chapter, this field is not limited to only your application's binary name. For example, Tap Tap Tap's Convert app uses a longer App Store application name that includes a keyword-searchable caption: "Convert—the unit calculator." The submitted name can be up to 255 characters long.

Unfortunately, like web site domains, iPhone application names are becoming a haven for squatters. Because of how applications are stored in iTunes Connect, application names must be unique. If someone else has already submitted an iPhone application with the same name as your app, you won't be able to submit your app with that name. Even if that other app has not been approved for sale in the App Store, it's still registered in the system as a "taken" name. The iTunes Connect form will present an error message, notifying you that your requested application name is already taken, forcing you to choose a different name in order to complete the submission process.

If someone has already registered a web site domain name that you wanted, it's often easy to look up the WHOIS domain registrant information so that you can at least contact the person to inquire about purchasing the domain name from them. With this application name issue, there's no way for you to find out who has taken the name, so you have no recourse. That other developer would probably have to delete the application listing from their Manage Your Applications section in order for the app name to become available again.

Because of this, there seems to be a panicked trend of iPhone developers creating partially completed New Application listings in their iTunes Connect accounts for app names that they plan to someday develop, for fear that if they don't do this now, those specific names may not be available in the future. Ideally, Apple will resolve this problem in the near future to prevent potential name-squatting abuse.

If the system reports that your app name is already taken (even though that name does not currently exist in the App Store), do not despair. You may not have a way to capture that name for use in your App Store application name field, but you can append a keyword-rich caption to the name to work around the issue. For example, the fictional app Breadcrumbs that has served as an example throughout this book is already a taken Application Name in iTunes Connect, but the longer name Breadcrumbs—Parked Car Locator was still available, and it makes the app listing that much more search-optimized in the App Store.

Here's the one major caveat to that solution. If there are two or more applications with the same name available live in the App Store, the identical app names could cause confusion in the marketplace, with consumers unsure as to which one is your app—especially if both apps provide similar functionality. Even though your added caption makes your submitted application name technically unique in the system, the app's actual name is still essentially the same as the others in the eyes of consumers. This could also lead to lawsuits if your app name is infringing upon an existing trademarked application name in the App Store. If you already trademarked your application's name, then the law is on your side (at least in your country). This is why creating a unique name is so important. Avoiding common words for your app name can prevent these kinds of problems from occurring.

Application Description

The description you painstakingly wrote earlier in this chapter should be pasted into this field. Just remember that the desktop version of the iTunes App Store only initially displays the first two to three lines of text with a More link to read the rest of it. This makes those first few lines of text very important, so be sure to use that limited space wisely, explaining what your app does. Since you are allowed a generous maximum of 4,000 characters, use the rest of the available characters to list features and benefits, awards, testimonials, and other key selling points. HTML tags are not supported, but lines breaks and special Unicode characters are acceptable.

Device Requirements

This drop-down menu allows you to select the hardware requirements for your app, such as supporting both the iPhone and the iPod touch, or the iPhone only. Be careful to choose the appropriate selection because if your application requires an iPhone-only feature and yet you selected both iPhone and iPod touch compatibility, that alone might delay your app review or even warrant a rejection.

Category

You must choose a primary category where you want your app to be located in the App Store. Selecting a secondary category is optional but can be beneficial as an alternative if Apple thinks your primary category choice is not appropriate based on your app's functionality.

If you choose Games as a category, then two more menus appear, allowing you to select two subcategories from the Games parent group, such as Action, Arcade, Board, Puzzle, Strategy, and other game genres.

Copyright

List your copyright line as you want it displayed in the App Store. There's no need to include the © symbol since the App Store automatically places it before your copyright line. So, for example, submitting the line "2009 Electric Butterfly, Inc. All rights reserved." would appear in the App Store as: "© 2009 Electric Butterfly, Inc. All rights reserved."

Version Number

This is a fairly self-explanatory field, listing your app's version number, such as "1.0" or "1.3.1." You should use the same version number as the value listed in your application

Info.plist file's CFBundleVersion and CFBundleShortVersionString properties, so avoid including alpha characters such as "Beta 1." Discrepancies between your actual app binary version and the version number you enter in this form might cause delays or problems during the app review process.

SKU Number

The SKU Number form field is often the source of the most confusion for iPhone developers, since Apple does not provide much explanation as to what format or syntax this string should adhere to. Contrary to popular belief, there is no defined template or numbering system for the SKU attribute. Even calling it a SKU number is somewhat misleading in that it does not have to consist of numerical characters. Your app's SKU is never shown to customers and never publically listed in the App Store.

Basically, the SKU is an internal, unique ID that is displayed in your iTunes Connect sales reports. So to help identify which apps are listed next to specific revenue earnings, it's often convenient to use an easily recognizable name vs. a string of only numbers. For example, if the app's name is Breadcrumbs, then an acceptable SKU number could be "BREADCRUMBS" or "BREADCRUMBS_01." I should point out that the SKU is independent of the version number, so it does not change with every version update. In fact, once submitted, that SKU number can never be changed, so pick a good identifying name that works for you. Including a number in your SKU like "BREADCRUMBS_01" can be helpful if you plan on releasing a sequel application as an entirely new application, such as atebits' move from the original Tweetie app to the separate, new product Tweetie 2.

Keywords

The keywords you crafted earlier in this chapter should be pasted into this field. As I've mentioned, whether or not you're using multiword phrases for some of your keywords, it's always recommended to separate them with commas for best results.

Application URL, Support URL, and Support Email Address

I discussed the importance of maintaining a dedicated web site for your iPhone app in Chapter 8, so even though the application URL appears as an optional form field here, you *should* include your site URL here. Not doing so will only hurt your app's marketability down the road, especially now that the Application URL link is displayed so prominently beneath the description text in the App Store page redesign of iTunes 9.

As a convenience for users, the Support URL and Support Email Address fields *are* required entries. The support email address you provide is used only by Apple's internal team and is not posted in the App Store, but you may also want to list it on your application web site for customers who need to reach you. If you choose to do that, then offering a dedicated email address for only support queries will aid in better managing and sorting customer support requests, especially if you're a independent developer. Besides, using a dedicated address like support@breadcrumbsapp.com lends a much more professional touch than a generic free email like dave123@hotmail.com. No one has to know you're a one-person shop!

As for the Support Site field, it should be an easy-to-type URL that's integrated with your application's main web site, such as http://support.breadcrumbsapp.com/ or http://www.breadcrumbsapp.com/support/. Even though the desktop version of iTunes supplies an active link to your support site from your product's App Store page, that's not the case in the mobile iPhone OS version of the App Store, which only lists the web site URL for a selected application. And with more than 90 percent of all iPhone and iPod touch users browsing and downloading apps directly from their device, if they encounter a support issue, they'll look up your web site in Mobile Safari in the hopes of finding online assistance. So, make life easier for both you and your customers by linking your app's web site directly to your support page.

So, what should you include on your support web page? It's important that your support URL points to a valid source for contacting you since Apple will check its existence during the app review process. At the very least, give site visitors some way to contact you directly, whether by an email link or by an HTML feedback form (if you'd rather hide your email address from spam harvester bots).

To help reduce the flood of support queries and provide 24/7 assistance even when you're offline, it's always a good idea to post a list of frequently asked questions (FAQs), especially if you find yourself answering the same email questions repeatedly.

For iPhone apps that enjoy an active and vibrant user community, then self-hosting an online forum, such as the popular open source phpBB—http://www.phpbb.com/—might be a beneficial addition to your support site. But be aware that maintaining any kind of live forum or message board of your own requires a lot of manual policing to weed out the spam and inappropriate posts that are bound to litter the site.

If you don't have the time or skill set to build your own custom support offerings, there are some amazing ready-made, third-party services available at very affordable monthly rates, such as the following:

- **Get Satisfaction** (http://getsatisfaction.com/): Offers an easy to set up, hosted customer care site for posting support queries and feature requests. The web interface of Get Satisfaction is designed to cultivate a thriving community between you and your customers, and even with each other. It has become a rather popular solution among a growing number of Mac and iPhone developers.

- **Tender Support** (http://tenderapp.com/): Offers a comprehensive, hosted customer support solution, complete with web-based discussion boards, FAQ/knowledge base, and direct support requests. Tender even provides an extensive password-protected admin dashboard site for you to easily organize and manage your customer support flow. The creators of the acclaimed Tweetie iPhone app, atebits, utilize Tender for their support system, so to see Tender in action, check out http://support.atebits.com/.

Even after providing an extensive support site, if you find too many customers misusing the App Store's Customer Reviews section as a place to post feature requests and bug reports, then it may be helpful to add some support information to your application description text. Anything you can do to redirect users to your support site may help reduce the number of unnecessary one-star reviews that are nothing more than feature wish lists! But never reprimand customers who do that. Phrase it in a positive manner that persuades customers into believing your support site is the best and fastest method of receiving quality assistance. For example, you could insert additional wording at the bottom of your application description text that reads: "For quick support assistance, please contact us directly at `http://support.breadcrumbsapp.com/` -OR- email us at `support@breadcrumbsapp.com`." And if you prefer connecting with users via Twitter, you can also add your Twitter URL to that sentence. Basically, the more customer care options you provide, the greater chance you have of reducing the clutter of support-related posts in the App Store's customer reviews (which in turn, may help boost your app's overall customer star rating).

Demo Account

Most iPhone developers won't need to fill out this optional field, but for those few applications that require creating a user account or logging into a password-protected web service, then you'll want to pay close attention here. These login features are definitely tested by Apple's app review team, so if they run into trouble accessing that in-app feature because you forgot to provide user account credentials or a working password in this Demo Account field, then this can delay the approval process because reviewers will reply to you, requesting that login data. Some apps have even been flat out rejected based on the inability of app reviewers to successfully log in to a test account or a members-only web service from within your app, so if even if you do supply the required login information in this field, be sure to first test that it's a working, valid demo account.

In fact, if there are unique features in your app that you worry the reviewers may misinterpret or have trouble accessing, including some additional notes in this field may help expedite the review process. Just be careful that whatever text you include here is clear and concise. The last thing you want is for your app to be rejected because the extra notes you added here proved to be more confusing than helpful.

End User License Agreement

By default, if you do not provide your own end user license agreement (EULA), then Apple's standard App Store EULA will be applied to your application. This appears to be the EULA that most iPhone developers choose to adopt, but if reading about end user agreements in Michael Schneider's Chapter 3 leads you to believe that specific features in your application warrant a custom EULA, then Apple does allow you to upload your own as long as it meets Apple's minimum terms (which are provided in a link at the end of the application form on this screen). Since Apple needs to review custom EULAs upon submission, that option could potentially slow down the approval process.

Step 3: Assign a Rating to Your App

After completing and double-checking the values you've entered in the application metadata form, click the Continue button to proceed to the next screen, Ratings. Here, you're presented with a survey-style list of questions that you must answer in order to complete the submission (see Figure 9–12). Apple requires all iPhone apps to be assigned a content rating so that the iPhone OS parental controls can filter out specified age-appropriate applications when children access the App Store.

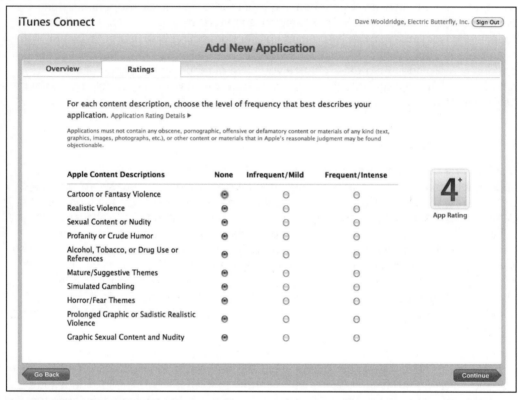

Figure 9–12. *Answering None to all of the content questions dynamically displays an age rating of 4+, labeling the application as suitable for both kids and adults.*

The possible age ratings are 4+, 9+, 12+, and 17+. As illustrated in Figure 9–12, answering None to all of the content questions will dynamically display an age rating of 4+. Experiment with various Infrequent/Mild and Frequent/Intense answers for some of the content types, and you'll see the displayed rating change to 9+, 12+, or even 17+. It's in your best interest to answer truthfully, selecting a rating that's appropriate for your app. Even if your submitted 12+ rating consists of only a few Infrequent/Mild answers, if Apple's review team thinks your app requires a more restrictive rating such as 17+, it can and will reclassify your rating before approving it for sale in the App Store.

Ratings may seem subjective, especially with vague, generalized content types like Mature/Suggestive Themes, which can mean different things to different people.

Nonetheless, Apple takes its ratings system very seriously, so there's not much wiggle room to complain if you don't like the approved rating your app has been given.

There are three major factors to be aware of when designing your iPhone application:

- If your app displays Internet-based sites via an embedded `UIWebView`, your app will probably be given a 17+ rating since this gives users the ability to access any web content, some of which may be deemed inappropriate for children.

- If your app retrieves data from a web service, such as an online catalog of digital comics or eBooks, especially public domain items that may contain inappropriate content, then your app will most likely be saddled with a 17+ rating.

- If your app features either Prolonged Graphic or Sadistic Realistic Violence or "Graphic Sexual Content and Nudity"—the bottom two criteria in Apple's list of content types—your app will be deemed unsuitable for the App Store and will not be approved (see the No Rating classification in Figure 9–13). Oddly enough, there does seem to be a slight gray area where a mild degree of sexually themed content is allowed since apps containing the third item on the list, Sexual Content or Nudity, are typically granted a 17+ rating.

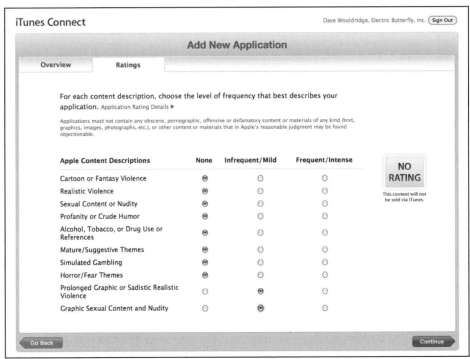

Figure 9–13. *If your app contains the bottom two content types, even an Infrequent/Mild answer for either of those items will render your product unsuitable for the App Store. The infamous No Rating label spells rejection.*

Take great care when answering the ten ratings questions because they cannot be modified after the app has been submitted for review. When you've completed this page, click the Continue button to move onto the next screen.

Step 4: Upload Your App Binary, Large Icon, and Screenshots

The Upload screen is where—yup, you guessed it—you upload your app's zip file, the large 512 by 512 pixel app icon, and your screenshots. To upload a particular element, click the related Choose File button below it to select the file from your hard drive (see Figure 9–14). Once selected, it will be listed on-screen with a new Upload File button, which you must click to complete the upload of that item into Apple's system.

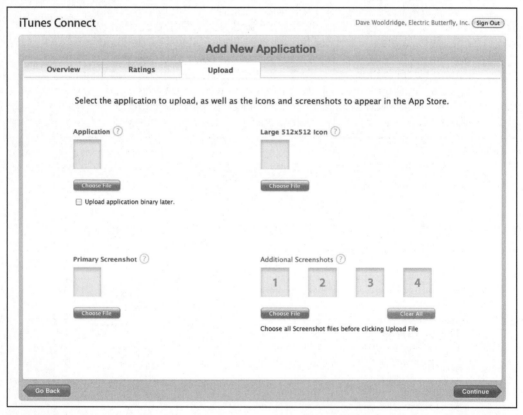

Figure 9–14. *This screen allows you to choose and then upload your application binary and related art materials.*

Since I discussed the need for creating a large, high-quality 512 by 512 pixel app icon way back in Chapter 4, you should already have this icon file prepared and ready to upload. Please note that this large icon must be the same graphic as the small 57 by 57 pixel app icon that's compiled in your iPhone application. Submitting small and large app icons that are not identical in design will quickly earn yourself a rejection letter. The 512 by 512 pixel icon should be delivered as a flat, square JPEG or TIF image with a 72 dpi resolution and RGB color mode. Do not include layers, masks, or transparencies of any kind. And this is the most important rule: do not add rounded corners or the beveled gloss yourself. The App Store automatically adds those icon effects dynamically but will honor the custom setting of the `UIPrerenderedIcon` key in your application's `Info.plist` file.

For best results when uploading your screenshots, it's recommended to first add your primary screenshot to iTunes Connect before selecting the additional four screenshots since doing the opposite has been rumored to sometimes cause the online form to exert erratic behavior. And for the additional screenshots, select all four in reverse order within the Choose File dialog box, and then click the Upload File button to upload them all at once. For full-screen portrait images, the required dimensions are 320 pixels wide by 480 pixels tall, and for wide landscape images, it's 480 pixels wide by 320 pixels tall. If you elect to remove the status bar from your screenshots (as Apple suggests), then the dimensions are 320 pixels wide by only 460 pixels tall for portrait, and 480 pixels wide by only 300 pixels tall for landscape. Like the app icon, screenshots should also be submitted in RGB color, 72 dpi with no transparencies, and saved as JPEG or TIF images (flattened, no layers). The system may not accept screenshot sizes and image formats that don't adhere to Apple's specifications.

Last, but certainly not least, it's time to upload your application binary's zip file. How big is your app? Did you check your application binary's Get Info properties window before compressing it into a zip archive? Ideally, it should be less than 10MB, since that's AT&T's official cut-off size for downloading applications from the App Store over its EDGE and 3G networks in the United States. So in this case, size *does* matter! If potential customers are limited to only downloading your iPhone app when connected via WiFi on their mobile device or computer, then that prevents impulse buys from travelers on the road between hotspots. Of course, if you've built a highly complex, visually immersive game, you may not be able to stay under the 10MB application file size, and iTunes Connect will certainly accept large app uploads. But if your application is relatively light on functionality and embedded resources, then it's always a good idea to optimize the compiled output into as small of a file size as possible.

Step 5: Set the Availability Date and Price

After uploading your app binary and related art files and clicking the Continue button, the next screen presents options to choose the availability date and price tier.

The Availability Date setting has proven to be one of the more frustrating elements of the app submission process. Within the main category pages of the App Store, consumers have the ability to sort the list by release date, which is a great source of exposure for new app releases. Once upon a time, developers used to be able to make quick changes to the availability date after being notified that their app had been approved, which would allow them to control when their app appears in that valuable list. This enabled developers to closely time the launch of press releases with the product's visibility in the App Store's new releases list. Unfortunately, Apple has made recent changes to the release date reflected in the App Store, rendering that little trick obsolete. Now, the actual release date of your app is the date it is approved by Apple, unless your availability date is earlier—whichever date comes sooner.

Confused? Yeah, I know, right? It's not exactly set up the way developers would envision such a feature to work, yet this is Apple's playground, so when in Rome.... To make the best of the current release date system, you should still set your availability date to a distant day in the future (such as a few months ahead), way beyond the estimated approval date. Then after you've completed the submission, remember to set your iTunes Connect user profile's preferences to notify you via email when your app submission status changes to Ready for Sale. This way, if you regularly check your email, the moment you're notified of your app's approval, you can quickly log into iTunes Connect and change your availability date to the approved date so that it instantly appears in the App Store and benefits from the fleeting exposure in the new releases list. This notification also serves as a nice head's up so you can send out your press release closely following the product's availability in the App Store.

If you don't change that future availability date until long after the app's approval date, then you'll miss that optimal window of visibility in the Sorted by Release Date list. Why? Because the app's release date is set to the earlier approved date and not your far future date. By the time your application appears in the App Store on your future availability date, it is pushed far down that list, below more recent releases and away from browsing consumers. Your best bet? Remember to set your notification preferences and check your email religiously so that you can immediately modify your availability date to the approved date when that day comes.

For paid applications, you'll also need to choose a price tier. Since regional App Stores support various currencies, the drop-down menu forces you to choose a tier instead of an actual price. When you choose a tier, the corresponding pricing is automatically displayed, revealing not only the currency conversions in several regions but also what your proceeds would be after Apple subtracts its 30 percent fee. To give you an idea of the prices for the most common tiers, here's a list in U.S. dollars:

- Tier 1 = $0.99
- Tier 2 = $1.99
- Tier 3 = $2.99
- Tier 4 = $3.99
- Tier 5 = $4.99
- Tier 6 = $5.99
- Tier 7 = $6.99
- Tier 8 = $7.99
- Tier 9 = $8.99
- Tier 10 = $9.99

As you've seen with higher-priced apps in the Navigation and Medical categories, there are additional tiers, but Tier 1 is the absolute minimum price (99 cents in the United States) that can be charged for paid applications and In-App Purchase items. Of course, for free apps, simply select the Free option in the Price Tier menu.

By default, your application will be available worldwide, unless you choose to select only specific individual countries from the checklist at the bottom of this screen.

Step 6: Supporting Multiple Languages

Moving on to the next screen will bring you to the Localization page. If your application currently supports your primary language only, then you can skip this stage by clicking the Continue button. Do not select additional languages until your application actually includes support for those languages. For those of you who did provide support for multiple languages in your uploaded app binary, don't go anywhere just yet!

Within this section, you can designate additional languages for display in regional App Stores that support those languages. For example, if your application already supports both English and Japanese, then you'd add Japanese from the Language dropdown menu. Since English was the primary language you selected back in step 1, there's no need to add English here.

Upon selecting an additional language and clicking the Continue button, the next screen will present a form that looks almost identical to the application metadata form you encountered in step 2. The only difference is that instead of English, you'll be submitting localized content for App Store metadata elements like the application name, description, keywords, support URL, and even an option to upload localized screenshots. If you opt not to submit new screenshots for the new language, then your primary language screenshots will be used by default.

Step 7: Confirm and Submit Your App for Review

The last screen in the app submission process is the Review page. This is similar to an order confirmation page on a shopping site in that it is a ready-only summary of your submitted application data. Take a deep breath and meticulously review the listed details, checking very carefully for any errors or typos. Once you hit that Submit Application button, it will be added to the queue for Apple to review, and only a select handful of elements can be later edited in iTunes Connect, so now is the time to make sure everything is correct!

If everything looks good, then you'll need to click the Submit Application button to complete the submission process. Now you'll see your new app listed in the Manage Your Applications section with the status Waiting for Review.

If you discover a problem or need to edit certain assets that are untouchable when in the submission queue, then you can pull the app from review by clicking the app listing's Reject Binary button. This will change your app's status to Developer Rejected. When you're ready, you'll need to resubmit a new app binary, which will start the review process from the very beginning, so it's recommended only to do this when in dire need.

When your app is being reviewed by Apple, the status changes to In Review. If you were required to upload a CCATS document, then you may see the status Waiting for Export Compliance while your CCATS is being evaluated.

We all cross our fingers, desperately hoping not to receive the dreaded Rejected status, but if your status reads Ready for Sale, then your app has been approved! Time to celebrate the momentous occasion!

But wait… don't forget to modify your iTunes Connect account settings so that you receive email notifications when your status changes. If your availability date was set to a future date, then your app won't appear in the App Store until you update your availability date to the current approved date. Receiving status updates via email will enable you to easily monitor this.

Submitting App Updates

When submitting a new version or a bug fix update for review, you're required to include a "What's New" description along with the standard app description. This "What's New" description is displayed when an app is listed in a customer's Updates tab in the iPhone App Store, as well as included just below the app description in the desktop iTunes App Store. This text is also read by Apple's team when reviewing your submitted update. This is yet another case where less is more. Be brief and very concise. If you go into too much long-winded detail, you run the risk of something being misunderstood by a reviewer, leading to possible approval delays or even rejections.

Using an immediate date for your availability date is the best choice for your app updates. What some developers don't realize is that the availability date is global for all versions of that application, not just the update you're submitting. If you set the availability date to a far future date and the update is approved much sooner than that, then all versions of that application will disappear from the App Store…until your specified availability date is reached. And that's definitely a situation to avoid!

It's also interesting to note that updated versions are no longer included in the App Store's new release lists, so the once common trick of pumping out continuous back-to-back updates to retain visibility in those App Store lists no longer works. Apple has limited the new release lists to only new applications. But updated versions are listed in the App Store's Updates tab, immediately notifying existing customers of the available downloads.

To avoid any conflicts when submitting updates, compile your new version with the same App Store distribution provisioning profile that was used in the current application that's available in the App Store. Also make sure the version number listed in the `CFBundleVersion` and `CFBundleShortVersionString` keys of your update's `Info.plist` file are identical to the new version number submitted in iTunes Connect.

Managing Your Own Expectations

Tom Petty was never wiser when singing "the waiting is the hardest part." You've worked so hard to get to this point that even if the app review process ends up being much shorter than expected, the slow passing of time until Apple's confirmation arrives can feel excruciatingly long. Patience, Grasshopper. It's best not to dwell on it; instead give yourself a project to focus on. Have you finished creating all of your marketing materials, such as your press release and video trailer? And how about researching and connecting with potential media sites for reviews and press opportunities, as discussed in Chapter 8? If so, then that's great! You'll be ready to rock when your app does become available in the App Store. But that's still no excuse to idly sit, feverishly watching the clock. There's no time like the present to dive into developing your next application or begin working on new features for the existing app. Just whatever you do, keep busy, and the time will fly.

For those of you who would rather not log into iTunes Connect a million times a day, obsessing over when that status message will change, you could always elect to have status updates sent directly to you via email. Within your iTunes Connect user profile, simply opt in to receive status update emails by updating the Notifications tab (see Figure 9–15).

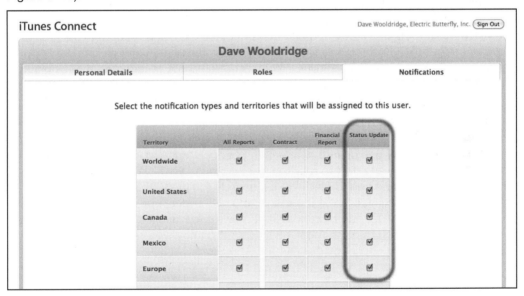

Figure 9–15. *Request to receive email notifications when your app's status changes by updating the Notifications tab in your iTunes Connect user profile.*

But if you're paranoid that you might miss that all-important email notification, Apple also provides a handy Status History feature. In the Manage Your Applications section of iTunes Connect, click the Status History link next to your app listing's current status. The Status History feature allows you to see exactly what stages of the review process have already transpired, as well as when specific actions happened and who initiated them (you or Apple).

In an effort to provide greater transparency and streamlined communication, Apple also created the iPhone Developer News and Announcements site as an online resource for app submission tips, iPhone Program updates, SDK news, and recommended programming techniques. The content can be accessed via the following links:

- Web site: `http://developer.apple.com/iphone/news/`

- RSS feed: `http://developer.apple.com/rss/iphonedevnews.rss`

This web site even posts the latest turnaround time for app reviews, such as "Based on the current volume of app submissions, 96% of applications are being approved within 14 days. Last Updated: November 20, 2009."

Try, Try Again: Dealing with App Store Rejections

If your submitted iPhone app is rejected by Apple, do not despair. Although painfully frustrating, it is not the end of the world. The nice thing about software is that it can always be modified and resubmitted! In the rejection letter that Apple sends, the reviewers usually explain why it was rejected, and if you're lucky, they sometimes even provide suggestions on how to remedy the issue. For simple things such as inappropriate icons or the incorrect usage of a UI element, making the necessary adjustments should be a no-brainer. It doesn't matter if you agree with the reason or not, the important thing is that you make the requested fixes and resubmit your application. Fortunately, there's no limit to how many times you can resubmit an app, so get back on that horse and keep trying. You've come this far, so don't let a tiny dispute prevent you from making money in the App Store.

For major rejection issues that are not so easily remedied, it's important to remain calm and deal with this as a professional business owner. I know that just the idea of several months of your life being thrown out the window because of an unacceptable app would be enough to drive any person into a screaming frenzy. Your first instinct may be to write a scathing blog post in an effort to rally the troops behind your cause. Social media networks like Twitter and FriendFeed make it entirely too easy to gather an angry mob of online followers, but raging against the machine won't endear you to Apple or the app review team. Yes, they do read blog posts and news sites just like you. Although it might feel personally satisfying to have TechCrunch report on how you're yet another victim of app rejection, that won't help you get into the App Store.

And if Apple's rejection was completely justified because your application violates its established terms and conditions, then you really don't have a good reason to complain. Your loud rants will only make you look unprofessional in the eyes of your peers: the developer community. And it certainly won't win you any points with consumers who read your blog or follow you on Twitter.

If you have a legitimate reason why your app rejection was unjust, then talk to Apple about it. Before pleading your case publically on blogs, Twitter, and even YouTube as some developers have done, try to establish a dialog with the app reviewers who evaluated your app. If that doesn't work, then try contacting the official app review team email address at `appreview@apple.com` or any Apple executives you personally know.

Always state your case in a thoughtful, clear manner to help them understand your reasoning. Several app rejections have been overturned because of persuasive developer arguments and a quick reevaluation.

No one has said the app review process is perfect. Just remember that the App Store is only a little over one year old. It's still a very young marketplace, and yet it grew in size much faster than Apple (or anyone else) ever anticipated. It's easy to get upset over rejection, but with more than 100,000 apps flooding the App Store, Apple's overworked review team is merely trying to do their job as best they can under such remarkable pressure. Mistakes do happen, but Apple is constantly working to improve the process. Although that kind of sentiment may make me sound like a glorified fanboy, please don't misinterpret my intentions. As a developer myself, I get just as frustrated if my creativity or ambition are limited by the restrictions of the business world, but then I remember that it *is* a business, and if I want to be a part of it, solving problems with etiquette and professionalism is the only way to truly succeed in the long run.

Apple holds the keys to the kingdom, so if you hope to someday thrive in the App Store, it's in your best interest to maintain a good working relationship with the company and its review team.

Approved! Making It to the Promised Land

So that miraculous day has finally come where your app has been approved and is now available in the App Store? Congratulations! It is indeed a worthy achievement that can bring you much success, especially if you've taken all the necessary steps to effectively market your app!

The immense value of in-app analytics was already discussed in Chapter 7, so once customers being downloading your app, you should be benefitting from the incoming analytics data that anonymously tracks usage behavior.

Checking on your application's performance in the App Store is as simple as logging into iTunes Connect to review reported sales and downloads on either a weekly or daily basis. *Beware: tracking sales can be utterly addictive and destroy your daily productivity level.* iTunes Connect also issues monthly financial reports that summarize your app sales and earned revenue.

Analyzing Your App Store Sales Statistics

But what if you want more? The iTunes Connect reports include a lot of raw data, so it's useful to apply an analytics model to Apple's data in order to really understand your product's life cycle and sales performance in the marketplace. Several third-party tools and web-based services can do just that. Depending on your needs—tracking your App Store statistics from an iPhone or desktop application, graphing your statistics to better educate your own marketing efforts, or merely needing to automate the task of retrieving and analyzing sales and download data (when you forget to do so yourself)—there's definitely a solution out there that will mesh well with your workflow. Although this may not be an exhaustive list, here are a handful of available solid options to explore.

AppFigures

http://www.appfigures.com/

This web-based solution supports the automated importing of your iTunes Connect sales reports, presenting the data in dynamic graphs and charts. Beyond tracking sales, trends, App Store rankings, and reviews, AppFigures will also automatically email you report summaries every day. You can choose either a free Basic account or upgrade to access all Premium features.

AppSales Mobile

http://github.com/omz/AppSales-Mobile

AppSales Mobile is an iPhone app that downloads and analyzes your iTunes Connect sales reports. Since it's available as open source from GitHub, you'll need to compile the project in Xcode and run it as a debug build in order to use it. But it gives you the flexibility to compile and install it on your own mobile iPhone device and even customize the code to suit your own needs.

AppStore Clerk

http://blog.fieryferret.com/2008/10/appstore-clerk.html

AppStore Clerk is a free Mac OS X application that parses your sales reports and displays your app downloads in a simple, easy-to-read spreadsheet table. It may not include the advanced graphing features of other solutions listed here, but it's generously offered as freeware (and the developer even provides the source code as well).

AppStore Sales

http://positiveteam.com/

Positive Team's Mac OS X application boasts a clean and simplified iTunes-style interface design. It supports the automatic download of reports from iTunes Connect, as well as tracking the ranking and sales of your iPhone apps and in-app purchase products. A 14-day trial of AppStore Sales is available for download.

AppViz

http://www.ideaswarm.com/products/appviz/

Ideaswarm's AppViz is a beautifully designed Mac OS X application that can download your iTunes Connect sales data as well as import reports that you've already downloaded to your hard drive. Like most of the other tools in this list, it can analyze and track your sales and downloads in visual graphs to reveal trends. It also monitors multiple apps and accounts, App Store category ranking, and customer reviews, plus sales tracking for your in-app purchase products as well. A trial version of this popular, feature-rich desktop app is available for download.

Heartbeat

http://www.heartbeatapp.com/

This is a very slick, remotely hosted web application that offers an extensive suite of sales tracking, trends, crash report monitoring, usage stats, App Store rankings, revenue payment management, and more. If you're looking for a comprehensive tool for managing your entire App Store business, then you might want to test-drive a Heartbeat trial account for 30 days.

My App Sales

http://www.drobnik.com/touch/my-app-sales/

Like AppSales Mobile, this sales-tracking product is also a convenient iPhone app, but it stands to offer quite a few more features because of the creator Oliver Drobnik's active development plans. A full source code license can be purchased online for only $15 US, and it allows you to compile and run this feature-packed app on your own iPhone devices.

TapMini from TapMetrics

http://www.tapmetrics.com/tapmini

If you're already using TapMetrics for your in-app analytics, then its free TapMini utility for Mac OS X can help save you time by automatically downloading your iTunes Connect sales reports and syncing the data with your TapMetrics account.

Other Resources for App Store Statistics

Beyond the solutions already mentioned here, don't forget to also check out the many App Store ranking tools that were profiled earlier in Chapter 2 such as APPlyzer and David Frampton's excellent (and free) MajicRank.

Rev Your Engines

You're in the App Store…now what? No, it's not time to take a break. I know you're tired from months of development, but you've got to capitalize on the short-lived momentum surrounding your app's launch! Chapter 10 cranks up the publicity engine to increase consumer awareness of your app's availability.

Chapter 10

Increasing Awareness for Your iPhone App

Your iPhone app has been approved and is available for sale in the App Store, so now what? First, I'd like to congratulate you on this milestone achievement! If you've worked your way through the entire book and finally have an application listed in the App Store, that in itself is quite an accomplishment. Only fellow developers truly know how much hard work and dedication goes into launching a new software product. After months of meticulously planning and programming your app, you deserve to celebrate. Although you'd probably love nothing more than to take a much needed vacation at this point, unfortunately, you can't rest yet.

It's time to rev up the publicity engine to increase consumer awareness of your app's availability. Even if you implemented the various business strategies from previous chapters and your prerelease marketing efforts resulted in an initial sales surge, there's still vital work to be done. It's your job to ensure that your iPhone application does not get buried amidst the thousands of new apps flooding into the App Store. This chapter reveals how to craft effective press releases, utilize promo codes, gain exposure through reviews and interviews, and sustain momentum in the App Store with promotions, giveaways, and carefully timed sale events.

Dedicating As Much Effort to Marketing Your App As You Put into Developing It

If your iPhone app was already available in the App Store when you bought this book and you decided to skip ahead to this chapter, then I highly recommend reading Chapter 8 first. In fact, I insist. This chapter will prove much more useful to you *after* you've read Chapter 8.

Even though Chapter 8 is aimed at prerelease marketing, its primary goal is to help you build a very solid foundation online: establishing a web site presence, a social media following via Twitter and Facebook, and relationships with prominent bloggers and influential iPhone app review sites. All of those elements will serve as the underlying backbone of your post-release marketing efforts as well, so having them in place long before your app goes live in the App Store is crucial to your success.

You want to capitalize on the initial visibility of your app's release in the App Store, so the trick is to get as many consumers and iPhone news outlets talking about your app at the same time. Think of it as a supernova of publicity in the hopes of creating a snowball effect. You want consumers thinking "Everyone is talking about that app, so it must be good!" With that in mind, when reading this chapter, don't tackle a single task each week. Read through all the topics and then try to implement as many of them as possible at the same time, in the hopes of sustaining that buzz well beyond the initial release.

How much time should you dedicate to marketing your app? Initially, only one or two hours a day is *not* enough. Yes, I know you're eager to start developing that next great app idea, but before you dive into any future projects, your new 1.0 app release needs attention. You should be prepared to set aside the first two weeks to focus on nothing but promoting your new iPhone app. Request reviews, publicize your app on Twitter and Facebook, set up media interviews, post blog articles, submit your app for awards, and the list goes on.... Once your marketing efforts start to pay off with an increase in sales and/or a rise in the App Store charts, then you can gradually ease back into your normal work life with only a couple hours a day spent on app marketing.

Unfortunately, there are no shortcuts in software marketing. For your iPhone app to have a chance at becoming successful, you have to be willing to invest just as much time and effort into promoting your app as you put into developing it.

If you're not able to dedicate the necessary hours to post-release marketing, then it's in your best interest to hire a third-party company to handle this job. Perform a search online for *iphone app marketing* or *iphone marketing agency*, and you'll find hundreds of marketing and PR firms around the world that specialize in mobile product launches. Here are just a few agencies to give you an idea of some of the services available:

- Appular: `http://appular.com/`
- App2Market: `http://www.app2market.com/`
- Appency: `http://www.appency.com/`

Of course, there are many more marketing agencies out there beyond the three listed here. Depending on where you live, you may feel more comfortable utilizing a local firm, so do several online searches to find one that meets your specific needs. As I've said before, whenever you're hiring third-party consultants or companies, always do ample research before selecting one. Not only should they be experts on the specific challenges of the App Store and marketing iPhone apps, but their practices, policies, and performance should also be very transparent. Since they are representing your company and products, their actions are a reflection of you and your application. For example, if an unscrupulous PR firm uses its own internal iTunes accounts to plant the same fake five-star reviews for all of its clients' apps in the App Store, it's only a matter of time before someone makes the connection and blows the whistle. Even if you were unaware that this was happening, ultimately it's your reputation that gets tarnished.

Apple has even been known to remove apps from the App Store that have abused the customer review system. Obviously, most PR agencies take their ethical responsibility very seriously and never cross that line. I only mention this so that you do your homework and ask the right questions before choosing a mobile marketing firm to promote your iPhone app.

Depending on the level of services provided, an experienced third-party marketing agency will cost at least $1,000 or even thousands more. If you're an independent developer who can't afford to outsource the marketing and publicity for your app, then you'll need to carve out the necessary time in your schedule to handle the job yourself. So, roll up your sleeves, and let's dive in!

> **Know when people are talking about your app!** Based on the latest relevant search results, Google Alerts is a fantastic free email notification service that enables you to monitor when a specific name or topic is discussed online on web sites, blogs, and even Twitter. I highly recommend setting up Google Alerts to track your iPhone app name and company name. You can even use the service to keep tabs on your competitors! Sign up for free at `http://www.google.com/alerts`.

The Art of Crafting Effective Press Releases

Once your app becomes available in the App Store, you'll want to tell the world about it! Sure, notifying your followers on Twitter, Facebook, and your blog are important first steps, but you'll also want to announce the news on a grander scale to reach as many iPhone and iPod touch users as possible. One way to accomplish this is to send out a press release to all the major iPhone news sites. Even if you're a well-established developer in the Mac or iPhone communities, don't assume that the major news outlets are watching your blog or Twitter posts. With the constant flood of tech news that comes across journalists' desks on a daily basis, take the time to deliver important announcements directly to their email inboxes.

The Essential Ingredients of a Press Release

So, how does one write an effective press release? Do not simply copy and paste the iPhone app announcement from your blog into an email message. Press releases consist of specific formatting. By following the standard rules and syntax for press releases, you'll be making it much easier for reporters to quickly scan your story for the pertinent facts.

Using Streaming Colour Studios' press release for Dapple as a visual example (see Figure 10–1), I'll walk you through each of the essential elements of a press release to convey the information that journalists need.

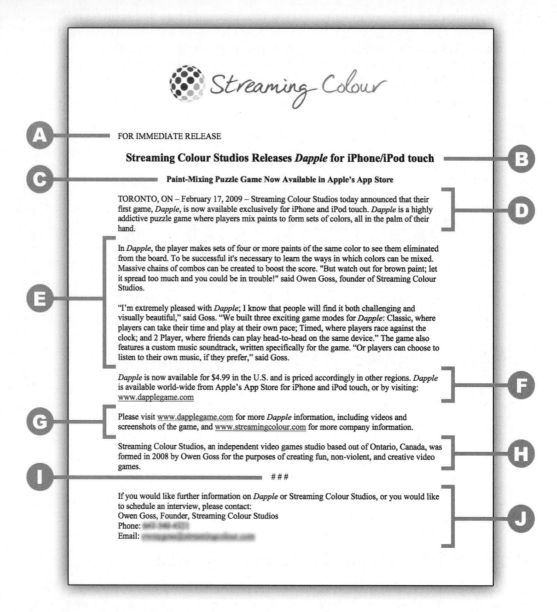

Figure 10–1. *Using Streaming Colour Studios' Dapple announcement as an example, this illustration pinpoints the essential ingredients for effective press releases.*

Referring to Figure 10–1, let's identity each component and its importance in the press release format.

- **A: Release instructions.** Typically, if your app is already available, then you'd use the phrase "FOR IMMEDIATE RELEASE" in all caps. If you're sending a press release in advance of the product's official launch and want the press to hold off on publishing the story until then, you could specify "UNDER EMBARGO UNTIL" and specify a date. Just be aware that many (if not most) news sites and blogs actively ignore embargoes, always eager to be the first to break new stories. If its imperative that your announcement remains under wraps until the product is available, then you may want to wait to send out the press release until the morning of the app's actual debut in the App Store. Some publicists recommend sending out the press release the night before, but with many news sites reporting around the clock, your press release just might get coverage in the middle of the night while your target audience is sleeping, and then the story is buried by newer stories in the morning. That's why its always a good idea to research the reporting habits of each of the iPhone-related news sites and blogs, so that you can get a better gauge for when to send them your press release.

- **B: Subject line.** The most important element of your press release is the subject line. This title needs to capture the attention of anyone who reads it, whether it's the subject line of an email or the headline of a hyperlink on a news site. Traditionally, the formula is *company releases product for platform*, replacing the generic *company*, *product*, and *platform* with your specifics. In Figure 10–1, this translates to "Streaming Colour Studios Releases Dapple for iPhone/iPod touch." Never, never, never add marketing adjectives like "amazing" or "exciting" to the subject line—doing so only makes your press release look like it was written by an amateur. Unlike your other marketing materials, a press release should stick to only the facts, without the flourish of marketing jargon. But at the same time, to compete with the hundreds of other press releases that arrive daily, your subject line should be both informative *and* captivating. If you're announcing a new version of an existing app that has previously won awards, it's perfectly acceptable to include "award-winning" in the subject line. Since the goal is to grab the attention of the media, if the app name is not reflective of its unique, pioneering features, then adjust the subject line accordingly. Instead of saying "Electric Butterfly Releases XRayMed for the iPhone," the subject might draw more attention if worded "Electric Butterfly Releases First X-Ray Reader App for the iPhone." You can always mention your app's name in the summary line below the subject title. If you do boast of being first to market with a particular app or feature, then just be sure it's true!

- **C: Summary line.** This is the second most important element of your press release. If journalists are remotely intrigued by your subject line, this brief one-sentence summary will help determine whether they continue to read the rest of the press release. Many developers opt not to include this line, using only the subject line to lead into the introductory paragraph, but I highly recommend including a summary line to help deliver the basics even if the reader stops there. In the case of the Dapple press release in Figure 10–1, the subject line and summary line together convey that Streaming Colour Studios released Dapple for iPhone and iPod touch and that this paint-mixing puzzle game is now available in Apple's App Store. If readers only bothered to read those two lines, they would still be aware of the most important information: what it is and where to get it.

- **D: Introduction.** The first paragraph begins with your location and release date, followed by a rehash of your subject and summary lines. This introduction should be a single paragraph with only a couple sentences, stating that your company announces the release of a specific product, what it is, who the target audience/platform is, and where it's available.

- **E: Description.** Remember when I talked about crafting an "elevator pitch" for your app description in Chapter 8? The next few paragraphs that follow the introductory paragraph are essentially your elevator pitch description without the flowery marketing adjectives. The main body of your press release should explain in concise detail exactly what your app does, what features and benefits it provides, and why people should care. The press love to include quotes in the stories they run, so it's also a good idea to include a good quote from a senior executive of your company (you?) on why the product was created or how it represents an important milestone for your company. Just remember that less is more. Unless your iPhone app represents some earth-shattering technology breakthrough that warrants a lengthy explanation, your press release should be no longer than one page. That means if you were using word processor software such as Microsoft Word to write your press release, the entire document would fit within a single 8.5" × 11" page with 1-inch margins.

- **F: Pricing and availability.** The next text block should include your iPhone app's price, any hardware or software requirements, and where the app can be purchased. Since most iPhone apps are available in multiple countries, if the price is listed in dollars, then mention that's the price in the U.S. App Store and is priced accordingly in other regions. Most news sites cater to a global audience, so it's important to mention if your app is available worldwide in all of Apple's regional App Stores. If you also offer a free lite version, then be sure to include that information as well so that interested readers can download it and try it risk-free.

- **G: Web site URL and additional information.** Since a one-page press release can't possibly include everything about your new iPhone app, it's absolutely crucial that you include a link to your app's web site or company web site so that interested consumers can access additional information, screenshots, and video demos. If the press are interested in writing about your product, they will also visit your listed URLs to better familiarize themselves with your company—yet another reason to make sure you have a professional, well-designed web site before your iPhone app is released.

- **H: About your company.** This last paragraph should describe your company. This is also a great place to briefly mention any relevant awards you've won and other well-known products you've produced. The press are consumers too, so if they recognize and admire your other software apps, they may be more inclined to write about your new product.

- **I: End of the press release.** The three number symbols centered on the page represent the end of the press release content. Anything that you include below that marker is regarded as information that should not be posted publically, such as your phone number and other media contact details. Of course, for those automated news sites that simply post the exact email announcement you send them, the entire message will be published, regardless of those markers. For those automated sites, be sure to omit any personal contact information that you don't want posted online for search engines to index and cache for all eternity.

- **J: Media contact information.** Always provide a way for the press to reach you. An email address is a must, and a phone number is also recommended. If you live in a country or region where phone calls from the United States can be quite expensive, then set up a Skype account or instant messaging account and list that in lieu of a landline phone number. The more avenues you provide for reaching you, the better, so it can't hurt to also include your Twitter handle as well. If they like your app, they may just decide to follow you! This section is also a great place to include download links for screenshot images, video trailers, an official press kit, and any other marketing materials that you've produced for your iPhone app. Journalists don't have time to hunt through your web site for screenshots, so always include direct links to media resources. And don't forget to state that you welcome all questions, interviews, and app reviews. Let the press know that you're openly accessible for additional inquiries and can provide promo codes for reviewing your app. If you're unfamiliar with promo codes and how they work, keep reading. I'll be discussing promo codes later in this chapter.

For those of you who think this all seems like common sense, then you're one step ahead of the game. You'd be surprised at just how many developers forget to include vital information in their press releases such as pricing, a web site URL, and even contact information. How is a journalist supposed to write a quality story on your new iPhone app announcement if they can't reach you with any additional questions they have? They won't. Incomplete press releases simply get discarded, and the media moves onto the next story. Don't let that happen to you!

Do you have to follow a standard press release format? No, some developers have found success with clever announcements, but take great care to ensure that the press release remains easy to read and contains all of the necessary information. Sometimes "too creative" can backfire, such as a press release formatted in Objective-C code syntax, which would receive quite a bit of attention and admiration from developer blogs but might prove extremely difficult for nonprogrammer journalists to decipher. If you have your heart set on creating a clever press release for select recipients, be sure to also prepare a normal one for those news sites that may not "get the joke" or are unable to accept nonstandard press releases.

Press releases are not limited to only new products. Send out a press release to announce anything that's newsworthy, such as new app versions and special limited-time sale offers and promotions. Since most of the dominant iPhone news sites are English-based, if English is not your native language, don't send them a press release in a foreign language, and certainly don't try converting your press release with an automated online tool like Google Translate. Either the journalists won't be able to translate it themselves or the auto-translated English will contain so much incorrect syntax and phrasing that it can render your announcement unreadable. Hire a professional translator to convert your press release to proper English, and do likewise for translations from English to any other language. First impressions are everything when dealing with the press, so it's a worthy investment.

The Virtual 24/7 Press Room

Although you'll be sending out your press release to as many iPhone-related news sites as possible, you'll also want to make your press release available on your web site or blog. You can't possibly reach everyone yourself, so for those journalists who were not included in your initial email list but discover your iPhone app on their own, provide access to your press release online. And don't just post it as an HTML page. Make it available as its own download that the press can save to their computers for later reference.

After looking at the Dapple press release in Figure 10–1, nicely formatted with a company logo letterhead and various font sizes and styles applied, you may be tempted to create something similar—and you should! This is easy enough to produce with most word processor software programs and makes your press release look that much more professional. Be sure to save the press release in several popular formats, such as DOC (Microsoft Word), RTF, and PDF to ensure that anyone can easily open and read your press release.

Create a dedicated section on your web site for posting all your press releases. Make it easily accessible from anywhere in your site by including a link to it from your main navigation menu or footer menu. Most developers tend to call this section something intuitive and simple, such as "Press" or "Press Room," so that it's extremely easy to find. Although providing a public archive of downloadable press releases online is great, don't stop there. Make it as easy as possible for journalists and reviewers to write about your iPhone app by also including download links of screenshots, video trailers, app icons and logos, and even your company logo! Any materials that might prove useful to the press should be included in your virtual online press room.

Streaming Colour Studios' online press page at `http://www.streamingcolour.com/press.html` accomplishes this and more. It offers a convenient downloadable press kit for each iPhone game that includes screenshots, an app icon, a company logo, and a press release, all compressed in a single zip archive. This press page also lists links to relevant awards, interviews, and app reviews to further spotlight its iPhone games.

Maintaining an online press section on your site will serve as a comprehensive resource for those journalists and bloggers who are interested in doing a story on your company or products, no matter what time zone they are located in. Reporters are often under tight deadlines, so your 24/7 virtual press room can help provide immediate answers even when you're unavailable!

Of course, don't wait for the media to find your web site. A dedicated press section is a good resource to offer, but you'll definitely want to actively send out your press release to the prominent iPhone-related news sites as well.

Who to Notify and How?

The nicely formatted press release with your company logo looks great, but don't send that out as a PDF attached to an email that merely asks journalists to read the attachment. Not only is that a surefire way to have your email ignored, but it's also a common flag for spam filters. If your email address hasn't been whitelisted by the press members you're attempting to reach (yet another reason to establish a relationship with them beforehand), sending an email with attachments may accidentally get marked as junk mail. And for those sites that automatically post press releases that are emailed to their mail bots, sending the press release in an email attachment makes it close to impossible for their automated scripts to parse your announcement text.

Your email should include your entire press release in the body of the message with the subject headline as the email's subject line. Don't format the text as styled rich text or as a fancy HTML email. To enable journalists and mail bots to easily copy the press release, use the tried-and-true plain-text email format. Since word processors such as Microsoft Word tend to insert curly quotes, curly apostrophes, long dashes, and other special characters, you'll want to ensure your press release is converted to standard ASCII plain text. Although your email application may support Unicode characters, many web sites still publish HTML pages with an ASCII text-related content type such as ISO-8859-1. If your press release contains special characters, often news sites copy and paste that text directly to the Web without first converting it into HTML entities. When that happens, your press release is displayed online with strange question mark symbols representing the unrecognizable special characters. This not only makes your press release look unprofessional, but it can also render it difficult to read.

For the same reasons you never want to include your press release as an email attachment, do not include screenshots of your iPhone app as attachments. If you know the journalist whose receiving your email, then attaching one or two screenshots is perfectly acceptable, but for most scenarios, only include direct URL links to your screenshots and video trailer. This provides immediate access to your screenshots and other press materials without the issues that often plague email attachments.

When listing URLs within your email message, always include the full URL, complete with the `http://` prefix. Most modern email programs will dynamically display full `http` URLs as clickable links, but that's not always the case for partial URLs that start only with `www`.

Now that your press release email is ready to go, whom should you send it to? Perform online searches for *iPhone news* and *iPhone app reviews* to find the sites and blogs that cover new iPhone app announcements. After scanning the search results, you'll quickly compile a list much more comprehensive than the collection of sites I've included here, but these should serve as a good starting point. This list consists of web sites that specialize in iPhone news and app reviews. And since some of the major Mac and PC news sites also cover iPhone app news, I've included a few of them here as well. This long list may seem daunting at first glance, but take the time to send your press release to as many relevant iPhone news sites as possible. Remember, they won't all report on your new app release, so the more sites you contact, the more potential coverage you'll get, compensating for any sites that ignore your emails.

- 148Apps: `http://www.148apps.com/`
- AppVee: `http://www.appvee.com/`
- AppCraver: `http://www.appcraver.com/`
- The Unofficial Apple Weblog: `http://www.tuaw.com/`
- Touch Arcade: `http://toucharcade.com/`
- Slide To Play: `http://www.slidetoplay.com/`
- Pocket Gamer: `http://www.pocketgamer.co.uk/`
- The Portable Gamer: `http://theportablegamer.com/`
- FingerGaming: `http://fingergaming.com/`
- App Store HQ: `http://www.appstorehq.com/`
- Appmodo: `http://appmodo.com/`
- AppAdvice: `http://appadvice.com/`
- iPhone Alley: `http://www.iphonealley.com/`

- iPhone.Appstorm: http://iphone.appstorm.net/

- The iPhone Blog: http://www.theiphoneblog.com/

- AppSafari: http://www.appsafari.com/

- iPhoneAppReviews: http://www.iphoneappreviews.net/

- iPhone Application List: http://iphoneapplicationlist.com/

- The iPhone App Review: http://www.theiphoneappreview.com/

- What's on iPhone?: http://www.whatsoniphone.com/

- iPhone App Ratings: http://www.iphoneappratings.org/

- AppChatter: http://www.appchatter.com/

- TouchMyApps: http://www.touchmyapps.com/

- Got Apps?: http://gotapps.com/

- All About iPhone: http://www.allaboutiphone.net/

- iPhone App Index: http://www.iphoneappindex.com/

- The Daily App Show: http://dailyappshow.com/

- iPhone Freak: http://www.iphonefreak.com/

- AppVersity: http://www.appversity.com/

- Talk iPhone: http://www.talkiphone.com/

- SlapApp: http://www.slapapp.com/

- iPhone Footprint: http://www.iphonefootprint.com/

- AppStoreApps.com: http://www.appstoreapps.com/

- iLounge: http://www.ilounge.com/

- Macworld's iPhone Central: http://iphone.macworld.com/

- Macworld AppGuide: http://www.macworld.com/appguide/

- Ars Technica's Infinite Loop: http://arstechnica.com/apple/

- TheAppleBlog: http://www.theappleblog.com/

- MacNN: http://www.macnn.com/

- Macsimum News: http://www.macsimumnews.com/

- The Mac Observer: http://www.macobserver.com/

- AppleTell:
  http://www.appletell.com/apple/archives/category/iphone/

- Mac User: http://www.macuser.co.uk/

- Mac|Life: http://www.maclife.com/

- MacTech: http://www.mactech.com/

- Daring Fireball: http://daringfireball.net/

- PC World: http://www.pcworld.com/

- Gizmodo: http://gizmodo.com/tag/iphoneapps/

Some of the iPhone app directory sites listed in Chapter 2 also post app reviews, so be sure to revisit those sites too. At the very least, you should make an effort to get your app listed in as many of the iPhone app directories and social recommendation sites as possible, such as Appolicious (http://appolicious.com/), Yammer (http://www.yappler.com/), and AppBoy (http://www.appboy.com/).

Before sending press releases and app review requests to any web site or blog, first explore the site to learn about any special submission policies that are enforced and which staff members handle iPhone app news and reviews. Don't send a press release or app review request to a site unseen. Doing so is not only a waste of your time, but it annoys those site administrators who don't cover iPhone app news or your particular app genre. For example, don't send a press release or review inquiry for a productivity app to a games-only site like TouchArcade.com. You never want anyone in the media to perceive your submissions as ignorant spam. Do your research before contacting specific sites or individual writers.

If your app targets a specific niche market, such as writing, yoga, or golf, then you should also make an effort to send your press release to related web sites and magazines in those fields. Those sites and magazines like to keep their readers informed on the latest related products, so even though not everyone will own an iPhone, targeted coverage in a specific field could help reach new customers who don't ordinarily visit tech sites.

Not everyone you send a press release to is going to post your announcement, but if you send it out to a large number of news outlets, you're bound to get some coverage. If your iPhone app doesn't get mentioned on one of your favorite news sites, don't despair. There's a lot of news out there, fighting for the attention of journalists. If you're having trouble reaching the right people or getting posted on mainstream sites like Google News (http://news.google.com/), then you may want to enlist the assistance of a third-party press release distribution service that specializes in technology news. Perform an online search for press release distribution, and you'll find dozens of free and commercial services, such as prMac (http://prmac.com/), PRWeb (http://www.prweb.com/), and PR Newswire (http://www.prnewswire.com/). Before signing up for a specific service, you'll want to verify that they'll distribute your press release to the mainstream news outlets you want to target. But don't expect them to adequately reach smaller, niche iPhone news sites—that's a job best suited for you.

When journalists and bloggers do post stories or reviews on your new iPhone app, be sure to email a personal thank-you to each one. Even if your press release didn't warrant a spot on their main news site but was mentioned as only a posted link on their Twitter account, that's still coverage that will drive additional traffic to your app's product page in the App Store. No matter how small, any publicity a third-party gives your app is worthy of a thank-you. Expressing your gratitude with a sincere email note also helps strengthen your relationship with those journalists and bloggers. Creating a dialogue with them also presents a great opportunity to ask if they'd like to receive a promo code to download your app and write a review.

Issuing Promo Codes: Soliciting App Reviews on Influential Blogs and Review Sites

For those iPhone sites that post app reviews, you won't want to send them only a press release. You should also contact them about writing a review of your app, which requires a slightly modified pitch. With more than 100,000 apps in the App Store, everyone wants their app reviewed, so how do you ensure that your app stands out from the crowd? This is where having an established relationship with prominent bloggers and app reviewers (as discussed in Chapter 8) can help move your app to the front of the queue. If you've already prepped them with sneak-preview screenshots and a video trailer of your app during your prerelease marketing efforts and they were impressed, then there's a good chance they'll want to review your app when it's released.

Providing Review Materials

Your app review pitch should contain all the information from your press release, plus additional media materials such as a few screenshots, a video trailer, and the app's icon—basically all of the elements that you included on your web site's press page and/or downloadable press kit. Depending on the submission rules of each web site, reviewers may ask you to include screenshots and other app-related images as email attachments or require URLs of your materials online. Some sites only accept app review requests through online web forms. Here's a rundown of the materials that most app reviewers require:

- **Your elevator pitch.** Why should reviewers care about your app or game? They need to be sold on why your new app is important to their readers. Remember when I talked about crafting an "elevator pitch" for your app description in Chapter 8? It's proving to be quite useful in almost all of your marketing efforts, such as your web site, App Store text, press release, and now app review requests! Use your elevator pitch to help construct an appealing email subject line and app description. Those two elements need to convey your passion and excitement as the creator of the app. Reviewers are extremely busy, so brevity is key. Like your press release, your app description should be short. And always remember to include your app's price!

- **Three to five screenshots.** Don't inundate reviewers with too many screenshots. Pick three that best represent your app, and only submit those. If a site requires that you submit more than that, then send the five screenshots that you had uploaded to the App Store, since those were obviously picked as the best representations of your app.

- **Video trailer.** If you've produced a video trailer that shows the app or game in action, then *always* include a URL link for viewing that as well. As I already mentioned in Chapter 8, pay close attention to production value because your video trailer is a direct reflection of your app's quality. A well-produced video trailer that's less than two minutes long can quickly educate a reviewer in less time than it would take to download and test-drive your app, so it can often be the deciding factor on whether your app gets reviewed.

- **App icon and App Store URL.** Although some reviewers don't require your app icon image, you should always include a direct link to your app in the App Store. This enables them to check out your App Store listing and link to it from their review. Instead of copying the long, complicated URL from the App Store, it is often easier to provide Apple's shortened iTunes link format of `http://itunes.com/apps/APPNAME`, replacing *APPNAME* with your application's official App Store name. For example, a link to the popular Bump app would be `http://itunes.com/apps/bump`. For those reviewers who do accept app icon images, submit the high-quality 512 × 512 pixel version for maximum flexibility.

- **App web site URL.** Definitely include a link to your app's web site so that reviewers can explore any additional online resources you offer. Don't be disappointed if a review does not link to your web site. The iTunes Affiliate Program is a major revenue source for many review sites, so typically the review will only direct readers to your app in the App Store via an affiliate link.

- **Contact information.** Just like your press release, make sure to always provide all your relevant contact information, such as your name, company name, email address, phone number, Skype, IM, and Twitter. The more options you provide, the better. It's surprising just how many developers forget to include these vital details. If a reviewer can't reach you with additional questions, then that alone could prevent a review from being written.

- **Promo code.** Many sites tell you not to include a promo code with your app review request, stating that if they're interested in reviewing the app after evaluating your submission, they'll ask for a promo code. It's nice that they don't want to unnecessarily waste promo codes for apps they don't plan on reviewing, but here's a little secret. If you provide a promo code with your initial review request, you've just made it incredibly convenient for them to download your app for free and try it immediately. Odds are they'll use the supplied promo code, and your chances of getting reviewed just got a little better! Obviously, Apple limits how many promo codes you can issue per app version, so you'll want to use your promo codes sparingly and supply them with the initial submission only to the most popular and influential review sites. Not sure what a promo code is? I explain what they are and how to acquire them in the following section.

Obtaining Promo Codes

For those new to iPhone development, promo codes are special codes that you can use to provide someone with a free copy of your iPhone app. Promo codes work just like iTunes gift card codes and are redeemed the same way. This is the easy and recommended way to provide journalists, bloggers, and app reviewers with a free download of your product!

A promo code is assigned to a specific item in the iTunes Store. In this case, it would be your iPhone application. If a user redeems a promo code provided by you, only the related app is downloaded free of charge. That promo code cannot be used to download any other item, and like gift cards, once a promo code is redeemed, it can never be used again, which prevents piracy.

Promo codes are not tied to an individual's iTunes account, so treat them like cash. A promo code can be given to anyone you want, but at the moment, they can only be redeemed in the U. S. iTunes Store. That won't pose a problem when dealing with the popular app review sites since most of them are based in the United States, but if you hold app giveaways via Twitter or Facebook, only your U.S. followers will be able to claim promo code prizes.

So, how do you obtain promo codes for your iPhone app? As with everything else associated with your App Store products, promo codes are managed in Apple's iTunes Connect site. Either log into the iPhone Dev Center online and select the iTunes Connect button in the far-right column or log in directly to iTunes Connect here:

`http://itunesconnect.apple.com/`

On the main page of iTunes Connect, visit the section called Request Promotional Codes. From that web page, select the application from which to issue promo codes. If you don't see your app listed there, then that means it has not yet been approved by Apple. Since promo codes are redeemed via iTunes, your app must be available for sale in the App Store before you can request promo codes for it. After selecting your app, enter the number of promo codes you need. Simply return to iTunes Connect any time you need additional promo codes issued to you.

It's important to note that Apple grants you only 50 promo codes per app update. So if you use up all 50 promo codes for your 1.0 version, you won't be able to request any more promo codes until after your next app update is uploaded and approved in the App Store. Although 50 may sound like a lot, they'll disappear much faster than you might expect. Everyone loves free apps, so you'll have a lot of people asking for promo codes, but use them sparingly. Your first priority is making sure you have enough promo codes for the press and app reviews. After that, you can use remaining ones for giveaways and promotions. But I recommend always hanging onto a handful of promo codes, just in case an exciting app review or marketing opportunity presents itself down the road.

If you want to send an advance copy of your app to someone to review before it's available in the App Store, then obviously you won't be able to issue a promo code. Your only option is to use ad hoc distribution to provide the app to that reviewer. Most, if not all, app review sites can provide their device IDs and will accept ad hoc distributed versions if they've agreed to do an advance review. And since sneak previews and exclusives for highly anticipated apps are greatly desired, they'll gladly deal with the irritating complexity of ad hoc distribution and expiring provision profiles. But keep in mind that you can register only 100 device IDs per year for all your apps combined, whereas Apple is much more generous with 50 promo codes per app update. If your app is already available in the App Store, then don't waste your precious ad hoc device ID allotment. Issue promo codes instead, which are preferred by reviewers anyway.

Publicity Requires Planning and Patience

Just because you sent someone a promo code, don't assume that automatically grants you an app review. And even if a reviewer does eventually write about your app, it may not be within the timetable you anticipated. As I've already mentioned, journalists and reviewers are extremely busy, receiving hundreds of new product releases and review requests every day. It may be days or even weeks before they reply to your inquiry, so be patient. I know I'm starting to sound like a broken record, but this is yet another reason why establishing relationships with the press during your early prerelease marketing efforts is so important. Everything takes time, and publicity is no different, so plan ahead.

If an important iPhone app review site does not respond to your submission in a timely manner, then whatever you do, never offer bribes, beg, or attempt to solicit sympathy. And certainly never hassle them with a mind-numbing barrage of emails and phone calls. Such behavior will not only ruin your chances at receiving coverage, but it may just get you and your company banned from their site.

You can preempt much of the mystery by asking two simple questions when you're initially contacting members of the press:

- "After receiving a new press release or app review inquiry, how long does it typically take for an article or review to be written and posted online?"

- "If I don't receive a response, may I check back with you in a week or two?"

If you push too hard, you may not like the result. If you're dealing with a fellow developer with a popular app review blog and you're having trouble getting him to commit to writing a review, tread carefully. Keep in mind that a possible reason could be that he didn't like your app and is reluctant to write a negative review because as a developer, he understands how much hard work went into its creation. If you continue to hound him, he may opt to publish the bad review just to get you off his back. And that certainly doesn't help you at all, so approach every potential opportunity with patience.

For those of you who are eager to speed up the app review process and move to the front of the line, there are a few sites such as iPhone Toolbox (http://iphonetoolbox.com/) and Fresh Apps (http://www.freshapps.com/) that offer expedited app reviews for a fee. For the record, I'm *not* a fan of buying reviews. Granted, I understand that the ethical quandary is alleviated since the fee only promises a quality review will be written with no guarantee that it will be positive. You could pay the fee and still receive a bad review. If you're going to go down this path, why not pay for an unbiased review to be posted where it can reach the most eyeballs: in the App Store! FuelMyApp (http://www.fuelmyapp.com/) offers just such a pay per review service, and you won't even have to waste any promo codes! It only costs you the price of your app plus a $2.99 service fee per review. When posted reviews show up in the App Store, the reviewers are then reimbursed the app cost, so they receive a free app for their efforts.

Even if you encourage happy customers to post App Store reviews, that won't help you the first day or two your app is available in the App Store. You'll be heavily promoting your app's release, driving as much traffic as possible to your product page in the App Store, and yet for the first couple days, it may have only a few customer reviews. Without a substantial number of reviews, consumers may be hesitant to buy your app. But if your app has more than a dozen reviews in the App Store, then that seems to change how it is perceived, causing people to be a little less reluctant to make a purchase. If you have several friends or peers who would be willing to post a review, it's worth sacrificing ten promo codes to ensure that your app has a decent number of reviews in the App Store during those crucial first few days after its debut. You could also give away a few promo codes on the Promo App Codes site (http://www.promoappcodes.com/), AppGiveaway.com (http://www.appgiveaway.com/), or via your Twitter and Facebook accounts in exchange for some App Store reviews. Just make sure the participants post honest, objective reviews. Having all five-star ratings on the very first day will look quite suspect!

Using Promotions and Giveaways to Improve App Discovery

Who doesn't love freebies? Giving away something of value is a great way to draw attention to your iPhone app, especially if it's your app that's being given away for free! Temporarily reducing your app's price to free for a single day or a weekend can help boost it higher in the App Store's Top Free Apps charts, especially if you notify all the iPhone news sites of this limited-time offer. Those sites love to report on price reductions and freebies, so the stunt should gain quite a bit of exposure. And if you partner with a popular giveaway site like FreeAppADay.com (http://www.freeappaday.com/), then the extra publicity should really improve your app's ranking and visibility in the App Store charts!

If you're scratching your head, wondering how you're supposed to profit by giving away your app, then you're not looking at the big picture. It's true that you won't be making any money from all those users who downloaded the app for free, and you won't see a huge spike in paid app sales after the free offer ends. So why do it? This strategy is all about the up-sell.

By removing the price barrier for a limited time, thousands of new users will have taken advantage of the free download. Those are new customers who probably would not have purchased it before anyway, not to mention the thousands of new users who are discovering your app for the first time. If they enjoy the free app, you've just expanded your customer base with an opportunity to up-sell future In-App Purchase content and other new apps. Even if you were already doing that within a free lite version, there's a big difference in audience size. The lite version of your relatively unknown app may reach 50,000 users, whereas a highly publicized weekend giveaway of your full paid version may add more than 100,000 new users to your existing customer base in only a few days. But this strategy only works if you have a way to eventually convert a large percentage of these new users into paying customers.

Robert Szeleney partnered with FreeAppADay.com to offer his popular Rope'N'Fly game as a free App Store download for one day. He did this with the express intent to spread awareness for the new sequel, Rope'N'Fly 2. He capitalized on the free download offer by promoting the sequel on the original game's main screen (see Figure 10–2), reaching a much larger audience in the process. This extra exposure helped propel Rope'N'Fly 2 into the App Store's Top 50 Paid Apps chart.

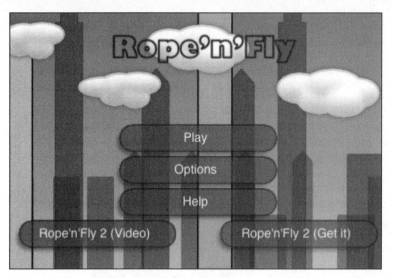

Figure 10–2. *By offering a free one-day download of Rope'N'Fly, the game's main screen helped promote the new sequel, Rope'N'Fly 2, to a much larger audience.*

If you currently have only one iPhone app available and do not have any plans to integrate In-App Purchase, then offering a limited-time free download will aid in app discovery and visibility within the App Store, but it may not improve your sales. Candy Cane was fortunate in that its gamble of giving away Fling! for a short time pushed the game to the #1 spot on the App Store's Top Free Apps chart. When Fling! returned to its normal price, the wave of positive word-of-mouth recommendations from users resulted in enough sales to catapult Fling! into the U.S. Top 50 Paid Apps chart. If you have faith in the quality of your app, then this strategy may work for you, but it's risky. For most apps that try this approach, the developers see a slight bump in sales after the free offer ends, but it doesn't last long. Without a way to up-sell In-App Purchase items or cross-promote other products, it's often hard to justify this kind of freebie strategy.

If you're worried about cannibalizing potential app sales, then why not give away something else? That's what Tap Tap Tap did. To promote the launch of the voice-morphing app Voices, Tap Tap Tap partnered with Potion Factory to offer a free copy of its Voice Candy application for Mac OS X. To leverage the software freebie to help promote the Voices iPhone app, consumers had to tweet about the special offer on Twitter in order to download their free copy of Voice Candy. Tap Tap Tap announced this "TweetBlast" promotion through MacHeist's email database and Twitter feed, initially reaching almost 600,000 members. By spreading the word via Twitter, more and more people found their way to the web site, who in turn tweeted about it to receive the free Mac software. It was a successful viral campaign that motivated tens of thousands of people to tweet about it, which resulted in hundreds of thousands of people checking out the Voices app. Besides providing the promotion details, the web site also beautifully showcased Tap Tap Tap's Voices app with demo videos and an App Store buy button (see Figure 10–3). And sure enough, the ploy worked. With an introductory price of only 99 cents, enough people purchased the app within the first few days that Voices skyrocketed to #1 in the U.S. Top Paid Apps chart.

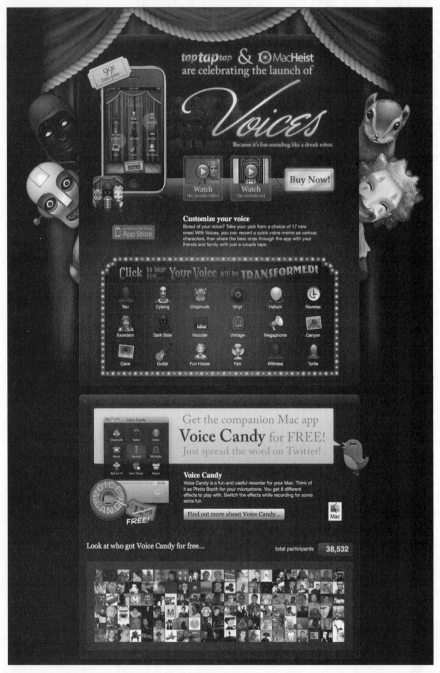

Figure 10–3. *By offering a free copy of Voice Candy for Mac to anyone who tweeted about the special promotion, Tap Tap Tap's clever TweetBlast campaign helped propel Voices to #1 in the U.S. App Store's Top Paid Apps chart.*

With Tap Tap Tap's John Casasanta being the creator of MacHeist, the company had unique access to an extremely large targeted audience. Obviously, most independent developers won't have mailing lists as large as MacHeist, but this kind of social media-based promotion can still work on a smaller level. If you followed my advice in Chapter 8 and have spent the past few months cultivating your own audience via Twitter, Facebook, email newsletters, and blog readers, you should have a sizable base for communicating special offers, giveaways, and other app-related news.

Any online promotion, especially one that utilizes social media, should always be designed to grow your audience. Don't give away free software, promo codes, or prizes without receiving a valuable connection in return. Even if they tweet about your iPhone app, there's no guarantee those tweets will turn into sales. But if people were required to follow you on Twitter or subscribe to your free email newsletter in order to participate in the promotion, then regardless of the outcome, your marketing efforts would be rewarded. That's exactly what Tap Tap Tap did with its Voices TweetBlast campaign. To get the free Voice Candy software, participants were required to first sign up for a free MacHeist account, follow @TapTapTap on Twitter, and then tweet a very specific message. Even if the promotion didn't pay off with a substantial boost in Voices sales, it added thousands of new Twitter followers and MacHeist members, enabling Tap Tap Tap to easily reach those people again in the future with special offers and new product announcements.

Timing a Good Sale to Rejuvenate App Downloads

Like freebies, sale prices are also heavily reported by many iPhone news sites, so the extra publicity can definitely drive more traffic to your app in the App Store. A carefully timed sale will attract new customers who ordinarily may not have purchased your app at its regular price. During a sale, you won't make as much profit per purchase, but ideally, the increase in sales volume will make up the difference.

The goal is to exceed your usual daily revenue and climb higher in the App Store charts. The higher you rank, the more visible your app is within the App Store, especially if your sale price has boosted the app into the Top 100. That visibility exposes your product to new consumers who may not have previously known about it. Seeing your app perform well in the App Store will prompt people to check it out. It's a bit of a vicious cycle. You've got to sell a lot of units to rank high in the App Store charts, but once you're in the Top 100, that visibility will help you sell even more. For as long as that position can be maintained, keep offering the discounted price. When your app eventually falls out of the charts, then you can evaluate whether to revert to the regular price.

Some iPhone developers offer a special introductory low price on a new app the moment it lands in the App Store. If it's a short-lived, hit-driven release like a game or a novelty app that requires higher placement in the App Store charts to survive, then an instant sale price can maximize its chance for success. But if you've developed a niche app that caters to a very targeted audience, then offering a discount right out of the gate could prove to be a bad move. Unlike many hit-driven games, productivity apps typically enjoy a much longer life cycle since they satisfy a distinct need. If there's a significant demand for your app's unique features, then early adopters won't hesitate to pay regular price. By offering a discount on day one, you'd be selling them the app for less money than they were prepared to spend (which is great for consumers but bad for your bottom line). Since most niche apps don't rank high in the overall App Store charts anyway, an introductory sale price will only reduce the amount of revenue you could have made selling the same number of downloads at regular price.

When the initial popularity of your app starts to decline and the weekly revenue begins to slide into the "long tail" of the product's life, that's a perfect time to hold a sales event. The reduced price will help lure new customers and rejuvenate interest in the app. If you find that the discount is sustaining an acceptable level of sales, you can always decide to permanently stick with that price point for the remainder of its time in the App Store.

A well-received sale offer on one app can also positively affect the rest of your product line in the App Store. Customers who enjoy their new purchase will be curious about your other offerings. If you're effectively cross-promoting your products within each app, then a spike in downloads for the discounted app will also drive more traffic to your other apps, which often results in more purchases.

Contemplating Sponsorships and Product Placement Deals

Similar to in-app advertising, sponsorships and product placement offer an innovative way to monetize a free lite version, but they're typically more tightly integrated within the app than traditional advertising. This provides a much more elegant solution for users, while enabling the sponsor to directly connect with a very targeted audience. Since the sponsor would be eager to promote their affiliation with the app, the added marketing support can help reinvigorate interest in an existing app, bringing a flood of new users that you can later up-sell additional paid content and other apps.

App Cubby's popular Gas Cubby app has been a prominent staple in the App Store for quite some time. Founder David Barnard was looking for a way to increase both value and revenue for this perennial product. In December 2009, he announced an exclusive sponsorship deal with Honeywell, the parent company of such famous automotive brands as FRAM, Prestone, and Autolite. Since Gas Cubby caters to the very audience those brands want to reach, it's a good alliance that benefits both App Cubby and Honeywell. The result is a new rebranded version called Gas Cubby by FRAM that's available for free in the App Store. With the back-end overhead costs associated with maintaining Gas Cubby's various features and services, offering enough value in a free lite version without losing money had always been a struggle, but the Honeywell sponsorship provided a way to properly monetize a free version. To test the waters, they've started with a basic advertising deal (see Figure 10–4) but have plans to integrate even more value and features in future releases.

Figure 10–4. *With an exclusive Honeywell sponsorship deal, the rebranded Gas Cubby by FRAM enables App Cubby to offer plenty of value for free, reaching a much larger audience.*

David Barnard remarked on App Cubby's blog, "I'm excited about the number of users who will get to use Gas Cubby. That alone will exponentially increase the value created by Gas Cubby. Had I given the app away for free without a partner like Honeywell, there's no way I could have managed the marginal costs. The advertising will help pay for the excellent tech support App Cubby is known for, and we've temporarily removed the online backup/sync feature in Gas Cubby by FRAM to keep other costs under control. Once we get a sense for how many people start using the app now that it's free, we'll be working toward scaling and redesigning our current sync architecture to accommodate the load."

For people who prefer to use the app without ads, the paid version of Gas Cubby is still available in the App Store. This way, App Cubby is able to provide users with a choice of either the free or paid option, while being able to monetize both versions to support continued development and future updates.

Product placement is a little different than a typical sponsored advertising deal. You may be familiar with product placement in other entertainment mediums such as television, where a show can be presented with fewer commercial breaks because the sponsors' products are actually integrated within the show itself. Ever notice how the cast of a show all drink the same beer or drive various car models made by the same auto maker? That's no accident. That's paid product placement.

Firemint's Real Racing is one of the most popular racing games in the App Store. Possibly for fear of cannibalizing sales of the paid version, a free lite app had never been released…that is, until recently. By partnering with Volkswagen, Firemint was able to offer a free Real Racing GTI version in the App Store. Real Racing GTI features the same game engine as the original Real Racing app, but all the featured race cars are the new 2010 Volkswagen GTI. Even the sponsor stickers and track billboards are all Volkswagen ads (see Figure 10–5). The game also includes a virtual showroom, providing a closer look at the GTI.

Figure 10–5. *Firemint's free Real Racing GTI game features 2010 Volkswagon GTI race cars and sponsored billboards on the race track.*

With this strategic product placement deal, Volkswagen can promote its new GTI model to this highly targeted audience, and Firemint now has a way to monetize the free lite version. With the free Real Racing GTI game available to a greater number of users, it also presents Firemint with a much bigger audience to up-sell the additional features in the paid version of Real Racing.

Firemint also receives a substantial marketing boost from Volkswagen's web site— http://www.vw.com/realracinggti/—which actively promotes Real Racing GTI, encouraging consumers to download the free game to take the new 2010 GTI for a virtual test-drive.

Even the app icons for both Gas Cubby and Real Racing were customized to better promote the sponsored versions. Not only do the altered app icons help differentiate the free versions from the original paid apps, but it's also an important visual element within the App Store that helps reinforce the sponsors' brands (see Figure 10–6).

Figure 10–6. *Not only do the custom icons (right) help differentiate the free versions from the original paid apps (left), but it's also an important visual element within the App Store that helps reinforce the sponsors' brands.*

As evident with Gas Cubby by FRAM and Real Racing GTI, partnering with a sponsor can breathe new life into an existing app by extending its reach to a larger audience with a free version. Obviously, these kinds of sponsorship deals are not appropriate for all apps. For example, if your iPhone app is a mobile guide to the latest movies and local theaters, then recruiting Warner Bros. as the exclusive sponsor would present a conflict of interest when listing new movies from other studios such as Universal and Paramount. And if your app's subject matter is too broad or your app does not currently reach enough people, then you may have trouble finding an interested sponsor. Companies are in the business of selling more products, so a sponsorship proposal would only be appealing if your app can deliver a large audience in a very targeted market.

Connecting with Customers: Delivering App Updates and Quality Support

Don't wait months before releasing updated versions of your app. Even without any reported bugs or crashes, you should update the app periodically, providing additional polish and value. A lack of updates can negatively affect your application's perception in the App Store. If consumers notice that your app hasn't been updated in several months, they may be reluctant to purchase the app for fear that it's no longer actively supported.

Maintaining consumer interest in your app is not just about attracting new customers; it's also about keeping your existing customers happy. Remember when I talked about loyal customers being the best customers in Chapter 6? The way to build customer loyalty is through delivering bug fixes and additional features/content in a timely manner. By continuing to update the app, you're enhancing the user experience and keeping your app top of mind. Even if your app's overall customer usage eventually declines because of distractions from new app purchases, whenever a new version shows up in a customer's Updates list, it serves as subtle reminder of your app's value and your commitment to supporting it.

If customers remain satisfied with your app, they will be that much more motivated to buy In-App Purchase items and other new products from you. A steady stream of updates also helps sustain customer usage, which is extremely important if your primary revenue stream is in-app advertising. As long as you keep delivering a rewarding and fun experience, people will continue to talk about your app. Continuous updates and quality support are big factors in driving word-of-mouth.

In previous chapters, I already discussed the importance of setting up a support site and email address for customers who need assistance or have questions, but how you utilize that communication channel will ultimately determine its effectiveness as a business tool. Customer relationship management is the most organic form of direct marketing and sales. People who feel good about your company will want to support you, not only by buying your apps and downloadable content but by becoming advocates who spread the word to others on Twitter, Facebook, and app recommendation services such as AppsFire (http://www.appsfire.com/), appSpace (http://appspace.com/), and Appolicious (http://appolicious.com/). Even hackers using pirated iPhone apps have been known to later become legitimate buyers of In-App Purchase content if they appreciate the developers' efforts.

Online word-of-mouth is a double-edged sword that can cut both ways with the power to catapult products from obscurity to overnight success, as well as destroy business reputations within a matter of hours, so always treat customer inquiries with absolute respect and care.

Take the time to implement an organized customer support system that enables you to not only respond quickly to bug reports and issues but also effectively track customer support histories and contact information. This usually goes beyond the capabilities of most email applications, requiring the use of a more feature-rich customer management solution such as help desk software or a web-based trouble ticket system. Perform a search online for *customer support software*, and you'll discover dozens of available products and services. Many of them, such as Zendesk (http://www.zendesk.com/), offer affordable pricing tiers that cater to both solo developers and large enterprises, depending on your specific needs.

What's especially interesting about Zendesk is that it provides several appealing features for iPhone developers. If you're already using GetSatisfaction.com as your online support solution, those community comments can be synced with Zendesk. For those of you using MailChimp to send out email newsletters, then it can be integrated with Zendesk for email-based customer support management. Want to access your help desk system remotely? Just download the free Zendesk Notifier iPhone app. Zendesk even provides an open source feedback form that you can embed into your Xcode project, enabling customers to submit support requests directly to your Zendesk account from within your iPhone app! You can download Zendesk's Cocoa library for iPhone at http://github.com/zendesk/zendesk-iphone-dropbox.

By tracking customer support histories, you'll be able to better serve each customer's unique needs and effectively monitor recurring issues. Always reply to every support email you receive, even if it's only a feature request. A quick thank-you reply is an easy way to establish a nice rapport with your customers. People like to know their voice has been heard.

When major bugs do surface, it's important to react quickly. The first thing you should do is immediately update your app's description in the App Store, notifying consumers that you're aware of the problem. By letting users know up front that the issue is being addressed and an updated version will be available soon, that should help reduce the flood of redundant support emails and—fingers crossed—help dissuade people from venting their frustrations in a public forum that can damage your app's reputation. At the very least, it should buy you enough time to investigate and resolve the showstopping bug.

If the reported issue is a severe crash affecting a large percentage of your customers and you need to get the fixed update into the App Store as soon as possible, then Apple does provide expedited reviews for special circumstances. After submitting your updated app in iTunes Connect, send an email to Apple's review team at appreview@apple.com, explaining the situation. In emergency cases, Apple can expedite the app review in a day or two, saving you several days of waiting. Apple will only perform expedited reviews for you once or twice (and Apple does keep track), so use this "get out of jail free card" very wisely. This is yet another reason why Chapter 7 placed such a strong emphasis on extensive testing before submitting to the App Store. The developer community is lucky to have this direct email line into Apple, so please don't use it to communicate anything other than critical app review issues.

Additional Tips for Sustaining Momentum in the App Store

Beyond soliciting app reviews, participating in iPhone-related web forums, growing your audience online via Twitter and Facebook, and the myriad of other marketing and publicity strategies already outlined in Chapter 8 and Chapter 10, here are a few more important topics worth mentioning.

Banking on the Prestige of Awards and Endorsements

Enter your app into as many high-profile iPhone awards competitions as possible. Winning an award can do wonders for both your app and your company, providing a landslide of publicity and prestige. And with all the press that reports on the winners, being included will increase consumer awareness and boost app sales. Even if you're only a semifinalist, that extra exposure and recognition will definitely benefit your app. Here are a few to consider:

- Apple Design Awards: http://developer.apple.com/wwdc/ada/
- 148Apps' Best App Ever Awards: http://bestappever.com/

- AppFire's App Star Awards: `http://appsfire.com/appstar`

- AppAdvice's App Awards: `http://appadvice.com/appawards/`

Although all the awards listed here are very influential, landing a renowned Apple Design Award is perceived as the highest honor a Mac or iPhone developer can achieve. Submitting your app to the Apple Design Awards is a great way to gain Apple's attention. Even if you don't win an ADA, if your app impresses Apple, it may just get selected as a featured app in the App Store. And we all know that being showcased in the App Store's "New & Noteworthy" and "What's Hot" has the power to transform apps into best-sellers.

Endorsements from respected developers and media personalities can also provide welcome sales spikes. The once little-known Simplenote was publically endorsed online by John Gruber as his favorite notes app. Because of the large readership of Gruber's DaringFireball.net site, sales for Simplenote shot through the roof in the days that followed.

As I mentioned in Chapter 8, high-profile awards and expert testimonials should be proudly displayed on your app's web site and App Store description like merit badges. Awards and endorsements offer validation and a seal of approval that influence consumer perception of your app.

Share Your Knowledge

In Chapter 8 I discussed the value of writing blog posts and articles about your iPhone app development experiences as a way to grow your online audience during the prerelease stage. By publishing your thoughts, insights, and lessons learned from the process, it helps bridge a connection between you and your readers. Ideally, they'll have a greater appreciation for your efforts and the finished product. But don't stop once the app is available in the App Store. iPhone developers love to read about the experiences of their peers and are often quick to retweet your URL if they think the blog post would be of interest to other fellow developers. Remember, many customers follow the blogs and tweets or their favorite app creators, so if those developers spread the word about your app, their customers could also become your customers! Other web sites and blogs may link to your articles as well. And if you're lucky enough to get some link love on Digg.com, Technorati.com, or even Slashdot.org, you could see traffic to your site rise exponentially in a matter of hours.

Streaming Colour Studios' Owen Goss saw that happen firsthand after publishing a blog article about his Dapple game's sales numbers. Slashdot posted a story about it, linking to his blog, and Owen got to witness the famous "Slashdot effect." The day of the Slashdot post, Streaming Colour Studios' site traffic increased 4,000 percent, and his Dapple sales were four times more than the usual daily sales! As you can see, publishing interesting articles of value on your blog (with links from your social media accounts) has the potential to dramatically boost both product awareness and app sales!

Participating in Interviews and Podcasts

It goes without saying that invitations by the press and the developer community to be interviewed for a story or a featured guest on a popular podcast should always be accepted when your schedule permits. This can have a similar effect to publishing frequent blog articles and Twitter posts, enabling consumers and peers to learn more about you as a person and business owner. It represents yet one more valuable audience for increasing sales and awareness for your app!

Be aware of the proposed topic before agreeing to participate. If the story takes a negative angle, then your involvement could ultimately tarnish your reputation. Also be very careful what you say in an interview. When you're on the record, speaking too casually about your opinions of other products, companies, and individuals can land you in hot water. Remember that most published articles remain online indefinitely, so your words can come back to haunt you again and again and again.

If you're charming and don't experience difficulties speaking in public, then this additional exposure can help endear new fans to your cause. If you're shy (like most programmers) with a distinct fear of public speaking, then it might be beneficial to first receive some media training. It's important that you're able to make a good impression when speaking to the press or chatting on podcasts. Sure, media training consultants and seminars cost money, but if you blow a high-profile interview, that could cost you even more.

Can Advertising Sell Apps?

This is one of the most commonly asked questions by iPhone developers. The answer is somewhat less definitive than you might expect. Advertising your app can result in enough sales to justify the expense if you choose the right medium and market, but that's easier said than done. It's extremely difficult to accurately track the conversion rate of your advertising campaign. Web and mobile ad networks track the click-throughs to the App Store and Apple tracks sales of your app, but how do you tie the two reports together to pinpoint just how many of those ad clicks turned into actual app sales? Currently, the only way to accomplish this is by using an iTunes Affiliate Program URL for your advertisement link. Beyond the benefit of earning a 5 percent commission on all sales derived from iTunes affiliate links (as discussed in Chapter 6), it's also a great way to track which ad click-throughs result in app sales. And if you're already using similar affiliate links on your web site, LinkShare allows you to assign a unique Signature ID to the iTunes affiliate link you employ for your advertisement, so that click-throughs and sales from your ad can be easily identified in your LinkShare reports.

If you're going to experiment with advertising, try your hand at mobile ads first since they're the most targeted. As I already said many times, more than 90 percent of iPhone users download apps directly from the mobile device's App Store. This is your target audience, so what better way to reach them than advertising within another iPhone app or on a mobile web site? And as I mentioned in Chapter 5, if you've already implemented in-app advertising in your own app with AdMob, then you'll be able to benefit from its Download Exchange program, which enables you to advertise your apps across other apps in their network by giving up some of your app's ad inventory. This can be a very cost-effective way to test some initial advertising. Of course, if your app doesn't feature in-app advertising, then you'll have to pay for the ad campaign.

Since you're paying per click, include the price and a short descriptor to prevent the curious from tapping the ad just to find out the price or what the app is. With advertising typically being fairly expensive, if your app is priced at only 99 cents, then you'll need to be very careful not to spend more than you could possibly make in new sales.

While your ad campaign is actively running, pay close attention to your daily sales reports in iTunes Connect to see whether you can recognize sales spikes that may have been caused by the ad. If your advertisement is using an iTunes Affiliate Program link, it's much easier to track the sales performance of your ad through your LinkShare reports. If you don't see any significant sales impact, then you can always modify your ad campaign to see whether the results improve. Don't be afraid to continuously tweak your ad text until you find a message that proves effective. It's important to give your campaign a solid amount of time before discontinuing it. Successful advertising is all about frequency and volume. If you advertise for only a couple days, then that's not enough time to properly evaluate its effectiveness. Repetition is the name of the game. People may need to see an ad a few times before they're motivated to tap it, especially if they're immersed in the current app and haven't been paying much attention to the embedded in-app ads.

Average click-throughs typically hover around 2 percent of ad views, and even then there's no guarantee those App Store visitors will purchase the app. Your ad campaign needs to be viewed by millions of iPhone users for it to generate enough traffic to your App Store page. And what if that massive traffic volume still doesn't result in sales? Many iPhone developers have found that advertising a free lite version produces a much higher conversion rate than the paid app, since there's no risk for the consumer to download a free app. If you've built a great app, the free lite version can help close the deal, acting as a much better sales tool than a static banner ad.

If you venture into web advertising, buying keywords and ads on search engines and popular portal sites is often too costly for low-priced mobile apps, not to mention that some of the people clicking your ad may not even own an iPhone. Your best bet is to focus your web advertising efforts on niche sites that specifically target your app's audience. For example, if it's a game, advertise on a popular iPhone gaming site such as TouchArcade.com.

Print advertising is difficult to justify for most iPhone apps. Not only is it expensive, but it's unable to deliver instant access to your App Store page like a clickable online ad. Your URL is listed in print, which requires interested readers to manually type the URL into their web browser the next time they are sitting at their computer or using their iPhone. And at that point, they may have already forgotten about your ad. If you work for a big company with a large advertising budget, then print advertising can be very effective in reinforcing your brand identity. Print magazines usually require a three-month lead, so by the time your print ad's issue hits newsstands, your app may have already fallen into the "long tail" of its life cycle—an opportune stage for the ad to revive consumer interest and app downloads. If you're an independent developer on a shoestring budget, then print advertising may be out of your league, so stick with web and mobile ads.

With that said, advertising can work when aimed at the right audience. Just tread carefully to see whether it's a good fit for your iPhone app before diving in with both feet. Keep in mind that no single marketing tactic will turn your app into a best-seller. By incorporating the many strategies you've learned here into an orchestrated marketing plan, you'll soon be on the road to achieving success in the App Store.

Looking Toward the Horizon

First, I'd like to thank you for reading this book. And second, I want to congratulate you for working so diligently through every chapter. Together, we've covered a vast number of important topics. You've learned about competitive research, in-app marketing strategies, alternative business models, the App Store submission process, online promotion, and much more. There was even a dedicated chapter on harnessing the power of In-App Purchase! This book was carefully designed to provide the essential tools, resources, and knowledge needed to transform your iPhone app development from a fun hobby into a successful, thriving business.

Beyond what you've read within these pages, there will always be new avenues that arise in the future for promoting your app. Study what other developers are doing to market their mobile products—not only what works but also which strategies fail and why. But don't limit your scope to only the iPhone community. It's important to stay well informed on current events in the entire mobile arena by reading all the latest technology news sites and blogs, such as TechCrunch.com, Techmeme.com, and Mashable.com (to name just a few). Even software marketing campaigns for Google Android, Palm webOS, and mobile web apps may inspire new ideas that would lend themselves well to your own efforts reaching iPhone and iPod touch users. The goal is to keep an open mind and embrace new strategies that can help grow your business.

With the App Store being such a phenomenal success, the iPhone OS platform will undoubtedly expand onto new devices. And forthcoming SDK updates will continue to roll out an endless array of innovative new features. It's a fascinating time to be in mobile software, and Apple has only just begun to tap into the possibilities. With new opportunities arising every day for iPhone developers, the future promises to be an exciting journey!

Index

You Need the Companion eBook

Your purchase of this book entitles you to buy the companion PDF-version eBook for only $10. Take the weightless companion with you anywhere.

We believe this Apress title will prove so indispensable that you'll want to carry it with you everywhere, which is why we are offering the companion eBook (in PDF format) for $10 to customers who purchase this book now. Convenient and fully searchable, the PDF version of any content-rich, page-heavy Apress book makes a valuable addition to your programming library. You can easily find and copy code—or perform examples by quickly toggling between instructions and the application. Even simultaneously tackling a donut, diet soda, and complex code becomes simplified with hands-free eBooks!

Once you purchase your book, getting the $10 companion eBook is simple:

❶ Visit **www.apress.com/promo/tendollars/**.

❷ Complete a basic registration form to receive a randomly generated question about this title.

❸ Answer the question correctly in 60 seconds, and you will receive a promotional code to redeem for the $10.00 eBook.

THE EXPERT'S VOICE™

233 Spring Street, New York, NY 10013

Offer valid through 2/2011.